STALINISM RELOADED

STALINISM RELOADED

Everyday Life in Stalin-City, Hungary

Sándor Horváth
Translated by Thomas Cooper

Indiana University Press

Bloomington and Indianapolis

This book is a publication of

Indiana University Press
Office of Scholarly Publishing
Herman B Wells Library 350
1320 East 10th Street
Bloomington, Indiana 47405 USA

iupress.indiana.edu

Translation funded by the László Tetmájer Fund of the Hungarian
Studies Program, Department of Central Eurasian Studies, Indiana
University–Bloomington.

Manufactured in the United States of America

Library of Congress Cataloging-in-Publication Data

Names: Horváth, Sándor, author. | Horváth, Sándor. Kapu és a határ,
    mindennapi Sztálinváros.
Title: Stalinism reloaded : everyday life in Stalin-City, Hungary /
    Sándor Horváth ; translated by Thomas Cooper.
Description: Bloomington : Indiana University Press, [2017] | Partially based
    on 2004 dissertation entitled A kapu és a határ, mindennapi
    Sztálinváros. | Includes bibliographical references and index.
Identifiers: LCCN 2016053492 (print) | LCCN 2016055324 (ebook) | ISBN
    9780253025746 (cloth : alkaline paper) | ISBN 9780253026811 (paperback :
    alkaline paper) | ISBN 9780253026866 (eb)
Subjects: LCSH: Dunaújváros (Hungary)—Social conditions—20th century. |
    Sztálinváros (Hungary)—Social conditions—20th century. | Dunaújváros
    (Hungary)—Social life and customs—20th century. | Sztálinváros
    (Hungary)—Social life and customs—20th century. | City and town
    life—Hungary—Dunaújváros—History—20th century. | Communism—Social
    aspects—Hungary—Dunaújváros—History—20th century. | Hungary—Social
    policy. | Hungary—Politics and government—1945–1989.
Classification: LCC HN420.5.D85 H68 2017 (print) | LCC HN420.5.D85 (ebook) |
    DDC 306.09439/7—dc23
LC record available at https://lccn.loc.gov/2016053492

1   2   3   4   5   22   21   20   19   18   17

To Gabriella

Contents

Acknowledgments

THE UNDERLYING IDEA of this book did not occur to me in an exotic or pleasant place on a sunny afternoon, but in an industrial city sometimes shrouded in fog from the ironworks. The inhabitants of this city, interestingly, do not complain about this fog, because it means they still have jobs. Initially, my aim was simply to try to understand this city, a place somehow both modern and old, a symbol of the hopes of one generation and, perhaps, the despairs of another. This book may have grown a bit slowly from its initial, embryonic form, but I modestly trust that this slow process of development has made it a more mature work in the end.

Over the course of my research and writing, I have enjoyed the support of several individuals and institutions. I would like to mention first and foremost two colleagues, Gábor Gyáni, my scholar-mentor, and László Borhi, a close colleague without whom this book would never have reached completion. The everyday conversations I had with them and with other colleagues at the Institute of History of the Hungarian Academy of Sciences helped me reassess the essential subject of my research from numerous additional perspectives and enriched my study with new lines of inquiry. Over the course of the past fifteen years, the Institute of History, fundamentally a workshop that provides crucial support for scientific endeavor, has provided me with the time and independence that are indispensable to any major research project.

I would also like to express my gratitude to several people who provided me with intellectual support and encouragement at various different stages. Vera Bácskai and György Kövér helped me consider innovative ways of using different types of sources and new means of adapting the scientific tools of urban history in contemporary history. I am indebted to my friends and colleagues György Majtényi and Eszter Zsófia Tóth, who in the course of long conversations patiently discussed with me my early findings on the topic and inspired me to pursue further research. My research was also considerably shaped by conversations with my friend and colleague, Mark Pittaway, a historian who died tragically young.

In the course of my research and writing, I have also benefited a great deal from comments made by a number of people in the broader profession. I am particularly grateful to Anne Applebaum, Mónika Baár, Ulf Brunnbauer, Pál Fodor, Tibor Hajdu, Paul Hanebrink, Dagmara Jajeśniak-Quast, Gábor Klaniczay, Árpád von Klimó, Katherine Lebow, Attila Pók, János M. Rainer, Heléna Tóth, Tibor Valuch, Zsuzsanna Varga, István Vida, and Rosemary Wakeman.

Archivists and colleagues in museums have also provided valuable assistance in my research. Let me express my sincerest thanks to Ferenc Erdős, Balázs Czetz, and the staff of the Fejér County Archive and also to Márta Lendvai Matussné, who tragically died since then, and Margit Kronaszt in the Intercisa Museum, Dunaújváros. A professional cartographer, Béla Nagy at the Institute of History, patiently helped me produce the maps in the book.

Funding for this project was provided mainly by the Institute of History of the Hungarian Academy of Sciences, and the translation was funded by the Tetmájer Fund at the Indiana University, but many other institutions provided me with financial and/or in-kind support during the process of writing and revising the manuscript: the Hungarian Scientific Research Fund (OTKA), School of International and Public Affairs at Columbia University in New York, the Mellon Foundation, the Institute for Human Sciences (IWM) in Vienna, the Center for Advanced Studies at Ludwig Maximilian University (LMU) in Munich, the Institute for East European Studies at the Free University in Berlin, and last but not least Imre Kertész Kolleg (IKK) at Friedrich Schiller University in Jena. I am grateful to these institutions for their generous support.

The origins of this book go back to my doctoral dissertation at Eötvös Loránd University, Budapest, which was published in Hungarian. Here I have completely revised and reconceptualized my dissertation, broadening its focus and adopting new lines of inquiry. I would like to express my sincerest gratitude to the readers of the manuscript, Steven E. Harris and Timothy C. Dowling, for their highly constructive comments, from which I have endeavored to learn. I also wish to thank the dedicated staff at the Indiana University Press, especially Jennika Baines and Janice Frisch, who made the publication process a pleasurable experience. A special thanks goes to Therese Malhame, who did an excellent job copyediting the manuscript.

I cannot express enough appreciation to Thomas Cooper, the translator and proofreader of the text, who was able to digest the original manuscript with patience and dispatch.

Thank you to my family for your patience and forbearance during this process, especially to my children, who helped me organize my time effectively and made and make every day exciting. Finally, thanks to you, Gabriella Erdélyi, my first and last reader, my honest critic and beloved wife.

STALINISM RELOADED

Introduction

I<small>T IS</small> 1960, at the Rácalmás Children's Home on the periphery of Sztálinváros, the Hungarian "Stalin-City." In one of the pictures a seven-year-old boy wearing a sweat suit provided by the institute is smiling. His name is Jancsi, after his father. In his hand he holds a copy of the *Arany ABC* (Golden ABC), his generation's first encounter with the world of letters. His sisters are sitting beside him. One of them is holding a stuffed bear, the other is cradling a plastic doll. There is a doll behind them on the shelf and, in the shadows in the back is a metal-frame bed for small children. On the shimmering tablecloth, which has been wiped clean, are a small rocking horse and an enormous plate of jam rolls. The little girls are stuffing themselves with the rolls. White glasses and flowers are on the table in front of them. The picture is complete, as a dramaturgical composition, with the crowning addition of hot chocolate. In the other picture taken in the Children's Home, two boys, one a year and a half old, the other two and a half, are sitting in a baby-walker. They have polka-dot balls in their hands. They are laughing.

The children's mother, Ilona, was born in Újpest, a working-class district of Budapest, in 1930, the beginning of the Great Depression. Most of the people who in 1950 went in search of work to Sztálinváros, the first new socialist city in Hungary, were members of her generation. She did not know her father's name. She bore her mother's family name. She had no memory of her mother, who had died when Ilona was one year old. She was raised by her grandparents, who told her that her father had been a "tradesman" (a house-painter) and her mother had been a housewife. With the launch of Stalinization in Hungary,[1] this pedigree was just barely "acceptable." Her grandmother had died when Ilona was nine years old, and in 1940 her grandfather put her in an alms house. She lived in many such houses and spent several years in the care of a family that she decided to leave. In the period between the end of World War II and the spring of 1948 she was raised in the nunnery of the Good Pastor Sisters Order in Budapest. Before the order was dissolved by the state, at the age of eighteen she was given a job working at one of the refreshment bars in the Ministry of Interior. She worked there for a year before finding a job in a bar in Angyalföld, an infamous working-class district in Budapest. Here she met her future husband, János, in 1949, and the two moved in together in 1950. By that time her "certificate of good character" (a document issued by the police) contained a few comments. She had been imprisoned several times, for periods of only a few days, for loitering and stealing. Between

1945 and 1948, her fate was "pending," as indeed was the fate of Hungary. In 1950, it seemed as if she might be able to begin a new life on new foundations, much as it seemed that Hungary might be able to begin anew with the launch of the first five-year plan.

In 1950, at the beginning of the construction of Sztálinváros, Ilona traveled to the city with János in the hope of finding work and beginning a new life. They were among the first "settlers" in this new, chaotic socialist urban world. In the periods between the births of her children she worked variously in a bar, as a cleaning lady, and sometimes as an administrator for a month or two. But there were never enough jobs for women in Sztálinváros, even toward the end of the decade. They were living in shared lodgings with several other families, in a half-finished temporary apartment building when their first son, Jancsi, was born in January 1952. In 1953 János completed his training to become an electrician. This enabled him to take better-paying work outside of Sztálinváros. In January 1955 their second child, Judit, was born and at the end of December Ilona gave birth to another girl, Magdolna. Ilona and János, having been residents of Sztálinváros for five years, found lodging in one of the unheated, half-finished apartments of the Technikum District, again in shared lodging. As an official and frequently used term, *shared lodging*, essentially meant that families were sharing individual apartments with other families.

In 1956 the family experienced a propitious change. After the 1956 Hungarian Revolution was crushed by the Soviets,[2] the couple got word that an apartment in the "prole" (*proli*) district of the city had been left empty. On November 30, 1956, they took possession of the apartment by moving into it—that is, they engaged in the practice of squatting, which was not uncommon at the time. It proved a prudent decision. The City Council of Sztálinváros followed widespread practice and granted them legal ownership of the apartment, thereby easing some of the tensions that arose because of the lack of apartments. This recognition of legal ownership was particularly common if the person who had taken possession of the apartment was a member of the people's army or an officer of the Ministry of Interior or the frontier guards. János was none of these, but he was an important part of the workforce in Sztálinváros, since he brought home 2,000 forints every month (considerably more than the average at the time, 1,500).[3]

Furthermore, after 1956 he was given work in the city. On May 1, 1957, at the dawn of the Kádár era, his fourth child, Zoltán, was born, and later that year Ilona and János married. This gave renewed cause for hope, and married couples had better chances of receiving official approval to reside in apartments they had obtained by squatting. But János fell ill for six months. In 1958, he began to travel regularly for work, in order to earn more money. In the fall of 1959 Ilona cheated on her husband with a soldier from the Soviet barrack outside the city. János stopped sending money home and then stopped coming home altogether. Ilona began spending more and more time in bars, the children were underfed, and there was no wood with which to heat the apartment (the central heating system planned for the district had not yet been completed). In 1959, one day before Christmas, proceedings were launched against Ilona for not providing proper care for her children (of whom there were now five) and hosting men in her apartment in exchange for money. She was arrested, and her children were put in the care of the state. Ilona clung fast to the youngest of her offspring when the police took the children from her. The police took pictures of the apartment, which was in disarray, and photographs of the children. The photographs taken in the Children's Home were included among the documents used at the trial.[4] Ilona's story is one of many stories of Sztálinváros that offer glimpses into the everyday lives of the families of the new socialist city, the stories with which I deal in this book.

This book presents the history of the Hungarian city of Sztálinváros [Staːlinvaːroʃ], in English, "Stalin-City," a city that was intended to be the paradigmatic urban community of the new socialist society. It explores the contradictions of the Stalinist policies and the reflections of the locals in a single city, as well as the ways in which tradition was simultaneously tossed aside and venerated, along with the competing rhetorics and imperatives of state officials, local bureaucrats, and the inhabitants of the city, all of whom exerted significant influences on one another. The story takes place in the first decade of the construction of the first socialist city in Hungary, beginning in 1950 and concluding in 1961, when as part of the second de-Stalinization campaign the city was renamed Dunaújváros (in English "New City by the Danube").

The protagonists of this book are not the politicians, political elites, or institutions, but rather the "ordinary people," such as local bureaucrats, drunken steelworkers, bricklayers, working women, angry teenagers, misbehaving children, and marginal people of various kinds.[5] Setting aside the "totalitarian paradigm," I reject the notion of a sharp divide between the "state" and "society," between supporters and agents of the regime on the one hand and victims on the other. Nor do I accept the "revisionist paradigm," which rests on an opposition between supporters of Stalinist policies and advocates of resistance (both paradigms have been persuasively challenged in recent scholarship).[6] Rather, I examine the ways in which the social discourses, values, everyday practices, family structures, uses of urban and social spaces, and leisure activities were shaped by the socialist regime, on the one hand, while these people exercised agency and exerted significant influences on the state that ruled them, on the other. They not only carved out "spaces of (relative) freedom," as Katherine Lebow writes of the Polish new town of Nowa Huta,[7] but by adapting to the Stalinist policies and even influencing the forms these policies took, they created a kind of "Stalinism reloaded," which contributed to the stabilization of the socialist regime.[8] The effects of de-Stalinization were palpable in Hungary in the 1950s. The Imre Nagy government (1953–55) sought to create a new kind of socialism with a "human face," and following the 1956 Revolution similar efforts were made by the Kádár regime, the leaders of which had learned the lessons of the first large uprising against Soviet and communist power in East Central Europe.

I will argue that the ordinary people engaged in, made use of, and transformed the social practices, tools, spaces, and languages that the state provided them in the course of constructing the city of Sztálinváros according to the expectations of the state. Furthermore, they were even able to shape the Stalinist policies. They were able to exert significant agency, because without their participation Stalinism would not have worked. To understand these mutual influences, we have to shift the focus from what the party mandated or prohibited to what the Stalinist policies made *possible* , and how the acts of ordinary people shaped these policies.[9]

In comparison with the first, "revolutionary years" of Stalinism in Hungary (1950–53), over the course of the rest of the 1950s both ordinary people and the regime seemed to follow a more socially traditional and conservative path. This conservative turn in social mores and beliefs between 1953 and 1957 helped them produce a more nuanced consensus on basic everyday-life values regarding social differences, urban spaces, and family life.[10] The conservative turn in everyday practices was one highly important factor in pushing both ordinary people and state officials more or less in the same direction, albeit for different reasons. This conservative "new deal" led to the notion of the "unplanned city" (socialism as chaos) and the "modern city" (socialism as modernity), which was also a brief trope of a compromise between the communist agenda and the construction of the city. As I will argue, the public rhetoric, mixed with official rhetoric and local public discourses, had a seminal role in this process. This public rhetoric drew a sharp distinction between the urban and rural, between proper and disorderly family life. In sum, both state and social actors contributed in different and contradictory ways to this distinctive story of urbanization and to the creation of the socialist city. In other words, Stalin-City and the socialist regime was envisioned, created, envisioned anew, and re-created both symbolically and in practice not only by the state but also by the ordinary people.

If we aim to arrive at a nuanced understanding of the past from the perspective of people's everyday experiences and relationships, the study of a model (and modeled) urban community like Stalin-City may yield answers to questions that remain inscrutable if examined from broader or more distant perspectives. How was it possible to transform social norms and Stalinist policies in a manner that enabled the residents of the city occasionally to experience the feeling of being free on the everyday level? How did the socialist regime remain sustainable so

Sztálinváros came into being, what the functions of these myths were in the formation of an identity for the residents of the city, and who created them and why. From this perspective, the myths were elements of the construction of the city that were no less important than the mortar and brick. In chapter 2, I examine how different images of the districts of the city were changed and shaped by the shifting official expectations after the mid-1950s, and how, in accordance with this, the people of Sztálinváros conceptually divided the spaces in their minds on the basis of a transformed social hierarchy. The sharp, official differentiation between rural and urban lifestyles had a significant role in the transformation of the cityscape and the traditional (prewar) social hierarchies. Accordingly, in chapter 3, I address this official distinction between rural and urban lifestyles, which on the ground was quite blurred, in strong contrast to the rhetoric of socialist ideology.

The second part of the book examines the conflicts that emerged on the micro level from the point of view of the families that inhabited the city, as well as the effects of the Stalinist policies on interpersonal relationships. In chapter 4, I examine how marriage customs changed in a city in which, because of the influx of immigrants, people either knew one another very well or not at all. I also consider the consequences of the rise of women in the workforce as salaried employees (which was and is considered one of the causes of high rates of abortion and divorce) and unemployment among women in Sztálinváros, as well as the shifts that took place in the circumstances of children. One of the recurring motifs of people's recollections of their lives in the city is the frequent mention of the high rates of abortion and divorce, topics I address in chapters 5 and 6, respectively.

Over the course of the decade, the spaces of freedom that the people of Sztálinváros managed to carve out of a world shaped by Stalinist policies and a conservative regime were increasingly discernible in the "growing" city, and they were reproduced in the social hierarchies as well,[24] a topic I examine in the third section of the book. Indulgence in censured forms of entertainment and recreation in semipublic and public spaces played a role in the creation of identity and community that strongly influenced the social lives of the people of Sztálinváros. The official condemnation of some bars, which represented social hierarchies (chapter 7), hooliganism, which was seen as a symbol of generational conflicts (chapter 8), slums, which were manifest cases of social injustice (chapter 9), and prostitution, which was a symptom of unequal gender relations (chapter 10), in general all contributed to the evolution of a new form of everyday life and to the reproduction of social hierarchies to make the renewed regime more sustainable.

In this new social order the residents of the city became members of a community that was compelled to adhere to new sets of rules and morals on the everyday level. This new form of everyday life shaped both the residents and the

Stalinist policies, and by the end of the decade had created a new order that hardly resembled the objectives that had been set in 1950, the year in which the city was founded. This new order, however, lasted until the end of the socialist regime. Like Ilona's children, who lived in the Children's Home on the periphery of the city after 1960, the residents of the city grew up on the boundaries of the Stalinist policies and Europe. They adapted to the state policies, but they also learned to use the tools provided by the regime to further their personal goals.

Notes

1. The communist takeover took place in Hungary between 1945 and 1948. The Communist Party took control of the country in 1948. For more on this process, see Pittaway, *The Workers' State*, 52–114; and Mevius, *Agents of Moscow*, 47–68.

2. On the reasons and consequences of the 1956 revolt, see Borhi, *Hungary in the Cold War*; and Békés, Byrne, and Rainer, *The 1956 Hungarian Revolution*.

3. *Statisztikai évkönyv 1985*, 17.

4. She was punished for failing in her duty to provide necessary care. FML, f. XXV-24, Criminal Proceedings, 1960, box (b.) 6, B I. 39/1960, Mrs. János B.

5. Although on closer look the residents of Sztálinváros could hardly have been considered "ordinary" from the perspective of traditional Hungarian habits, customs, and social values, in the perspective I adopt (where they are the protagonists of this historical narrative), their experiences did become elements of the widely shared lifestyle of the emerging socialist urban community—thus warranting the use of the term *ordinary people* to describe them—however novel this lifestyle may have been at the time. This perspective was used also by Christopher Browning in his seminal book, *Ordinary Men*, on the experiences of the members of reserve police battalion 101 in Poland during World War II. For the critical meanings of the term *ordinary people* in Sovietology, see Kotsonis, "Ordinary People."

6. On the development of the totalitarian and revisionist paradigm, see Siegel, *The Totalitarian Paradigm*; Fitzpatrick, *Stalinism*, 1–14; and Hoffmann, *Stalinism*, 1–7.

7. Lebow, *Unfinished Utopia*, 6.

8. The most important reason for this was that the East Central European versions of Stalinism were not able to guarantee stability, and this "led to a near complete collapse of industrialization and collectivization drives by the mid-1950s." Pittaway, *Eastern Europe*, 7.

9. As Stephen Kotkin writes of the Soviet new town of Magnitogorsk, "power relations created effects—of experience, identity, resistances. Concentrating on the rule articulation process in the encounters of daily life involves shifting the focus from what the party and its programs prevented to what they made possible, intentionally and unintentionally." Kotkin, *Magnetic Mountain*, 22. Kotkin's work is significant from the perspective of this inquiry in part because he was the first person to examine, through a study of the history of a new socialist city, how the people of the city adapted to and exerted an influence on "speaking Bolshevik," and how the practice of "speaking Bolshevik" transformed their social practices and the Stalinist policies (ibid., 198–237). "Speaking Bolshevik" in Kotkin's *Magnetic Mountain* functions "as an analytical trope capturing the essence of the Bolshevik project—the process of 'Bolshevization' of individuals' lives. . . . In Kotkin's scenario, socialist ideology is continuously adaptable and at the same time recyclable." Krylova, "Soviet Modernity," 178.

10. This delayed conservative turn was similar to the Soviet one in the early 1930s, which reasserted the most conservative "family values" as Stalin "steadily began to , , , pull back from egalitarianism and collectivism toward a promotion of hierarchy, cultural traditionalism, and social conservatism that has come to be known as the 'Great Retreat'." Suny, "Stalin and His Stalinism," 44. However, the course of Stalinist policies in East Central Europe (including Hungary) was different in the sense of intensity, and these policies were implemented mostly in the 1950s.

11. Peltonen, "Clues, Margins, and Monads," 359.

12. For these limits in a different social context, see Lüdtke, *Eigen-Sinn*; Bessel and Jessen, *Die Grenzen der Diktatur.* These scholars were among the first to reexamine the relationship between the individual and power in a dictatorship, which according to the totalitarian paradigm was the struggle between the "oppressed" and the "oppressor." In contrast, the notion of *Eigen-Sinn* (self-will or self-reliance) gives back to historical agents their historical spaces (scope for action, spaces of agency) and makes it possible to analyze the boundaries of these spaces.

13. On the theories of social actions and historical agency, see Cabrera, *Postsocial History*, 95–122.

14. On the new towns in history, see Galantay, *New Towns*; for an overview of the new-town movement in postwar Britain, see Alexander, *Britain's New Towns*; in Europe, Gaborit, *European New Towns*; for the postwar United States, see Bloom, *Suburban Alchemy*; for the changing images of a new town of steel in the United States, see O'Hara, *Gary*, 121–43.

15. On "statistical thinking" and the enumeration and classification of citizens, see Scott, *Seeing Like a State*, 193–222.

16. Bauman, *Socialism, the Active Utopia*, 17.

17. Cf. Kotkin, *Magnetic Mountain*, 21–22, and Krylova, "Soviet Modernity," 174.

18. Cf. Lebow, *Unfinished Utopia*, 7.

19. "Among the particular features of Stalinism were the abolition of private property and free trade; the collectivization of agriculture; a planned, state-run economy and rapid industrialization; the wholesale liquidation of so-called exploiting classes, involving massive deportations and incarcerations; large-scale political terror against alleged enemies, including those within the Communist Party itself; a cult of personality deifying Stalin." Hoffmann, *Stalinism*, 2.

20. Recent trends in the historiography on East Central European socialist regimes broadly confirm these concepts; see, for example, Kenney, *Rebuilding Poland*; Brunnbauer, *"Die sozialistische Lebensweise"*; Davis, Lindenberger, and Wildt, *Alltag, Erfahrung, Eigensinn*; Fidelis, *Women, Communism, and Industrialization*; Lebow, *Unfinished Utopia*; Pittaway, *The Workers' State*.

21. I use the terms *centrally planned economy* and *state paternalism* in the sense in which János Kornai uses them. Kornai's theory concerning the economics of shortage is also useful in arriving at an understanding of the society of Sztálinváros because the rapid, dynamic changes that took place in this society were often occasioned by the rapid alternation of investment cycles. See Kornai, *The Socialist System*. On the origins of this kind of state paternalism, see Hoffmann, *Cultivating the Masses*, 306–8.

22. Apart from me, only one social historian has intensively studied the documents of Sztálinváros, my friend and colleague, the late Mark Pittaway. I am indebted to him for the conversations we had on the topic. Pittaway's articles and book on Hungarian workers are seminal works in the social historical research on the socialist era in Hungary. See Pittaway, *The Workers' State*. When I began to pursue research on Sztálinváros, there were a few books, including

more recent inquiries, that touched on the history of the city in the course of analyses of national settlement policies, labor policies, and macrosocial processes, such as Belényi, *Az alföldi városok*; Germuska, *A szocialista városok*; and Valuch, *Magyarország társadalomtörténete*, 52–53; Erdős, "Dunapentelétől Sztálinvárosig."

23. For more on the process of dismantling the cult, see Jones, *Myth, Memory, Trauma*.

24. The reproduction of hierarchy on the shop-floor level among the industrial workers was similar to this process. See Pittaway, *The Workers' State*, 254–55.

PART I

IDENTITIES

1　Myths

Whores from Budapest were brought by the train-load, and the dry dredge
sometimes lifted the corpses of infants from the ground.

　　István Örkény on Sztálinváros

For many, the history of Sztálinváros began with a ride on a *fapados*, or
"wooden-benched" (meaning cheap or third-class) train car.[1] People heading to
the city and those departing from it perceived the settlement from different
distances, and their accounts of Sztálinváros evoked various impressions. They
thereby exerted a continuous influence on the expectations people had of the regime, as well as what they thought of socialism itself, the most expensive Hungarian symbol of which was this city. To the outside world, Sztálinváros was as
varied as the many accounts of the city, and despite the fact that it represented a
new phenomenon, the image of the city was nonetheless a mix of the narrative
styles of traditional national myths.[2] In addition, in Hungary, Sztálinváros was
considered a city of "immigrants," similar to New York for Americans. Thus the
great diversity of its residents became a core component of its image and the identity of its denizens.[3]

　　The third-class train, dubbed the "Sztálinváros express," played a meta-
phorical role. The image of Sztálinváros was shaped by the depictions and descriptions of the people who traveled to the city and those for whom it became
home. The majority of the official accounts, recollections, newspaper articles,
short stories, and propaganda literature characterized the birth and expansion of
Sztálinváros as a straight but bumpy path in a clearly defined direction, very much
like the journeys by "wooden-benched" train that had brought so many people to
it. These notions and views that found expression in literary forums or the print
media shaped the image of Sztálinváros, which in turn influenced the physical
transformation of the city and people's memories of it.

　　A city is not created exclusively by administrative orders or by dredging machines and cranes, but also by people's imaginations, their ideas of a new urban
community, and the myths that nurture the notion of unity.[4] I argue in this chapter that the myths that provided an interpretative framework for the history of
Sztálinváros had already been fashioned well before the actual construction of
the city was under way.[5] The establishment of the settlement, its planned and

unplanned growth, and the ever-changing nature of its inhabitants nurtured myths that facilitated the creation of a history of the city, which at first was difficult to grasp (i.e., to read and interpret). The historic definition of a city and the ideas of the "socialist city planners" who had been charged with the task of reforming and reinvigorating it created the foundations of the first myths of Sztálinváros. The myths of the city shaped not only the images of the city but also the local identities of the residents and the municipal policies. A conservative turn can be also detected in the new myths regarding the short history of the city, which helped represent the local, Sztálinváros identity as a distinct one. This identity included the myths of the heroic years as well as representations of the freedom, the chaos, and the melting pot of diverse people coming to the city. The transformation of the myths of the city helped create the distinct identity of the city-builders and the inhabitants of the city, which made it easier to represent Sztálinváros as a city for both the locals and the officials. The conservative turn showed not only that Stalinist policies shaped the people's vision of the city but also that the residents were able to influence what the officials thought about the image of the city and, indeed, the image of the socialist regime.

The City from "Scratch"

The idea of creating Sztálinváros and a new integrated steel factory did not come from the Communists. During World War II the idea of building an ironworks to meet the needs of the munitions industry was raised. Originally the Ministry of Industry suggested constructing a new ironworks in the industrial district of the city of Győr near the western border of the country, a district that had already grown because of the expansion of the wartime industry, and arrangements were even made with a German-affiliated firm of an American company.[6] Because of bombings, however, the work had to be discontinued and a new site had to be found. At the time, the city of Mohács in the southern part of the country was considered appropriate.[7] Following the war, the need for an ironworks was even direr, if simply to enable the country to meet its obligations for reparations to the Soviet Union, and the new leaders also considered Mohács. The city, however, which had been the site of the defeat of the Hungarian armies in a crucial battle against the Ottoman Empire in 1526 and therefore was a symbol of the Turkish occupation of the country, was not to become home to the largest state investment in Hungary of the twentieth century. Although construction began in Mohács in 1949 with the help of Soviet engineers, by the end of the year, relations between Hungary and Yugoslavia were so bad that the decision was made not to build the ironworks so near the southern border, a move supported by the Soviet specialists as well.[8]

Map 1.1. Map of Hungary, 1950.

At a December 1949 meeting of the Political Committee of the Hungarian Workers' Party (the ruling Communist Party at that time) it was suggested that the construction site be moved to Dunapentele, a town that was only seventy kilometers south of Budapest, the capital of Hungary. A decision was also reached at the same meeting regarding the pace of the nationalization of the industrial and transport enterprises. In other words, the decision to build a new city was made in parallel with the Stalinist expropriation of private property.[9]

Sztálinváros was a unique city in Hungarian history, even if the state referred to it simply as a *socialist city*, a term that was used for many other cities too. Construction was begun on muddy ground in the spring of 1950, in accordance with resolution 94/11/1950 of the People's Economic Council, and the city that was built to be a home for those who worked at the ironworks was named after Stalin on November 7, 1951 (before that it was called Dunapentele, the village neighboring the construction site). Dunapentele got its name from Saint Pantaleo, a medieval Greek who was the patron saint of an abbacy located on an island in the Danube near the city. By that time, the nationalization of private enterprises had been implemented in Hungary. The multiparty system that seemed to be prospering after 1945 were dissolved. Many Church leaders were imprisoned and denominational schools were taken over by the state. And very much in line with the purges that took place within the party in the Soviet Union in the 1930s, the Hungarian Communists began with increasing frequency to liquidate "internal enemies."

The real or alleged offspring of former industrialists and aristocrats were resettled from the capital city to the deserted areas of the Hungarian plains. In the factories a system of work norms was introduced on the basis of which earnings were calculated. In 1948 a system of rewards was introduced for "outstanding workers," and in 1950 the so-called Stakhanovite system was adopted (a reference to Aleksei Grigorievich Stakhanov, a Russian worker who in 1935 allegedly set an example by mining more than fourteen times the amount of coal set by the quota). In the villages, as a system was being introduced that obliged village dwellers to deliver agricultural products to the state (this was called *beszolgáltatási rendszer*, which means "delivery system"), lists of so-called kulaks (wealthy peasants) were being made.[10] Every year on May 1 parades were held beneath enormous portraits of Stalin and Mátyás Rákosi, the first secretary of the Communist Hungarian Workers' Party, while people who had been found guilty of committing political crimes worked in labor camps.[11] In addition to introducing Stalinist principles of property ownership and provisions of law, one of the most important tasks of the party was to spread Bolshevik rituals. With the exception of the brief period of the 1956 Revolution, Sztálinváros bore this name until 1961, when it became Dunaújváros (which means New City by the Danube). By that time the city had thirty thousand inhabitants and, like other newly minted (as it were) East Central European cities (such as Magnitogorsk in the Soviet Union, Nowa Huta in Poland, Stalinstadt in the German Democratic Republic [GDR], and Dimitrovgrad in Bulgaria), it played a significant role in the symbolic language of the building of socialism and the actual output of the iron industry as well.[12]

The office of the City Council equivalent of the Soviet administrative model was formally organized when the settlement acquired the status of a city.[13] This approach consequently entailed that a settlement would be regarded as a city once it was declared to be one: so on April 29, 1951, the Council of Ministers hastily turned the construction site into a city, temporarily naming it Dunapentele, before the official opening of the first street (May 1 Street was only partially completed on May 1, 1951).[14] The settlement could not have been graced with the permanent name "Sztálinváros," not only because it dramatically failed to meet the expectations regarding a "socialist city" but also because it did not yet have a single paved road. The establishment of autonomous local administration (the City Council) was declared, but in vain, insofar as the state-owned building enterprises continued to make the decisions regarding the sums allocated for urban development. The jurisdiction of the council began to grow only in 1954, by the time the majority of the planned industrial investments had been completed. The pace of urbanization was not determined by local administrative authorities, but by the investments in industry. Having been declared a city, on November 7, 1951 (at the time a public holiday in commemoration of the October Revolution of 1917), the settlement was dubbed Sztálinváros, the clear significance of which established the framework for its growth.

The physical borders of Sztálinváros were significantly shaped by not only the legal urban concept but also a statistical urban concept. The size of the city's population was established ahead of time as an important criterion of the envisioned urban community. Contemporary architects agreed that the ideal population of a city was between 50,000 and 100,000.[15] Plans were initially based on the number of workers in the ironworks (estimated at somewhere between 11,000 and 12,000). The required numbers of administrative and other employees were added, as were the numbers of family members. The total sum was thus 35,000–40,000 people, which the architects believed "would increase over the course of the following 15–20 years." Architects calculated the proportion of breadwinners and dependents to be 50–50 percent.[16] According to the National Statistical Office, the population was 31,000 in 1960 and 43,000 in 1966.[17]

In the world of the socialist planned economy, the general architectural appearance of Sztálinváros had to serve as an expression of fundamental socialist principles.[18] On the drawing board the city represented modernization, equal social opportunities, residential areas planned and arranged in accordance with modern expectations, and fully equipped apartments. The city, which would provide the backdrop for the lives of the similarly "planned" urban citizens, the "socialist man" (in Hungarian *szocialista embertípus*), had to create first and foremost the conditions necessary in order to ensure a new kind of "collective" life. One of the important roles of the city was to "rear" and "educate" its inhabitants for life as part of a kind of collective, with its public squares, the structures and arrangement of the buildings, and the edifices of public administration. From the perspective of the planners, the socialist city had to fulfill new functions, such as providing collective eateries that would replace home cooking in the life of the (idealized) "socialist man." Another significant task of the new socialist urban settlement was to play a role in child rearing (day cares, kindergartens, schools) and to provide cultural and sport facilities and recreational areas. The communist visions of collective life had a significant role in the first myths of the city, which determined the everyday life and later the local identity of the inhabitants.

The Myth of Collective Life

The myth of collective life, which was crafted on the drawing board, made spacious apartments where people would spend the greater part of their free time with family members superfluous (and equally significantly, masses of people needed housing). Needed instead of large homes were gigantic roads and squares for processions, sites where residents would gather, live active social lives, and "freely" discuss their opinions.[19] The opposition of the collective and the individual

Figure 1.1. Master plan of Sztálinváros, 1953. Photo used by permission of the Intercisa Museum, Dunaújváros.

was one of the central elements of official ideology, and one could discern its influence in both holiday and party convention rituals, and even in urban architecture. The rituals of political socialization required space.[20] Having studied habits and practices in the Soviet Union, Oleg Kharkhordin concluded that to a certain extent collective rituals of party meetings originated in the institutions and rituals of the Orthodox Church, which were built on the continuous self-reflection ("self-criticism") of the individual and the community.[21]

In the eyes of the city planners, to make the "socialist lifestyle" of its denizens possible, a socialist city had to be, first and foremost, comprehensible. This was manifested in its clearly functional structure.[22] The city was designed to consist of relatively small neighborhood units housing approximately six thousand people. These neighborhood units were all to have their own, individual centers.[23]

The concept of neighborhood units originated with American urban planner Clarence Perry, who developed it in detail in the "Regional Plan" for the city of New York in the 1920s. The essence of the concept is that the neighborhood unit is amenable to pedestrian life. With the exception of the workplace, everything that one might need can be found within walking distance. The borders of a residential district circumscribe an area comparable in size to an elementary school district. In Perry's view, this distance is approximately a quarter of a mile, or a ten-minute walk, the distance a child can comfortably walk to school.[24] Perry's views on children's walk to school exerted an influence on newly constructed cityscapes all over the world, and thus not surprisingly in East Central Europe as well. The concept of the residential district set the borders of the everyday lives of Sztálinváros residents similarly to way it determined the borders of everyday life in Radburn, a planned city in New Jersey.

The emergence of this notion of the neighborhood unit was one of the consequences of a shift that took place in the 1920s as the "aesthetic" approach to urban planning was replaced by the "scientific" approach.[25] After World War II, the concept of neighborhood units spread all over Europe, including to socialist countries. Neighborhood units also formed the basic architectural districts of "new cities" in England. The US city of Columbia, Maryland, was also constructed in accordance with the notion of neighborhood units, with the "denizens' tree" in the center to symbolize urban community spirit.[26] The public spaces in the new cities in England (which consisted of neighborhood units) bear striking resemblances to the public spaces of the socialist cities of Eastern Europe. In both cases, these spaces were intended to symbolize the communal lives of the new urban communities.

In the layout of socialist cities specific functions were attributed to the center, with particular focus on Main Street. First and foremost, this street connected residential districts with industrial plants (for example, in Sztálinváros, Stalin Avenue and its extension connected the city with the ironworks).

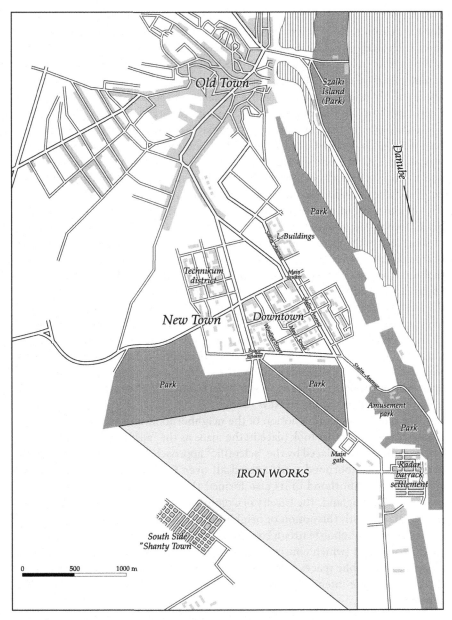

Map 1.2. Map of Sztálinváros, 1959.

This also gave physical expression to the fundamental notion that in a socialist city work is the principal factor around which society and, by extension, the cityscape should be shaped. Accordingly, the connection between the residential area and the industrial plant was a symbol for the relationship between the individual and work.[27] The so-called Radburn principle (the aforementioned New Jersey planned city) was also realized. The essence of the Radburn principle is that ground plots of residential buildings adjoin a footpath in one direction and a motorway in the other (as the buildings of Stalin Avenue in Sztálinváros did).[28] The enormous squares of Sztálinváros thus served propaganda needs and harmonized with plans for motorization: the wide roads were suitable for pomp and processions and for heavy traffic.

In Sztálinváros (as in other socialist cities), the proposed main street, Stalin Avenue, was to serve as both a background for the events of everyday life and a stage for processions and rituals. This found expression in the width of the thoroughfare, which was 85–110 meters.[29] This constituted a comparatively grandiose plan, as indicated for instance by the fact that Stalinallee (which in 1961 was renamed Karl-Marx-Allee), the main avenue of the Stalin baroque style in Berlin (constructed at the same time), was only designed to be 75–80 meters in width.[30] According to the initial designs, the city planners envisioned a tower-like building at the end of Stalin Avenue, in the main square in front of the party headquarters, at least 30 meters high. This was to be home to the City Council. However, as early as 1952 the plan failed to meet the expectations of contemporary official urban planning ideas. The pinnacled tower was replaced by a high-rise building that created a modernist impression. In addition, the local "skyscraper" brought traditional cultural anxieties regarding modern urban life to the fore.[31] The construction of the council hall also created conflicts because of its height. Originally, it would have been significantly higher than the party headquarters completed in 1951. Local party leaders disapproved of this plan. Eventually, in the 1956 construction plan a building was approved that was tall, but significantly lower than the one envisioned in the initial plans.[32]

The development plan of the main square was constantly being changed, and debates persisted from year to year regarding the question of the height of the buildings (which were designed to be monumental).[33] For this reason, the square remained unfinished even after a significant number of the residential districts had been built. In 1956 the area in front of the Béla Bartók House of Culture, which according to the original plans was to be the "minor center" of a residential district, was still the "most imposing" square of Sztálinváros. Although this square was not intended as a site for demonstrations, on October 25, 1956, participants in the local revolutionary rally held a protest there, and not in the incomplete "main square" (which allegedly had been "designed for the proclamation of political will") or on Stalin Avenue, which was still only half-completed.[34]

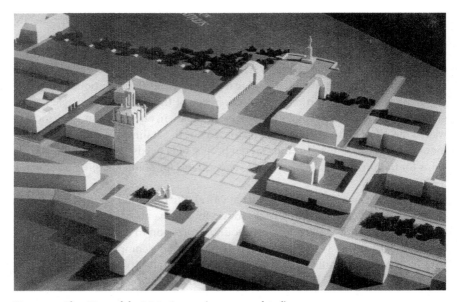

Figure 1.2. Plan No. 1 of the Main Square (never completed).

The implementation and realization of the monumental plans for public spaces was a recurring problem in other socialist countries as well, since shifts in the political winds (occasioned by the death or fall of political leaders) brought about changes in the plans and the available funding. Thus, in most instances by the time one plan was about to be implemented, a new one was already being formulated. As a consequence, in socialist cities "of high importance" visitors encountered an incomplete main square or a half-finished statue. The statue of Marx in Chemnitz (Karl-Marx-Stadt) offers an illustration of this: only Marx's head was displayed on the pedestal because the pedestal itself came out too tall, thus only the boots of a full-scale statue would have been clearly visible to viewers. Local residents were bewildered upon first seeing the statue, and the city acquired the derisive nickname "Stadt mit Köpfchen," or city with a little head (in German *Köpfchen* also means a resourceful person). The leaders of the totalitarian state were unable to circumvent the wishes of local city leaders and have a monument to Marx erected in the city bearing his name that would have harmonized with their expectations.[35] The main square of Sztálinváros is also an excellent illustration of the fact that the state, which strove to depict itself as all-powerful, could not even exert complete control over the symbolic city spaces.

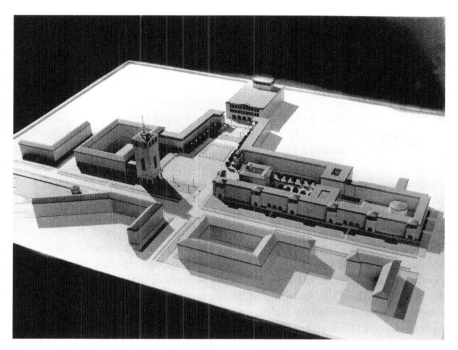

Figure 1.3. Plan No. 2 of the Main Square (never completed).

By building residential areas in accordance with clearly structured designs and delineating the borders of a city center that served a function as a symbol of collective urban identity,[36] the city planners also established the border between public and semipublic spaces. The "socialist individual" was expected to behave differently on the streets of residential districts, in the yards of L-shaped residential buildings, or on downtown playgrounds than he or she would on Stalin Avenue or the main city square. The image suggested by the plans for Sztálinváros envisioned collective life on Stalin Avenue and the main square, while the intimacy found lacking in socialist cities would be assured by the constellations of the residential blocks or deliberately winding streets. Görbe (Winding) Street in the center was intentionally planned not to be parallel with the other streets. A winding street was also deliberately included in the plans for the city in order to ensure that, its planned nature notwithstanding, the layout of the model urban community not seem too monotonous. After the mid-1950s, however, both the understandings of collective life and the myths of the city-builders had to be transformed.

Heroes and Rearing: Transforming the Stalinist Visions

Several accounts represented Sztálinváros in the first years as a peculiar kind of "educational institution" where people themselves changed and, "having overcome adversities, new socialist heroes [would be] born."[37] The image of this educational function was transformed after the mid-1950s. The most effective representation of this new depiction of the educational role of Sztálinváros is the 1959 feature film *A kölyök* (The kid). The main character is a young, scatterbrained girl who falls in love with her new foreman in Sztálinváros. After numerous misunderstandings and pranks she becomes "properly reared."[38] The image of Sztálinváros was shaped by the ways in which propaganda literature and people's recollections (which bore the influences of the propaganda literature) cast the creation of the city as a kind of miracle brought about by the "common will." Skits and formulaic poems on this topic often began with the image of "stone walls" arising in the place of cornfields and man overcoming nature and human weaknesses. The miracle of the construction of a city has been a literary topos since antiquity, so the existing clichés were more than adequate to fashion the official myth of the founding of Sztálinváros. The only difference was that heroism was represented by Stakhanovites instead of Gilgamesh (for instance), and the party, Rákosi, and Stalin replaced distant "guardian" gods. The "creation story" of the city, a story replete with wonders, prompted some denizens of Sztálinváros to refer to these miracles in their requests for an apartment (even when the person in question was not thoroughly versed in the official ideology in 1954): "I could only part from my children after having soothed their pain with the words of the Lord Jesus Christ. I promised that we would be reunited as soon as I found accommodation. I made this promise based on the Word and we believe it will be answered. Soon I will receive an apartment. Please, do not make us apostates. For we are enlightened to know that this city was built through the power of the Scriptures."[39]

The creation of socialist heroes was also a narrative means of fashioning a kind of Stalinist individualism, which had an effect on the ways in which individuals represented their personal goals by building the city.[40] The heroes—and the creation of the new socialist individual—originated in the myth of collective life.[41] In 1953, when reflecting on the recent past, István Örkény summarized the presentation of the hero as: "Heroism—that's all my eyes could see. They wanted to see heroism, and nothing but heroism."[42] Not long before this, Örkény planned to portray the city as a "school." On the basis of his experiences of the city of Sztálinváros, "he was planning to write a grand saga on the lives of three generations. The main character would have been Antal Bónis, an engineer, who, influenced by the heroic romanticism of the construction of Sztálinváros, becomes a new man."[43] Örkény published excerpts from the novel, but he never finished it. As his literary works demonstrate, by the end of 1953—probably due in part to the June reforms of de-Stalinization—his attitude had changed. In 1954 he began work on a narrative titled *Babik*, the story of a fictive Stakhanovite, an "outstanding worker." Working together with Hungarian directors and screenwriters Péter Bacsó and Károly Makk, Örkény completed the script for a film based on the story, but it was rejected by the authorities because it offered a depiction of socialism as an entirely absurd world.[44] Örkény later continued work on the story as a novella, the unfinished text of which was published in 1982.

Nonetheless, images of prosperity, a monumental new settlement, and the "heroism" of the era of its construction were deeply ingrained in the public imagination regarding Sztálinváros, and whenever the city was mentioned, these notions regularly came to the fore. One discerns this in Örkény, who rejected the works he had written in the early 1950s. Even in the 1970s his memories of Sztálinváros were based on earlier topoi:

> Whatever was created there, it was a monumental enterprise. Nothing like it had happened in Hungary before: to build a district, move the people in to build the plants, begin to construct the plants, at the same time develop the city, while the plant is also being developed—this all had a great romantic atmosphere. . . . At the time we were not aware that it could have been done better, in a better place, in a better way. The crowd that gathered there was terribly exciting. Some of the worst of the country came and some of the best, for example, whores from Budapest were brought by the trainload, and the dry dredge sometimes lifted the corpses of infants from the ground. . . . The building operations had the feel of a gold rush.[45]

In people's recollections of the city, in addition to frequent mention of the diversity of the new arrivals in the city, one finds an emphasis on the presence of numerous prostitutes, criminals, and "déclassé elements," all of which strengthened the gold rush myth of construction. The notion of the power of the "common will," which was promoted by the political system, was replaced by the positive image of the "liberty" of the founding years. This was also combined with the notion of liberation from allegedly antiquated social constraints and the domination of "the old order." This is very similar to what Katherine Lebow found in the case of Nowa Huta, where "de-Stalinization was thus, among other things, an attempt to rein in some of those social forces that Stalinism had unleashed."[46] The origins of this shift in imagery (toward a notion of individual liberty) lie in the fact that after the 1956 Revolution, the Kádár regime partially attempted to secure its legitimization by emphasizing discontinuity with the Rákosi regime. Kádár was trying to present himself as a frontline soldier in the struggle for de-Stalinization in Hungary, so the new order strove to distance itself from the pre-1956 "abuses." Heroic construction was thus transformed by the myth of the gold rush, which also stressed the melting pot character of Sztálinváros.[47]

The "gold rush myth" can be traced back to the early beginnings of the construction of the city. In its portrayals of Sztálinváros as an "educational institution," the propaganda literature told of characters who did not want to live and work according to the "socialist way," but who, when placed in the brigades, learned from their comrades and became good socialist citizens.[48] In these narratives, fellow workers always play the role of instructors or mentors, never neighbors or family members. The melting pot and the gold rush myths were also supported later by local criminal statistics after the mid-1950s. Police officers were indirectly motivated to increase police control and thus create an increase in "criminal statistics" because if they failed to produce a sufficient number of "criminal reports" they were reprimanded.[49]

Diversity and liberty became the new catchphrases, transforming the earlier mythos of heroism. After 1956, the new government tried to represent itself as not Stalinist. Official discourses sought to depict the early history of Sztálinváros as a city in which chaos had prevailed as a consequence of Stalinism and the "former Stalinist governments" in Hungary at the beginning of the 1950s. The function of this dichotomy (essentially replacing earlier mythos of heroism with a new vision of the city as a place where disorder had reigned) was to impose greater control on everyday life after 1956 in the city. Accordingly the "chaos" of the early story of the city was "unleashed because of Stalinism."[50] Whereas in Nowa Huta the Stalinism before 1956 represented a version of "liberty" because it brought with it a shakeup of social relations, in Sztálinváros it also became a symbol of chaos and gold rush for people who entered the city without a "proper lifestyle."

Chaos and Gold Rush

On the arrival of the first city-builders, the most striking feature included bustle and tumult, which became persistent stereotypes in regard to the city, thus generating a "chaos myth" of Sztálinváros. Heavy traffic, construction debris, and the cavalcade of people represented the inscrutable nature of the city, both for villagers and for visitors from Budapest. Neither spatial nor social reference points were unambiguous for visitors to the new settlement. According to memoirs, for the first few years Sztálinváros was not an "easily comprehensible" city. In spite of this, when people described the city or conjured memories of their visits, they were nonetheless able to discern some clear boundaries between spaces and people—boundaries that were palpable in general consciousness as well.

As Hungarian author István Örkény wrote of Sztálinváros in his propagandistic "reportage" of the early 1950s:

> Upon arrival in Sztálinváros, my first impression was that I had landed in a gigantic metropolis. On my way from the train station on the level plains I suddenly found myself surrounded by five-story residential buildings. The

plaster was crumbling from their walls, but electric lights still shone in all of the windows. And I had the impression, as I asked passersby for directions and made several unnecessary detours in search of my accommodations, that I had wandered the long, breathtaking avenues for hours. It was only the next day, in the light of day, that I realized I had walked down only two or three streets.[51]

Later Örkény emerged as one of the most original voices of the Hungarian literary pantheon of the twentieth century, reinventing the genre of epigrammatic storytelling with his so-called one-minute short stories.[52] According to his memoirs, at the invitation of Márton Horváth, one of the most prominent figures of Hungarian Stalinist cultural politics before 1956, he paid regular visits to Sztálinváros.[53] A narrative titled *Sztálinvárosi képeskönyv* (Sztálinváros picture book) was the fruit of these visits. In compliance with the spirit of the times, the work is a propagandistic fable about labor competition, so-called Peace Loan subscriptions ("peace loans" were like war bonds, allegedly raised by the people as an expression of patriotic duty), and the burgeoning socialist city. As a standard method of the era, "sociography" sank to "reportage." Its function was to bring "victorious statistics," which were published on a daily basis, closer to people, in other words to render them in a literary style that was readable, engaging, and exciting. Thus reports on "the achievements of the party" would reach a wider reading public. Örkény did not intone the laudatory discourses himself, but rather attributed the acclamations of the state to the subjects of his reports, as was customary at the time.

In the *Sztálinvárosi képeskönyv*, literary subjectivism and an impressionistic documentary style are mixed with propagandistic "reportage." The work is composed of several one- or two-page stories structurally similar to Örkény's one-minute short stories. The first part, titled "The Journey," describes the voyage in the "wooden-benched" train car to Sztálinváros from the author's point of view. Örkény begins to gather a sense of the city on the train.[54] This old topos, the bustle of the "workers' train," also inspired many authors to write on the plights of the industrial workers, among them Zoltán Szabó, one of the founders of Hungarian sociography, who authored a presentation of the commuters' journey.[55]

The author attempts to personalize the people traveling to Sztálinváros by highlighting their differences. Several characters are described: a man who was imprisoned for illegal pig slaughter; Mari's husband, who left her and moved in with a "piece of filth" (Mari does not spare the details); and the wedding of a daughter of an in-law, "who married a council member." A dispute even breaks out because in Mari's view sooner or later every husband will cheat on his wife, an opinion that the lady giving the account of the wedding reception flatly rejects. But "though an eternal disservice to the human race, the debate remains unsettled" because they have to change trains in Pusztaszabolcs. These are the lines with which Örkény closes the first section of the work. The human cavalcade, the emphasis on the heterogeneous yet solidary nature of the immigrants to the city is a recurring topos in descriptions of Sztálinváros.

The recollections of solidarity and chaos remained much steadier than the myth of the collective life and constituted a basic element of the local identity. The bustle and the bewilderment of the new arrivals and the topos of the "wooden-benched" train also appear thirty years later, in a 1980 "reminiscence short story" submitted as part of a literary contest organized by the City Council. The story, titled "Solus eris," begins with the following description: "Mara arrived on the 'Sztálinváros express,' which was mixed with Pullman cattle cars. Smoke was rising from the engine. The train stopped between the mechanical plant under construction and the groundwork of the future administration office. Passengers were slowly getting ready to get off. The girl looked around, hesitating in the tumult."[56]

Looking back in 1980 on his arrival in Sztálinváros, József Bodor, a middle-rank local official, recollected finding not a city, but rather chaos and muddy puddles:

> I went there, unofficially.[57] I was looking for the city. I crossed the village and found myself in the middle of a muddy pool. It was a gigantic sea of mud, immense quantities of materials were being delivered, trucks were coming and going, there was a great bustle. We were swept to the edge of the road, right in the mud. . . . Workers watched on with a bit of Schadenfreude as a man with a briefcase—at the time many of these men came bringing directives—got his little car stuck in the mud. In a word, things were chaotic. Crowds of people swarmed through the city; nobody knew who anyone was.[58]

The bustle, "the gold rush myth,"[59] and the emphasis on the flood of immigrants into the city in the propaganda literature and memoirs served to portray the foundation of Sztálinváros as a manifestation of the collective "heroic" will. The bulk of reminiscences on the history of the city and the majority of the propaganda literature and commemorative volumes all dealt with the circumstances of its creation. The people who authored recollections of the city were primarily encouraged to record their very first memories from the period 1950–51. One of the principal reasons for this was that the self-image of Sztálinváros—as in the case of other socialist cities—was grounded first and foremost in the myth of the years of its foundation, which was due in no small part to the fact that the political power that had resolved to construct the city stressed the "solidarity" of these years. The "myth of collectivity" was intertwined with the myth of the "heroic act" of founding the new settlement, and it became one of the central elements of the official depictions of Sztálinváros. One of its most important functions was to highlight the fundamentally positive components of the political system. National propaganda, with its continuous proclamations of the accomplish-

Figure 1.4. The sea of mud and the first buildings.

ments of Sztálinváros Stakhanovites, also served this goal.[60] The creation of a heroic mythos also prompted the inhabitants of the city to build their local identity in part around the memory of the initial period of the construction of the city.[61]

Written at the beginning of the 1950s, the propagandistic literature by István Örkény, Boris Palotai, András Sándor, and Tibor Tardos essentially shaped later discourse on Sztálinváros. The "Stakhanovite hero," elevated by these writers to the role of the protagonist, later (though as early as 1954) gradually became something of a "déclassé" element of the narratives or even a "recidivist" (for example, in the writings of Örkény after the death of Stalin). When Sztálinváros was part of the focus of economic policy, the residents of the city were represented in the schematic characterizations either as heroes or as misguided but essentially decent people. In contrast, after the death of Stalin and partly as a consequence of Imre Nagy's 1953 reform program, which represented de-Stalinization in Hungary, some literary works criticized the "abnormality" of Sztálinváros and labeled the residents vagrant opportunists.[62] Because of the reforms introduced by Nagy, which slowed the pace of agricultural collectivization and reduced investment in heavy industry, state investment in Sztálinváros dropped in 1954. This had two immediate consequences. The pace of construction slowed, leaving the city littered with unfinished buildings, and the city acquired a different image in the official propaganda.

Until 1954, one was not permitted to refer to higher wages as a reason for moving to Sztálinváros. Nonetheless, the Sztálinváros City Council received numerous letters in which residents of distant villages requested well-paid jobs and apartments, because both were readily available in the new city (or so they had heard). In fact, in 1959 local officials complained that "several times a patient of a psychiatric ward or a convict of the Employment Squad was sent to Sztálinváros to find a job and given the promise that later they would receive accommodation."[63]

When looking back on their decisions to move to the city, most people explain that they were motivated by the hope of finding better wages and better lodgings. This perception was not due exclusively to the propaganda literature, but actually had a basis in reality. Between 1951 and 1953 the city was better supplied with foodstuffs and manufactured goods than other cities outside Budapest, which is amply attested to in retail business statistics as well as people's recollections.[64] Similarly, wages were higher, otherwise no one would have relocated to the new city. Furthermore, skilled workers and white-collar technical workers (technical staff representing lower-level managers) were given housing quickly, and this was a significant factor for those who wished to move. In contrast, for the residents of the barrack-like dwellings surrounding the ironworks, who flocked in from villages and scraped together a living as unskilled workers doing odd jobs in Sztálinváros, one of the largest construction sites in the country, the city simply represented a place to flee from the poverty of rural life. Naturally, both the myth of "poverty" and the myth of "abundance" had their own individual functions. While the myth of poverty became a motif of criticism of the political system and the private discourse that flourished alongside the prevailing state discourse, the myth of abundance became an element of favorable views of the regime that contributed to shaping the identity of the city's residents. The myth of abundance also played an important role in the propaganda on local cultural life, partly as an effort to demonstrate that in a "socialist city" people enjoyed higher standards of living than they had under "capitalism."[65]

The various points of orientation that people emphasized in their recollections of arrival in Sztálinváros depended in part on whether or not they regarded the construction of the city as negative or positive. While the socialist realist literature mentioned Stalin Avenue, which in places reminded the authors of a metropolitan boulevard (András Sándor), the first street (István Örkény), or party headquarters (Boris Palotai), others, the unofficial storytellers, found their bearings by orienting themselves around the infamous bar named "The Dive" (*Késdobáló*), the tumult at the market, or the stacks of rafters and beams. However, the Stalinist image of the "heroism" of the first builders was transformed and used again as an important element after the de-Stalinization campaign. The state officials needed a new and legitimate image of Sztálinváros after the mid-1950s, but the locals also participated in this identity-building process. The Stalinist images and the local rumors regarding the construction of the city were mixed in a new way to transform the myths of the city and create a new local identity after the mid-1950s, which was convenient for both the officials and the local inhabitants.

The Melting Pot and Rootlessness: The Visions of the New Intelligentsia

The Ministry of Interior also inherited this social image, as indicated by the fact that the first pages of the dossier on Sztálinváros begin with a 1959 document by András Sándor in which Sándor examines the society of the city and its role in 1956. It was a telling choice, for Sándor had shown himself to be a reliable minion for the intelligence services. Sándor's perception of Sztálinváros society was not without antecedents, and his statements summarize myths about the city that had already become deeply ingrained in the public imagination. Sándor wrote of the sharp contrasts of Sztálinváros in his report for the intelligence services: "From the outset, the diverse nature of the citizenry found manifestation in sharp contrasts. The most valuable creative geniuses alongside opportunists, outstanding skilled workers alongside lumpen proletarians, peasant laborers still attached to the land alongside former counts, socialist soldiers alongside fascists, ambitious youngsters alongside déclassé individuals, nuns alongside prostitutes, earnest members of centuries-old foundry dynasties alongside gold diggers, all were mixed in the city like pure raw iron and the rusty iron scrap in a blast-furnace."[66]

These sharp contrasts (rural/urban, working-class aristocracy/lumpen proletariat, young/old, skilled/unskilled workers) were recurring motifs in representations of the city, and they reinforced the official discourse, which expressed the significance of the state's mission to create a "classless society" by emphasizing existing differences and promising that the city will strip away social differences.

András Sándor, a man compelled to rewrite the story of his life many times, was one of the most captivating creators of the myth of Sztálinváros rootlessness. His life was a representation of the "new intelligentsia," which was constantly searching for new strongholds and for a short time found them in the peculiarities of the melting pot.

The definition of "new intelligentsia" became much broader, and came to include a wider spectrum of people, ranging from technical professionals to anyone who had completed a degree in higher education. In short, it came to designate a new administrative and specialist elite. In other words, the concept of the "intelligentsia" changed. It no longer designated a lifestyle, but referred instead to schooling, qualifications, and family background, and thereby became easier to use as a statistical category. As a statistical category, the members of the "new intelligentsia" were the descendants of workers and peasants or hailed from these "classes."[67]

In 1950, Sándor went to Sztálinváros, a city still under construction. He became one of the so-called people's educators, who would travel, often from village to village, spreading communist teachings (*népművelő*). He was considered an adherent of Imre Nagy, the prime minister in 1953, who later became the symbol of de-Stalinization in Hungary. In May 1956, Sándor organized an intellectual club in Sztálinváros based on the model of the Petőfi Circle in Budapest (the "antechamber" of the revolt in October), the function of which was to organize debates on the new model of socialism. After the suppression of the revolt against Stalinism and Soviet occupation in October 1956,[68] Sándor was arrested on November 22, but released in January 1957. He was arrested again on February 18. On March 3, 1958, he was sentenced to serve eight years in prison by the court of first instance. On October 4, 1958, the sentence was reduced to six years by the Supreme Court.[69]

The following year he was compelled to compose a confession (as was common practice with political prisoners at the time) that also included a history of Sztálinváros. His principal aim may have been to meet official expectations in order to have his sentence reduced. As he was an adept writer, this cannot have been a terribly difficult task, particularly since he knew that his liberty was at stake. His confession turned out to be so persuasive and paradigmatic that it became a point of departure for the Ministry of Interior's presentations on the city. In April 1960, as part of the first general amnesty, he was released from jail.[70] Sándor's representation of Sztálinváros, paradigmatic in the eyes of the authorities, was based on a model of discontinuity. In compliance with this image, in his view and the view of many others even as late as 1956, the major issue for Sztálinváros society remained "rootlessness." According to Sándor, "even in 1956 the majority of the population regarded the city as a temporary or secondary residence, and they were more inclined to take advantage of the opportunities they found in the city than to consider themselves residents."[71]

This characterization resurfaces in the 1970s recollections of Jenő Tapolczai, the charismatic local council head, and in a 1980 interview with Ferenc Lombos, the first party secretary of the Stalin Ironworks construction. The same stereotype is reinforced in his memoirs (published in 1984) by his successor, László Földes, who was also the author of a 1980 sociography on Sztálinváros compiled at official request. In addition to stressing the "heroic" nature of the foundation of Sztálinváros, the emphasis on the charismatic character of the council chair, Tapolczai—who in contrast to the city party secretary better represented local identity—also served to cast him as a central character in the events.[72] The "myth of rootlessness" bore a role similar to the exaggeration of local social conflicts: it served primarily to confirm the notion that, in contrast to the "old regime," a "new order" was rising in the city (and by implication in the country).

This, however, did not mean that the heroic founders of the city were deprived of their mythic aura. On the contrary, the imaginative presentation of the crowds of "criminals," "prostitutes," "déclassé individuals," and "transitory residents" cast the efforts of the "real builders" in an even more emphatic light. As a well-worn literary topos, the exaggeration of adversities and inimical forces always amplifies the valor of the triumphant hero. In the case of Sztálinváros, the exaggerated presentations of natural hardships such as loess, mud, insufficient infrastructure, and the presence of swarms of antagonists, "criminals," and "the déclassé" also served this function. With the changing political perceptions of the city, however, the topos, the initial function of which was to highlight the greatness of "heroes," began to acquire contrary connotations, and in private discourse that was carried on in opposition to the regime it bore a different meaning. Primarily due to the growing image of the city as a twentieth-century Potemkin village, the exaggerations seemed to express the weakness of the political regime, and they gradually became objects of derision.

The main character of a novella (submitted in 1980 to a literary contest held by the Sztálinváros City Council), Mara, who "arrived on the 'Sztálinváros express,' which was mixed with Pullman cattle cars," had also been a prostitute from "Franzstadt" (a Hungarian nickname for the Ferencváros, a "working class district" of Budapest). In the story she flees from the oppressive "madam" and "pimps" to Sztálinváros, which symbolizes freedom.[73] The presentation of the only female character in the story exemplifies the prejudices regarding the women who arrived in Sztálinváros in the early years. According to public opinion, "a decent woman would hardly come to the city." Many thought that, given the city's bad reputation, at least until 1954, no married man would have brought his family there. If a woman came to the city by herself to work, she was considered "lascivious." Although she hopes to start a new life, Mara behaves lasciviously, both in the apartment in the old district and at the New Year's party. "A young man wearing a lambskin hat" also appears, and he invites the male protagonist to "amuse himself" with "the girls," where "debauchery hardly needed to be forced."[74]

In various representations, two myths of "Sztálinváros women" emerge. One is the aforementioned "lascivious woman," the other is the myth of the "heroic working woman" who overcomes the difficulties of the weather and other adversities. This working woman was also a central element in the official propaganda. In the Örkény reportage cited above, Marika represents this mythic character. "It would be difficult to tell whether she is thin or plump, because she wears as many layers of clothes as an onion has peels. Because of the continuous winds, she dons thick trousers, tucks in a long-sleeved dark blue sweater, on top of this she wears a light-blue quilted jacket as thick as a blanket. She ties them all together with a narrow belt around her waist."[75]

Figure 1.5. Zsófia Tevan, the engineer at the so-called "female workers' construction site."

The "heroic working women" of Sztálinváros popped up the most frequently in portrayals of "female" construction projects. The construction work was referred to as "female" because all those involved, from the members of the brigades to the directors of the projects, were female. By creating this model, the political regime intended to demonstrate that women were perfectly able to undertake building and construction work, which were generally considered "men's occupations." Even today Johanna Wolf, the engineer in chief of the National Construction Enterprise no. 26. (which carried out the aboveground construction in Sztálinváros), and Zsófia Tevan, the overseer of the "female construction workers," are both referred to in people's recollections and in the literature on the history of women as female representatives of professional expertise in their fields.[76] The contradictory representations of the women of Sztálinváros in short stories was also intended to present the city as a site of liberation from the norms based on traditional perceptions of gender roles. In addition, this fit the narratives according to which the new arrivals in the city of Sztálinváros, having broken free from public scrutiny, lived according to new norms. These new norms, however, were mostly created not by the planned city, but by the new, growing city

Figure 1.6. Propaganda representation of the "female workers' construction site."

according to the recollections of not only the authors of propaganda but also the architects and planners of the city.

The Growing City and the Planned City: The Visions of the Planners

The notion that one could plan the ideal "socialist city" entirely from scratch was based on a distinction between a planned city and a city that was the product of growth over time.[77] According to this distinction, within a specified period of time (in this case the first five-year plan), it would be possible to complete a project (the city) that would be a physical embodiment of the uniform, rigid architectural conceptions characteristic of the period. However, as early as 1959 Tibor Weiner, the local chief architect, acknowledged that "planning launched the construction of a 'planned' city, but with the creation of temporary buildings such as residential barracks and buildings to serve public purposes, as well as the multitude of preparatory sites, the state-owned enterprise directing the investment prompted the organic development of a 'growing' settlement. . . . The difference between the *ultimate objectives* that had been drawn up in the plans and *the process of the natural growth of the organism* resulted in the *realistic development of the organism.*"[78]

In Weiner's view, city planners had already recognized this in the early stages. This suggests that planners envisioned the city in two radically different ways: the city as a whole could be given shape and form, as could the social processes within its boundaries, while according to the builders it could only arise as a product of "organic" development.

Only after 1956 did Weiner publicly announce this contraposition between the planned city and the growing city, a decision that was partially due to the fact that after 1956 the Kádár regime wished to distance itself from the Rákosi regime, which had come to be seen as the embodiment of Hungarian Stalinism. In 1929 Weiner spent two semesters at the Dessau Bauhaus and worked under the supervision of Hannes Meyer. The same year, at the invitation of Walter Gropius, he participated in the founding congress of CIAM,[79] the leading figure of which was Le Corbusier. In 1931, following the expulsion of his supervisor, he traveled to the Soviet Union with Meyer and some of his students to plan cities there.[80] After working on several school buildings, he contributed to the Moscow organization plan and the underground project. Beginning in 1937 he lived in Paris, and because of the war, then fled to Chile, where he designed private residences and public buildings as an independent architect until 1946. After his return to Hungary he worked on his most grandiose plan, the Sztálinváros project, until his death in 1963.[81] For the highly experienced, internationally well-known, widely traveled architect, Sztálinváros was not merely an experimental site, but also a chance to realize his dreams. However, it also represented the limit to these dreams. For this reason, Sztálinváros bears the signs of modernist, functionalist, and Bauhaus architecture, but also socialist realist "Stalin baroque," which was most visible after 1954. In a peculiar twist, the plans that were drawn up at the beginning of the 1950s, well after the heyday of modernist architectural, were only realized in the city after the death of Stalin in 1953.

One of the primary functions of Sztálinváros in the visions of its planners was to "secure the placement of workers in factories working together with the ironworks, at the same time it should serve as a district seat, and as an organizing force it should involve the population of surrounding underdeveloped settlements in the building of socialism."[82] This definition of scope and tasks sheds light on the territorial division of labor between the city and the region. Architects believed that as a central site Sztálinváros would affect surrounding settlements, and those hierarchically subordinated to it would be modernized by the industrialization of the city. In the course of planning, the hierarchical subordination of the surrounding settlements was maintained through the specification of the functions of the city. The estimated number of people "residing in the farther outskirts, who will be administratively, culturally, and socially served by the central

Figure 1.7. Tibor Weiner, chief architect of Sztálinváros.

nature of Sztálinváros," is fifty thousand.[83] Only gradually, however, with the establishment of infrastructure, did Sztálinváros begin to fulfill central functions (such as marketplace and urban workplace) for the surrounding settlements.

Writings by Weiner and his fellow architects reveal an ongoing conflict between faith in the omnipotence of planning and skepticism springing from the unpredictability of the "growing" city. Due to the symbolic nature of Sztálinváros, these two approaches have survived into the present, and have even been accorded considerable attention in historic representations. This is also due partly to perceptions of the 1950s. Sztálinváros became more than a symbol of the "socialist city" in Hungary, it also came to represent the 1950s. In this interpretative framework, the Hungarian society of the 1950s "drifted off" the course of natural development, Stalinism ran counter to "authentic" Hungarian history, and in 1956 the "subdued masses" attempted to right these wrongs.[84]

According to this, Weiner depicted Sztálinváros as a kaleidoscope of the trends of the 1950s: "This city was laden with contradictions. It became a kaleidoscope of stylistic trends that changed year to year, experiments, research into new tools and new forms of expression, solutions adopted because of compulsion, which within a traditional architectural framework strove to achieve both the economical and the luxurious."[85]

The city remained in this kaleidoscopic state, just as its society, "the socialist city," or "the 1950s" continued to be associated with Stalinism. The portrayal of Sztálinváros as a torso fits the interpretation according to which the 1950s was a jumble of unfinished historical and social processes that alternately represented continuity and discontinuity.

Conclusion

In 1970 the local museum was moved into the building of the former party headquarters. In 1975 it was named "Intercisa" after the former Roman settlement near the city. There is some irony to the fact that, because of the excavations undertaken in the process of building Sztálinváros, Intercisa became one of the most thoroughly examined settlements of the Roman borderlands in Hungary. Thus Intercisa owes its status as a historical site (a symbolic historical site at that) to Sztálinváros.[86]

In the case of Sztálinváros, any interrogation of historical continuity constituted an interrogation of the essential purpose of the creation of the city itself. Not coincidentally, local historical publications and museum exhibitions partly responsible for creating the history of Sztálinváros attempted to emphasize the continuity between Sztálinváros and the past of Dunapentele quite early on. One of the first local exhibitions in 1954 displayed the history of the settlement from prehistoric times. Only one of the three showrooms dealt with "the new city," and only one-tenth of the exhibition brochure included information on the recent past.[87] Up to the present day, the fact that a Roman settlement existed on the territory of Sztálinváros (or Dunaújváros) is considered an "organic" part of local history. One of the districts built in the 1960s was named the "Roman" district not simply to call attention to archaeological findings, but rather—and more important—to emphasize this "continuity" and thus provide justification for the establishment of the settlement as a city.[88]

Nonetheless, references to the ancient past of the settlement played a key role in the creation of local identity. One of the most enduring elements of representations of the city of Sztálinváros became the emphasis not on its socialist past but rather on ancient antecedents as symbols of its organic history, independent of the regime, as if the origins of the city had not lain in the policies of Stalinism. The discontinuity of Stalinism on the one hand and the continuity of the "ancient past" on the other became basic, if controversial elements of the official narratives of the history of the city after the late 1950s.

In 1959 András Sándor wrote on Sztálinváros: "Rootlessness in itself is a hazard. Few people were able to strike root in the course of only a few years (eventually, they became the sprouting plasma, the drop of protein)."[89] What was presented as rootlessness in the local newspaper, people's recollections, and the documents of the council bodies was rather a process of transformation, changes that were difficult for the people at the time to grasp, shaped by a discourse that strove to separate the past from the future, "the village" from "the city."

The emphasis on rootlessness and the separation of "old" (traditional) and "modern" (meeting official expectations) elements of life played a crucial role in the creation of a distinctive identity for residents of Sztálinváros. This is palpable in the propagandistic description by the local journalist, Miklós Miskolczi, in which he attempts to portray the identity of the Sztálinváros citizen as displayed in different situations:

> A person who struggled to learn to read and write in the evenings in order to learn a trade at the national enterprise and rise in the world was a Sztálinváros citizen. The man who had arrived in Sztálinváros as a distinguished master of a profession and was managing dangerous machinery with one hand and downing ten pitchers of beer with the other after he had finished his shift was also a Sztálinváros citizen. A Sztálinváros citizen had arrived as a scared member of the petite bourgeoisie, but then, having discovered his true identity, he reinvented his life and within a few years did not even remember his former self. A Sztálinváros citizen would try to take a seat in the restaurant of the hotel wearing a checkered shirt and a quilted jacket with plaster stains on it, and when refused service, would slap the manager. . . . A citizen of Sztálinváros might be someone who himself tortured the poor accordion, but nonetheless paid for music lessons for his son and daughter.[90]

Sztálinváros could only be regarded as a city if the concept of a city itself, and with it, the ways in which the inhabitants of the city perceived everyday life were changed. Myths woven around the radically novel urban image became a starting point for the creation of a distinct identity of the denizens of the burgeoning community. Myths of the heroic persistence of the city's founders, a gold rush, rootlessness, a melting pot and cosmopolitanism, the planned city and the growing city were divided along differing perceptions of the political regime, providing positive and negative frames for stories of the city. Incompleteness was a significant component of the Sztálinváros image. It implied that the city was always changing and changeable, and was furthermore capable of representing not only chaos but also freedom in the communist chaos in a contradictory way that was also shaped by the agency of ordinary people. It also enabled residents to define their local identity in accordance with whatever political myth happened to be the most suitable at the time. After the mid-1950s, the myths of collective life and the heroic founders were transformed into myths of chaos and gold rush to create a common basis for local identity. These new myths were acceptable for both the locals and the official expectations. This process reloaded the early myths of the city and helped to build new identities based on the effects of Stalinist policies, which were also shaped by the local denizens and the visitors who described the city.

Recalling their experiences, people created various frames for their stories and histories depending in part on the social spaces they chose to depict and the theatrical scenes on which they dwelt. These choices played a significant role in the processes of myth formation, since the creation of space is itself an important narrative act. For this reason, in what follows I examine several significant characteristics of this narrative act by analyzing the narrative spaces of the city and the accounts of the people who moved in, made use of, and interpreted these spaces. More specifically, I examine the process whereby urban space and Clarence Perry's theory of neighborhood units became a means of representing social distances and diversities in a city in which social inequalities were theoretically nonexistent.

Notes

Epigraph: Lázár, *Örkény István*, 168.

1. Miskolczi, *Város lesz csakazértis*, 17.

2. On Hungarian national myths, see Gyáni, "Sorskérdések és az önmegértés."

3. By no means was the social composition of Sztálinváros typical of Hungarian cities or the envisioned urban "lifestyle." For this very reason it was considered a city of "immigrants." Euphemistically put, it was considered as "cosmopolitan" as New York. Cf. Bender, *The Unfinished City*, 185–97. Its cosmopolitan nature was particularly evident in comparison with the county seat, which was seen as being rather conservative. See. for example. Miskolczi, *Város lesz csakazértis*, or the "confession" of András Sándor regarding downtown intelligentsia, cited later in this chapter.

4. For decades, research on urban representations (images) has been a significant component of urban history. It includes the examination of spatial (primarily architectural) structures as well as literary, artistic, and even film representations of given communities. For the most widely known work on the analysis of spatial structures and images of the city, see Lynch, *The Image of the City*. A similar topic is explored by Strauss, *Images of the American City*. Burton Pike offers an outstanding summary of topics in relation to literary representations of cities in, *The Image of the City in Modern Literature*.

5. I use the term *myth* as defined by Jan Assmann, who regards myth as a story that serves as the basis for an understanding of the present and cultural memory. Myth is often contrasted to the notion of history. In addition, myth formulates normative claims and has a creative force. In this case the process of creating myths is the interpretation of individual or collective memory as core stories, which does not question the reality of past stories constructed into events. See Assmann, *Das kulturelle Gedächtnis*, 76.

6. The Deutsche Brassert GmbH was an affiliated firm of H. A. Brassert & Company. Kántor, *Így épült a vas és acél országa*. For more on Brassert & Company, see Glenn, *The Washingtons*, 149; Chandler, *Scale and Scope*, 325.

7. Korompay, *40 éves a Dunai Vasmű*, 12.

8. For Soviet policy in Hungary, see Borhi, *Hungary in the Cold War*, 47–75.

9. Magyar Nemzeti Levéltár Országos Levéltára (MNL OL [Hungarian National Archives]), f. M-KS 276, description (*csomó*) 53, preservation unit (*őrzési egység*) 42. Minutes of the meeting

from the December 27, 1949, session of the Political Committee of the Magyar Dolgozók Pártja (=MDP [Hungarian Workers' Party].

10. The term *kulak* was borrowed in Hungary from discourses in the Soviet Union during the first collectivization campaign at the beginning of the 1950s, and it became a social category consisting of relatively affluent independent farmers. Officially, every independent farmer in Hungary who owned more than 25 cadastral acres (1.42 acres) was labeled a kulak after 1948 and had his land expropriated.

11. For a good summary of this period of Hungarian history, see Gyáni, Kövér, and Valuch, *Social History of Hungary*. Gyarmati and Valuch, *Hungary under Soviet Domination*. On the position of the country in the international constellation, see Borhi, *Hungary in the Cold War*.

12. On the economic history of new towns in East Central Europe, see Jajeśniak-Quast, *Stahlgiganten in der sozialistischen Transformation*. For a social and cultural history of Nowa Huta, see Lebow, *Unfinished Utopia*. For Dimitrovgrad, see Brunnbauer, "'The Town of the Youth,'"; on the planning history of Stalinstadt in the GDR, see May, *Planstadt Stalinstadt*.

13. The Soviet administrative model was introduced in Hungary in 1950 in a bill concerning local councils.

14. Minisztertanács 1007/1951. (1951.IV.29.) sz. határozata [Cabinet Resolution no. 1007/1951. April 29, 1951].

15. French and Hamilton, *The Socialist City*, 11.

16. MNL OL, f. XXVI-D-8-f, b. 88, f. 2. Proposition for the approbation of the Sztálinváros development plan.

17. *Dunaújváros: 1950–1965*, 8–11. The proportions of breadwinners and dependents were 58 percent and 42 percent, respectively, in 1960. Since then the population of the city has scarcely increased. In 2009 48,000 people resided in Dunaújváros, which was considered host to the most rapidly "aging" society of the region. *Megyei jogú városok a Közép-Dunántúlon, 2009*.

18. On these economic models, see Kornai, *The Socialist System*. Miskolczi begins his sociographical analysis of Sztálinváros's "demystified history" by introducing the program and five-year plan of the MKP (Hungarian Communist Party); see Miskolczi, *Város lesz csakazértis*, 47–54. Valuch presents Sztálinváros through the politics of forced industrialization and settlement development, see Valuch, *Magyarország társadalomtörténete*, 52–53. Other examples include Romsics, *Magyarország története a XX. században*, and Pető and Szakács, *A hazai gazdaság négy évtizedének története*.

19. Weiner, "Sztálinváros," 85.

20. On the function of Soviet rituals in demonstrating the contrast between the collective and the individual, see Lane, *The Rites of Rulers*, 61–64.

21. Kharkhordin, *The Collective and the Individual in Russia*, 76.

22. In his 1930 fundamental work on socialist urban planning, Nikolai Miliutin contends that "'The new way of life must be born as a natural result of the new organization of labor and housing and of the proper organization of institutions for collectivized social services to meet the needs of the population." Miliutin, *Sotsgorod*, 79.

23. MNL OL, f. XXVI-D-8, Várostervezési Intézet [Institute for City Planning], b. 88, Proposition for sanctioning Sztálinváros urban planning. In the Soviet plans the city center is surrounded by micro districts (*microraion*) housing 8,000–12,000 residents.

24. Perry, *The Rebuilding of Blighted Areas*; Perry, *The School as a Factor*.

25. Hannerz, *Exploring the City*, 19–58.

26. See Anderson, "Columbia Association to Drop 'People Tree' from Logo," and Bailey, *New Towns in America*, 16–17. For additional examples, see Power, *Estates on the Edge*. Although historic sources tend to lump new cities together, there are considerable differences

between them. For example, some are built as satellite towns around a city while others are created to serve a new industrial plant. On these differences and comparisons of several new cities in America, see Bailey, *New Towns in America*, 115–53.

27. Weiner, "Sztálinváros," 39.

28. For a detailed explanation of the Radburn principle, see Relph, *The Modern Urban Landscape*, 65–67.

29. Matussné and Pongrácz, *Dunaújváros története képeslapokon*, 98.

30. Heineberg, "Service Centres in East and West Berlin," 311.

31. Skyscrapers are often symbols of fears related to modern urban development. See Lindner, "The Death and Return of the New York Skyscraper," 122–26.

32. By this time architects were concerned less with monumentality and more with ensuring that the tower "would provide, from different perspectives, essential junctions to various directions of development." MNL OL, f. XXVI-D-8, b. 89, file 745, Title: Sztálinváros building plans. The construction schedule of the second five-year plan.

33. One example of this is the 1953 proposition made to the Political Committee of the Hungarian Workers' Party. MNL OL, f. 276, cs. 53, ő.e. 142 (October 21, 1953).

34. Állambiztonsági Szolgálatok Történeti Levéltára (ÁSZTL) [Historical Archives of the Hungarian State Security], 3.1.5, file O-13582, page 12.

35. For the history of the statue and the ideas related to it, see von Plato, "(K)ein Platz für Karl Marx." In addition to Sztálinváros, Eisenhüttenstadt (Stalinstadt) also offers an example of a half-finished main square. May, *Planstadt Stalinstadt*, 210–313, provides a detailed account of the history of planning and construction. In Nowa Huta a monumental theater was planned on the southern side of the main square on the one hand to mark the end of the square and on the other to stress its grandiosity. On the planning process of the main square in Nowa Huta, see Lebow, *Unfinished Utopia*, 30–32, 40.

36. On the sides of houses opposite the streets, quadrangles were formulated partly in accordance with the Radburn principle and partly because architects unintentionally copied the row of working-class houses built in the nineteenth century in Port Sunlight, Liverpool. These houses also form quadrangles. For more, see Crouch, *Design Culture in Liverpool*, 16–19.

37. Cf. Palotai, "Egy nap Dunapentelén," and Ember, *Sztálinvárosiak*.

38. *A kölyök* [The kid] (1959), directed by Mihály Szemes. The "socialist city" also figured in Soviet propaganda as an "educational site." In the local Komsomol, or youth division of the Communist Party of the Soviet Union, the city of Magnitogorsk was claimed "to have taught us how to work. Magnitka taught us to live." Kotkin, *Magnetic Mountain*, 198. In reference to the analysis of the official discourse in the German Democratic Republic, German social history discusses this locution as part of an "educational autocracy" (*Erziehungsdiktatur*). Ludwig, *Fortschritt, Norm und Eigensinn*, and Haeder, *Schülerkindheit in Ost-Berlin*.

39. FML, f. XXIII-510, b. 2, 1954, Petition for an apartment submitted to the Sztálinváros City Council Social Division of Health Department.

40. Several works describe how some people accepted and internalized the official Stalinist worldview. One important work among these is Hellbeck, *Revolution on My Mind*.

41. Kharkhordin, *The Collective and the Individual in Russia*, 190–200.

42. Örkény, *Visszanézve*, 381–86.

43. Simon, *A groteszktől a groteszkig*, 51.

44. Ibid., 52–54.

45. Lázár, *Örkény István*, 168.

46. Lebow, *Unfinished Utopia*, 183.

47. Cf. the melting pot character of the American "steel city," Gary, in O'Hara, *Gary*, 105.

48. The educational function of the city can be traced back to the concept of *kul'turnost'*, "the personal attributes of a 'cultured' person. Kul'turnost' was reflected in the way one spoke, ate, dressed, made love, and went to the bathroom." Lebow, *"Kontra Kultura,"* 74.

49. FML, f. XXIV-11, b. 9, 1957–58, report on police achievements of 1957–58.

50. Cf. Lebow, *Unfinished Utopia,* 6.

51. Örkény, "Sztálinvárosi képeskönyv," 346.

52. For a more detailed discussion of Örkény's significance, see Szirák, "A Grotesque Allegory of Human Dignity."

53. Lázár, *Örkény István,* 167.

54. Örkény, "Sztálinvárosi képeskönyv," 346.

55. Szabó, *Cifra nyomorúság,* 110–15. For more representations of this topos, see László-Bencsik, *Történelem alulnézetben*; Tar, "6714-es személy"; Ember, *Sztálinvárosiak,* 32;the 1970 film, *The Black Train,* directed by Pál Schiffer.

56. FML, f. XXIII-508, box 60. A 1980 short story, "I Live in a Young City," submitted to the literary contest under the password "Solus eris." Similarly, arrival and bustle are emphasized in in the memoir of István Sudár (who served as secretary of the Fejér County Party Council in 1975), "Két nyár és az első tavasz."

57. This expression may seem comic today, but recollections of the time often draw a clear distinction between "official" and "unofficial" visits and meetings.

58. Interview with József Bodor, in Miskolczi, *Új tavasz,* 47–50.

59. The same myth is reinforced in the fictitious reminiscence of the wife of István Angyal: "I packed my belongings, and with a fiber bag and a sheepskin cover I traveled to Dunapentele, where construction was just beginning. I was attracted by *the romanticism of the gold digger city.* I was given accommodation in a hostel for young women, and as a standard unskilled construction worker in the Adamovszki brigade I was making concrete and carrying bricks.... People tend to talk about this age disparagingly today. But he and I both—he especially—sincerely believed that we were building a new world. There were no exaggerations of exceeding production norms" (emphasis added). Lukácsy, *Felismerem-e Angyal Istvánt?* 55.

60. Sztálinváros Stakhanovites in *Szabad Nép,* October 20, 1950; February 10, 1951; March 6, 1951; April 8, 21, and 25, 1951; July 28, 1951; August 29, 1951; September 28, 1951; October 28, 1951; November 3, 1951; December 23 and 31, 1951; April 4, 1952; July 27, 1952; August 7, 1952; October 11 and 20, 1952; April 6 and 15, 1953; May 17 and 18, 1953; and June 4, 1953. From the second half of 1953 Sztálinváros Stakhanovites are quoted less frequently in the columns of *Szabad Nép,* which may be attributed to the effects of Imre Nagy's government program.

61. One notes the same phenomenon in the case of Stalinstadt in the German Democratic Republic, since the circumstances of the foundation of the city also played an important role in stories about it. Ludwig, "'Traum der Zukunft—Wirklichkeit.'"

62. See, for example, Örkény, *Babik,* originally written as a screenplay in 1954, but the screenplay was never made into a film.

63. FML, f. XXIII-506,b. 21, 1957, and FML, f. XXIII-502, b. 16, Minutes of Execute Committee Meeting, June 26, 1959.

64. MNL OL, f. XIX-G-4-rr, b. 14, Documents of the Management of Domestic Trade Mine Supplies, and FML, f. XXIII-509, b. 1-2, Department of Trade and Distribution.

65. A similar process was observed in Magnitogorsk and Stalinstadt, see Kotkin, *Magnetic Mountain,* 198–237, and Vogel, "Kulturelles Leben in Stalinstadt."

66. ÁSZTL, 3.1.5, file O-13582, Hostile entities residing in the municipality of Sztálinváros, The history of the counterrevolution and the immediate period before the counterrevolution

in Sztálinváros, An overview of Sztálinváros social and class relations in 1956, Report on April 3, 1959 (hereafter, An overview of Sztálinváros in 1956).

67. On the definition of "new intelligentsia" in the Soviet Union, see Fitzpatrick, *The Cultural Front*, 177; On the adaptation of the term regarding the "new intelligentsia" in Hungary, see Majtényi, *A tudomány lajtorjája*, 51–90.

68. For a short overview of the 1956 Revolution, see Rainer, "The Hungarian Revolution of 1956," and on the role of 1956 in the Cold War, see Kramer, "New Evidence on Soviet Decision-Making."

69. For a short biography of András Sándor, see Standeisky, "Egy literátus ügynökről."

70. In 1966 he began working under the code name "Sárdi" as an unofficial informant (secret police agent), zealously reporting on his coworkers and writers. ÁSZTL, file M-35897 and M-35897/1, codename "Sárdi."

71. ÁSZTL, 3.1.5, file O-13582, An overview of Sztálinváros in 1956.

72. Tapolczai, *Egy elnök naplója*, 41; interview with Ferenc Lombos, in Miskolczi, *Új tavasz*, 19–23; Földes, *A második vonalban*, 197–98; and Miskolczi, *Város lesz csakazértis*, 13–30.

73. FML, f. XXIII-508, b. 60. The short story submitted under the password "Solus eris."

74. Ibid.

75. Örkény, "Sztálinváros képeskönyv," 355.

76. Vámos, "Wolf Johanna"; and Interview with Tibor V., March 28, 2001 by the author.

77. Weiner, "Sztálinváros," 37.

78. Ibid., 38.

79. Congrès Internationaux d'Architecture Moderne, the most influential international modernist architects' organization between 1928 and 1959.

80. For an outstanding documentary on this trip, see *Sotzgorod: Cities for Utopia*, directed by Anna Abrahams, 1995.

81. Gábor, *A CIAM magyar csoportja*; Prakfalvi and Hajdú, *Építészet és tervezés Magyarországon*.

82. MNL OL, f. XXVI-D-8-f, b. 88, unit 1, Proposition for the approbation of the Sztálinváros development plan.

83. Ibid., unit 2.

84. For a critique of this literature, see Pittaway, "Control and Consent." For Hungarian historical studies on Stalinism, see Rainer, "Revisiting Hungarian Stalinism."

85. Weiner, "Új forma új tartalom," 83.

86. In addition to the local museum, several other institutions in today's Dunaújvaros are named after the Roman settlement, including one of the largest Hungarian housing and loan associations, several local enterprises, and a local humanitarian organization. Intercisa Lakásszövetkezet [Intercisa Housing and Loan Association], Modern Intercisa 2005 Kft, and Dunaújvárosi Intercisa Lions Klub [Dunaújváros Intercisa Lions Club].

87. *Sztálinvárosi helytörténeti kiállítás*, 36–41.

88. Erdős and Pongrácz, *Dunaújváros története*, 5.

89. ÁSZTL, 3.1.5, file O-13582.

90. Miskolczi, *Az első évtized*, 106.

2 Downtown America

While the downtown area is being turned into America, . . . the walls of
buildings in the Technikum District have not yet been plastered.

Sztálinváros Hírlap, 1958

A CITY IS teeming with strangers. This is especially true if the majority of the
residents are newcomers from various regions of the country. To get by, residents
must learn to read the codes of the new city. Using a poignant metaphor for urban life, Kevin Lynch writes, "We stare into the jungle and see only the sunlight
on the green leaves, but a warning noise tells us that an animal is hidden there. . . .
In the same way, we must learn to see the hidden forms in the vast sprawl of our
cities."[1]

According to the official data, over the course of the first three years the population of Sztálinváros grew from 4,000 to 27,000.[2] The majority of new arrivals
in the city came from industrial regions, but the actual settlements from which
they hailed were nonetheless very different. Gossip, social control of the community, and the consideration of the opinions of others are not sufficient in and of
themselves to enable people to determine at first glance the extent to which a person's social status differs from their own. In any city people's physical appearances play crucial roles in the representation of their value systems and social
orientations (as I discuss later in the chapter on teddy boys in Sztálinváros). In
addition, to facilitate their own orientation in social spaces, residents designate
imaginary borders in the urban space surrounding them. They also do this in order to know what is acceptable and what is forbidden in a given space, and to
enable themselves to determine a person's social status by their home address or
even their daily route.

In this chapter, I demonstrate how the images and official depictions of individual districts of the city were transformed and shaped to create a common
narrative of the city spaces acceptable for both the officials and the inhabitants of
Sztálinváros. The transformation of this interpretation was influenced partly by
newspaper articles regarding the different districts and partly by the changing
expectations of officials and inhabitants. The function of this process was to create a more enduring narrative of the city and its social composition and to reproduce former social hierarchies in a new way.

The planners of the city, as I will discuss, wanted to create similar districts, but the different neighborhood units acquired strikingly different images. I situate the origins of this differentiation in the changes made to investment projects after Stalin's death. These changes determined not only the migration patterns of the denizens but also the images of the unfinished districts in the long run. The other reason for this differentiation was the conservative turn in the mid-1950s, which helped raise the notions of social differences in the city, in both unofficial and official perceptions and depictions of everyday life. I argue that the ways in which the inhabitants perceived the different parts of the city created an opportunity to represent social inequalities. These inequalities were in principle incompatible with the fundamental objectives of communism, but the city became more comprehensible because of this process. This division of the city districts in the popular imagination made it possible for the residents of the new urban world, who came from different social backgrounds, to orient themselves more easily and feel more at home in the city and also to accommodate to the new order of the Stalinist policies.

In the first years the city seemed chaotic and incomprehensible to its residents. When they encountered a stranger in the streets (which were still under construction), they could hardly determine the person's social ties and social place at first sight, even if his or her attire or speech offered some indications. One reason was that everyone was "covered in mud up to the ears," but more important, residents had not yet created the imaginary urban spatial divisions that would have helped them anticipate with whom they might meet in a given area. Unlike in the majority of Hungarian provincial cities, because of the high proportion of new arrivals in the city, the bulk of the population of Sztálinváros encountered far more strangers than they had in their former places of residence (with the possible exception of immigrants from Budapest). The association of residential districts with different social strata was virtually absent from official and public urban policy ideas. I will explore how the social differences became more visible in the city after the mid-1950s, not only because of the system of centralized housing allocations, the local press, and the contrast of rural and urban norms, but also because of the images that emerged in relation to the various districts.

Segregation and the System of Distributing Housing

Sztálinváros was to be "the first city in Hungary with no poor, no beggars, and no neglected outskirts," writes András Sándor in 1951.[3] According to a brochure printed in 1952: "The most eye-catching characteristic of the construction of socialist cities is that they lack both a separate downtown area and separate outlying areas. The whole city is constructed in a style as homogeneous as possible, the same modern and comfortable residential buildings can be found in the city cen-

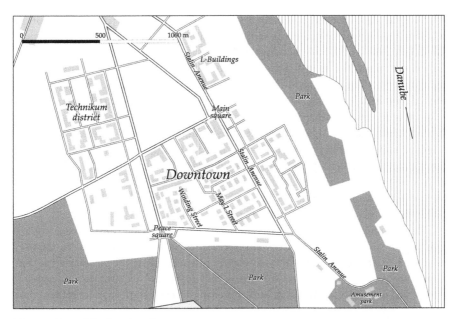

Map 2.1. Map of Sztálinváros Downtown, 1959.

ter as are found in the outlying districts. There are no separate suburbs with detached villa-like buildings, but flowerbeds and grassy, wooded parks in front of every single residential building."[4]

According to the same brochure, however, the buildings "should not all look alike."[5] One of the most significant differences between a "socialist" and a "capitalist city" in official ideas regarding urban policy was that in the socialist cities there were no social differences, in other words there was no residential separation or segregation along class lines. In the views of the urban policymakers, centralized allocation of housing would prevent residential segregation. As it so happened, the system produced quite the opposite.

Conflicts between representatives of "modernist" and "socialist realist" architectural trends left their mark on districts completed before 1956.[6] This was not the primary reason behind the segregation that began to develop in the city, however, not only because of the Stalinist policies but also because the traditional social hierarchies could survive in these forms of inequality. Architects of both Western and Eastern European "new cities" shared the fundamental view that in the new cities there should be neither poverty nor segregation. Yet the "new" planned cities proved less malleable than planners and architects had imagined, and in the end they became as segregated as the "old" cities.[7]

Regardless of their income, for the residents of Sztálinváros the question of whether they were allotted an apartment by the state was of crucial importance. The conditions on the basis of which a family was given an apartment fundamentally determined the stratification and status of the people of the city, though most of the pertinent sources were drawn up by the national enterprises and later the administrative department of the City Council. Although it is true that according to the statistics there was a serious dearth of apartments (because of the large influx of immigrants into the new industrial center), this affected various layers of the inhabitants differently. In part through informal connections, often a skilled worker whose abilities were indispensable in the workplace (even if his or her salary was hardly more than that of an unskilled worker) could obtain an apartment with considerably less difficulty than an untrained worker who had come to the city from a rural setting.[8]

In an analysis of the social composition of housing estates, Iván Szelényi, a Hungarian sociologist, demonstrated that since the end of the 1960s segregation processes existed even in the total absence or limited presence of market mechanisms. In his view, one reason for this is that "various institutions . . . employ a workforce variously structured, and therefore, a residential district attached to such a 'symbiotic complex' is potentially different in its social composition."[9] The Sztálinváros of the 1950s is a typical illustration of how, even with a limited presence of market mechanisms, perceptions concerning the segregation of districts still arise.

Sztálinváros apartments were built according to standard designs that were considered "fully developed" by the time the architectural debates concluded in the early 1950s. As early as 1946 the shortage of housing caused by the war was to be remedied by the mass production, and thus standardization, of housing.[10] At the outset, standardization and mass production were not synonymous with the construction of urban multistory complexes. In his 1948 book, Lajos Gádoros, a significant architect of the era, still insisted that the most suitable kind of accommodation for families with children was the "detached house."[11] The tide quickly turned in the field of design, however. Detached houses with their own separate gardens proved too expensive, "not only in view of actual building costs but also because their tenants tended to lose contact with the community, and became individualistic in order to protect their fences," Gádoros claimed in 1949, only a year after the publication of his argument in favor of detached houses.[12] The course had been set: standard designs for urban multistory apartment complexes had to be drawn up.

The apartments that were built according to a standard design in 1948 generally consisted of a living room and an alcove, in addition to the kitchen, hallway, bathroom, and separate toilet. Floor space was approximately fifty square meters.

Figure 2.1. The ideal and standardized apartment in Sztálinváros consisted of a living room and an alcove.

By 1949, primarily by reducing the hallway space, and later by combining the toilet and the bathroom, reducing the size of the kitchen, and finally getting rid of separate pantries, the "alcove" was made bigger and the apartments could be called two-room accommodations. New terms were introduced in housing, such as "little room," "alcove," "dinette," and "hip-bath." By 1949 the "two-room" design (in fact one-and-a-half-room) apartments prevailed, and this became the basic type of standardized housing.[13]

Rejecting "bourgeois" and "working class" types of housing, city planners emphasized a type of accommodation with characteristic features of the "modern household" and multifunctional rooms.[14] A peculiar mix of multiroom and studio apartments, "the fully equipped two-room apartment" became the dominant new type of housing after 1948. One of the fundamental principles of the program was that housing arrangements were determined not on the basis of the wealth, income, or social standing of the prospective tenants, but on the size, customs, and occupation of the family. Essentially, according to the architects of the socialist future, an ideal apartment consisted of a living room of 18–20 square meters, one (possibly two) 10–12-square-meter smaller room(s) with a separate entrance, a kitchen 7.5–10 square meters in size, and a hallway, pantry, bathroom, toilet (each of which would be as small as possible), and generally a balcony.[15] The designs used at Sztálinváros construction sites were created in accordance with this ideal.

In Sztálinváros new arrivals were socially segregated by being housed in an abundance of concentrated masses of cheap apartments. The newcomers were given different housing depending on their employment status. There were two main reasons for this, apart from the cyclical nature of Sztálinváros construction. On the one hand, in various periods apartments of differing quality were built in a given section; for example, the apartments completed after Stalin's death were of a much lower quality because of the decrease of investment funds after 1953. On the other hand, the apartments were distributed according to national enterprises. The employees of one enterprise were generally given housing in the same area of the city (sometimes in the same new building).[16] The position of the tenant in the factory employment hierarchy also played a crucial role. The majority of the best apartments were allocated to managers, high-level employees,[17] and skilled workers who were considered particularly important in the ironworks. At the other extreme, barrack apartments were assigned to construction workers who were generally already in a disadvantageous position. Thus distribution of housing contributed to the accumulation of advantages and the preservation of disadvantages and, consequently, social inequalities.[18]

At a construction enterprise committee meeting on February 23, 1951, the following problem was addressed: "Accommodation for workers must be equally distributed. How is it possible that the quality of residences for Civil Engineering employees is much higher—indeed some members of the local intelligentsia dwell in downright luxury apartments. Inequality among workers still exists. There are also considerable differences in state subsidies for white- and blue-collar workers."[19]

The differences in housing distribution addressed right after the beginning of construction grew more pronounced in later descriptions. Social segregation is not exclusively a metropolitan or market economy phenomenon. It emerged as palpably in newly built socialist cities as it did in Budapest.[20] Furthermore, research carried out in the 1960s and 1970s suggests that the social composition of various districts in medium-size Hungarian provincial cities was also characterized by segregation.[21] In provincial cities segregation did not cease after 1945. On the contrary, this was when it began to emerge in the newly built cities. The main explanation for this lies in the fact that in the socialist housing distribution system the various social groups had unequal access to apartments.[22] This inequality was not merely a factor of bureaucratic mechanisms. Rather, it also enabled members of city society to preserve, if in a different form, the social hierarchies that had existed before. Reproducing social hierarchies helped the inhabitants to accommodate to the Stalinist policies, which were shaped through this process and became more acceptable after the mid-1950s, both for officials and inhabitants of the city.

While segregation and the models describing it may represent *separation and movement* of urban social groups in physical space, the study of mental maps brings spatial and social *orientation* into focus.[23] How did residents of Sztálin-város perceive given districts of their city, and how was this perception influenced by the local print media? A city becomes visually comprehensible and "imaginable" if its districts, roads, and the social affiliations of its denizens are easily identifiable and can be properly integrated in the imaginary system people fashion regarding their city. In what follows, I examine the forces that influenced the identification process of the different parts of the city and the transformation of images that arose of the various districts of Sztálinváros.

Downtown: "Sztálinváros, Switzerland"

When May 1 Street was inaugurated as the first completed street of the city on May 1, 1951, everyone thought it was the main street of the city, though it had not been presented as such in the plans. The unfinished Stalin Avenue, the major avenue in the plans, was peripheral in 1952, as was Görbe utca (Winding Street), a meandering street that had been designed deliberately to break the monotony of the straight roads. Barracks at the verge of the downtown area were everyday sights at the time. They functioned as small outskirts. As architect in chief Tibor Weiner recalled, "In this heroic-romantic age of roads covered with mud amid the maze of drays and trucks, for the people stumbling alongside the open ditches dug by public utilities the first paved road, May 1 Street, which seemed to have sprung into bloom overnight, did indeed become main street."[24]

People may well have wondered why the main street had been built to look like any other residential street. The answer is simple: it was designed and planned to be a residential street and not the main avenue. According to the prevailing architectural ideas of the time, the main street should be bordered by block buildings of the exact same height with representative ornamentation. It should be wide and suitable for processions. Residential streets were bordered by various types of smaller dwellings. Although dwellings were built on May 1 Street, since it was the first street befitting a large city, local offices, the local branch of the Heavy Industry Investment Enterprise (which was supervising the construction), the local council, and party organs all took quarters there. In addition, the first permanent accommodations for leading members of the intelligentsia and highly skilled workers arriving in Sztálinváros were also established there.

As was the case elsewhere, avenues determined the significance in the cognitive maps of the downtown area of Sztálinváros. Kevin Lynch distinguishes five

Figure 2.2. May 1 Street.

categories that help differentiate given elements of cognitive maps. These are paths, edges, districts, nodes, and landmarks.[25] Applied to Sztálinváros, these categories suggest that May 1 Street did not simply function as a route, but also played the distinctive role of a symbol and point of orientation in descriptions of Sztálinváros.

By the summer of 1952 it had become fashionable in Sztálinváros to live on or in the immediate vicinity of May 1 Street. In a letter published in the Communist Party daily (*Szabad Nép*) rendering an account of his changes of address in Sztálinváros, one writer describes his experience of ascent in social standing by referring to his move into the "prestigious" downtown Beloiannisz Street (and it is worth noting, this "ascent" was not exclusively associated with an increase in the size or furnishings of an apartment): "I started out in the L barrack. Forty of us shared these living quarters. My next apartment was in 'cube three' (today 4 May 1 Street): I shared the first floor with seventeen tenants. Then I was given a small room in 'cube seven' (Ady Endre Street, a residential building next to May 1 Street). Finally, with my family I was able to move into I/1. Section (16 Beloiannisz Street, next to May 1 Street). It was an apartment with three rooms, central heating, and a bathroom and study."[26]

Figure 2.3. May 1 Street and the city lights.

As illustrated by an official photograph taken in May 1951, May 1 Street acquired such an atmosphere of "downtown" life that it was frequented primarily by smartly dressed people (although it is quite possible that this was true only of the time at which the photo was taken). In addition, the sidewalk and the roadway were not separated for traffic, so pedestrians strolled both on the sidewalk and on the roadway. In the daytime the street was packed primarily with pedestrians rushing to offices or people working on it.[27] The buildings lining the street were also the first in the city to have electricity installed.[28] However, in 1951 May 1 Street still gave the impression of being the center of a gigantic construction site, and it hardly had the atmosphere of a downtown street.

Opened in the summer of 1951, Béke (Peace) Restaurant, an establishment at the end of May 1 Street, attracted individuals considered undesirable by the residents, who had numerous conflicts with them. Béke Restaurant figured as a spatial and social center in mental maps of Sztálinváros. Conflicts began when offices started to move out of the buildings on May 1 Street and higher-level employees and highly skilled workers began to move in, people who in general had been used to a "quiet" life. Residents of May 1 Street bombarded the office of the local newspaper with letters of complaint, and these letters were published by editors, the majority of whom were also downtown residents. The primary sources of conflict described in the paper were the two restaurants at the end of the street: "At one end of May 1 Street there is Kossuth Restaurant, at the other Béke. From 11:00 PM until 3:00 AM these places disturb the rest of the residents, who are exhausted after a day of hard and honest work, with horrible brawling, fighting, 'singing' and obscenities," lamented one letter writer.[29] In 1951–52, Peace Square (Béke tér), a public space at the corner of the downtown area, was a place of upheaval and chaos. Only the people who lived on May 1 Street were characterized as living an "exemplary" life by the local newspaper. This situation changed in 1953 with the opening of the ironworks, when the population of Sztálinváros, which had been relatively homogeneous, began to become more diverse. The social cleansing of the downtown area began, much to the delight of the people of higher social status who lived in it. The social intermixing of the early years was less acceptable after the conservative turn and the segregation of the districts. Segregation became characteristic of the city as each of the districts acquired a distinct place in the reemerging social hierarchy.

This was all a consequence of the fact that people of innumerable social backgrounds had settled in a relatively small area. The residents of the downtown area, who had arrived there in the early years, were on the whole very different from those who came after 1953. They were primarily unskilled workers with little or no education who had come to the city to work in construction. After 1953, with the opening of the ironworks, ironworkers with more formal education settled in Sztálinváros. The Sztálinváros City Council played an increasingly important role in the distribution of housing, so the social cleansing of the downtown area was also supported by a more important administrative institution.

From several perspectives, 1953 was a turning point in the history of Sztálinváros. Resolution number 78/1952, passed by the People's Economic Council, commissioned Hungarian enterprises to transfer highly skilled and well-trained employees to the Stalin Ironworks.[30] Although most of the companies were reluctant to implement the resolution, several thousand highly skilled workers arrived in Sztálinváros in the hope of earning higher incomes and being given housing promptly. As the ironworks was in need of skilled workers to launch production, these experts generally received accommodation and high wages within a few months. Construction workers, most of whom had come from villages and who until then had dominated the city, did not receive permanent housing because there was a surplus of unskilled labor. They continued to reside in barracks and were gradually driven out of downtown restaurants and bars.

The process of "cleansing" the downtown area of undesirable people and events and the conflicts that arose between social groups with different social habits were part of a larger process whereby social conflicts were channeled at the level of discourse, and the urban spaces were linked to groups with diverging lifestyles. In 1954, according to the local newspaper, the City Council, under pressure from downtown residents, issued several statutes that were intended primarily to make the downtown area a residential neighborhood for "respectable lifestyles." Of course, the requests of the local residents were taken into consideration only if they overlapped with the goals of the local bureaucrats, who also sought to "cleanse" the downtown area (where many of them lived as well). Both groups wanted to create a "socially cleaner" downtown in part to demonstrate the success of the construction of the city and in part to strengthen the social status of the downtown inhabitants. The same year the management of the Béke Restaurant decided to ban intoxicated, slovenly customers.[31] In the downtown district several dozen people were fined for breaches of the peace, or, to be more precise, for "howling up and down" the street.[32] In the fall of 1954, people who "kept dogs, rabbits, and other animals without permission" in downtown residential apartments were also fined.[33] The same year saw the beginning of full-scale landscaping in downtown Sztálinváros.[34]

According to a report in the local newspaper in December 1954, a member of the Sztálinváros City Council representing the downtown area was not kept very busy by his district. Allegedly, his most daunting challenges were to protect flower beds and keep construction debris from more distant building sites away from downtown. The report stated that the supervision of the cleanliness of the district was to be achieved with the creation of residential councils.[35] Although the newspaper offered rather illusory images of the situation, in comparison with other Sztálinváros districts it reported far fewer problems and more positive aspects of life in the vicinity of May 1 Street. In 1954 apartments designated as temporary accommodation were beginning to be allocated as permanent housing. According to the narratives of the newspaper reports, the area slowly became a neighborhood for Sztálinváros residents with a consolidated lifestyle. "Troublemakers" were gradually driven out from the Béke Restaurant, and this was depicted as a positive development. Üzletház, essentially "department store," at the end of May 1 Street was the first shop in Hungary to carry nylon stockings.[36] The Hotel Arany Csillag (Golden Star) and the Dózsa movie theater opened at the end of 1951. The housewives of May 1 Street could collectively use the "modern washing machine" installed at 6 May 1 Street.[37]

The December 31, 1953, opening of the Béla Bartók House of Culture at the end of May 1 Street, placed the cultural center of the area in a representative space. By November 1954, the hall had become home to ballet and literature clubs, a chamber orchestra, and a doctors-teachers club.[38] By 1956 it was hosting opera and theatrical performances.[39] The building had a movie theater, and dances were organized as well, thus residents from the outskirts also visited the hall. The

Figure 2.4. The first ballet exam in the House of Culture (Sztálinváros, 1955).

Béla Bartók House of Culture was considered the informal center of Sztálinváros, even in 1956.

The value of downtown apartments was steadily increasing, a change one can discern in advertisements for apartment transfers. Residents were given apartments to rent from the state through the local City Council, and if one were assigned an apartment, this could last a lifetime and indeed later even became inheritable. Nonetheless, a practice of bartering emerged that resembled a sort of marketplace transaction. For example, residents would offer their claim to an apartment for exchange in the classified ads. The value of the apartment depended on its location, size, and cost of rent. By 1956 people were offering to trade an apartment in Budapest in a prestigious district, on the so-called Szabadság Hegy (or "liberation hill"), for an apartment in downtown Sztálinváros, in all probability because of a well-paid job opening in Sztálinváros.[40] Whatever the case, the advertisement itself indicates that people of diverse social backgrounds were arriving in Sztálinváros. In accordance with their social place, newcomers of the most privileged backgrounds attempted to obtain housing downtown.

Figure 2.5. Stalin Avenue.

The number of downtown locales hosting intellectual meetings further increased with the opening of the Fáklya (Torch) Club in May 1956.[41] Numerous private balls were held in the restaurant of Hotel Arany Csillag and the "social column" (a regular section of the paper that reported local news) of the *Sztálinváros Hírlap* provided continuous coverage of these events.[42] In 1959 András Sándor described the hotel and restaurant as "bearers of a kind of provincial cosmopolitanism and fashionableness, as if providing a substitute for diversions of the capital city for certain circles of the intelligentsia and the emerging class of skilled professionals."[43]

In 1957 Stalin Avenue, which according to the initial plans was to be the main road of the city, began to come into use. In 1952 it was still full of bushes, mounds of dirt, and construction debris.[44] As had been done in the areas on and around May 1 Street in 1954, first the status of the apartments as "temporary housing" was terminated and then they were allocated to people with "good connections." As reported with enthusiasm in the local newspaper, the district was then cleansed (as it were) of people who had committed breaches of downtown norms.[45] In 1957 the "no-man's-land" in the middle of the road (which had been designed for processions and thus made too wide) was landscaped,[46] thereby creating a dividing line between the downtown area and Dunasor (Danube Lane), which at the time was considered an outlying district.

Campaigns against "drunkards" and "those who had committed breaches of the peace" were launched in other parts of the downtown area as well (Iskola Square, Kossuth Lajos Street, and Szórád Márton Street). Tenants at 27 Iskola Square (School Square) asked the council to evict one of their neighbors for his "inappropriate" behavior.[47] In 1958, with the division of the city into districts, the downtown area (the area bordered by Szórád Márton Street, Kossuth Lajos Street, Stalin Avenue, and Építők Street [Builders Street]) was designated as an independent administrative unit separate from other quarters. As local journalist Miklós Miskolczi describes in his later recollections, the downtown area was increasingly seen as the "Switzerland" of Sztálinváros.[48]

According to a 1958 report in the "social column," many of the girls and women of the city had besieged hairdressers and beauty parlors before a fancy dress party in Béke Restaurant, and not in vain. The majority of the guests entered the hall, which had been decorated with Chinese lanterns, wearing evening gowns fitting the latest fashion. Well-known artists from Budapest performed, and the hit song "Que sera sera" (Whatever Will Be, Will Be) was the most popular at the dance (which lasted into the wee hours of the night).[49] For the local newspaper, in 1957 this was all characteristic of the "refined" diversions of the "socialist man," as well as his "freedom" as a consumer.

The local newspaper depicted the life of an ideal downtown resident who was employed at the ironworks. According to the article, he leads "a sober life, has two grown-up sons. . . . He never enters a bar, and avoids parties, but loves movies, theater plays, and he spends his evenings listening to the radio or attending rehearsals by the ironworks choir. He loves taking walks. . . . He [has] furnished his apartment with new furniture."[50]

This article demonstrates that the newspaper characterized the changes made to the downtown area as a good thing, squarely in line with socialist ideals, in this case represented by a worker who has improved himself by engaging in more refined cultural pastimes and forms of consumption.

According to the newspaper, the relative prosperity attracted swindlers to the downtown area. They primarily targeted May 1 Street, where, as was commonly known, housewives were mostly at home in the mornings while their husbands were working. One of these swindlers visited May 1 Street posing as an architect and acquaintance of the women's husbands. He said his child was suffering from paralysis and he had come to Sztálinváros to purchase medication. The story sounded so plausible that several people gave him 100 forints before the police arrested him.[51] The story indicates that the women of May 1 Street did not find the idea of people coming to Sztálinváros in search of medication unbelievable, since at the time public supplies were remarkably good in comparison with availability in other parts of Hungary. Moreover, the women of May 1 Street were so well-to-do that several of them could afford to give 100 forints to a complete stranger (the average monthly wage at the time was approximately 1,500 forints).[52]

Downtown and, more specifically, the area around May 1 Street was considered a more illustrious neighborhood than any other place in the city, not far away from the workers' districts such as the L-buildings.[53]

L-Buildings: The Skilled Workers District

The L-buildings got their name from their shape: two L-shaped buildings situated opposite each other created a long courtyard where the residents were able to carry on their social lives. According to Miklós Miskolczi, a former tenant of the Sztálinváros L-buildings:

> In no part of our neighborhood did we ever have engineers or physicians as neighbors, and we hardly would have wanted them. We and the majority of tenants in the L-buildings lived in a better and more open social community than any of us ever had, anywhere, before moving to Sztálinváros. . . . Only a few of the children who grew up in our neighborhood earned university degrees. Boys became workmen and, in an ideal case, girls worked as clerks. . . . Thus, the L-building lost nothing of its proletarian character. It was like a working-class district for skilled workers.[54]

The members of the intelligentsia who exercise an influence on public opinion have often subscribed to the stereotype of the working class according to which overcrowded residences, privation, and excessive "sociability" are a hotbed for "deviance."[55] Furthermore, in the imaginary division of working-class dwellings a stereotype prevailed that the working class could be separated into the good and the bad, the working-class aristocracy and the "Lumpenproletariat." This division was also applied to residences in the view according to which the "orderly," "traditional" lifestyles of the districts where skilled workers had been provided with housing could be contrasted with the "immoral," "disorderly" family life of tenants in the slums. In Sztálinváros narratives the press, the administrative authorities, and the police similarly juxtaposed the L-buildings with, for example, the barracks of the Déliváros (South Side). Images of the L-buildings and the neighborhoods in which they were found developed in contrast to images of the downtown area and the barracks, while the "colony-myth" of the L-buildings began to emerge only in the late 1950s according to the conservative turn in the depiction of everyday life in the city.

The L-buildings were built in 1952–53, but their infrastructure remained incomplete for years. The majority of the heads of families who had children living with them were skilled workers who, however, did not hold prominent positions.

Courtyards evoked the idea of a collective living space that, with the stairways opening from the quadrangle and through them onto individual apartments, created one unit.[56]

The L-buildings were inaugurated at the turn of 1953 and 1954, which was precisely when the city began a period of "four years of scarcity" due to radical cuts in Sztálinváros investment funds as a result of changes in government policies.[57] Because of the reductions, the final completion of buildings was protracted, and tenants were moved into "temporary" situations for a long period of time. The asphalting of roads was delayed and quadrangles were littered with piecemeal beams and construction debris awaiting removal. Because the central heating system had been left unfinished, gigantic holes obstructed traffic in and around the blocks. Time and again the inadequate infrastructure resulted in fatal accidents.[58] For years street lighting was not installed, people were compelled to use the "outhouse" instead of an indoor toilet, and trash of dubious origin was thrown out of the windows.[59] At that time, the quadrangle, which was intended to serve as a theater for community life, was little more than a site for children's "gang fights" amid the weeds and refuse.

Under the circumstances, people would gladly have traded a two-room apartment in the L-buildings for any one-room apartment in Budapest.[60] But there was no single image of the "orderly working class district." Some believed that the neighborhood was in danger of "ghettoization." In a letter to the local newspaper one writer contended that "certain tenants disregard their neighbors, they brawl, chop wood, and listen to the radio at earsplitting volumes. They ignore tenant regulations and noise regulations, though it's true that the latter are not posted in the building."[61] Stealing wood was an everyday practice among the tenants of the L-buildings, as it was in the poorer neighborhoods, simply due to the shortage of fuel.[62]

Until 1957 children from the Technikum District, which had an even worse reputation than the L-buildings, frequently visited the latter to fight with the kids there. Children from as far away as the Óváros (Old Town) were attracted by the heaps of construction debris because they provided wonderful opportunities to "play." Landscaping began only in 1958,[63] but by then the area had such a bad reputation that the neighborhood liquor store was one of the most ill-famed in Sztálinváros.[64] Advertisements for mutual apartment transfers suggest that flats in the L-buildings were still considered somewhat more respectable than those in the Technikum District. Some of the people posting ads, however, were willing to move anywhere other than the Technikum District and the L-buildings.[65]

This was hardly surprising insofar as much of the landscaping construction begun in 1958 was progressing very slowly. Sidewalks were left unfinished, and those that were finished were under fifty centimeters of water due to lack of drainage. Most of the stairway windows were broken, and children had smeared the walls with grime, stamped the grass flat, and pulled out the shrubs. Because of its width, the road in front of the L-buildings was used as a speed track, and as letter writers complained, "all the people who had purchased motorcycles in the city brought them there to test them."[66] The local newspaper considered this part of the city worse than the downtown district. However, on account of the relatively high status of the tenants, and comparatively good business and educational services (there were nurseries and kindergartens in the quadrangles of the buildings and the downtown area was not far away, especially Stalin Avenue, with its shops), the L-buildings were still considered better dwelling places than the other working-class district, Technikum.

Technikum: The "Prole" District

In the local urban discourse the residents of slums were more often referred to as "deviant" and "morally corrupt" than were the denizens of other districts.[67] In Sztálinváros the "temporary" barracks and the buildings of the Technikum District were considered slums, and this contributed to the widespread conviction among the people of Sztálinváros that in these parts of the city they were likely to encounter "deviants" and "profligates."

Technikum, which was later renamed the Ságvári District, was the third largest residential district completed after the downtown area and the L-buildings. People began moving into Technikum in late 1953,[68] but because of the cutbacks in investment funds residential buildings remained unfinished for more years than the L-buildings. In one of the letters of complaint a writer argued that the infrastructure of the Technikum District should be given the same importance as the infrastructure of May 1 Street, but it was not.[69]

Sidewalks were left unfinished and plaster was missing from the buildings for years. Generally former residents of workers' hostels, which were located on the far edges of the downtown area and were being closed down, were given apartments in Technikum, and they found themselves living in worse conditions than in their former dwellings. There was no central heating, so people often chopped wood indoors.[70] Street lighting as well as supply of electricity in the apartments were everyday problems.[71] Newspaper reports suggest that in all likelihood the proportion of workers who had previously lived in villages was probably the highest in Technikum. Workmen from villages continued to keep animals, for which the "fully equipped two-room" flats were hardly suitable. According to an article that was printed in the local newspaper in October 1954, someone walking the streets in the early hours of the morning might be charmed by the sound of roosters crowing and hens clucking, but he would also hear the bleating of sheep in the hallways and ducks quacking in the bathrooms.[72]

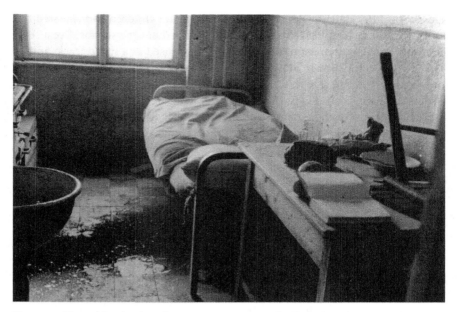

Figure 2.6. Photo taken by the police in an apartment in the Technikum District.

Most often, the newspaper highlighted the disadvantages and problems faced by people living in Technikum. These articles in the local press concerning the problems of this district were published mostly after the autumn of 1956 as a kind of "reform journalism" dealing with social problems in the city. One of the first articles mentioned that fistfights were allegedly common in Technikum District.[73] The streets were covered with mud (residents repeatedly complained about this).[74] The mud was so deep that parents had to carry children on their backs to distant kindergartens because, for a long time, Technikum had no kindergartens.[75] Buildings that remained half-completed for years were flooded with people fleeing the barracks. In several cases they caused further damage to the apartments. Wooden flooring was torn up and used for fuel, and poultry was raised in the bathrooms, so after having been subjected to this kind of use the apartments often seemed far worse than rooms in the barracks.[76]

By the fall of 1957, some six thousand people were living in the unplastered, half-finished buildings, yet not a single new store had opened in the district. The butcher's and the greengrocer's were still located in the barracks, and there were no other shops nearby. Thus there were long queues at the grocer's, which resembled a village shop.[77]

The design of the apartments, which had been planned to conform to urban life, compelled many of the new tenants, who were accustomed to large pantries, to adopt new habits and customs. Their rural lifestyles often prompted them to remodel the apartments: many tenants were fined for keeping animals in the pantry and enlarging vent-holes for this purpose.[78] After the conservative turn, and especially after 1956, the district became a common topic in the local press. By 1958 the Technikum District had become known as the "prole quarter." In a letter of complaint one writer protested that "while the downtown area is being turned into America, . . . the walls of buildings in the Technikum District have not yet been plastered."[79] According to a 1958 report, the district "deserved" its ill-fame: "unkempt buildings, broken window frames, and dirty walls all told the story of stairways without owners. A pig was slaughtered in front of 3 Rákóczi Street [a street in the district]. People were wading in the mud until István F. came up with an idea of what to put under the hog. He went into the stairways and unhinged the door of an electric meter board. . . . On our journey we visited a building where pork was smoked in the storeroom."[80]

In these articles, the Technikum District was depicted as if it were a target for immigrants coming from a rural background. The de-Stalinization campaign that was under way after 1956 blamed the poor infrastructure of the district on the investment strategies of the early 1950s, essentially implying that the cause of the palpable differences in lifestyles in the city was the overly rapid Stalinist industrial campaign. These articles were also intended to demonstrate that the new system would deal with these problems.

Apartment advertisements indicate that in 1958 a one-room downtown flat was considered as valuable as a two-room apartment in the Technikum District. Some people even rejected the offer of an apartment in Technikum, although it would have been the first apartment they had ever occupied. In advertisements for apartment trades people often expressed willingness to move anywhere except Technikum, an indication that the district had already begun to become segregated from the rest of the city. According to the reports, no one wanted to move there and those who could afford to leave did so quickly, but very few people were actually able to do this.[81]

For a period of roughly ten years following their construction, the quality and infrastructure of the Technikum apartments differed significantly from the apartments downtown, but by then the Technikum's reputation as the "prole district" had become fixed in public opinion. Indeed this view was so firmly established that even as late as the 1970s people believed that not a single high ranking industrial manager or well-paid skilled worker resided in the district.[82] The slow infrastructural development of individual districts branded the neglected areas for a long time, and this became something of a self-fulfilling prophecy. The Technikum District, however, did not have the worst reputation in the city. The barrack districts around the city had the image and function of settlements for the people deemed by both the local authorities and the inhabitants of the inner city districts as unable to follow the "proper way of life."

Radar: "Abandon All Hope, Ye Who Enter Here!"

In the public discourse on Sztálinváros districts the barracks represented the slums. They were seen as similar to the shantytowns of the third world. The difficulties faced in the slums were often characterized as central problems in the local media in large cities. One of the primary roles of the horror stories about the poorer areas was to contrast modern urban norms with the norms of the slums.[83] This reinforced the perception that denizens of modern districts of the city were beneficiaries of state social welfare, whereas tenants of the barracks were not.

The Radar barrack settlement was the oldest Sztálinváros slum. It was built on the site of a former World War II military observation post (radar), hence the name. For long years construction workers employed primarily by the Civil Engineering Enterprise who had not been allocated urban accommodation lived in the buildings, which had been constructed for temporary use only. Originally construction brigades inhabited the barracks. These brigades were composed of people from the same village and were formed along friendship and kinship ties. Later the barrack apartments were gradually distributed among employees of the same enterprises.[84]

The majority of the construction workers were from villages in northeastern Hungary and the Hungarian Plains (the most underdeveloped regions of Hungary). The newspaper portrayed them as people who continued in their village lifestyle, encountering the urban lifestyle only when they began to meet with members of the intelligentsia and skilled workers.[85]

One finds this stereotype in the recollections of local journalist Miskolczi, according to which barracks had been and remained flophouses, even if the author was aware that some of the barracks had been transformed into family housing.

> Barracks were built of bricks. The single-story, thin-walled houses had a single window. The roof was mostly gable, or it was covered with tar board and insulated with tar. Upon entering the standard residential barrack one found oneself in a long hallway. As in a hotel, rooms and restrooms opened off the hallways. Six to eight, and occasionally sixteen to twenty-two people shared a room. As necessity demanded, tenants slept on bunks or simple iron bedsteads. The room was furnished with a plain kitchen table, four chairs at most, and as many plywood cabinets as there were tenants.[86]

According to the newspaper portrayals, open pits and the absence of street lighting was the norm in Radar.[87] By 1953 the arrival of family members—that is, the wives and children who were reunited with the workmen already living in Radar—made it necessary to remodel the barracks. By this time more than 3,300 people resided in Radar, and construction workers constituted 70 percent of the population.[88] Thirty barracks were altered to accommodate the families of married workmen. Bigger rooms were converted into smaller ones with an "entrance hall," which made it possible to separate the kitchen space from the living area, as was typical in "traditional working-class homes." Running water was installed in the northern section of the district and the plumbing was connected, making it possible to include indoor bathrooms and toilets in the barracks. In apartments owned by married couples drapes replaced pages of *Szabad Nép* (Free People, the Communist Party daily) on the windows and concrete walkways were even built in front of some of the buildings. These alterations indicate that by that time the bureaucrats and planners of the city had begun to reckon with the long-term existence of the barracks.[89] The barrack city, which was the consequence of "growth" instead of "planning," was seen as a real problem that sometimes demanded the attention of the authorities.

In 1953–54, the years in which the "cleansing" of the downtown area began, several families with small children were moved to Radar as the accommodations were rearranged. A few families were offered apartments inhabited by people who were sick with infectious diseases. Because of the increasing number of children, teachers were also relocated to Radar and found themselves living in similarly bad conditions.[90]

By 1953–54 the number of families had increased, and barrack apartments were transformed into family residences. The population was perceptibly growing, the number of children was increasing, and slowly but steadily Radar became one of the residential areas of the city of Sztálinváros. The ironworks and construction industry were fighting over who should bear the responsibility of renovating the barracks. Eventually, the 1953 renovation financed by the Construction Industry Trust somewhat improved the situation and gradually more and more families moved into the "spruced up" barracks. The majority of the tenants in Radar were lower-rank workmen employed by local enterprises, but most of them still took construction jobs if they had the chance. Since 1954 fewer and fewer job openings were available in the construction industry in Sztálinváros, and thus many of the city's residents had no jobs.

As the years passed, the buildings began to deteriorate again. In 1956 construction industries and the ironworks repaired walls, roofing, and the water and electric systems, but time proved more tenacious than the maintenance units. Some of the barracks, originally built to serve as temporary workers' lodgings for the larger construction projects, were no longer usable. In the fall of 1956 maintenance work was canceled because of the outbreak of the revolution, and this contributed to the fact that in 1957 part of Radar was utterly dilapidated. Barracks owned by the 26/5 National Road and Sewage Construction Enterprise were an exception. According to the local newspaper, they stuck out like a bit of nice new decor against an otherwise crumbling backdrop.

By 1957 furrow weed covered the walkways connecting the barracks, and heaps of debris and garbage flooded the vacant lots between the buildings. The sunlight shone through several hundred broken windows, and many of the window and door frames were missing. Wooden planks and boards "escaped through the chimneys to heaven," as residents would tell visitors in their local "jargon." The distinctive still life was made all the more unusual by the many black and gray hogs leisurely strolling about, either individually or in herds. Radar offered them plenty of slop and rubbish through which to rummage. On April 15, 1957, the City Council attempted to put an end to this "Pig Paradise," but the efforts were ineffective. The banks of the Danube were lined with pigsties. Some people kept entire herds of swine.[91] According to one article, "In addition to its metallurgy, our city could also be famous for its pig farming. Visitors arriving in the city would realize that in comparison with Sztálinváros, Nagytétény [a settlement famous for its pig farming] smells like a perfume shop."[92] Following 1956 the number of articles in the local press on the Sztálinváros shantytowns increased. Extreme poverty had become more visible. This was partly because the new regime intended to legitimize itself by attributing horrible residential conditions to the "abuses" of the Rákosi era, and the new officials wanted to show that they were following a new kind of socialism.

In the summer of 1957 a hygiene supervision raid was organized to ensure that the residents of Radar would not grow "complacent." Having last been cleaned in 1954, the sewer system was clogged with sewage and waste. Refuse water gushed to the surface in front of many of the buildings and there were fetid puddles in front of the apartments. The chief medical officer of the city decreed that unless the sewage problem was solved, Radar was to be evacuated; however, this did not happen because there was no place to send the residents.[93]

A journalist hungry for a sensational story for the local newspaper stated that if a gate were to be erected at the entrance to Radar the inscription should be the citation from Dante: "Abandon all hope, ye who enter here!" Although the majority of the buildings and land belonged to the 26th Construction Industry Trust, operation costs were not covered by anyone. The reason for this was simple. Nobody needed the workforce residing in the district anymore, because the ironworks had started to produce iron and less work remained in the city for the construction workers. After the sewage system became clogged the toilets ceased to work, so dozens of public lavatories were scattered everywhere. In the quarters housing more than a thousand tenants, typhoid broke out. In the bathrooms the names of the "owners" were inscribed over their faucets so that everyone would use their own washbasin. This was essentially the extent of "medical care" in the district.

According to the police, although the crime rates in Radar were not as high as the those in the South Side District of Sztálinváros, nonetheless there were prostitutes and various criminal gangs. They supported this contention by quoting residents who on several occasions requested the establishment of a permanent Radar police station instead of the occasional patrols (these requests were made in vain).[94] In the local newspaper the story of a twenty-three-year-old woman who was branded a prostitute by the court and her neighbors (although the police had found no evidence of this) embodied the lifestyle of Radar residents. The core argument of the article was that Radar was a hotbed of "deviance," and this reinforced the stereotype according to which visitors would encounter "deviant" people at every step.[95]

Hardly any descriptions of apartment interiors in the city went into as much detail as those described of the Sztálinvárosi Hírlap. After 1956 sensational presentations of poverty by the Sztálinváros press were common, and the primary cause of privation was almost always allegedly the "immoral" conduct of barrack residents. Sensationalist articles in the *Sztálinvárosi Hírlap* all suggested that it was easy to end up in Radar, but hard to get out. The descriptions painted a negative picture of the lifestyles of the several thousand tenants in Radar, in contrast to the lifestyles of the residents of the downtown area. The residents of Radar only came into contact with residents of the downtown area at construction sites or in the factory, since Radar was located right next to the factory. The newspaper articles about the districts on the outskirts of the city shaped the image of these areas for the officials and engineers living in the downtown area. Moreover, these articles may also have reassured them in regard to their own social positions.

Sensationalism was expected from the *Sztálinváros Hírlap* after 1956 because it needed readers. Readers and party employees sponsoring the newspaper were more willing to read the paper if it was written in the moderate critical tone characteristic of the party. The Agitation and Propaganda Department of the Hungarian Socialist Workers' Party also attributed increasing circulation numbers to reports on so-called social problems.[96] This was all decisively influenced by the discourses of the de-Stalinization campaign that came after 1956, according to which the Stalinism of the early 1950s was to blame for the social problems in the city, the social inequalities, and the inadequate infrastructure. Thus, the image of the Sztálinváros barracks was strongly influenced by the fact that the political system after 1956 strove to present itself as having severed all ties with Stalinism. By this time, the imaginary world that had been built on the "old" Stalinist foundations in Sztálinváros was seen as bad even by the authorities.

The South Side: The Sztálinváros "Shantytown"

The so-called South Side emerged south of the ironworks as a residential area for construction workers, in the opposite direction of the planned city. From the outset residents of the barrack launched several complaints. The opening hours of

Figure 2.7. The South Side barracks.

the store were inconvenient because workers only arrived home from their shifts after the store had closed, no events were organized in the house of culture, doctors did not make house calls so far away, even when asked, and buses did not stop at designated stops.[97]

At the end of 1953, together with Radar the South Side barracks were altered to provide accommodation for the families of married workmen.[98] On average twelve people shared a room in the South Side apartments.[99] In 1953 and 1954, with the closing of barracks in the proximity of the downtown area, the population in the South Side began to increase. Visitors encountered a peculiar subculture here. For residents, the majority of whom were male, the most popular recreational activities were drinking and listening to accordion music. The city newspaper portrayed this district as the one that was the most provincial. Besides Radar and the South Side, the so-called "old village" (later a district of Sztálinváros) next to which the city had been built was officially represented as the most traditional and provincial in the city.

There were woodpiles in the barracks underneath the beds. Tenants confessed that although stealing wood was forbidden, the foreman knew well that this was their only way of finding fuel, so he turned a blind eye. The local grocer did not carry any fresh meat. Tenants had to go into the city to purchase meat and vegetables. The market, located on Béke Square, was a brisk twenty- to twenty-five-minute walk from the South Side. Taking a bus was complicated because it involved a great deal of waiting.[100]

One of the most prevalent stereotypes regarding ghettos and poor areas is that street and neighborhood life are much more vibrant than elsewhere.[101] Characterizations of the sociocultural functions of slums are often linked to discussions of street life.[102] In the case of the South Side, the articles published in the *Sztálinváros Hírlap* generally characterized the distinctive aspects of its residential life by portraying the allegedly bustling street life of the district.

Alongside photographs of politicians, after 1956 newspapers began to include more scenes of city life (a child, sometimes beside a woman, lovers in sentimental urban backdrops), pictures of city traffic (accidents, traffic police officers), and pictures taken at police raids.[103] Photographs, used as one of the most effective means of creating the impression of authenticity, primarily represented the particular urban environment in the area where the newspapers carrying the pictures were sold.

Papers sold in the streets attempted to influence readers to identify with the newspaper through photographic themes and the reconstruction of images of urban spaces considered significant. In addition to the idyllic pictures and portrayals of the thronging traffic of the city, many images also disturbed the harmony of everyday life, images of the "deviant" elements of society who were violating social norms, such as juvenile hooligans,[104] or unskilled workers making a living by doing odd jobs and continuing to practice animal husbandry in the urban environment.

Around 1954 the local newspaper painted the following picture of the South Side: during the day, the district gives the impression of a desolate "bedroom community"; in the evening, one hears the music from the megaphone of the house of culture; crowded buses stop regularly at the bus stop; passengers quickly disperse after getting off; they go to the cigar store, the grocer, or home; smoke begins to rise from the chimneys and the streets become lively; loud clattering can be heard from the area behind the house of culture; people are bowling; there is no pit at the end of the lane, the bowling balls roll freely and bounce back onto the ground with great energy; they are playing with three pins; some thirty people are standing next to the players; in addition to the music from the megaphone, a guitar and a contrabass can be heard from the restaurant; the merciless musicians play very loud, the noise makes one's eardrums throb; several people are chatting in front of a door; they are talking about where they would like to move in the future; because, as they say, this year, in 1954, even employees of the Ship-Store Enterprise have left;[105] those who stay do not have much choice; the most momentous event in the neighborhood is the grape harvest ball in the fall.[106]

The South Side played a distinctive role in the life of the city. It was relatively far from the downtown area and, as the *Sztálinvárosi Hírlap* claimed, institutions and national enterprises viewed it as the "naughty child," if not the "stepchild." The perception was shaped by the fact that over the course of the years several hundred families moved into the barracks. The construction of the buildings began in 1950, and they were intended to last for five years, but they remained in use for far longer. At the beginning of 1956, 3,500 people were living in them, under extremely harsh circumstances. The twenty-five-centimeter-thick walls became damp and the roofing leaked. The majority of the barracks had uneven brick flooring and the doors and windows were loose. Though reluctantly, construction enterprises did renovate their properties, unlike most national enterprises of the ironworks, which paid little attention to the living conditions of tenants. After October and November 1956, virtually every family living in the South Side remained there. The majority of the people had no other place to go. The barracks were the only place where they were sure to have at least a roof over their heads.[107]

As early as 1957, there were calls to separate the people living in the barracks from the people living in the downtown areas on the bus lines. Indicating the dawn of a "new era," the local newspaper reported on this with indignation. Passengers were classified according to residence and clothing. Both the residents of the downtown area and the conductors looked down on the Radar and South Side passengers, who boarded wearing dirty work clothes, so a separate bus line was opened for them.[108]

According to the *Sztálinvárosi Hírlap*, thieving, brawls, and scandals were everyday events in the South Side. Doors, windows, electric wires, and even locks of buildings that had been closed down were stolen. According to the newspaper, these items were used by construction workers to build their own houses in settlements neighboring Sztálinváros.[109] These stereotypes had an effect, as indicated, for instance, by the actions taken by the police. As of 1957–58, the police made regular raids in the South Side. People were asked to produce their identity papers in the night and several former convicts wearing "suspicious clothing" were taken to the police station. According to the report in the *Sztálinvárosi Hírlap*, one of them had "thick rubber-sole shoes, drainpipe trousers, greased-up hair, and sideburns," considered typical marks of a teddy boy.[110] A few days earlier he had been released after having served his two-year jail sentence. His family had been living in the South Side for years before he was imprisoned.[111] Reports and recollections described the South Side as a safe haven for former convicts because they could easily "blend in."

This stereotype not only applied to the South Side but also surfaced in the national perception of Sztálinváros. The local newspaper generated varying images of the different districts in part to challenge these stereotypes of the city by presenting them as characteristic of only certain areas, primarily the barracks, which were to be closed down.

In 1958 more than 4,000 people lived in the South Side. This figure includes 410 families and 800 children. Having arrived in the barracks, hundreds of families found themselves unable to leave. Wives, and in many cases female family members of other generations, arrived with the hope of obtaining permanent residence, but this was available only to employees of the ironworks. Anyone who lacked a permanent place of work (and this included the majority of women) did not get an apartment, and thus wives lived in apartments only because of the advantages afforded their husbands. According to one survey done by the local council, 190 of the more than 400 couples "cohabited," that is, shared the same living spaces. The newspaper also described the practice of "illegal occupation of houses" as a characteristic feature of life in the district, but those who failed to find accommodation could move in with a family already living there and sublease a room. Several families, often with six or eight children, arrived from various regions of Hungary. The City Council intended to send them back, but no such measures were actually taken.[112]

The problem of alcoholism in the South Side, an attribute of the allegedly "deviant" behavior of the area, was given considerably more emphasis than elsewhere. The *Sztálinvárosi Hírlap* struck a rather negative tone when stating that "the smoky bar" was the only place to socialize and mothers would even take their infant children there. The bar also served as a meeting place for thirteen- to sixteen-year-old adolescent girls and boys.[113]

Only in the 1960s were the residents of the barracks finally moved to "reduced value" apartments, which had been built specifically for them. These apartments had kitchens that opened onto the hallway, one or two rooms opening from the kitchen, a shower stall with no door, and no gas or central heating.[114]

As portrayed in the *Sztálinvárosi Hírlap*, Radar and the South Side resembled third world shantytowns. According to contemporary unofficial discourse, "peasants" fleeing from the destitution of villages often ended up in these slums. The seasonal nature of construction work frequently entailed unemployment.[115] These "irregular" districts did not establish strong ties with the essential urban network. Stereotypes suggested that the destitute areas were a transitory station between urban and rural environments.

After 1956 the number of articles on the two slums increased dramatically, and not by accident. The journalists were expected to work to increase the popularity of the *Sztálinvárosi Hírlap*, because during the Kádár era the communist journals had to sell well. The policymakers realized that the newspapers could not do as they had done in the early 1950s, when most of the articles included pure propaganda. Thus the new form of journalism included critiques of the regime (especially regarding the Rákosi-era policies), because one of the important functions of the party newspapers was now to convince the people in a widely accessible forum of the legitimacy of the post-1956 government. The publication of articles critical of aspects of city life (for instance, descriptions of the social conflicts in the city) and writings that resembled what one would expect to find in the tabloid press today (touching on topics such as romantic relationships or criminal cases) helped newspapers increase readership, and many local papers ceased to be seen simply as propaganda tools.[116]

The increase in the number of articles on the poorer districts after 1956 was not a sign of greater concern for the residents of the South Side or Radar, nor should it be seen as an indication that the area had more problems than there were earlier. The goal was simply to increase circulation, and one way of doing this was to reinforce stereotypes regarding people living in poverty. Thus the local media largely contributed to an increased awareness of segregation and the emergence of ghettos in Sztálinváros. Differences in the images and perceptions of the various districts of the city were also reinforced by the efforts of the new regime to distance itself from Stalinism and its "abuses," of which Sztálinváros was a manifest example. It was as if the authorities had passed through a new gate, beyond which all memory of the recent past faded.

The Old Town and Commuter Villages

According to the *Sztálinvárosi Hírlap*, in Dunapentele, referred to as the old town or old village, the features of village life still prevailed. The majority of residents still worked in agriculture. They held holiday feasts separate from the urban population, and they even participated independently in the processions. The image of the old village suggested by the newspaper completely separated the rural past from the modern, urban future. One finds only occasional mention of lodgers employed in industries who connected the old village with the city, or visits by residents of the new city to the old village for religious holidays and funerals. This latter phenomenon is explained by the fact that in the new districts of the city neither churches nor cemeteries were built.

The picture painted in the *Sztálinvárosi Hírlap* reveals that the old village differed from Sztálinváros with regard to its infrastructure and the occupations of its residents. It was related to the city in much the same way as the villages from which people commuted to work in Sztálinváros. The newspaper said virtually nothing about how in the early years the majority of city builders, factory workers, and managers had sought accommodation in the "old town" or the neighboring villages because they had found the urban accommodations unsatisfactory.[117]

In 1960, of the 11,600 industrial workers in Sztálinváros, more than 2,800 commuted to the city daily. A significant proportion of the workforce employed by the industrial enterprises traveled to the city every day from sixteen different settlements. The majority came from the neighboring Dunavecse district and a few northern villages of Tolna County. Sztálinváros was the most attractive destination for work for the people of Dunaföldvár, Rácalmás, Perkáta, and Nagyvenyim (nearby villages around Sztálinváros). In the beginning, the majority of workmen arrived in trucks or wagons and occasionally by train. Later most of them would take the bus to Sztálinváros.[118] Commuting created a chain of "overnight communities" around Sztálinváros.[119] At the same time, officially this type of commuting found mention only in the discourse contrasting urban and rural lifestyles, which I discuss in the next chapter.

Conclusion

Although the residential areas of Sztálinváros and the quality of the housing and furnishings underwent changes, the images of various districts of the city changed only slowly. When people were thinking of moving to a new apartment, they could take into consideration what they had read in the newspaper or what people had said of the area in question, rather than the actual quality of the apartment. This process had a spontaneous effect on the development of the city, which did not resemble the ideas of its planners. Furthermore, people with larger social networks could orient themselves more easily in the growing urban community because they had more sources of information about Sztálinváros and therefore a more nuanced image of the city.

In spite of the planners' efforts to establish a kind of social uniformity, the dissimilarities among the communities of immigrants to Sztálinváros inevitably led to the formation of residential districts with divergent norms. The evidence from the newspaper suggests that the regime was quite comfortable with revealing and promoting such social differences. The image (or projection) of a given district came into being at the same time as, if not earlier than an actual "realistic" image of the district, and exerted a longer-lasting effect on the development of the city.

In the interests of nurturing the popularity of the local newspaper, the editors had to be sure that the local headlines and reports concerning the various districts harmonized reasonably well with the experiences of the residents of the city. Indeed this enabled them to increase their own credibility, which was not at all true of the newspapers that were published before 1953, which included almost exclusively state propaganda. Both the popularity and the credibility of the newspaper became important after 1953 and in particular after 1956. An article could be published in the local newspaper only after having gone through several filters, and only if it was acceptable both to the party members who exerted an influence on the image of the city and the general readership (and, of course, there was considerable overlap between these two groups). Because of the de-Stalinization campaign, it was again acceptable to write about social differences, which earlier would have been inconceivable. This was part of the conservative turn that was taking place in the norms of the city, which contributed to the "reloading" of and acceptance of Stalinism and also helped prompt the residents of the city to accommodate to state policies. Social differences that earlier had been given no official acknowledgment were not only recognized but even accepted officially. Indeed, a few "sensational" reports on the "anomalies" found in the city may have increased the newspaper's popularity. (Naturally these anomalies were blamed on the party leadership of the earlier era, which allegedly had taken communism in the wrong direction.)

Presentations in the newspaper of social conflicts in the city also suggested the possibility of taking independent action, since the community of a given part of the city did not evolve as a homogeneous block (as had been envisioned by the city planners), but rather was influenced by numerous other factors that originated first and foremost in the ways in which the state distributed goods and property (e.g., housing, but also including spending on infrastructure). The division of the city in the popular imagination into "desirable" and "undesirable" areas made it apparent that the population of the new urban community was nowhere near as homogeneous as the plans for the city and the propaganda of the regime suggested; both portrayed the people of the city as a homogeneous, faceless mass. It also made the city a place in which people felt more "at home," since everyone knew where everyone else fell on the social hierarchy simply on the basis of his or her address. However, this process was also significantly furthered by the fact that the urban–rural dichotomy, which was blurred at the everyday level, was emphasized by the state policies to establish a new mode of social differentiation that in turn created a more acceptable social diversification for both the officials and ordinary people.

Notes

Epigraph: *Sztálinváros Hírlap* [Sztálinváros Herald], September 9, 1958, 3.

1. Lynch, *The Image of the City*, 12.

2. According to the findings of the official survey in 1960, 9.9 percent of the population immigrated from Fejér County, 23.6 percent from other counties of the Dunántúl (Transdanubia), 38 percent from the mid, Duna-Tisza and the Tiszántúl regions (in the Eastern part of Hungary), and 16.2 percent from Budapest (immigrants constituted 87 percent of the total population in Sztálinváros). *Dunaújváros. 1950–1965*, 8. Based on requests for residence permits, between 1951 and 1954, of those who were granted permits (and the numbers do not equal the sum total of immigrants), 28.2 percent immigrated from Budapest, 9 percent from Fejér County, 26.7 percent from other counties of the Dunántúl, and 36.1 percent from other counties (15.4 percent of whom came from Borsod-Abaúj-Zemplén). Data collected from Erdős, "Dunapentelétől Sztálinvárosig," 260.

3. Sándor, *Sztálinváros*, 23.

4. *Sztálinváros. Első szocialista városépítkezésünk Sztálinváros*, 6.

5. Ibid., 7.

6. In this case "modernist" means architecture that is nonrepresentational and functional, made largely of industrial materials and processes, and committed to the transformation of society along "egalitarian" lines. However, "socialist realist" means the Stalin-era emphasis on neoclassical, representational architecture committed to monumental displays of state power.

For more on the meaning of modernist architecture in a "socialist" context, see Harris, *Communism on Tomorrow Street*, 52–53, 66,

7. On segregation in American new cities, see Kato, "Planning and Social Diversity."

8. For a comparison of the conflicts concerning housing, see Harris, *Communism on Tomorrow Street*, 111–15.

9. Szelényi, *Városi társadalmi egyenlőtlenségek*, 99–102. For more on this allocation process, see Szelényi, *Urban Inequalities under State Socialism*, 63. For the survival of these inequalities after 1989, see Bodnár, *Fin de Millénaire Budapest*, 35–58.

10. Gádoros, *A korszerű lakás térszükséglete és berendezése*, 6.

11. Gádoros, Kismarty-Lechner Jr., and Perényi, *Családi lakóház*, 13.

12. Gádoros, "Lakásépítkezésünk eredményei és tanulságai," 11–18.

13. Ibid.

14. Major, "Preface," 6.

15. Kismarty-Lechner Jr., *Városi lakástípusok*, 13.

16. For a comparison, see the segregation according to occupational and social origin of residents in Ufa and Pskov in the Soviet Union. Matthews, "Social Dimensions in Soviet Urban Housing," 111–13.

17. Here one should draw a clear distinction between the relatively large number of primarily female "administrative" employees and technical or top position employees holding a degree or a certificate of technical engineering.

18. This tendency not only characterized Sztálinváros and the 1950s but also persisted later. For more, see Mihályi, "Történeti szempontok a magyarországi lakáshiány értékeléséhez"; Dániel, "Lakáspolitika, lakbér, lakáshiány"; and Hamilton and Burnett, "Social Processes and Residential Structure," 283; on the operation of the Budapest housing distribution and its reinforcing inequalities, see Horváth, *Két emelet boldogság*, 75–141.

19. Politikatörténeti és Szakszervezeti Levéltár (PSzTL) [Political History and Trade Union Archives], f. XII.-33. Építők, unit 658, 1951.

20. Cf. French and Hamilton, "Is There a Socialist City?" 16–17, who deny the existence of segregation in socialist cities. On segregation in present-day Budapest and its antecedents in the socialist era, see Konrád and Szelényi, *Az új lakótelepek szociológiai problémái*; Csanádi and Ladányi, *Budapest térbeni-társadalmi erezetének változásai*; and Ladányi, *Lakóhelyi szegregáció Budapesten*.

21. Researchers discovered similar patterns in many other Hungarian small or middle-size towns such as Pécs, Szeged, Salgótarján, Veszprém, Miskolc, Debrecen, Békés, and Dunaújváros; see Szelényi, *Városi társadalmi egyenlőtlenségek*, 114; Béres, *A városfejlődés fordulópontján*; Saád, "A lakosság területi szegregálódása"; Tóth, *Társadalmi kapcsolatok szerveződése*; Papp, "Békés város tagozódása"; and Szirmai, *Csinált városok*."

22. On segregation in "socialist cities," see Weclawowitz, "A városok térbeni-társadalmi erezete," and Szelényi, *A szocialista városok és a szociológia*.

23. Massey and Denton, "The Dimensions of Residential Segregation." On the relationship between segregation and housing conditions, see Szelényi, *Városi társadalmi egyenlőtlenségek*, 86. On the notion of mental maps, see Lynch, *The Image of the City*; Downs et al., *Maps in Mind*; Kuipers, "The 'Map in the Head' Metaphor."

24. Weiner, "Sztálinváros," 82.

25. Lynch, *The Image of the City*, 47–48.

26. *Szabad Nép*, August 20, 1952, 3.

27. *Dunai Vasmű Építője*, May 8, 1951, 2.

28. Ibid., May 29, 1951, 3.

29. *Sztálin Vasmű Építője*, August 4, 1953, 4.

30. Miskolczi, *Az első évtized*, 83.

31. *Sztálinvárosi Hírlap*, February 23, 1954, 2.

32. Ibid., September 17, 1954, 4.

33. Ibid., September 10, 1954, 2. There are no data on regulations regarding cats, probably because cats were considered "urban" pets.

34. *Sztálinvárosi Hírlap*, January 15, 1954, 1.

35. Ibid., December 10, 1954, 3.

36. Ibid., December 24, 1954, 3.

37. Ibid., December 10, 1954, 4.

38. Miskolczi, *Város lesz csakazértis*, 105.

39. *Sztálinvárosi Hírlap*, December 19, 1956, 4.

40. Ibid., 3.

41. Ibid., January 10, 1957, 4.

42. Ibid., January 19, 1957, 4; February 12, 1957, 4; February 26, 1957, 4.

43. ÁSZTL, file O-13582.

44. *Szabad Nép*, August 20, 1952, 3.

45. *Sztálinvárosi Hírlap*, January 19, 1957, 3; April 16, 1957, 2; March 22, 1957, 2.

46. Ibid., February 12, 1957, 2.

47. Ibid., June 11, 1957, 2.

48. Miskolczi, *Város lesz csakazértis*, 208.

49. This Doris Day song from 1956 had a special political meaning and it was very popular after the 1956 Revolution in Hungary. *Sztálinvárosi Hírlap*, January 21, 1958, 3.

50. Ibid., February 7, 1958, 2. For a description of similar tenants, see ibid., November 14, 1958, 5.

51. Ibid., May 9, 1958, 2.

52. *Statisztikai évkönyv 1985*, 17.

53. Miskolczi, *Város lesz csakazértis*, 29.

54. Ibid., 29–31.

55. Keating, *The Working Classes in Victorian Fiction*, 103; Gyáni, *Az utca és a szalon*, 183; Gyáni, *Bérkaszárnya és nyomortelep*, 146–47.

56. Weiner, "Sztálinváros," 60.

57. The term is employed by Miklós Miskolczi to describe the years between 1954 and 1958.

58. *Sztálinvárosi Hírlap*, January 29, 1957, 3.

59. Ibid., April 19, 1957, 2.

60. Ibid., March 26, 1957, 3.

61. Ibid., February 26, 1957, 3.

62. Miskolczi, *Város lesz csakazértis*, 29.

63. *Sztálinvárosi Hírlap*, April 24, 1957, 3.

64. Ibid., May 23, 1958, 2.

65. Ibid., December 12, 1958, 6.

66. Ibid., May 9, 1958, 4.

67. Suttles, *The Social Order of the Slum*, 5–6.

68. *Sztálinvárosi Hírlap*, December 29, 1953, 1.

69. Ibid., April 2, 1954, 2.

70. Ibid., November 9, 1954, 2.

71. Ibid., November 19, 1954, 3.

72. Ibid., October 1, 1954, 2.

73. Ibid., December 15, 1956, 3.

74. Ibid., January 10, 1957, 3.

75. Ibid., February 12, 1957, 2.

76. Ibid., March 8, 1957, 5.

77. Ibid., October 1, 1957, 3.

78. Ibid., 4.

79. Ibid., September 9, 1958, 3.

80. Ibid., January 16, 1958, 3.

81. Ibid., June 20, 1958, 6; August 29, 1958, 6; February 15, 1957, 6; December 12, 1958, 3, 6; May 6, 1958, 2.

82. Miskolczi, *Város lesz csakazértis*, 208.

83. Mayne, *The Imagined Slum*, 10.

84. PSzTL, f. XII-33. 143. ő.e., 939, 1953, and MNL OL, f. XXIX-F-2-a, b. 76.

85. *Sztálinvárosi Hírlap*, September 11, 1953, 2.

86. Miskolczi, *Az első évtized*, 70.

87. *Sztálinvárosi Hírlap*, September 11, 1953, 2.

88. PSzTL, f. XII-33. 143. ő.e., 939, 1953, and MNL OL f. XXIX-F-2-a, b. 76.

89. *Sztálinvárosi Hírlap*, December 31, 1953, 5.

90. Ibid., September 10, 1954, 2.

91. FML, f. XXIII-502, b. 13, December 27, 1957.

92. *Sztálinvárosi Hírlap*, February 22, 1957, 4. The incompatibility of keeping animals and urban life was not exclusively emphasized in articles on Sztálinváros. The issue was an important theme in the discursive contrasting of urban and rural lifestyles, discussed in chapter 3.

93. *Sztálinvárosi Hírlap*, June 14, 1957, 3.

94. Ibid., July 2, 1957, 2–3.

95. Ibid., July 18, 1958, 2; September 12, 1958.

96. MNL OL. f. 288–41, 1959, unit 6. According to information on the operation of the *Sztálinvárosi Hírlap*, 160–65, 161: "Circulation and the educational impact of the Herald have considerably increased due to the articles, reports, feuilletons, and commentaries that addressed significant, oftentimes national social problems. They included series of articles on collective property protection, juvenile delinquency, ideological education, the fight against alcoholism, and so on. By publishing these articles, the newspaper has assisted the work of authorities responsible for criminal investigations." The increase in the popularity of the Herald is verified by the fact that in June, July, and August of 1958 only 1.1 percent of the 130,800 copies were not sold. Ibid., 165.

97. *Sztálinvárosi Hírlap*, October 9, 1953, 2; April 23, 1953; October 23, 2; December 12, 2; December 15, 1953, 2.

98. Ibid., December 31, 1953, 5.

99. Ibid., March 19, 1954, 2.

100. Ibid., January 19, 1954, 3.

101. Suttles, *The Social Order of the Slum*, 73.

102. Welz, *Street Life*, 50–54.

103. Especially in early 1957 the latter was a popular photographic theme in *Esti Hírlap* (Evening Post), a newspaper of national circulation. See, for example, February 14, 1957, 3; March 3, 1957, 3; March 8, 1957, 3.

104. Illustrated reports on youth subcultures played a significant role in the development of English journalistic photography. Harrison, *Young Meteors*, 34–37.

105. Abbreviation of the Shipping and Stocking National Enterprise. Employees of this enterprise were considered more capable and earned better wages than other barracks tenants.

106. *Sztálinvárosi Hírlap*, July 9, 1954, 2; October 22, 1954, 3.

107. Ibid., December 15, 1956, 4.

108. Ibid., February 8, 1957, 4; March 26, 1957, 2; June 21, 1957, 2; March 11, 1958, 1.

109. Ibid., June 7, 1957, 1.

110. This term refers to a 1950s British subculture characterized by young men wearing clothes that were based on styles from the Edwardian era. I use the term as a rough translation of the Hungarian term *jampec*, which represented a somewhat analogous trend in Hungary at the time.

111. *Sztálinvárosi Hírlap*, September 19, 1958, 5.

112. Ibid., November 4, 1958, 2.

113. Ibid., May 9, 1958, 4.

114. Miskolczi, *Város lesz csakazértis*, 209.

115. Since officially, as one of the ideological requirements, there was no unemployment under the socialist regime, very few works addressed the topic of socialist unemployment. Rottenberg, "Unemployment in Socialist Countries"; Gregory and Collier, "Unemployment in the Soviet Union." Zoltán Baksay discusses unemployment emerging in parallel with the introduction of planned economy; naturally the primary focus is on "stopping" unemployment. Baksay, *A munkaerőhelyzet alakulása*.

116. For more on the establishment of the tabloid press at the end of the 1950s (a phenomenon that closely intertwined with the new expectations of the reorganized Communist Party), see Horváth, *Kádár gyermekei*, 98–123.

117. Tibor V. recalled that the top managers of the project owned houses in Kulcs (about fifteen kilometers from Sztálinváros to the north), from where they commuted.

118. Dallos and Szabady, *Magyar városok*, 90.

119. Ibid. Statistics on commuters from the villages neighboring Sztálinváros.

3 Urban Villagers

Socialist settlements will differ markedly from that which we see today in our city or countryside: they will be neither the one nor the other.

Nikolai Miliutin, 1930

In addition to its metallurgy, our city could also be famous for its pig farming.

Sztálinvárosi Hírlap, 1957

Emphasis on the creation of a new home from nothing played an important role in the identity of the people of Sztálinváros. A local journalist, Miklós Miskolczi, who later left the city, offered a characterization of this distinctive local identity with a portrayal of the "typical" Sztálinváros man as "brave and self-assured, since he had not simply left the village of his birth, his onetime residence, but had also undertaken the exhaustive work of creating a home. He brought with him not only his past but also the morals, traditions, and tastes of his background. He let himself be transformed by the new while at the same time exerting an influence himself on the newly forming community. People saw one another as strangers, but we all felt at home because we all knew that everyone was both a stranger and at home."[1]

Those who moved to Sztálinváros did not become "rootless." They brought their ties to the past with them in the form of kinship and neighborhood relationships, norms and ways of life. At the same time, the re-created and transformed community networks of immigrants took advantage of the strivings of individuals to maintain themselves and strengthen the group identities of their members. In addition, communities adapted to local modern behavioral patterns or the expectations of the authorities. In a peculiar way, precisely by referring to conduct that did not conform to official expectations (for instance, using the catchwords of the party in the course of a court proceeding over a neighborhood spat), they adopted the official language, including the urban–rural dichotomy, to reach their personal goals. They had some help in this: they were able to exert some horizontal control over communal life by reporting people who overstepped boundaries to the authorities.[2]

The image of quarters made up of residential districts exerted a strong influence on the expectations placed on residents. Immigrants with diverse pasts and origins adapted to official expectations when submitting applications for housing or complaints, but in their daily routines they strove to assert their own interests. Conflicts originating in the varied lifestyles of new arrivals in the city most often surfaced in discussions of the differences between "urban" and "rural" lifestyles in the official discourse.

Urban anthropology has long addressed the issue of how immigrants who were earlier accustomed to rural life adapt to urban environments. Virtually every large city has at least one district that is perceived by the public as a village within city limits.[3] The primary reason for this is not necessarily that the buildings of the district resemble village houses in their architecture, but that the lifestyles of its residents differ. Recounting his first visit to the West End in Boston, Herbert J. Gans claims that the bustling street life, the multitude of tiny shops, and the streets littered with garbage gave him the impression that he was in an exotic place. According to his book, which is based on research carried out in 1957 and 1958, the distinctive lifestyle of the residents makes them "urban villagers." In Gans's view, immigrants adapt to the urban lifestyle primarily in the transformation and formation of kinship relations, local community life, neighborhood relationships, local institutions, and subcultures characteristic of the area in which they live.[4]

Several districts in Sztálinváros (Technikum, the South Side, and Radar) were considered "village-like" due to the lifestyles of their residents. In this chapter I will argue that to control immigration to the city, the authorities declared the rural lifestyles undesirable, especially after 1953, so in the official discourse the social problems related to immigration were embodied in the contrast between "urban" and "rural" norms. The primary function of this contraposition was to cast the transformation of immigrant lifestyles as part of the official plan (and ideology) according to which "socialism" would bring an end to the differences between the village and town. Most sources offering accounts of the traditions of immigrant "villagers" analyze the adaptation to an urban lifestyle within the framework of this opposition. As a result, they are rather biased and they emphasize elements that indicate some conflict, the origins of which allegedly lie in the difference in lifestyles, thereby presenting the resettlement of "villagers" and "urbanites" in the city as a constant struggle. The sharp urban–rural dichotomy in the official language helped make the earlier Rákosi regime seem responsible for the social conflicts in the city. Thus the propaganda was able to demonstrate that the Kádár regime was much more concerned with the needs and grievances of society.

Sztálinváros bequests suggest that, in terms of material culture the differences between "village" and "urban" lifestyles were not as clear as they might seem on the basis of the official discourse of council bodies, the police, the court, and the press. In fact, the amalgamation of "village" and "urban" lifestyles, and the transformations that took place in the value systems of immigrants resulted in the coexistence of "village" and "urban" values in many families. This often found manifestation in a kind of "mythic" respect for real estate and the idea of keeping real estate in the family. It was also palpable in bequests, since quite often even after the collectivization of land in 1959–61, residents of the downtown area of Sztálinváros owned arable land,[5] while village migrants owned equipment and personal tools that were considered "urban" at the time.[6] This chapter demonstrates that the discourse on the urban–rural dichotomy was energized by the de-Stalinization campaign in order to depict everyday life during the establishment of the city as chaotic. This urban–rural dichotomy also served to represent the "modernist objectives" of the regime and to legitimize the "new way of socialism" (especially after 1956).[7] In other words, it served to "reload" Stalinism.

Producing the Urban–Rural Dichotomy

The creation of a city bearing and befitting Stalin's name was a project of primary importance to Hungary, so the residents of the new metropolis would have to be subjected to a careful selection process. The September 23, 1951 resolution of the Ministry of Interior was an attempt to do this. Immigration to Sztálinváros was brought under the supervision of the authorities, thereby strengthening the impression of order and control.[8] However, residency permits were mandatory only for the allocation of apartments, and the majority of the people who might have been denied residency according to the stipulations of the resolution lived in barracks for years without the slightest hope of being given an apartment. Indeed, the residency permits yield only tentative conclusions concerning the social backgrounds of new arrivals in the city, all the more so because requests for residency can hardly be regarded as reliable sources (since it was in the applicant's interest to embellish his or her social background to improve the chances of receiving a residency permit). Residency permits provide some information on well-educated individuals who unofficially held relatively good positions: white-collar workers and skilled workers were overrepresented among the permits granted between 1951 and 1954, whereas those categorized (according to their original occupations) as "agricultural laborers" and "unskilled workers" made up only 20 percent (although the majority of workers must have been employed in simple tasks such as digging and moving earth to create foundations).[9] The social image of new arrivals in the city on the basis of the residency permits met official expectations, and thus functionaries in the offices that issued the permits achieved their goal. This is, of course, also true of newcomers in the city who filled out the petitions according to official expectations.

Although there is a widespread stereotype according to which Stalinization strove to control migration by enforcing a new system of identity cards and residency permits, neither personal experiences nor primary sources suggest that this plan was effective.[10] In contrast, networks based on kinship and friendship ties, and trust, also had a crucial influence on the decisions of immigrants to Sztálinváros, and migration was accompanied by considerable social mobility.[11]

Moshe Lewin argues that "ruralization" of the Soviet cities forged new forms of social structures. He also points out that the adoption of "urban ways of cultural life" did not happen instantaneously: "the cultural level of workers in large cities . . . showed that in European Russia the time workers dedicated weekly to 'culture' was falling."[12] As Stephen Kotkin puts it in his critique of Lewin's thesis on the ruralization of the cities, "Lewin sees a clash 'of almost two nations or two civilizations' whose outcome turned out to be tragic for both. In Magnitogorsk, however, such 'ruralization'—if that is the appropriate term—appears to have been largely beneficial, both materially and in terms of social cohesion."[13]

This discourse on ruralization had its roots in the debates about *kul'turnost'*, which informed the debates on the rural population's capacity to adapt to urban life. "East European intellectuals placed a high premium on kul'turnost' and since the nineteenth century had considered it part of what they believed was their mission to educate and uplift the downtrodden peasant masses. To do so was considered an essential step toward national revitalization."[14] The debates about the rural population and their "uncivilized life" were also rooted in the Soviet definition of culture as an evolutionary phenomenon and the revolutionary goals of "modernization" (i.e., industrialization and urbanization).[15]

In the experience of urban anthropologists in the West and communist cadres in the East, in almost every large city one district was regarded in the popular consciousness as a village within the city.[16] In the East, the inhabitants of housing estates in particular were seen as villagers in the eyes of the local authorities, and the myth of the ruralization of cities was created in the first reports of the strange new habits of migrants. The discourse of ruralization also served a political purpose. After Stalin's death the new-old cadres (who served in their positions both before and after Stalin's death) often suggested that all the problems of the cities derived from the industrialization process, claiming that the migrants who had arrived in those years had blighted the life of the cities.[17] The Stalinist industrial campaign—which in some East Central European countries lasted less than a decade—was blamed for the problems deriving from this period for almost forty years. De-Stalinization saw a new wave of calls for "communist social reform." At the end of the 1950s it was common for local administrations to point to the ruralization of cities and the social problems arising from it in order to receive more investment for infrastructure and housing. This cemented the perception that ruralization was a local social policy problem.[18]

The term *ruralization* was also easily absorbed into the totalitarian paradigm because it was a counternarrative to the representation of socialism as modernist. The narrative of the ruralization and proletarianization of socialist cities in East Central Europe stemmed partly from narratives of de-Stalinization that tried to represent the new regime as modernist, and it shaped the language of local party officials who had to write reports on ruralization. Thus, the discourse of ruralization was a tool with which to represent discontinuity between the regimes before and after Stalin's death and to claim a new legitimacy based on the "language of modernization."

In Sztálinváros the persistence of practices traditionally viewed as characteristic of "rural" or "industrial workers" presumably varied according to family background, educational level, occupational status, and gender. Older migrants (in particular older women), who moved in with relatives and found themselves isolated with few or no friends or workplace acquaintances, seemed to cling most fervently to traditions considered "rural" even by their close communities. Ilona Dobos, an ethnographer and the wife of András Sándor, describes an old immigrant woman who wore her headscarf and daytime clothes when she slept even after having moved to Sztálinváros because,

> she respects her grandson Jóska as an urban gentleman, because he is a man who wears trousers [and not overalls, so by implication he has an important position], and he carries a briefcase. She hardly dares to address him. She would never sit down with him at the dinner table; she rather withdraws to the cooker and holds her plate in her hands. . . . She talks about death a lot and spends a lot of time arranging her funeral attire. She has a beautiful apron for the long journey because she believes the Virgin Mary would weep with disappointment if she were to show up not wearing it.[19]

She even thought her identity card would have to be buried with her. The opposition between "village" and "urban" behavior was depicted in descriptions of individual Sztálinváros streets too. Peter Schneider, who compared images of the "boulevard" and "village street" (*Dorfstraße*) in the nineteenth and twentieth centuries in Europe, claims that in contrast to the "village street," the "boulevard" (the typical urban street) strengthens the notion that the people who use it are socially farther removed from one another.[20]

For the denizens of the city, "residential streets" that had been designed to be narrow, the "village" streets of the barracks, and the wide "boulevards" (like Stalin Avenue) represented the dichotomies of modern/traditional, alienated/sociable, and urban/rural. May 1 Street,[21] the first street to be declared "urban," attracted migrants arriving from cities. The majority of Budapest intelligentsia, who were seen as the "most urban" residents, were allocated apartments on this street or managed to obtain them. Traffic was first regulated in an "urban manner" here: the

Figure 3.1. Typical image representing the downtown area as a modern urban place.

separation of the sidewalk and the road, landscaping and infrastructure symbolically implied the urban nature of the street. However, a couple of dozen meters from the street the area was dominated by construction workers and half-finished buildings.

Tenants who led "decent" lives were among the prerequisites for the creation of an urban community. The border separating the buildings on May 1 Street from the "nonurban" outside world was embodied in the institution of "locking-up time" (when the superintendents of the buildings locked the gates at night and did not let anyone in) and the employment of superintendents who not only cared for the buildings but also kept watch over the inhabitants. One of the basic tasks of the superintendents was to push people who had lifestyles that were seen as incompatible with urban norms to dwellings in distant streets. The "rules of the house" were a kind of textual embodiment of this control of norms. These rules were compatible with "socialist morals," and they were revised by the City Council almost every year.

The series of measures implemented in 1954 in the downtown area (fines for breaches of the peace and for keeping animals, accompanied by the creation of parks and planting gardens (*parkosítás*),[22] designated the fundamental norms that, according to public opinion, an urban citizen had to embrace. The clash of norms perceived as urban and rural became a serious problem for the public. Municipal ordinances offered urban "villagers" two possibilities: either to be excluded from "urban" life or to adopt urban norms. The idea of concentrating the "residential sites" that failed to conform to urban norms in one part of Sztálinváros emerged as early as 1955.[23] The market, the pawnshop, restaurants, and temporary lodgings were considered the most "contagious" sites (this was true not only of socialist cities), places where urban norms were most likely to be compromised, and were therefore to be under ever stricter control.[24] The urban nature of downtown life was manifested in the Golden Star Hotel, which opened at the end of 1954, and the Dózsa movie theater. To meet the demands of intelligentsia relocating to Sztálinváros from Budapest, "urban" institutions and programs hosted by the Béla Bartók House of Culture to a large extent replaced dances considered "rural" (dances organized in the barracks in the early years).[25] "Urban" dances, such as waltzes, the tango, and later the twist (which was seen as flashy and fashionable) dominated the most popular balls.

In *Sztálinvárosi Hírlap*, the "urban" resident was portrayed as someone who lived a decent life, attending theater performances or listening to the radio instead of going to the bar. The urban man loved "going for walks," and would go to the swimming pool to put his free time to good use. He furnished his apartment with modern, functional furniture, he purchased entire furniture sets instead of individual items built by carpenters (which were seen as "rural"), and he slept on an immensely practical sofa bed. According to the 1954 report of the Council Trade Department, however, residents of neighboring villages also purchased furniture in Sztálinváros.[26] Mass-produced furniture, which was seen as both modern and functional, also became fashionable.

According to the articles in the *Sztálinvárosi Hírlap*, the urban man regularly used his bathroom to shower or bathe and used the pantry of his apartment to store food, not to "keep animals." He spent time in the kitchen only when cooking or eating. Otherwise during the day he stayed in the designated "living room" with his family. He sunbathed or took his child out to the balcony for fresh air, where he also occasionally did needlework, but he did not use the balcony to hang laundry. This was done in the public washroom (which, of course, either did not exist or was used for other purposes). From 1958 to 1959 the council's Minor Offense Department imposed fines on some people (they would not have been able to fine everyone) for drying clothes on balconies, contending that they were ruining the cityscape. Many people believed that the balconies should be used to beautify the cityscape, so they were careful to ensure that uniform flower boxes were placed on the balconies, instead of clothes.[27]

Similarly, according to an article in *Sztálinvárosi Hírlap*, the "urban" woman wore factory-tailored clothes, and by no means would she be seen in the street

Figure 3.2. Official representation of the "urban man" of Sztálinváros in his living room.

wearing a "dressing gown" or "housecoat" (in fact many housewives were seen wearing dressing gowns and housecoats when they popped out to the store for something). When cold weather set in, a short coat, a cardigan, or some other "sweater" was worn over the long dressing gown, and the "ladies" would queue in this attire in the butcher shop or walk as far as four blocks from their apartments. According to the newspaper, having nothing else to wear was a poor excuse for wearing a long gown, since if someone could afford a long dressing gown then they could also afford to buy a print dress. Allegedly the "cityscape" was "further spoiled" by the sight of an unbuttoned gown, which in her rush a slovenly woman might have left "open to the breeze."[28] The implicit message of the article indicated that Sztálinváros was not a village where women could be seen wearing only a long chemise and children ran barefoot in the street.

"Urban" girls and women were "working women" who frequently visited the hairdresser and the beautician but, again according to the *Sztálinvárosi Hírlap*, they were also familiar with cosmetics. They attended fancy dress balls in party dresses and wore suits to work.[29] These portrayals ignored the women who worked in clothing factories or did construction work, but their attire was not considered "urban." The lack of paved roads turned some Sztálinváros districts into a sea of mud, so residents often could not leave their homes without rubber boots. In contrast, since the sidewalks had been completed relatively early in the area, downtown residents were able to wear shoes. The difference between "the booted" and "the shod" was most visible in restaurants and bars. For a while the authorities attempted to prohibit people wearing boots and work clothes from entering Béke Restaurant, but with little success. Likewise, the contrast between "urban" and "nonurban" was manifest in the visible difference between the group of people wearing green quilted jackets and people wearing suits.

According to popular stereotypes, those who failed to adhere to "urban" norms, people who in the majority of cases were "village" people, tended to partake in brawls, chop wood in their apartments, throw garbage out of the windows (or allow it to pile up in their cellars), keep animals in the bathroom, frequent bars, and shop on the black market instead of in city stores.[30] The general public regarded districts populated predominantly by people from "villages" (such as the Technikum, Radar, and the South Side) as scenes of repeated fights, where apartments were frequently occupied by squatters, and stores resembled village grocery shops.[31] The stigmatization of people living in these districts simultaneously represented the stigmatization of people who had come from villages.

Furniture made for mass consumption, however, can be found both in the bequests of agricultural workers in Ófalu (Old Village) and in the bequests of downtown engineers. The same traditional three-door cabinet was spacious enough to hold three sets of overalls, a loden coat, a balloon coat, a leather jacket, a winter coat, another coat for the spring, three sets of pajamas, three sweaters, a rabbit-fur hat, and a raincoat.[32] The bequest of a village-born seamstress contained a leather purse, a mirror for a dressing table, and a dressing table. In addition to the pin cushion, there was a flannel bed gown, a satin dressing gown, a leather jacket, a "petticoat," a worn cardigan, and a tracksuit in the cabinet.[33] The bequest of a village-born downtown crane operator included five copperplate engravings, two suits, and a bicycle.[34] A nurse who resided in the Technikum District and died at the age of thirty-five bequeathed twenty-nine doilies, a complete set of chrome frame furniture, two runners, an electric iron, modern kitchen furniture, and a wristwatch to her heirs.[35] A clerk who was born in Szombathely, lived in the L-buildings, and passed away at the age of twenty-nine had 23 books, 4 framed pictures, 2 suits, 5 summer dresses, 4 woolen dresses, 4 blouses, 5 pairs of shoes, 3 nightgowns, and 8 petticoats recorded in her bequest. This list was hardly characteristic of the possessions of a young wife in the "colony."[36] There are no significant general differences in the bequests of people who had lived in the Old Village, Technikum, and the downtown area that would indicate the prevalence of either predominantly "village" or predominantly "urban" possessions in the households of a given area. The list of items in the bequests was determined much more by the occupational status and income of the head of the family than by the place of birth or the presumed lifestyle of the deceased based on his or her place of origin.

"Civilizing" the Urban Villagers

For years the Sztálinváros authorities struggled with street vendors and scattered stalls in the name of controlling public space and creating an "urban" cityscape. Street stalls and vendors were to be concentrated in one place, the market. This was justified by "aesthetic considerations" and "the protection of law and order." In early 1954 council employees and the police organized a raid on Stalin Avenue, which had been invaded by black marketeers. "Educative propaganda" was used to persuade the vendors to move to the marketplace. However, the "educative propaganda" was not entirely effective. Vendors remained on Stalin Avenue, the wide and bustling boulevard designed for processions.[37] "Peddlers" sold their wares across from the officially sanctioned stores with shiny shop windows, and although it was suggested that shop employees be authorized to "drive them away,"[38] the authorities never managed to rid Stalin Avenue entirely of peddlers. After a time the number of peddlers on the monumental thoroughfare dropped simply because traffic had declined (sellers had either been banned from peddling their wares on the Avenue or had moved to the marketplace) and the middle of the avenue had been landscaped. Furthermore, the council managed to prevent many of them from working unless they had the proper retail licenses. The retail licenses issued to "legal vendors" offer a rough picture of the people who were vending their wares on Stalin Avenue and at the market and the products and goods they were selling.

The Sztálinváros market resembled a "village" fair (the market was next to Peace Square; see the Map of Downtown in chapter 2). Handmade knives, cheap toys, candy and gingerbread, knitted fabrics, parrots, doormats, women's sandals, dyed shawls, rubber blade window cleaners, leather goods, "oriental sweets," bratwurst and sausages, shoes, hats and caps, headscarves, secondhand clothes, cotton candy, woodwork, nylon wallets, textile paintings, photo frames, and handmade wares were all for sale.[39] The fact that many of the birth registries recorded parents as "circus performer" suggests that appearances by performers were not at all uncommon in this socialist city.[40] It is therefore understandable that the city leaders wanted to drive away the stall-keepers and peddlers, who allegedly gave the area a distinctly "village" feel, to the periphery of the city next to the amusement park. In 1957 this area was designated the "marketplace and circus."[41]

The assignment of names to streets and numbers to the various buildings was also seen as an essential step in maintaining control over public space and giv-

Figure 3.3. Vendors at the Sztálinváros market.

ing the city an urban profile. At the beginning of the period of construction (but even as late as 1957), several Sztálinváros streets were only identified by a letter, both in the public discourse and by the Management Division of the City Council, which supervised housing distribution. Buildings identified by codes (such as L/1, Ü/1, C/2) made it difficult for visitors to navigate and "map" the city. For the local residents, however, this was a perfectly logical way of identifying the buildings, since the designations referred to the time of their construction.[42] In the South Side barracks, streets had been given names, whereas in the Radar barracks they were numbered. The practice of numbering streets instead of naming them (quite unusual in Hungary at the time and even today) does not seem to have created much, if any, confusion in everyday life. In spite of all this, one of the features of an "urban" community, at least in the eyes of the authorities, was that streets had names and buildings had numbers. The first numbers of street addresses were posted on the walls of the buildings in 1954, but as late as 1957 there were streets in the Technikum District that still had not been named.[43]

The creation of parks in Sztálinváros was also intended to add to the "urban" profile of the city. In this respect, the function of parks and playgrounds was to serve as theaters for urban recreational activities and to limit the play of children to specifically designated areas. The importance of the function of Sztálinváros parks is highlighted by the fact that a portion of the saplings and flower beds were brought from Budapest, and playing ball in a landscaped area was considered a form of vandalism. The clerk responsible for cases involving minor offenses struck a somewhat doleful tone when remarking that offenders could not be fined because they were under fourteen years old. Jenő Tapolczai, the president of the local council, reported indignantly that "children were playing ball and playing on the grass under their parents' and teachers' noses, and the adults do not do anything to stop them."[44]

Council members believed that by creating a "play street," they would be able to drive the "street urchins" into one place. Their scheme, however, which involved closing a downtown street and designating it for play, was of little avail. Children continued to roam the town, so the "play street," which had been named after the famous Hungarian poet Attila József (who had himself had been something of a "street urchin" as a child) was converted back into a normal thoroughfare.[45]

The former village (Dunapentele, which was adjacent to the new city and later became a district of Sztálinváros) had been designed to foster an urban lifestyle, but parks located in the Old Town were ruined by goats and geese. At a meeting of the Council Executive Committee, Tapolczai demanded that "the peasants of the Old Town" "be more careful with regard to cityscape. Residents of the Old Town should also feel that they live in Sztálinváros."[46] The ambitious president also planned to establish a park on the site of the barracks on Szalki Island to serve as the "Margaret Island of Sztálinváros," to be modeled on the well-known park in Budapest. Eventually a fish restaurant (which remains popular to this day) and a campsite for children were built.[47] Because the residential buildings were crowded, one function of the Sztálinváros parks was to provide a place for young couples to meet. A 1957 article states that at dusk "only one kind of person is visiting" the park. "Soft whispers are heard here and there, sometimes the sand crunches under the feet of couples looking for a bench. Of course, the search is futile, all the benches are taken."[48]

As of 1954 leaders of the city began paying more attention to the "urban" regulation of traffic. Speed limits of 50 kilometers per hour were introduced within city limits, and due to the heavy traffic, 25 kilometers per hour on Stalin Avenue. Signposts were set up and pedestrian crossings were marked.[49] To make the downtown area and Stalin Avenue appear more "grandiose," according to the plans, trucks and horse-drawn vehicles were to be barred from Stalin Avenue, May 1 Street, Ady Endre Street, and József Attila Street (all are streets between May 1 Street and Stalin Avenue). Eventually pragmatic arguments prevailed, however. Trucks were forbidden to use only Ady and József Attila streets, because this allowed them to avoid taking a detour to reach the ironworks. To make the image of the city rosier to the outside world, the long-distance buses were diverted so that they would not pass by the unplastered houses of Szórád Márton Street, which was lined by barracks, but instead drove to the front of the Golden Star Hotel.[50] Visitors taking the coach from Budapest to Sztálinváros arrived right in front of the "Stalin baroque" hotel (as they do today).

The installation of street lighting was also considered a fundamental criterion of urbanity. In 1957 the council president listed clean streets free of mud, adequate street lighting, and heated apartments as necessary features of "civilized urban life."[51] Streetlamps were first installed in the downtown area and then on Stalin Avenue, and in the sparsely lit L-buildings and the Technikum District, and finally in the Old Town. With regard to the barracks, a few streetlamps were installed on the South Side, but the streets of Radar remained unlit. The order of installation indicates which districts officials saw as important parts of the city. The Old Town and the barracks remained "rural," not just in the public imagination but also, specifically, in regard to street lighting.[52]

Reproducing Social Barriers

Quite early on, the establishment of a Sanitary Station served as a "hygienic border" that separated Sztálinváros and immigrants, in particular new arrivals from villages. Theoretically, everyone who "moved" to the city had to undergo a general medical examination (focusing in particular on contagious diseases) and a "disinfecting" process. Symbolically, the Sztálinváros Sanitary Station, where checks for venereal diseases were an especially high priority, became the Ellis Island of the city. In practice, of course, this process of "disinfecting" was applied differently to new arrivals from Budapest and migrants from the agricultural towns and settlements of the Great Plains, and because of geographical and social circumstances, the authorities could not subject every single immigrant to a medical examination. In addition, since the majority of new arrivals from villages were housed in residential quarters, they were generally subject to stigmatizing inspections by the police, sanitary supervisors, and the vice squad. The "hygienic border" separating immigrants from the city was relocated from the outskirts to an area within the city limits. For residents of the barracks, night-time identity checks, washing with a disinfectant cyanide solution in order to prevent the spread of disease (in particular the spread of sexually transmitted diseases), and similar practices were everyday occurrences. In public thinking, notions of an immoral lifestyle were linked to the residential quarters and the barracks that were home to new arrivals from villages, who generally took odd jobs or worked as unskilled laborers.[53]

When construction was completed and industrial production began, Sztálinváros gradually became "fully populated," and employees of the sanitary station also had to find new jobs. "Luckily" twenty to thirty Roma families resided in the city, and the thousands of residents of the barracks also "required constant supervision," so the Sanitary Station workers were not left idle.[54]

At local council meetings, the Old Town "Gypsy ghetto" had long been referred to as a disgrace, yet attempts to address this problem were continuously postponed. The language of documents produced by many of the official organs was discriminatory. For example, in the internal reports of the Sanitary Station the inspections held in the city were referred to as "louse inspections" and "Gypsy inspections."[55] A suggestion made at a local council meeting recommended that the Roma living in what had been wine cellars and cave-dwellings should be relocated to South Side barracks several kilometers from the downtown area, but the leader of the barracks protested, arguing that this would jeopardize hard-won public order. Roma families were living in wine cellars and cave-dwellings because when the construction of the city began the properties they were occupying had been expropriated as the building site for the bridge to Szalki Island. At the time, farmers of the Old Town rented out the dilapidated cellars southeast of the village to them. The Roma were stuck in the cellars for decades, while to the south of their dwellings the new city had been completed. Thus visitors arriving in Sztálinváros from the direction of the village—including visitors from Budapest, who should have crossed the Old Town before they arrived in front of the Golden Star Hotel—were confronted with the sight of their squalid hovels. This "tainted" Sztálinváros's "reputation." From time to time the issue of the twenty to thirty families surfaced, but apart from frequent "disinfecting baths" no measures were adopted to address the problem.[56]

One explanation for this may be that the Old Town was not considered part of Sztálinváros proper, so problems that affected the "villagers" of the Old Town were of less concern to municipal leaders. A report written in July 1956 states, "a view has come to prevail among workers according to which Sztálinváros has a separate inner city and outskirts."[57] Founded on the village–urban dichotomy, this downtown–outskirts dichotomy appeared both in everyday life and in the series of measures taken by the council. The treatment of the "otherness" of the Roma as a form of cultural backwardness made the decision to settle them in a single block outside of the downtown area seem entirely self-explanatory. One

Figure 3.4. The Sztálinváros "Old Town" (the former village of Dunapentele, which was adjacent to the new city and later became a district of Sztálinváros).

finds no traces in the documents of the council, either before or after 1953, of any attempt to integrate members of this community by changing the ways in which dwelling places were assigned, in contrast to Nowa Huta, where sustained efforts were made to promote integration until the mid-1950s.[58] Attempts to further the integration of the Roma in Sztálinváros amounted to little more than calls to demolish their dwellings and put them in barracks in an area on the far side of the factory and to expose them regularly to harassment by the administration, which claimed to be acting in the interests of protecting the health of the community (often referring to the need to "disinfect" people). Furthermore, because of the lack of an adequate labor force at the construction site, Roma were able to find work more easily than they had previously been, even if the positions they were given were hardly held in high esteem.

Protests by owners of barrack apartments against the centrally planned and executed "disinfecting" and "lime washing" were not terribly effective. A request filed by János K. in which he asked that his apartment in "barrack 1,000" not be "lime-washed" was rejected. According to K., "the walls were not dirty, because he had not heated the apartment at all throughout the entire winter." However, the sanitary inspector contended that "not only are the walls of the apartment owned by the aforementioned dirty, but the apartment itself is disorderly and unclean, and the protests of the proprietor against the summer-time house-cleaning and whitewashing necessary to maintain order and cleanliness in residential quarters are incomprehensible."[59]

The church was incompatible with the image of a "socialist city." The Christian burials made the old cemetery in the Old Town, as a scene of religious rituals, a site that was "unbecoming" of the new metropolis. In Sztálinváros the functions of the church and cemetery were fulfilled by the church and cemetery of the Old Town. Since both institutions had been created to meet the needs of a village of a few thousand inhabitants, they failed to address the demands of a growing population. The church was packed on religious holidays, and especially at Christmas time. The morgue was so crowded with corpses that rats occasionally consumed the flesh of the deceased prior to burial.[60]

The infrastructure of the Old Town, which would have been adequate for a single village, was hardly sufficient to meet the needs of the people who were moving to the city. Although religion and the question of religious funerals were important issues in Sztálinváros, because the city administration made the topic taboo there are almost no sources concerning it. If an issue was not regarded as a social problem, then it was not dealt with and no documents were created pertaining to it. Of course, in memoirs one finds the myth according to which the people of the city contained to practice their religion in spite of the prohibitions, but we have no other sources that confirm these contentions and thus can do little more than speculate as to their credibility.[61]

This all served the purpose of presenting the absence of religious life with portrayals of the community that missed it. For instance, according to a widespread rumor most members of the party attended church, particularly on church holidays. According to another widespread rumor, party members took their children to nearby villages to be baptized, fearful lest they be seen engaging in a religious ceremony in the socialist city. The documents of the City Council do not contain a single mention of any plans or even suggestions regarding the construction of a city church. The 1956 Revolution was too short-lived to have allowed enough time for the institutions of traditional religious life to be established in the city. In contrast, the rituals held in the churches of the Old Town were constant subjects of harsh criticism in the city newspaper, especially as of early 1957. Before this, the question was raised only rarely.

The reason for this was the distinctive policy of the state regarding the church, a policy characteristic of the Kádár regime, which did not prohibit but only frowned upon participation in religious rituals, though it vigorously propagated new social rituals through the councils. Of these, alongside church weddings so-called council weddings, which were festive and ceremonious, began to enjoy popularity in the 1960s. A "name-giving ceremony," which was intended to replace baptism, gradually gained ground, but people remained hesitant to make any changes to the funeral ceremonies and rites.[62] Conclusions concerning religious life in the city can be made primarily on the basis of debates held in the 1980s, particularly toward the end of the decade. This was the case in Nowa Huta, where, as in Dunaújváros, religious life had political significance.[63]

The construction of at least one high-rise building in the city was also seen as a prerequisite for the creation of a genuinely urban settlement. The eight-story apartment block, which for years had hosted offices, had long been the tallest building in Sztálinváros. The turreted city hall designed to be built on the main square (and always shrinking as new plans were devised) was also intended to symbolize Sztálinváros "urbanity."

The Sztálinváros soccer team was supposed to help foster a spirit of local patriotism. In reports on Sztálinváros sports activities the local team always held a place of prestige because according to local potentates the "quality sport" of the city was represented by the Vasas SK (Ironworks Sport Club) in national public opinion. When Sztálinváros, as a "favored child of the planned economy," was still the beneficiary of centralized investment, the city had a soccer team in the national first league. With the establishment of the Sztálinváros soccer team at the end of 1951, players from illustrious Budapest teams, such as Bástya (Bastion), Dózsa, and the Vasas of Csepel, were signed, so the Stalin Ironworks Builders managed to make it into the first league. At first, because the city lacked a proper soccer field, the team played at other locations and players occasionally visited the construction site. After 1954, when Sztálinváros investment funds were reduced, the team was eliminated from the first league and the best players signed with other teams.[64]

Residents of the city who kept animals were seen as "rural" in public opinion. Several times the local council attempted to prohibit pig farming in the Radar barracks, but to no avail.[65] In the washrooms of the multistory block houses, slaughtered pigs were frequently processed by the residents of fully equipped apartments. According to the plans for the gardens (which were built by residents at their own expense), woodsheds or poultry houses were allowed, but not pigsties.[66] It is worth noting, however, that people were taking out loans from the Országos Takarék Pénztár (National Savings Bank) to purchase refrigerators, radios, and utility furniture, but also pigs. Many residents of apartments that were fully equipped and furnished raised pigs in buildings in the Old Town, then processed the pig (which sometimes had been slaughtered in front of the building) in the washroom of the block house.[67]

To foster the spread of an urban lifestyle, barracks that had been built on the marketplace at the beginning of the construction of the city were demolished, a public restroom was planned on Stalin Avenue, clocks were placed all over the city, "bistros" were opened to replace "bars," and neon-sign advertisements for the National Savings Bank and the Lottery were planned to give the Sztálinváros cityscape a more urban air. But the barracks remained, in the Technikum District apartments were still cold in the winter due to the lack of heating, and one-third of the stores owned by the Kiskereskedelmi Vállalat (Small Retail Enterprise) were located in barracks in 1960.[68]

Transformation from "rural" into "urban" not only affected the traditions of migrants arriving in Sztálinváros from villages but also changed the "urban" environment and the definition of "urbanity." In the summer of 1959 an article in *Nők Lapja* (Women's Magazine) wrote of the Technikum District (which was viewed as the "most rural" of the planned neighborhoods): "Indeed, the newest district of the young town does not have district heating, and gas has not been installed. The store has not been opened yet, some of the houses are still unplastered, and the roads are not paved. But it is vigorously and powerfully demanding all the [urban] rights of the favored child. And it will obtain them, it will get them."[69]

Thus, block heating, gas, a store, plaster, and paved roads were not prerequisites for the district to be seen as an integral part of the city: in spite of its rural infrastructure, the Technikum District was declared "urban" in the official discourse.

Ten years after construction began, Sztálinváros still remained a mixture of "urban" and "rural" lifestyles. Based on various characteristic features, however, public opinion did draw an explicit distinction between the two. A person was considered "urban" or "provincial" depending on the perceptions of those in his immediate environment, and the criteria on which these perceptions were based were to a great extent influenced by official discourse. Yet it is also possible that someone might participate in a pig slaughtering on Saturday, but on Sunday he would put on his factory tailored suit and go for a "stroll" to window-shop on Stalin Avenue.

Networks of Migration

The subjects of migration are not individuals but social networks. Although scholars agree that one of the most significant mass phenomena of the twentieth century was the migration of villagers to urban areas, in Central and Eastern

Europe no clear, consistent definition of rural–urban migration emerged, particularly after World War II. One of the reasons for this is simply that the very notions of urban and rural were defined differently in the various countries.[70]

The majority of migrants adopt personal and group-oriented strategies at the same time. However, George Gmelch argues that personal strategies dominate among middle-class, better-educated immigrants, who are quicker to adapt to the urban environment. In Gmelch's view, group-oriented strategies are used primarily by rural immigrants with less education.[71] This is palpable in the contrasting recollections of people who took jobs in Sztálinváros. Memoirs of less-educated migrants from villages identify kinship bonds and the assistance of relatives as the most significant incentives to move to the city. In contrast, better-educated people with higher-ranking jobs generally emphasize opportunities for personal professional or financial success.[72] Migration and a high degree of social mobility, however, were linked as much in the case of Sztálinváros as in other growing urban communities. In inheritance cases heard by the Sztálinváros notary in 1960 and 1961, many of the parties with higher occupational and residential status had migrated from or been born in villages.[73]

In the early 1950s Ilona Dobos interviewed an elderly woman in Sztálinváros. The woman in question complained primarily about her lack of acquaintances, although she admitted that "there are several people from the village working at the construction sites. . . . I could have a good life here; there is no hard agricultural labor as back in the village. But it is so strange for me. The houses all look identical. . . . Everybody is wearing quilted jackets. How beautiful it was back at home, when we were still not married, and on Sundays my sister and I would put on our finest clothes and go to church. And probably the worst thing here is that no one knows me."[74]

In contrast, in his recollections a member of the intelligentsia emphasized the range of social connections, which partly strengthened his positive image of the city. According to him, in the early period even people who made trips to Budapest to see an opera or theater performance on weekends found friends in the city.

> We had lots of friends. They were primarily local physicians, and editors and journalists working for the local paper. Members of the intelligentsia who were not really engineers or technicians, but rather intellectuals in the humanities living in the city. There were a couple of really outstanding people. It was very interesting. The city exerted an unprecedented attraction on people. . . . There was a group who had houses in Kulcs. Johanna Wolf and a couple of managers.[75] But it was a more exclusive circle, a different generation. . . . They were among the leading members of the intelligentsia of the 1930s. And this was a different worldview. At home we were the young revolutionaries, something we fortunately did not actually carry out, but we had a different view of the world.[76]

According to this interpretation of the city, even representatives of 1930s intelligentsia formed their own separate circle of friends. Influenced by the official discourse, however, people looking back on their experiences in Sztálinváros categorized migrants according to their lifestyles. When immigration is discussed, the narrative focuses on conflicts between various lifestyle groups.[77]

Despite the depiction of the circles of local intelligentsia, a significant proportion of the members of the intelligentsia did not even request residency permits until 1955.[78] The majority of immigrants fleeing from the shortage of housing in industrial cities or the poverty of rural settlements had no choice other than to relocate to Sztálinváros. Thus immigrants from villages, with little or no education, were not simply unlikely to leave Sztálinváros—on the contrary, having left they would write letters pleading for a job and accommodation in the barracks of the city. When most of the construction work had been completed and industrial production had begun, however, the unskilled workforce was no longer needed.

Local authorities closed the gates of the city by implementing various anti-immigration regulations. The fate of a request submitted to the local council for a permit to return to Sztálinváros in 1960 shows how seriously these regulations were taken. The request was written by a woman who lost her parents at an early age and lived in dire poverty since childhood. She did hard manual labor and met her husband in Sztálinváros while working at one of the construction sites. They had three children, but according to her account the husband's stepparent had lured them back to the village of Nagykálló.[79] They were soon driven out of the house and the family of five had to move into a stable, from where she had sent the letter. The worker at the Health Department of the City Council personally wrote on the long application, "they'd better stay in Nagykálló," a response that was a sign of the crowded conditions in Sztálinváros. In a more detailed response the social worker wrote, "It would be a grave mistake if we were to tell you to pack up your children and come back when we know that we would not be able to provide accommodation for your family, thus we would be incapable of taking responsibility. . . . Joy and happiness do not derive from a city—they thrive in us or in our immediate surroundings, in the smiles of our children, in the love of our husbands; we must simply take care not to lose them."[80]

In Sztálinváros a significant proportion of the women who had newly arrived in the city worked in lower-ranking jobs or remained unemployed for long periods of time.[81] Alongside the expectations placed on women regarding social roles, this was one of the main reasons that the women of Sztálinváros integrated differently into local society than the men. Although the first wave of migrants to any settlement is usually predominantly male, after a time the number of women grows and the proportion becomes roughly equal, as indeed was the case in

Figure 3.5. The Görbe utca (Winding Street) neighborhood in 1951.

Sztálinváros. Single female migrants maintained much stronger ties with their mothers, sisters, daughters, and nieces than usual.[82]

In general, single women in Sztálinváros offered their female relatives support or asked them for assistance. It is difficult to draw conclusions regarding the depth of family ties in retrospect, yet aging mothers seem to have been taken in and cared for by their married daughters, which is hardly surprising given the expectations placed on women. This conclusion is based on the applications submitted to the social department of the local council, in which parents petitioned for support to be paid by their children or requested to be placed in homes for the elderly.[83] Divorce cases reveal that husbands and their attorneys were inclined to emphasize the conflicts that arose because of wives having taken the side of their mothers or sisters instead of their husbands.[84] Wives living without their spouses (separated, divorced, or widowed) often allowed their mothers, who also lived alone, to move in with them. For example, Mrs. Géza P., although she was poor and living in the barracks, took in her mother in order to care for her.[85] There were even cases when an unwed mother abandoned by the father of her child asked for and received help from the paternal grandmother.[86]

Immigrant narratives often describe arrival in a new community and the processes of settling down as a series of struggles.[87] In various applications addressed to the Sztálinváros Council one finds innumerable dramatic laments, such as "my wife has left her native village and her parents, and everything" or "some people are insulting us by asking why the hell we came here from Upper Hungary,[88] because now we are stealing the bread of the locals."[89]

In contrast to narratives that emphasize conflicts, some stories (often of the same person) highlight the help offered by relatives. Those who move set a persuasive example for others, and family members help one another in the migration process, so from the very outset they have kinship ties in their new places of residence. If a member of a family migrates he or she functions as a kind of magnet attracting others to follow (a process referred to as chain migration).[90]

Kinship-related chain migration was also part of the history of Sztálinváros. Applications for settlement, which include descriptions of the processes of resettlement and brief biographical sketches, almost always mention a relative who helped the family relocate. The recollections of people who came from rural backgrounds usually mention the help of a "distant relative" and other "country people" as well. For example, János B. recalls, "There was a machinist born in Kápolnásnyék who helped my father obtain accommodation in Sztálinváros. He knew the B. family, I mean in Kápolnásnyék. They were well-to-do, boot makers, they were very close. There were three extended families, and he was close with them. But, of course, in those days you had to lie in your résumé as much as you possibly could. So this is how he managed, through some family or village inside help. We were given housing immediately; he arranged that too."[91]

In their recollections, people with a higher level of education placed considerably less emphasis on relatives when describing their decisions to migrate to Sztálinváros. Job opportunities, higher wages, and even "professional challenges" were the pivotal factors in their narratives. The deputy manager of the Ironworks Power Plant project stated that for him the years spent in Sztálinváros had been the true years of "apprenticeship" (*Wanderjahre*, a year in which an apprentice traveled to improve his skills) before he had actually launched his career: "I believed I needed some technical experience before I began my scientific career. I wanted to learn about life, that's why I went to the building site of the power plant. It was an extremely complex and exciting task, and also a wonderful technical experience."[92] The other significant motif, the importance of family and kinship, surfaces in his narrative as well: "The construction of the power plant had just begun. I must add that my first wife, who is still alive, was a building engineer. She had arrived earlier. That's why I also wanted to go there."[93] Kinship-related immigration (which can be considered group-oriented) blended with individual immigration motivations, depending largely on occupational status and level of education.

In most cases immigrants are described as people who gradually adapt to urban life and adopt local norms. In Sztálinváros, however, before the waves of immigrants arrived, the only "lifestyle" was the Dunapentele rural way of living, which hardly met the official and the unofficial expectations of the city. In the early years, for the immigrants from Budapest, Ózd, and the Hungarian Great Plains, the notion of an "urban culture" did not exist because every single "urban" resident had been a new arrival. The urban norm was created partly by the sharp official distinction between urban and rural ways of life. The official depiction of the urban–rural dichotomy significantly influenced urbanization, the official discourse, and the language used in requests concerning neighborhood conflicts.[94]

Neighborhood Conflicts

In Sztálinváros, alongside the norms created by immigrants, the expectations of authorities also determined what were considered "acceptable" and "intolerable." The neighborhood lawsuits that were routinely launched by residents of the L-buildings in the workers district against one another demonstrate how the local norms were shaped both by the authorities and by the migrant communities.[95] The prevalence of neighborhood conflicts among immigrants indicates the increasing—not decreasing—intensity of neighborhood relationships and control in Sztálinváros.[96] According to a fundamental thesis of the scholarship on neighborhood relationships, traditional houses with a quadrangular courtyard enhance the intensity of these relationships, in contrast to more recently built square blocks, residents of which have less opportunity to meet one another (see the Map of the Downtown districts in chapter 2). However, several studies have concluded that neighborhood relationships can remain as intense in the newer buildings as in the older ones.[97]

The design of the L-buildings in Sztálinváros, with their gigantic quadrangular courtyards and the institutions (nursery schools, stores) and playgrounds located in them, created numerous occasions for neighbors to meet. Widespread unemployment among women also augmented the significance of neighborhood relationships. "Dependent" women built most of their social connections in the semipublic space of the quadrangle. In the course of tending to their daily tasks, with the possible exception of going shopping,[98] these women hardly ever left this space, which was under the close watch of their neighbors.

Conflict between the women living in the L-buildings began with a relatively trivial case. In the summer of 1956, Gyula R. was regularly working night shifts as a welder for the ironworks, so he had to sleep during the day. He moved to Sztálinváros with his wife (who was originally from Budapest) by trading the apartment he had been allocated by the local council of the city of Nyíregyháza (located in the northeastern part of Hungary, a poor area of the country) for a first-floor flat in the L-buildings of Erkel Garden (the word *kert* [garden] was used to refer to many of the building complexes). One source of conflict was that children always played in the playground next to the window of his apartment. On several occasions Mrs. R. drove the children away so her husband could rest. Because of the earsplitting wood chopping coming from one of the apartments upstairs, she quarreled with the tenant, Mrs. György O.

Tenants routinely borrowed household utensils, food items, or money from one another, and they babysat for one another's children, sometimes for free, sometimes not. They often bought things on credit in the neighboring grocery store. As a "housewife," Mrs. R. spent much of the day sewing clothes at home, and this, in all likelihood, provided her and her husband with a substantial income. Mrs. R.'s husband regularly repaired radios and other "household" appliances, which also added to the family's earnings. After a while Mrs. R. refused to mend some of her neighbors' clothes for free, and her husband seems to have stopped doing repairs without being paid. Husbands in the majority of tenant families worked for the ironworks, and wives were "homemakers," but they were not likely to earn any income in addition to their wages (discounting occasional housecleaning and babysitting). Presumably, Mr. and Mrs. R.'s neighbors envied them, in part because of their incomes as "self-employed" people.

According to the attorney's petition, Mrs. R. had lived in a detached house in Budapest. The attorney believed that when she moved to Erkel Garden, she was surprised to discover that the plaintiff in the case, Mrs. O., was continuously ringing the doorbell, as were other tenants. One requested an egg, the second asked to borrow a grinder, and the third had another request. Neighbors learned she could sew and Mrs. R. was bombarded with requests to make clothes for tenants and their children. "When she grew tired of being pestered, she refused to help. And the tenants of the building began to unite against her. All of a sudden, she became the worst tenant in the building."[99]

Claiming that her offspring were always "neat and clean," while other children were "unkempt and dirty," Mrs. R. forbade her children to play with them. This only made people ostracize her even more. The women in the building began to refer to her as a "lady," to which Mrs. R. responded by calling them "filthy communists." The party secretary in the house organized "voluntary work" to dig ditches for district heating pipes in front of the house. Gyula R. did not volunteer. The wife of the secretary demanded an explanation. Mrs. R. responded: "Let the filthy communists do the work, let them dig the pits. My husband surely will not." In the L-buildings calling someone a "filthy communist" was hardly an offense that would get one reported. Such an outburst would not have been sufficient grounds for an accusation of "character assassination" or "slander." But in a conflict that was building up into a court case people were inclined to cite their opponents' political views. However, her neighbors did not bring any action against Mrs. R. for this.

On the basis of occasionally contradictory testimony, the conflict may have turned into a court case because of the following, seemingly simple circumstance: according to an unwritten law of the building, for want of a drying room, families hung their clothes to dry in the quadrangular courtyard. The seemingly spontaneous community life in the courtyard was regulated by strict (yet unwritten) rules. For instance, one woman could not use another woman's drying space. In the summer of 1956, by which time Mrs. R. had essentially been entirely excluded from the community of tenants, Mrs. O. hung her clothes in Mrs. R.'s spot several times. For the women of the building, disregarding someone's "territorial" rights was the same as disregarding and even denying her presence. One day, when Mrs. O. was yet again using Mrs. R.'s spot, Mrs. R. yelled at her from the window, saying that if Mrs. O. did not remove her clothesline, she would cut it down. Knowing that Mrs. R. was hardly popular among the people in the building, Mrs. O. had retorted, "I'd like to see you try." Mrs. R. rushed out to the yard and without saying another word cut the clothesline, on which Mrs. O. had not yet even hung any clothes. Mrs. O. went to her apartment in tears.

Mrs. R. believed that order had been restored and she replaced Mrs. O.'s clothesline with her own. She hung the freshly washed laundry and returned to her apartment. Meanwhile Mrs. O was lying in wait. She watched Mrs. R. return to her apartment, then she cut the clothesline and all the clothes fell in the mud. After this she hung her own laundry out to dry. Mrs. R. only noticed this later. She cut Mrs. O.'s clothesline, causing her clothes to fall into the mud. Finally, when all the clothes lay in the mud, Mrs. O. and her husband began to call out to all the tenants of the building from their window. As her petition reveals, Mrs. R was particularly offended by a remark about how she had "come out with that horrible figure." She had replied by telling Mrs. O. that no matter how "bony" she was, her husband still "visited whores secretly." This statement incited Mrs. István M., wife of the party secretary, to shout at Mrs. R. that "she would have her relocated to the South Side because that was where she belonged." In what followed, Mrs. O. brought charges of defamation (for "bony") and slander (for the accusation that Mr. O. secretly visited whores). On August 14, 1956, the Municipal Court found Mrs. R. guilty of the charges and fined her 500 forints. The sum of the fine was mitigated by the court of appeal to 300 forints (Gyula R.'s official income was 1,500 forints a month, an average wage at that time in Sztálinváros, thus the fine was a serious sum).

Presumably encouraged by the success of the trial, on September 12, 1956, thirteen other women in the building visited the Housing Office of the City Council and requested that the R. family be evicted on the grounds of "unsociability." In response to the request, on September 22, 1956, the Housing Allocation Enterprise

(Ingatlankezelő Vállalat) ordered the family to vacate the apartment with their two children within eight days. Thus, the neighborhood community managed to obtain "official support," which shows that Mrs. R., who attempted to defy neighborhood norms, was forced to move out. Neighbors succeeded in presenting their rules so that they would be acceptable to and even win the support of the authorities, such as the council and the court. The strategy they adopted was to emphasize elements of Mrs. R.'s behavior that they knew were reprehensible in the official discourse ("anticommunist," "anticommunity," "unsociable," "bourgeois"). Thus they adapted their own norms to the expectations of the authorities ("communal," "loyal"), at the same time preserving some elements of their value system.

For example, Mrs. Gyula R. cited the norms of her earlier "Budapest detached house" residence, contrasting it with the "crowds" of the L-buildings. Her defense attorney expanded on this, contending that the primary cause of the conflict lay simply in the fact that "without any consideration people with the most diverse mentalities and manners had been placed in the same buildings."[100] This reasoning resembled the officially accepted thesis that immigrants were in a continuous "struggle" against the new environment and one another because of their different "urban" or "rural" lifestyles. In this case as well, the people who used the officially endorsed opposition between an "urban" and a "rural" way of life in their petitions reached their goals.

Conclusion

Migration to Sztálinváros can only partially be explained by poverty and the labor market. Members of the immigrant communities who arrived in the city as part of a process of chain migration first adopted a lifestyle—which the authorities considered provincial—in the barracks created for construction workers. The first immigrants, as people who worked in construction, were less educated, more provincial laborers; after 1953–54 the more educated ironworkers, engineers, and bureaucrats who came to work in the city ironworks found themselves in a settlement that resembled a chaotic rural construction site. Everyday customs and the differences between the various communities of immigrants bore the seeds of conflict, even if social status in this unusually mobile society was constantly changing. In the 1950s, several changes took place in the lives and behavioral ideals of "village" people who until then had worked in agriculture but found themselves moving to cities or taking jobs in urban areas. Such changes could be interpreted through the dichotomy based on stereotypes of "rural" and "urban" after the mid-1950s. How might one characterize a turner (a person who operates a lathe in the factory) who was born in a small village, whose parents were day laborers before 1945 and then became factory workers, who worked and rented an apartment in Csepel (an industrial district of Budapest), and who, upon arrival in

Sztálinváros, were not immediately given an apartment but found lodgings in a nearby village?[101] Based on his previous residence, he would be considered half urban; by birth he was rural; occupationally he was urban; and then, according to residence, he was again rural. If one categorizes him on the basis of his parents' occupations he could be considered either urban or rural, depending on the moment of history in question. On the basis of what characteristics and features of lifestyle can one establish a clear, meaningful dichotomy between "urban" and "rural"? Given the many abrupt upheavals of the time, this question is more complex than it may initially seem.

In the 1950s, this question arose as part of the general consciousness in Sztálinváros, where it found manifestation in a blend of urban and rural elements of life on the one hand, but in an emphasis on the allegedly sharp contrast between "urban" and "rural" life on the other. The notion of a clear urban–rural dichotomy played a central role in narratives in the local press and in discourses of the government offices. It fit the official ideology, according to which one of the primary duties of the state was to reduce and eventually abolish the differences between cities and villages. In this discourse the city represented the future and modernity, whereas the village stood for the past and anachronism. By implementing the sharp division between "rural" and "urban" in official depictions of city life, the socialist regime could portray itself as a warrior fighting for the cause of modernity. This public transformation of the Stalinist principles sustained the short legacy of Stalinist policies after the mid-1950s, which included the construction of a new city from scratch. However, alongside the use of public discourse on modernity, the renovation of family norms and the reproduction of social hierarchies in a new way, which I will explore in the next two parts of the book, also helped "reload" Stalinism after the mid-1950s.

Notes

Epigraph: Nikolai Miliutin, *Sotzgorod: The Problem of Building Socialist Cities*, 1930, 59–60.

1. Miskolczi, *Az első évtized*, 105–6.

2. Katerina Gerasimova draws attention to the common practice of reporting in neighborhood relationships, in "Public Privacy in the Soviet Communal Apartment," 214.

3. From the beginning of the nineteenth century until about the 1930s Tabán, a neighborhood in Budapest, was a good example of a "village" within a city. Gyáni, *Bérkaszárnya és nyomortelep*, 139–46.

4. Gans, *The Urban Villagers*, 11–12, and especially chapters 3, 5, and 11.

5. In the course of the collectivization that took place in Hungary in 1959–61, the vast majority of the lands ended up in the hands of the state. Smaller holdings were allowed to remain in private hands, particularly in the areas around industrial cities, where fewer agricultural cooperatives were formed. Varga, "The Appropriation and Modification of the 'Soviet Model' of Collectivization."

6. The 1962 bequest of a man who was born in Mezőkövesd, worked as a "raw material division manager," and lived in downtown Sztálinváros indicated that property (a plow and a shed) was as valuable as the Pobjeda wristwatch and the set of chrome frame furniture, including a settee, which signified urbanity. FML, f. XXV-151, b. 3, 1962.

7. For the debates on the relationship between socialism and modernity, see Hoffmann, "European Modernity and Soviet Socialism."

8. 138. sz. 5.440 / 1951. B. M. (1951.IX.23.) sz. rendelet a Dunapentele városban történő letelepedés szabályozásáról. [Nr. 138. 5.440 / 1951. Ministry of Interior (September 23, 1951). Resolution on the regulation of residence in the city of Dunapentele].

9. For a summary of data found in residency permits, see Erdős, "Dunapentelétől Sztálinvárosig," 260–61. The proportionate representations of immigrants who received residential permits between 1951 and 1954 by former place of residence were: Budapest (28.2%), Baranya (5%), Bács-Kiskun (9%), Békés (2.1%), BAZ (15.4%), Csongrád (2%), Fejér (9%), Győr-Sopron (0.9%), Hajdú-Bihar (1.5%), Heves (1.3%), Komárom (1.6%), Nógrád (1.5%), Pest (6.5%), Somogy (3.5%), Szabolcs-Szatmár (1.3%), Szolnok (2%), Tolna (5%), Vas (1.3%), Veszprém (1.6%), and Zala (1.3%). Original occupation: (greater than 0.5%): home employed (28.7%); minor, student (19.5%), construction laborer, tumbrel driver, unskilled worker (13.1%), agricultural laborer (7.7%), administrative employee (5.2%), locksmith (3.4%), transportation and postal service employee (2.7%), electrician, operator (2%), shopkeeper (1.4%), dressmaker, textile worker (1.4%), mason (1.1%), teacher (1.1%), turner (1%), party worker, soldier, police officer (0.9%), bakery and food industry employee (0.9%), carpenter (0.8%), shoemaker (0.7%), engineer, technician (0.6%), and blacksmith (0.6%).

10. Cf. Hoffmann, "Moving to Moscow," 847–51. Hoffmann argues that peasant migration to Soviet cities was neither totally controlled by the state nor chaotic. Cf. "The Myth of Managed Migration," in which Cynthia Buckley states that even the most severe Soviet residential restrictions in the communist bloc did not significantly influence migration patterns because if migrants from villages to cities failed to receive the necessary official documents, they obtained them semiofficially or "on the black market."

11. Cf. Tilly, "Trust Networks in Transnational Migration," 6–9; Simić, "Bogdan's Story."

12. Lewin, *The Making of the Soviet System*, 39.

13. Kotkin, *Magnetic Mountain*, 107–8.

14. Lebow, *"Kontra Kultura,"* 74.

15. Fitzpatrick, *The Cultural Front*, 5.

16. From the early nineteenth century until the 1930s the Budapest district of Tabán, close to the Castle on the Buda side of the River Danube, was regarded as such. See Gyáni, *Bérkaszárnya és nyomortelep*, 139–46.

17. At this time in Budapest social problems were redefined in the documents of the local administration and the term *social policy* was reinvented by party bureaucrats to legitimize their power. See Horváth, *Két emelet boldogság*, 21–73, chapter 1, "A látogató: A szociálpolitika fogalmának változása" [The visitor: changes to the term "social policy"].

18. This was the case in Sztálinváros, the first "socialist city" in Hungary, which had a lower budget for investment after Stalin's death. FML, f. XXIII-501, file 11, February 4, 1956; and in Budapest, where the "reinvention of social policy" after 1956 had its roots in the de-Stalinist narrative that tried to represent the difference between the social policy of the "Stalinist" (Rákosi) period and the "de-Stalinist" (Kádár) era. Budapest Főváros Levéltára (BFL) [Budapest City Archives], Fővárosi Tanács [City Council], f. XXIII-101-a. Jelentés a Szociálpolitikai Állandó Bizottság munkájáról [Report on the Work of the Permanent Committee on Social Policy], September 27, 1957, 146–47.

19. Dobos, *Áldozatok*, 92.
20. Schneider, "Straßenfluchten und Fluchtstraßen."
21. Weiner, "Sztálinváros", 82.
22. See the detailed discussion in chapter 2 in the sections on the downtown area.
23. FML, f. XXIII-502, b. 10, January 6, 1955.
24. FML, f. XXIII-502, b. 8, November 11, 1954.
25. *Sztálinvárosi Hírlap*, December 19, 1956, 4.
26. FML, f. XXIII-502, b. 7, March 17, 1954.
27. FML, f. XXIII-502, b. 16, July 17, 1959; *Sztálinvárosi Hírlap*, July 2, 1958, 2; November 14, 1958, 5.
28. *Sztálinvárosi Hírlap*, December 24, 1957, 4.
29. *Sztálinvárosi Hírlap*, January 21, 1958, 3.
30. *Sztálinvárosi Hírlap*, April 19, 1957, 2; February 26, 1957, 3.
31. *Sztálinvárosi Hírlap*, December 15, 1956, 3; March 8, 1957, 5.
32. FML, f. XXV-151, b. 2, 1961, János K., August 30, 1961, Bequest hearing.
33. FML, f. XXV-151, b. 2, 1961. Mrs. László B., June 21, 1961, Bequest hearing.
34. FML, f. XXV-151, b. 2, 1961, József T. July 14, 1961, Bequest hearing.
35. FML, f. XXV-151, b. 2, 1961, Mrs. Károly T., April 28, 1961, Bequest hearing.
36. FML, f. XXV-151, b. 2, 1961, Mrs. Jenő G., Inventory of estate no. 1961 / 3131.
37. FML, f. XXIII-502, b. 7, January 13, 1954; March 17, 1954.
38. FML, f. XXIII-502, b. 7, May 5, 1954.
39. FML, f. XXIII-509, b. 1, Retail licenses.
40. FML, Sztálinváros, Register of births, 1954–55.
41. FML, f. XXIII-502, b. 13, March 19, 1957.
42. One example of a Sztálinváros address is L/I/13/II/3. It indicates that the resident lived in the first of the L-buildings, stairway 13, apartment number 3 on the second floor.
43. FML, f. XXIII-502, b. 7, March 24, 1954; b. 13, February 7, 1957.
44. FML, f. XXIII-502, b. 7, May 5, 1954.
45. FML, f. XXIII-502, b. 7, May 26, 1954; b. 10, February 24, 1955.
46. FML, f. XXIII-502, b. 11, April 12, 1956; May 17, 1956; b. 10, September 9, 1955; b. 7, April 21, 1954.
47. FML, f. XXIII-502, b. 10, March 10, 1955; b. 11, April 12, 1956.
48. *Sztálinvárosi Hírlap*, December 10, 1957, 3.
49. FML, f. XXIII-502, b. 7, May 26, 1954; June 23, 1954.
50. FML, f. XXIII-502, b. 10, May 10, 1955; June 9, 1955; August 4, 1955.
51. FML, f. XXIII-502, b. 13, June 6, 1957.
52. FML, f. XXIII-502, b. 11, April 12, 1956; b. 18, March 11, 1960.
53. FML, f. XXIII-502, b. b. 11, April 26, 1956; b. 13, July 6, 1957; b. 15; December 28, 1958.
54. FML, f. XXIII-510, b. 3.
55. "In addition to the regular lice and Gypsy control, in January 1958 the entire staff of the Sanitary Station will assemble in the Gypsy-populated part of the Old Town and will check every single Gypsy for lice." FML, XXIII-510, b. 3.
56. FML, XXIII-502, b. 11, April 26, 1956. The police kept separate records on Roma. FML, XXIV-11, b. 2, 1952. After 1945 forced bathing became all the more systematic and inclusive. According to council reports, measures against the Roma community were primarily motivated by the goal of protecting the majority. At the same time, forced bathing symbolized humiliation and power. On the ignominious health and police procedures against the Roma community after 1945 and the characteristic practice of forced bathing, see Bernáth and

Polyák, "Kényszermosdatások Magyarországon." See also Majtényi and Majtényi, *A Contemporary History of Exclusion.*

57. FML, f. XXIII-502, b. 11, July 27, 1956.

58. Lebow, *Unfinished Utopia*, 106–12.

59. FML, f. XXIII-510, b. 4.

60. *Sztálinvárosi Hírlap*, June 7, 1957, 3.

61. Cf. Report of András Sándor. ÁSZTL, file O-13582, and Miskolczy, *Város lesz csakazértis.*

62. On the changing roles of social rituals, see Tóth, "Névadó, KISZ-esküvő, temetés."

63. Religious life in Nowa Huta is far more thoroughly documented because of the plans to build a church after 1956. Lebow, *Unfinished Utopia*, 163–64. There were no such plans in Sztálinváros in the 1950s.

64. FML, FML, f. XXIII-502, b. 11, February 4, 1956. and b. 16, October 27, 1959.

65. FML, f. XXIII-502, b. 16, November 9, 1959.

66. FML, f. XXIII-502, b. 13, December 27, 1957.

67. FML, f. XXIII-502, b. 16, December 14, 1959; *Sztálinvárosi Hírlap*, January 16, 1958, 3.

68. FML, f. XXIII-502, b. 18, January 19, 1960; February 16, 1960; March 1, 1960; May 24, 1960; July 3, 1960.

69. *Nők Lapja* [Women's Magazine], August 27, 1959.

70. Clout, "Rural–Urban Migration in Western Europe," 30–36.

71. Gmelch, "Migration and the Adaptation of Migrants." Cf. Mlinár, "A bevándorlók baráti kapcsolatai Velenjében." In the course of research pursued in Novo Velenje of Yugoslavia (today Slovenia), Mlinár argues that the formation of friendships among migrants is closely related to social status.

72. Miskolczi, *Város lesz csakazértis*, 337–43; Dobos, *Áldozatok*, 91–93, 112–16, 171; Tapolczai, *Egy elnök naplója*; and recollections of Tibor V. and János B.

73. FML, f. XXV-151. Documents of the Sztálinváros Notary, Inheritance cases.

74. Dobos, *Áldozatok*, 92–93.

75. Johanna Wolf was born in 1903. In 1931, she became one of the first women to earn a degree in engineering under the administrative restrictions that were applied to women in 1927. (The Technical University of Budapest offered a degree to women in architecture only, and the proportion of female students was set at 5 percent.) Wolf primarily worked at industrial projects as a building engineer. In 1951 she became chief engineer for the Twenty-Sixth National Construction Industry Trust, the national enterprise responsible for the construction of buildings in Sztálinváros. She is remembered as a strict and demanding boss whose favorite hobby was driving. (She drove her own car from the age of eighteen until she turned ninety.) Vámos, "Wolf Johanna."

76. Recollections of Tibor V.

77. Cf. Tapolczai, *Egy elnök naplója*; Miskolczi, *Az első évtized*, 105–6.

78. FML, f. XXIII-502, b. 10, September 9, 1955.

79. Three hundred kilometers from Sztálinváros, Nagykálló is an agricultural town located in the easternmost county of Hungary, Szabolcs-Szatmár-Bereg County, which borders Ukraine.

80. FML, f. XXIII-510, b. 4.

81. Even in 1960, by which time several factories founded specifically to create jobs for women had been in operation for two years, 60 percent of the women of Sztálinváros (as recorded by the Central Statistical Office) were dependent, in comparison with 27 percent among the male population. *Dunaújváros. 1950–1965*, 11.

82. Cf. Young and Willmott, *Family and Kinship*, 188; and Nelson, "Surviving in the City."

83. FML, f. XXIII-510, b. 3.

84. FML, f. XXXI-18, b. 10, the case of Vince Cs.

85. FML, f. XXV-24, Criminal Proceedings, b. 4, 1958. B. 314 / 1958, the case of Mrs. Géza P. See more on her in the chapter on slums.

86. FML, f. XXXI-18, b. 6, 6/17. Letters by the father and the father's mother addressed to the "unwed mother."

87. Zaborowska, *How We Found America*, 81.

88. Referring to present-day Slovakia, from where many Hungarians fled or were forcefully relocated following World War II. See Pertti et al., *Peoples on the Move*, 83.

89. FML, f. XXIII / 510, b. 4.

90. Young, *Family and Kinship*, 120–21. Gyula Benda points out a similar phenomenon in Budapest: "Generally, it is the husband who temporarily moves to Budapest, finds a job there, and if it turns out to be going well, he strikes root, receives accommodation, and then he moves his family to Budapest." Benda, "Budapest társadalma," 18.

91. Interview with János B., March 26, 2001; July 18, 2001.

92. Interview with Tibor V., March 28, 2001,

93. Ibid.

94. Cf. Compton, "Migration in Eastern Europe," 177.

95. FML, f. XXXI-18, b. 1, unit 1/8 and 1/9.

96. Neighborhood relationships have served as substitutes for kinship ties in other "socialist cities" as well, for example after World War II in Progresul, one of the Bucharest districts most affected by immigration, even if migrants did keep in close touch with residents of their native villages (as was also the case in Sztálinváros). Ogrezeanu, "Mahala: The Slums of Bucharest."

97. Zibell, *Frauen in Wohnumfeld*, 20–23; Engelhard, *Nachbarschaft in der Großstadt*.

98. Cf. Zibell, *Frauen in Wohnumfeld*, 115.

99. FML, f. XXXI-18, b. 1, unit 1/9.

100. Ibid.

101. FML, f. XXIII-506, b. 24, 1958 housing requests.

PART II

RELATIONSHIPS

The screeching comes not from the foundry, please,
We just arrived at school, you see.
This is School Square. Covered with scaffolding,
Heaps of bricks, pipes, lime, and tar pools.
Everything is being built. An ideal place
For innocently playing young children.
They bang one another's heads with a clamp,
They mix cement with lime.
Here they thrust a weld in the ditch,
There one is tumbling in sewage.
Some are eating parget, others sipping gas,
And one shoving tar up another's ass.

Excerpt from an "anti-skit" on Sztálinváros, 1954
(FML, f. XXIII-508, b. 60)

4 Family

As is usually the case, before the wedding my husband promised my parents
that he would take care of me and would be good to me ... on our wedding
night he acted like a village butcher. He was very rough, he aggressively
attacked me, like a hungry tiger goes for the meat. ... I request that he be
immediately forbidden from entering the apartment, since it was his family
that was allocated housing, and not him alone.

Testimony of Mrs. Mihály V. at the Divorce Trial, 1957

THE ACCOUNT ABOVE is one of the Sztálinváros courtship stories, and it is typical in that instead of telling the tale of the growth of a family, it exemplifies a cliché accepted at the time, according to which the urban lifestyle alienates people
from one another, and in the shadows of factory smoke stacks people will find
only loneliness, never sincere partners with whom to share their lives. In this narrative the family disintegrates, children grow up without parents, women are
abandoned, and finding a spouse is incidental and arbitrary.

Sztálinváros is one of the most striking examples in East Central Europe of
rapid industrialization and urbanization through state intervention after World
War II. Accordingly, for many people Sztálinváros also represented the disintegration of family life. The idea that the state intervened in every sphere of life—very
much a part of the totalitarian paradigm—played a significant role in depictions
of family life.[1] This may explain why, despite decades of arguments to the contrary, the myth of rootlessness and family disintegration occasionally surfaces
today, even in scholarly discussions, and has an effect on people's personal narratives of their life stories.[2]

The transformation of family life was included in the goals of communist
ideology, but the main objectives of Stalinist policies did not include basic renewal of family life in Hungary. The authorities and the state-owned enterprises
needed first and foremost a workforce with which they could fulfill their plan.
Thus family life was depicted as a partial problem by the local administration
until 1953. According to the documents regarding family life in Sztálinváros, the
significance of familial and kinship ties did not decrease in Sztálinváros and
families did not disintegrate. The families became basic targets of the official
steps only after the mid-1950s, but despite the state intervention in family life,

the family as a basic unit of society received a seminal role in the new policies after 1953.

In this chapter I will discuss how the families of Sztálinváros not only adapted to the new environment—such as the couples who for decades would meet in the park between the city and the Ironworks until they were able to request an apartment—but also were able to shape the Stalinist policies regarding families, especially after the conservative turn in the mid-1950s. I will demonstrate that the so-called petit bourgeois norms that were officially rejected at the beginning of the construction were tolerated by the mid-1950s, and at the end of the 1950s these norms were included in official depictions of the ideal gender roles and family life. I situate this transformation not only in the changing ideological objectives but also in the efforts of the officials to create a more stable local society to get rid of the Stalinist legacy themselves and at the same time to legitimate the socialist regime. In addition to demonstrating the survival of social hierarchies through marriages, this chapter also explores how the official depictions of ideal gender roles were changed accordingly and how official depictions of "working women" transformed them into fashionably dressed housewives, which was more acceptable for contemporaries. The transformation of the Stalinist policies regarding families not only contributed to the creation of a more stable regime but also helped the government better meet some of the expectations of the locals.

The Transformation of a "Gold Digger Camp" to the City of Families

The majority of the people who arrived in the city when it was founded were unlikely to have thought they would settle and start a family in Sztálinváros. Most immigrants arrived at the construction site with the simple hope of earning better wages. Girls wanted to make enough to cover their dowries, and older fathers wanted to make enough money to provide their daughters with dowries and then leave. (The giving of a dowry, which refers to money, goods, or even estates brought by a woman to her husband or his family at the time of her marriage, remained common practice for decades under socialism.) In 1952–53 even the local paper indicated that a dowry was considered a prerequisite for marriage. At the beginning of 1952 a Stakhanovite bricklayer was boasting to a local journalist about how he had made enough money working in Sztálinváros to marry off his daughter and purchase furniture worth 13,000 forints for her living room and kitchen.[3] Many of the young men who had no income flocked to Sztálinváros like "gold diggers," and indeed the prevailing conditions in the early years were more characteristic of a "gold digger camp" than a city.

For a while migrants from the same village remained under the "supervision" of the old community, especially when they shared the same lodgings. As they began to move into separate accommodations and the community of urban resi-

Figure 4.1. Typical image of a man and a woman with the construction site representing prosperity (1952).

dents became less homogeneous, the rigidity of former "village" rules gradually loosened, a change that was palpable in the customs pertaining to courtship and marriage. At the beginning of the period of construction, Ferenc P. arrived in the city from Berettyóújfalu (an agricultural town situated close to the eastern border of Hungary) with his daughter and son in the hope of earning enough money to be able to continue farming and to give his daughter an opportunity to collect money for her dowry. The following year the daughter became financially independent, and although she was still setting aside money for her dowry, she bought a new dress every month with her own money, which indicated that she had gradually adopted consumer habits that could well be considered urban.[4]

From the perspective of the changing composition of immigrants as well as from the perspective of marriages and parenthood, 1953–54 was a turning point. The number of marriages and births skyrocketed. It was around this time that masses of migrants with families came to settle in Sztálinváros, and more and more people viewed Sztálinváros as a place to move to and start a family because they could get apartments and steady jobs in the factory, which began operation in 1953. In early 1954, 100 babies were born in a single month; women in labor had to wait in the "hospital" hallways because there were not enough beds. At the beginning of 1954, within a single month the number of beds in the maternity ward increased from 12 to 62. While in the spring of 1952, 240 children were enrolled in Sztálinváros schools (and they lived almost exclusively in the Old Town), in 1953 this number had grown to more than 1,000, and by the beginning of 1954 it reached almost 2,000.[5]

At the beginning of the period of construction, Sztálinváros was populated primarily by single men and women, but by 1960 there were hardly any unmarried men or women of marriageable age (to be more exact, nine out of ten people of marriageable age were married).[6] The proportion of people living in wedlock in Sztálinváros exceeded the national average. As early as the beginning of 1957, the *Sztálinvárosi Hírlap* reported that the marriage registrar was having difficulty performing her duties for lack of the two necessary rooms. At the time, when "grand weddings" were held in the council hall of the Executive Committee of the Local Council even the banquet hall proved too small to host the crowds of guests.[7]

It is tempting to think that the "gold digging" men and "adventure hungry" women who arrived in the city became husbands and wives as the community became increasingly urban because according to the cliché, widespread at the time and persistent to this day, someone who gets married becomes an "upright" person. Of course, many of the immigrants married too. However, the fact that since 1953 vast numbers of families had been arriving in Sztálinváros to find jobs and accommodations significantly contributed to the increased proportion of married people in the city. In addition, unskilled workers, the majority of whom were unmarried and changed place of residence more rapidly, never really struck root in Sztálinváros, but left in the hope of finding better jobs. Families did not follow this pattern. Many of them were "stuck" in the Sztálinváros barracks, or, if they were more fortunate, in one of the newly built apartments.

Another basic reason to get married was that permanent housing was allocated only to married couples (and those with children generally had better chances of getting housing). On the housing request form issued by the local council, applicants were asked in a separate set of questions how long they had been married and how many children they had. In practice, unmarried people were thus excluded from housing allocations. If a single person still managed to obtain housing, he or she had to contend with a series of complaints launched by married couples and families who believed themselves to be much more in need of accommodation and bewailed their destitution, contrasting their misfortunes with the happy fate of the unmarried tenant who had the good luck to have been given an apartment.[8]

Common-law couples had even less chance than singles of being given housing, because living together out of wedlock was stigmatized both socially and

Figure 4.2. Idealized image of relationships in the factory restaurant (1952).

officially. Put simply, discriminative allocation and shortages of housing were incentives to marry. In addition, in some cases an apartment that had already been allocated to someone could not be kept unless the person obtained a marriage certificate. Families were more difficult to evict. So in some cases a single man would marry his common-law wife as a response to the threat of eviction by the council.[9] Thus the state officially encouraged the people of Sztálinváros to live together in nuclear families in which the mother and father were also husband and wife. The system for distributing apartments was one of the tools with which the government attempted to reach this goal.

As a consequence the average age of newlyweds went down, because most immigrants wanted to get an apartment as quickly as possible. Because of the inequalities in state redistribution of property, members of several social groups (primarily people with less education and training and those working in jobs of lower social status) were not allocated housing, so for these groups this pattern was not reversed—in other words, they continued to postpone marriage until after having secured an apartment.[10] It was easier to obtain housing in Sztálinváros in the early years than at the end of the 1950s. This may explain why people with occupations of a higher social status married at an older age. At the beginning of

the 1950s, members of the intelligentsia were allocated housing virtually immediately, but by the end of the decade they too had to wait for years before being
given an apartment.

Statistics reveal that Sztálinváros in 1960 was characterized mainly by the so-
called nuclear family model of a parent or parents living with an unmarried
child or children.[11] However, the data do not include co-tenancy, families with
their own supplies of foodstuffs, grandparents raising children in villages, or
married people visiting their parents on weekends to collect foodstuffs. For several new arrivals in the city kinship ties became informal work relationships. The
first brigades of arrivals, which in many cases included men from the same family,
were only one of the ways in which kinship ties subsisted. The two-home lifestyle,
which in the beginning meant a shortage of labor at the construction sites during
harvest time, was one of the new forms of the family-based economy, as were the
worker's hostels (which lay empty in the cold months of the year because residents returned to their home villages to spend the winter) and the role of nepo-
tism in the search for a job. In the "city of youths" the elderly and people who were
"less capable of work" received positions that involved less-demanding physical
labor (as cleaning women or in domestic industry).[12] Since very few older people
were living in Sztálinváros, their placement did not cause many problems. Only
in the 1970s did the number of pensioners skyrocket, as the majority of 1950s immigrants to the city began to reach retirement age. In 1961 only 450 pensioners
resided in Sztálinváros (less than 1.5 percent of the total population).[13]

Because of the state-regulated housing distribution, courtship, marriage, and
family life were part of a private sphere while at the same time representing
a chance to secure an independent home.[14] The housing distribution system
strongly affected the ways in which people chose partners and decided to have
families, and also influenced the timing of these decisions. The husband's social
status depended partly on income, but mostly on his place in the workplace hierarchy. The marriage and divorce rates, both of which were higher than the national
average, were strongly influenced by the system of centralized housing distribution. But who were these couples, and how did age, place of birth, and occupational status influence the decisions they made before the marriage registrar of
Sztálinváros?

Before the Registrar

To obtain better overview of the origins and social composition of families in
Sztálinváros, I compared the marriage registries of 1953 and 1958. In Sztálinváros
1953 was the first year in which a large number of new arrivals married, but by
1958, due to the conservative turn in state policies, the conventions pertaining to
courtship and marriage had changed.[15]

Based on samples from 1958, the average age of men at the time of marriage was twenty-eight and the average age of women was twenty-four. The national average did not differ radically.[16] The slight difference in men's ages from the national average in Hungary was part of a larger process whereby the average age of marriage gradually decreased after the end of World War II.[17] This applied primarily to blue-collar workers and people formerly from villages, who, prior to the launch of production, composed the vast majority of the population in Sztálinváros. The average difference in age between men and women did not vary according to place of birth: it was 3.2 years, approximately the same as the national average,[18] thus the officially propagated, sharp distinction between urban and rural lifestyles did not work in this case either. People born in villages were more likely to marry others born in villages (60 percent of men and 65 percent of women), whereas the majority of women from provincial cities married village-born men (53 percent). The influence of birthplace on the selection of a spouse suggests that men generally married women who were familiar with more urban lifestyles, whereas women mostly married men who were less accustomed to urban life. In other words, in regard to place of birth, women often married "down."

The average age at marriage for men in top positions (department heads, foremen, and men in upper management) was far above the average—33.4 years old—and they tended to marry women of much lower status, in most cases women working in office and administrative positions, and only rarely members of the intelligentsia.[19] In contrast, the average age at the time of marriage for male members of the intelligentsia was far below the average: 23.4 years. They married at the youngest age, in all probability right after obtaining their degrees in higher education. These men were presumably first-generation members of the intelligentsia, since 80 percent of them had been born in villages. Among their wives, the proportion of women belonging to the intelligentsia and office and administrative workers (*irodisták*, which refers mainly to bureaucrats and their secretaries, typists, etc.) is the same (each 40 percent of the total).

Of the various groups, skilled workmen were the most numerous. They married slightly younger than the average (at age 26.6) and tended to choose wives who were born in settlements similar to their own. They generally married women working in unskilled jobs or jobs requiring virtually no training (50 percent), including semiskilled and unskilled laborers, as well as temporary employees in catering or commerce. They were less likely to marry skilled workwomen or women employed in administrative and office jobs (each 18 percent both).

The average age at marriage of unskilled male workers was closest to the average (28 years). This group seems the most homogeneous of all, as virtually all the wives were also unskilled workers (69 percent). According to these data, from the perspective of age, place of birth, and occupational status, most of the marriages in Sztálinváros were homogeneous.

Professional soldiers, police officers, and employees of the Ministry of Interior made up a distinctive group of men. The majority of them were village-born. The average age at the time of marriage was 24.9—almost the youngest average age among men. The explanation may lie in the fact that, as the most faithful "employees" of the party, they had far less difficulty obtaining housing than people of other occupational categories, and this may have affected their marriages to a greater extent. The majority of their wives were unskilled workers (46 percent), although men of this category also married a relatively high proportion of women working in administrative and office positions (31 percent).

Women's occupational status also influenced their selection of a spouse. Like men of the local intelligentsia, women of this category married at an age significantly lower than the national average (22.9). Their husbands belonged to three major occupational categories, in similar proportions: top managerial positions in the steel factory, members of the intelligentsia, or officers employed directly by the state such as professional soldiers, police officers, or "employees of the Ministry of Interior." Thus women belonging to the intelligentsia mostly married men who—according to their occupational positions—had very high chances of obtaining an apartment from the local council.

Female skilled workers also married at a young age, in most cases marrying skilled workmen, usually workmen who had been born in cities, not in villages. Women working in unskilled jobs also married at a young age, but their husbands were usually village-born men (65 percent), unskilled laborers (41 percent), or skilled workers (36 percent).

As a group, women employed in office and administrative jobs had the most diverse array of spouses. They married a year later than the average age (25.4). Most of them married skilled workers, but they also married office and administrative employees, unskilled workers, men in managerial positions, professional soldiers, or police officers as spouses. Indeed a disproportionately large number of marriages were between women in office and administrative jobs and men who were members of the intelligentsia.[20] In regard to their spouses, women working in office and administrative positions seem to have been the most open to various professional backgrounds, while blue-collar women as a group were the most closed. This can also be explained by the fact that women who worked in administrative positions in Sztálinváros had the best educations and the best connections of the women in the city, and they were therefore among the most independent women as well. They had more opportunity to make decisions—not only in the labor market as job seekers market but also in their private lives—and were of higher social status.

A woman employed in an office or administrative position was as likely, or more likely, to marry a man in a managerial position than she was to marry an unskilled worker, but none of the skilled or unskilled workwomen married a man holding a top position. Although a secretary and a female construction worker earned approximately the same incomes, their status was fundamentally determined by whether they worked jobs considered blue-collar ("dirty") or white-collar ("clean"), and this seems to have affected their chances of finding a spouse with a particular professional background. In addition, due to the circular mobility characteristic of the 1950s, a secretary might have been a descendant of a family of a much higher social status.

Among Sztálinváros blue-collar workmen, only skilled workers had a chance of marrying an "office clerk," and a female blue-collar worker had little chance of marrying anyone other than a male blue-collar worker. Female office clerks seem to have had the greatest range of choices. The status of the majority of women depended on their husbands, and this was particularly significant for women in office and administrative jobs, although they also had a chance to achieve a higher professional status, and not simply through their husbands.

The older a man was when he decided to marry, the more likely he was to choose a much younger wife. In contrast, the older a woman was at the time of her marriage (especially if she was older than twenty-five), the more often she would marry someone only slightly older or even significantly younger. If a woman did not marry by the age of twenty-five, she was likely to be called a spinster. Due to the "pressure to marry," a prevalent social expectation, for an older woman it was less "shameful" to marry a much younger man than it was to remain a "spinster." It was not uncommon for women over twenty-five to have husbands who were six or seven years younger. Social status was determined to a large extent by whether a person, either man or woman, was married or single. Thus by the late 1950s, society may have seemed far more conservative than it was at the beginning of the decade, when according to state propaganda a woman's willingness to accept work would determine her social status in the future.

Between 1953 and 1958, marriages became more conservative in terms of both social status and the days on which it was possible to hold a wedding. Before World War II, village weddings were generally held in the late fall and winter, mostly on Mondays or Tuesdays, and less frequently on Saturdays or Sundays.[21] In contrast, after 1945 wedding ceremonies gradually became more frequent on Saturdays, and also spread more evenly throughout the course of a year.[22] For an urban population, the timing of a wedding was less dependent on the seasons. This shift in scheduling also characterized Sztálinváros weddings: in 1953 the majority of Sztálinváros weddings took place in the fall and spring, though the records indicate a relatively large number of weddings in the summer.[23] In 1954, responding to letters of complaint addressed to the *Sztálinvárosi Hírlap*, the editors of the local paper asked the registrar why weddings could not take place on Saturday afternoons. The terse response was that wedding ceremonies could only be conducted during office hours.[24] Two weeks later, the local *Sztálinváros Hírlap* reported that on Saturday afternoon the registrar, in a gesture of selfless magnanimity (though in all likelihood simply under pressure from above and below), had united two couples in wedlock.[25] From this point on wedding ceremonies became possible on Saturday afternoons, and increasing numbers of people took advantage of this. Indeed, within a short period of time it became almost fashionable.[26] Sztálinváros was also part of this national trend, and Saturday became the most popular day for weddings there.

Between 1948 and 1960 the proportion of marriages between spouses of different social and occupational categories began to increase across the country (from 27.7 percent to 32.4 percent). The greatest mobility can be observed among male agricultural manual laborers, whereas the lowest was among nonagricultural manual laborers.[27] In 1953 and 1958 an insignificant number of agricultural manual workers lived in Sztálinváros; therefore, the prevalence of homogeneous marriages among blue-collar workers (a kind of "endogamy" from a professional point of view) of this group fundamentally determined the marriages of the 1950s. In other words, alongside the marriages that seemed to indicate greater mixing between the social and professional classes and therefore constituted a kind of social mobility, "homogeneous" marriages, which were the most common among nonagricultural manual workers, constituted the largest part of "family life" in Sztálinváros.

Based on the contemporary research of György Vukovich, approximately 60 percent of the marriages of 1959–60 can be considered "homogeneous," and—surprisingly—"homogeneous" marriages were more common in Budapest.[28] Using the same occupational categories, according to the 1953 Sztálinváros samples 61 percent of all marriages were "homogeneous." Based on the same sample, 75 percent of marriages in which one member was either a skilled or unskilled worker were homogeneous. The 1958 samples reveal that 67 percent of marriages were homogenous, among which 84 percent of skilled and unskilled workers married spouses of similar occupational status. Thus, one can conclude that Sztálinváros marriages were much more homogeneous than the national average, and they became increasingly so over the course of the 1950s. On this basis, Sztálinváros society could be considered more professionally "exclusive" than the rest of Hungary. As in Budapest, although the population fluctuated more significantly in Sztálinváros, migration did not result in the heterogenization of Sztálinváros marriages. On the contrary, marriages became even more "endogamous."[29]

As an examination of the marriage registries makes clear, the selection of a spouse was not a haphazard affair. In spite of considerable social mobility and social fluctuations, the people of Sztálinváros tended to choose mates with whom they shared similar social backgrounds (though men tended to marry "down" and women tended to marry "up"). A woman's professional status also influenced her "value" (to use a vulgar metaphor) on the marriage market, although job or career remained less significant factors of identity for a woman. The marriages in Sztálinváros, which from the perspective of occupation and place of birth were relatively homogeneous, were not stable, as marriages were not stable in other industrial cities.

Marriages in Sztálinváros held far fewer surprises than one might have supposed on the basis of myths concerning the licentious and chaotic lifestyle that allegedly characterized the city. The patterns by which people chose spouses were far more predictable and in line with social expectations than they were "revolutionary," even if there were many single mothers or divorcées in the city. In regard to family life, 1953 and 1956 brought a conservative shift only from one perspective—specifically, marriage to someone of a similar social status became officially accepted. Parallel to this, by the end of the 1950s the image of the ideal husband and wife that was acceptable to both the state and ordinary people of the city had shifted and come to correspond more closely to the norms prevailing at the beginning of the decade, which were considered "petit bourgeois."

The "Ideal" Man and the "Ideal" Woman

In 1958 the local newspaper conducted a survey and asked five young women about their conceptions of the "ideal" man.[30] Their answers primarily reflect the preconceptions of the editors, who were trying to meet official expectations, but such surveys may have increased the paper's circulation, very much to the satisfaction of the party officials. The newspaper quotes K. B., a young "working woman":

> With regard to his appearance he should not be dashing. I imagine the man I would choose to be simple and serious. I don't want him to be better looking than other men. As for his inner qualities: I'd like him to love me, be good to me, and consider me a little better than other girls. He should be somewhat smarter than me so that I can learn from him. . . . We both should work, and we should share household chores and spend our free time together. I like sports so I expect him to be a sportsman. In sum: he must be a quiet, serious youth, but should the need arise he must be able to take a stand for himself.[31]

Women were expected to consider the appearance of their "ideal man" secondary. However, three of the respondents, although they emphasized that looks were not the most important factor, nonetheless highlighted aspects of appearance that they found essential: "I'd like him to have dark hair," "he should be good looking," "he should be clean and smartly dressed," "my ideal man is tall and brown-haired," "it wouldn't hurt if he were handsome."[32] Some of these "external characteristics" can be interpreted as indications of social status. Given the nature of their jobs, for most of the Sztálinváros blue-collar workers (who constituted the majority of the city's population) being "clean and smartly dressed" on weekdays was no easy task, certainly not as simple as it was for white-collar workers, members of the intelligentsia, and those in managerial positions.

Every response included "affection," "love of family," and "shared time at home and leisure time spent together." At the same time, even female respondents viewed men who stayed home or actively participated in household chores as "henpecked": "he should have male friends with whom he spends free time," "I could not live with a 'henpecked husband.' I'd never ask him to do the dishes or needlework." Another respondent noted, "He should be helpful around the house, do some of the household chores, but Lord save me from a 'henpecked husband.' I don't want him to be a man who sits around at home. I want him to go out often, and take me with him." The responses show a distinctive conservative turn related to the image of the independent working woman. The ideal man of the late 1950s could not be a "henpecked husband," so the household was the responsibility of women.

In their responses the women mentioned playing cards, drinking, and spending too much time with friends as negative attributes of male behavior. In contrast, an interest in sports and reading were both considered useful and explicitly positive characteristics in a man. When mentioning shared leisure-time activities, respondents listed markedly urban habits, such as going to the theater and the movies and listening to music. According to the *Sztálinvárosi Hírlap*, the urban lifestyle created numerous advantages for people seeking partners and spouses.

In their replies, alongside traditional conceptions of women's roles, the female respondents also expressed expectations that implied a degree of women's emancipation. "He should not interfere in my work and should not order me around," one teacher said. A hairdresser commented, "I'd like him to support me in keeping a modern house. (We would not cook at home, and would take laundry to the cleaner's, etc.)."

A week after the above article, another article was published in the paper containing the responses of five men to a question regarding their views of the "ideal" woman.[33] Though not always explicitly, the men placed considerably more emphasis on aspects of appearance that corresponded to stereotypes of female beauty, noting that the ideal woman was "slim," "long-haired," "blond," and "blue-eyed," her "attire should be tasteful," and she should "want to be attractive at home too, unlike some women who only care about their appearance when leaving the house." In addition to emphasizing external characteristics, almost all the male respondents specified the criteria for considering a woman a "decent girl." She should be only moderately attractive and should not have a bad reputation. The importance of "chastity" is best illustrated by the response of an army officer, who insisted, "my ideal is a woman who blushes when I kiss her and embraces me as if she were still my bride."

In the respondents' answers, "smoker, jealous, overly fashion conscious, slothful, and boastful" all figured as the worst characteristics, though at the same time they all expected the ideal woman to behave according to traditional roles: "she should be a good homemaker," "she should be a good cook," "she should be proud of my reputation," "she should be naively sentimental," and "she should be a good mother."

The only expectation that clashed with the role of "domestic ingénue" (and was included in almost every answer) was that the ideal woman should be educated, erudite, and have good communication skills. One respondent even added that she should have "the ability to debate." An interest in arts was often mentioned as an important attribute. This fit the stereotype from the prewar period, whereby female intellectual talents should find expression in an interest in the arts, since the world of art was regarded as "emotional," in contrast to the sciences, business, work, and politics (in other words, spheres of power), which represented the world of "rational" people, meaning first and foremost men. According to this stereotype, which was also adopted by the local, official party newspaper, the ideal woman is emotional and affectionate and avoids conflicts, which are aspects implying that she subordinate herself to the "ideal man" (i.e., rational, ambitious, and able to grapple with conflicts). Regarding housework, the reply given by a teacher proved the most "modern": "I believe in the mechanization of housework." Of course in the 1950s in Sztálinváros the notion of "mechanization of housework" in practice meant little more than hand-operated washing machines—and the idea of men using household appliances never even occurred to the respondents.[34] In general these kinds of articles offered little more than models compatible with official expectations, and were not actual accounts of varied, personal expectations; nevertheless, the values and expectations expressed sound as if they would have resonated with most people.

An article published in the women's column of the *Hírlap* contained letters written by readers suggesting that "a father with the stroller," "a man who is always clean-shaven and well-mannered, wearing ironed trousers" was the most attractive to the female readership.[35] As imagined by the women of Sztálinváros, the "prince" would not arrive on a white horse, but rather pushing a pram.[36]

And at the same time, according to classified advertisements in the spring of 1957, women were looking for men who fit conventional expectations. They sought men of an appropriate status who were serious and for whom home life was important, and they emphasized their looks. Similarly, men were seeking "slim and pretty" women, and they emphasized their own professional status. "In need of company, 25-year-old young intellectual man is seeking . . . ," one man wrote, and in a similar vein another specified, "I am a clerk and I own a boat. I am looking for a blond girl with a good figure." In comparison, women wrote things like, "a 26-year old plump, said to be pretty divorced woman is seeking a sincere man . . ."; "a 32-year-old plump, said to be pretty widow . . . is looking for a man of 40–50 for whom home life is important . . . only men with good jobs need reply"; "a 24-year-old tall and slim woman separated from her husband is seeking a man 10 years her senior and with a serious occupation."[37]

Before 1956, the working woman appeared first and foremost in the heroic narratives on the construction of the city. She was a figure who performed work traditionally done by men, for instance in construction, and she conquered the forces of nature and fought shoulder to shoulder to usher in a new utopia. In contrast, after 1956 the newspapers had to do more than simply meet party expectations. They had to be popular among readers. The emergence of the official mass media made it possible to project an image of the ideal woman that much more closely resembled the everyday experiences of the city's residents. This helped boost the newspaper's sales. The editorial staff had to take into consideration that most women in Sztálinváros did not work, and women worked in industry only very rarely in the 1950s. This change after 1956 in the official image of the ideal woman was connected to the decreasing need for women on the labor market. With the completion of the construction of the city, there was no longer any work for the women who were used as unskilled laborers. In official portrayals and discourses, women could return to the kitchen, which beginning in the late 1950s was depicted as increasingly modern.

The transformation of the official image of the ideal woman in a conservative direction had its roots in the overlapping of the interests of state and society and in the changing role of women in the workforce. A similar conservative turn in the state policies regarding gender roles can be observed in other socialist countries in the 1950s,[38] but the case of Sztálinváros demonstrates that the reproduction of social hierarchies in marriages had begun well before the mid-1950s. The Stalinist and post-Stalinist policies regarding family life were influenced and shaped, on the one hand, by the need for women as an industrial workforce, but on the other hand, these policies were also based on a consensus between the locals and the authorities.

Working Women and Fashion Plates

In 1960 *Nők Lapja* (Women's Magazine) published the views of students at the Food Products Commercial Trade School. " 'A woman who does not work cannot be modern,' small, dark and plump Berta declares orally and in writing. 'Don't get me wrong, I do not wish to underestimate a woman's tasks. But if I only did domestic chores, I would feel as if I were in jail.' "[39] Female employment was one of the symbols of Stalinist modernity; officially the state provided jobs for women or helped them find employment. This was manifested in themes that were ad-

Figure 4.3. Typical image of man and woman with the construction site after urbanization in the second half of the 1950s.

dressed in political life, including women's rights as one of the major political issues after 1945,[40] and in the fact that women began to work in paid positions in ever larger numbers after World War II.[41]

In Sztálinváros women demanded more opportunities for employment, but national enterprises determined by the cyclical nature of investment occasionally had less need for female employees. When investment funds decreased, women were the first to be dismissed, officially to enable them to fulfill their "duties as mothers." In 1953, when investment funds for construction were reduced, the first people to experience the consequences were pregnant women working in low-level construction jobs, performing tasks such as digging and transporting dirt. The justification given for laying them off clearly illustrates the belief rooted in fundamentally conservative attitudes and perpetuated by the socialist state: a pregnant woman should not work because in doing so she is jeopardizing her most important communal function. These women who were expecting and working as construction workers for a much higher wage were transferred to the national enterprise's headquarters as cleaners in order to "spare" them. They complained about the transfer because as low-level construction workers they earned

Figure 4.4. Idealized image of women workers at the construction site (1952).

700–800 forints a month, but as cleaners they made only 492 forints on average. The *Sztálinvárosi Hírlap* attributed this to their "irresponsible" attitudes.[42]

Especially after 1953, local officials started to mystify motherhood when the female workforce became superfluous. This surfaced in the official celebrations of International Women's Day (March 8) too, when feminist slogans representing the struggle for equality in the workplace were replaced with praise for "motherhood" and "femininity," as well as gifts of flowers. The prevalence of this fundamental attitude (the mystification of women as wives and mothers) is also indicated by the startling fact that the high point of the 1960 celebration of International Women's Day in Sztálinváros was a gathering of physicians' wives, which was even covered in *Nők Lapja*.[43] On a day intended to celebrate women's equality, these women asserted their status by referring to their husbands' professions.

Between 1954 and 1958, when the number of construction jobs was decreasing, most unskilled women were not given jobs. Unemployment among women rose also because of the increasing number of (male) workers who brought their wives and families to Sztálinváros. In 1957, six hundred unemployed women submitted job requests to the Social Department of the City Council in the hope of being given a job.[44] In January 1957 the head of the City Council was happy to announce to his colleagues that "there is no longer any concern regarding what will become of the construction of the city. Comrade Apró informed us that Dunapentele is alive and will thrive."[45] An on the spot directive was issued according to which the Sztálinváros soccer team had to qualify again for the national first division. The winds of a new beginning were also felt by the local leadership. It therefore became necessary to create jobs for women too. Negotiations were begun with the state officials on the establishment of a confectionery and meat processing plant, though in May the plans were changed to involve the creation of a foodstuffs plant, a clothing factory, and an undergarment factory in order to provide job opportunities for women.[46] The local policy of creating jobs mostly for unemployed women met the expectations of the city's residents.

Within a few months of the negotiations, the Sztálinváros divisions of the Undergarment Factory and Red October Men's Wear Factory (partially relocated from Budapest) began production, but they did not provide an adequate number of jobs. In the Undergarment Factory, on November 15, 1957 only 15 of the 243 workers were male, but several hundred Sztálinváros women in need of a job remained unemployed. They bombarded the City Council and higher "forums" with letters requesting jobs. Most of the time the rejection letters sent in response referred specifically to high unemployment among women.[47]

A large proportion of the jobs given to women were offered by the Catering Trade Enterprise, but even this sector was unable to employ every woman in need of a job. In April 1959 young women seeking jobs had the least chance of finding one. Only 10 percent of the women applying for jobs were employed that year. The City Council recorded 577 unemployed women seeking paid jobs, 136 of whom were supporting their families. The number must have been higher since not everyone submitted a request to the council.[48] In other words, it was considerably more difficult for women than for men to find a job in Sztálinváros, and many women remained unemployed for want of training or qualifications. A sixteen-year-old woman wrote, "I believe it is high time that I took charge of my own future. So I beg you, please help me find a job. I have heard rumors that it is impossible to find a job opening unless one has connections. So someone without connections cannot and will not have a future where she would like? I do not believe this, so I put my trust in you and turn to you for help."[49]

Her request was rejected on the grounds that many young women were out of work in Sztálinváros. Because the failure of universal employment in Sztálinváros was an everyday experience for women, many of them, although officially they were not recorded as unemployed, took domestic jobs or were dependent on their spouses.

Women employed in paid positions did not appear in statistics because many of them took supplementary jobs not related to state enterprises. Women often worked as part-time maids, housekeepers, or babysitters. Housekeepers were primarily employed by unmarried members of the intelligentsia of higher social status or people working in leading positions (e.g., physicians), but sometimes an expectant mother of two would also take out an ad seeking the help of a maid after she had given birth. Single men were numerous in Sztálinváros, and many of them took advantage of the services of laundresses instead of using the facilities of the Laundry Enterprise. Many people reluctant to use the Laundry Enterprise or public catering in general hired laundresses and home help instead. One shrewd housekeeper took advantage of this. She took dirty clothes to the Laundry Enterprise and then returned the clean clothes to the person who had hired her as if she had done the work.[50]

Women complained about unemployment, while state enterprises complained that women were unwilling to remain in the same jobs for extended periods of time.[51] According to their rhetoric, "many female employees have an aversion to serious, continuous work," and "women do not show respect for the positions that have been made available to them." This explanation, of course, provided a pretext for hastily hiring and laying off women, which was particularly convenient for enterprises working in light industry, which needed to mobilize the workforce periodically, in rhythm with the investment cycles characteristic of a planned economy (the year-end and quarter-end rushes).[52]

According to the director of the local Men's Wear Factory, women who sought employment only for a limited period of time in order to make money for some specific purpose were the ones who tended to change jobs more frequently: "Before purchasing furniture, a motorcycle, or some items of clothing, they were willing to work for a few months, and when they had saved the necessary amount, they would quit."[53]

The majority of the women in Sztálinváros were given positions as unskilled workers or clerks, and even if they had higher qualifications they were nonetheless assigned to positions lower than what they would have been qualified for or they were simply treated as inferiors at the workplace. This was essentially rooted in the fact that even though the presence of women in the workplace was tolerated, paid work was by no means viewed as a primary female duty, although the requests submitted to the local council demonstrate that women preferred even the most monotonous, physically exhausting positions.[54] The interpretations of paid work as a sphere in which women had a place only appeared in the official arguments concerning women in the workplace when the increase in investment funds entailed the need for a large female workforce.

What was expected of a woman in Sztálinváros? What did a Sztálinváros wife have to do to merit the title of "perfect mother" officially? Alongside the articles carried by the local newspaper, contemporary housekeeping guides also offer insights into the official expectations placed on women. The so-called double burden shouldered by women who worked in industry as well as in the household was celebrated in the propaganda at the beginning of the 1950s. In

Figure 4.5. A woman worker reading a fashion magazine at the Sztálinváros construction site (1952).

1950, at the start of the first five-year plan, a book was published by Mrs. Mária Pataki Keresztes, who advised "working women" on housekeeping at a time when high levels of investment had created a demand for women in the work-force. In her view, "today it is no longer fashionable or necessary to play the role of the 'busy housewife.' The working woman, the working housewife re-lates differently to family and society." In the chapter titled "Stakhanovite Methods in the Kitchen," she advises housewives to organize their household work in the same manner the exemplary Stakhanovites do in the workplace. She presents an example of the good and the bad housewife: it took 145 minutes for Mrs. Kovács, who allegedly worked without a clear method or plan, to prepare the vegetable stew and plum dumplings for lunch, while the "Stakhanovite"

Figure 4.6. A "fashionable woman" in the Sztálinváros cinema.

housewife Mrs. Szabó, who had an efficient plan, performed the same tasks in a mere 88 minutes.[55]

It is hardly surprising that Mrs. Szabó had little time to tend to her appearance, not that she should, lest she end up mimicking the deplorable vanities of the "excessively decked-out," stiletto-heel-wearing women decried in the newspaper articles. According to Keresztes, "one should wash one's hair every second or third week, using high-quality soap or shampoo." A working woman does not have to bother with old fashions. She should not spend time on anything other than caring for her hands and washing her hair. Keresztes pronounces that coloring one's hair "is a wanton, senseless thing to do."[56]

In stark contrast to the advice given in 1950, as of the mid-1950s the *Sztálinvárosi Hírlap* regularly published beauty tips for women. Keresztes's exhortations notwithstanding, at the beginning of 1957 hair curling became so popular that trade in the alcohol required for the procedure had to be banned. Owing to the scarcity of alcohol, only hospitals were allowed to request it. In letters addressed to the *Sztálinvárosi Hírlap*, women complained that "they had to go to the workplace with unkempt hair" because the hair salons did not carry alcohol.[57]

Articles in the local newspaper celebrating the "fashionable woman who tended to her looks" gradually replaced articles on working women, and from the mid-1950s the women's column, which was starting to occupy increasing space in the paper, carried more articles on fashion, "social life," child care, and cooking. These articles offered readers advice regarding a woman's ideal appearance: "Today Sztálinváros women care about their appearance. The number of women who would go to a bar or a restaurant wearing men's pants and checkered flannel shirts is minute." The article vaguely implied that men dressed "less elegantly," but by no means was this due to any kind of fault or blunder on their part.[58] The fact that women faced unemployment was sidestepped by emphasizing the importance of traditional gender roles.

In 1954–57, the period in which it was the most difficult for a woman in Sztálinváros to find a job,[59] the social column strove to popularize female roles that did not involve paid work. Regular accounts of dances presented the "fashionably dressed" women of Sztálinváros as the cream of city society. The newspaper articles defined a woman's status not by her workplace or occupation, but rather by her appearance, clothes, or husband.[60]

Live-in Lovers and Single Mothers

Families, of course, came into being outside marriage as well. The local administration produced more and more reports on cohabiting couples and single mothers with children after the mid-1950s. The conservative turn regarding family policies brought with it new methods of disciplining and transforming the families of Sztálinváros. This was manifested primarily in the practice of housing distribution. By stigmatizing unmarried couples in Sztálinváros propaganda, the state used marriage as a legal means of exerting more control over family life.

Discrimination against cohabitation was exacerbated in part because of the official belief that the largest proportion of cohabiting couples resided in the barracks, which had to be demolished.[61] Despite pronatalist demographic policies, the lifestyle of a large family was not unanimously seen as positive. In official reports on families issued by the local authorities, large families represented "rural" lifestyles, not "respectable" family life. For example, a survey done by the local council of South Side families explicitly emphasized that the families residing in the barracks had a particularly large number of children. In this survey, a large family was considered especially negative if the children had been born to an unwed couple. At the same time, according to the report on families residing in the barracks, one serious social problem was that unwed couples arriving in the city who already had six to eight children were not given housing, their large families notwithstanding, usually because they did not have a permanent place of work. The majority of them were compelled to reside in the barracks for years.[62]

According to one article in the local newspaper, "the development of Sztálin-város attracted wives, in many cases even grandmothers, nieces, etc., who hoped to receive permanent housing there. People who used the lodgings with which they were provided as family housing also married, or simply cohabitated."[63] Cohabitation and apartment sharing as a necessary solution to the dearth of apartments made it possible for local administrators to classify and use classifications as a justification for exclusions. They could refer to overcrowding as evidence of an improper family life.

Cohabitation was used by the officials in Sztálinváros as a synonym for disorderly family life. One council report attributed school problems faced by South Side children to cohabitation: "Cohabitation is very common, which makes it easier for one partner to abandon the other from one day to the next, and the single mother or father is unable to find care for the child, so children can be left without appropriate supervision."[64]

Cohabiting couples had to undergo special official procedures in order to be able to "legally" share a barrack apartment. In 1957 Lajos T., a resident in the South Side, specifically requested that his dependent partner, who was living in the same household, be allowed to register at his address, first, because "she was taking care of four children" and second, because he was going to marry her after his divorce case was settled.[65] The cohabiting couples often did not obtain a marriage certificate because their divorces were not final or they were only separated from former spouses. Their marital status qualified them as married (and this is how they were registered in statistics), but they lived separately from their de jure spouses. Consequently, wives and husbands may have had children from previous marriages.[66] Cohabitation in Sztálinváros did not mean the cohabitation of single men and single women, an institution increasingly popular in modern societies, but rather referred primarily to cohabitation of divorced people or those in the process of divorce. In other words, couples often lived together out of wedlock not because they did not intend to marry (since state housing policies provided ample motivation to marry, as did the usual social stigmas), but because their previous marriages made it impossible for them to remarry. For couples residing in barracks, dissolving a marriage seems to have been more complicated than entering one.[67]

The majority of people living in the South Side, including cohabiting couples, worked in blue-collar jobs that required little training. Women were generally housewives and the number of children was higher than average in these families. The children in these families were also discriminated against in the documents of the local administration.[68]

Although it was by no means seen as acceptable in the official or public discourses, premarital sex was clearly not unheard of, as indicated for instance by the short period of time between marriages and childbearing and the large proportion of unmarried mothers. However, the latter statistic may not constitute conclusive evidence regarding premarital sex since a divorced woman living with a man out of wedlock was also considered an unmarried mother. At the beginning of 1952, in the early period of construction when the majority of the new arrivals were men, the gynecologist's records indicate 430 pregnant women, 300 of whom were unmarried.[69] In 1952 more than 80 paternity affidavits were issued, and at the beginning of 1953, 80 children were in the care of the state.[70]

At a council meeting held at the beginning of May 1954, registry problems were noted indicating that of the three hundred newborn children whose family status was unsettled, fifty-six were recorded in the birth registry of those without paternity affidavits.[71] Taking the largest base of comparison into consideration (approximately one thousand children were born in Sztálinváros between November 1952 and March 1954), at least one-third of the newborns were born to "families with unsettled status." In the summer of the same year, when it was declared that "there are grave problems with regard to morals" at the workmen's quarters, the council concluded on the basis of various reports that "the number of single mothers is increasing."[72]

As a proportion of all births, the number of children born to single mothers did not increase in the subsequent years, but approximately 250 babies born each year were "fatherless," the term used by the City Council, which meant that the father was not willing to contribute to childrearing unless compelled to do so.[73] In contrast, the number of children in the care of the state significantly decreased. While in the first half of 1954, 20 children were turned over to state care within two months (the approximate number of births in this period was 160–70), in the first nine months of 1957 this number dropped to "only" 12.[74] Stereotypes notwithstanding, childbirth outside of wedlock was common not only among single women under the age of twenty but also among women past the age of thirty-five to forty. The majority of single mothers cohabited with someone to whom they were not married.[75] The cohabiting couples, single mothers and their children became visible in the official documents in 1954 and 1957–58 according to the transformation of the state policies regarding families. The local council started new campaigns in these years to "protect" children living in families regarded as disorderly.

Children and State Care

Although the state had assumed increasing authority over children's socialization prior to 1945, the process intensified after World War II. Through laws and welfare institutions the state exercised greater control over child care. However, due to the high rate of female unemployment, Sztálinváros children nonetheless spent more time with their mothers than with employees of state institutions. In

Sztálinváros the state introduced several institutions that transformed the everyday lives of children. District nurses, nurseries, day-care centers, kindergartens, schools, so-called pioneer organizations (similar to the Boy Scouts and Girl Scouts), and parents' associations all brought changes in family roles and childhood socialization, even if the family remained the primary sphere of socialization for children. Although precursors to these institutions in the precommunist era had similar ideological functions (for instance, kindergartens and the scouts), they were never attended in such huge numbers as after 1945. This was particularly characteristic of the people who came to Sztálinváros from industrial or agricultural areas. For the latter, these institutions had only been accessible with significant limitations before the war.

Conflicts between parents and state institutions arose virtually at the time of birth, as illustrated by disputes between district nurses and mothers. In extreme cases these conflicts ended in state intervention and the placement of a child in the care of the state. From the outset the number of children in Sztálinváros who were placed in state care was high. The rise in the number of problems with child welfare at the end of the 1950s was presumably not a consequence of any collapse or corruption of the institution of the family, but rather an indication that by then the institutional system of child protection, which at least took notice of problems within the family, had been created.

At the beginning of the 1950s families arriving at the Sztálinváros construction sites had voluntarily placed their children in the Rácalmás Children's Home, but by the end of the decade this home had become an institution of child welfare where in the majority of cases the children had either been abandoned by their parents or had been taken into state care due to parental negligence. In 1951, at the beginning of the construction of the city, the initial aim of establishing the Rácalmás Children's Home was to provide temporary paid accommodation for the children of ironworks laborers (who were doing "superb work"), and who themselves lived in temporary lodgings.[76] However, many of the workers did not take their children with them when they left the construction jobs, but simply left them at Rácalmás. In the summer of 1953, 235 of the approximately 900 children in Sztálinváros were housed either at Rácalmás or in the local nurseries (others were cared for by their families).[77] In January 1953, 80 children in Sztálinváros were in the care of the state,[78] but at the beginning of 1954 the Local Council Executive Committee meeting declared that the Rácalmás Day Nursery should be regarded as a 75 percent State Child Welfare Institution, since 75 percent of the children living there had been abandoned by their parents.[79] Characteristically, in April and May of 1954, 20 children were placed in state care, which constitutes 12 percent of the children born in the course of these two months.[80] Even the adoption of an abandoned infant was complicated, because the parents' place of residence was generally unknown and adoption was impossible without their consent.[81] In February 1957 the *Sztálinvárosi Hírlap* reported on the "masses" of abandoned children at the Rácalmás day-care institute.[82] The two years, 1954 and 1957, indicate the two waves of child care driven by the local administration, when the problems of the city's children were formulated at the level of the local authorities. Each of these years can be characterized as years in which the local council demonstrated by example that state policies could also be shaped by the city's residents.

With regard to child welfare, the City Council designated barrack apartments as the "major target," where families with up to five or six children moved into dwellings in which the conditions were unhealthy.[83] By doing so, the council stigmatized primarily parents and children living in the slums, and the expectations of ideal child care were developed with reference to them.

A 1957 report cited "financial motives" as the reason for turning a child over to state care by families in which the father's residence was unknown because he had abandoned the mother and child or children in Sztálinváros. Like the majority of mothers in the city, the women in such cases did not have permanent jobs and were unable to find work quickly because of high rates of female unemployment. In addition, since the men were no longer employees of the national enterprise, the mothers also had to leave their places of residence. Any attempts on the part of the mothers to find paid work were hindered by the presence of the children, and so, since the mothers had neither accommodations nor income, the authorities saw state care as the "most satisfactory" solution.[84]

Child welfare authorities placed children in the care of the state mainly on "moral grounds" due to the negligence shown by their parents. For example, one mother and father did not concern themselves with the continuing education and care of their fourteen-year-old girl and the child began to spend time with people of questionable repute and consequently set off down the "path to corruption."[85] In 1954 the case of a thirteen-year-old female student "caused an uproar" all over the city. The school noticed that she was often truant. Eventually it came to light that together with her nineteen-year-old girlfriend she had regularly visited and reveled in the apartments of young men with whom she went to the movies in the evenings.[86] Increased control of young girls' sexuality was rooted in the expectation that the major duty of a woman was to marry and bear children. Parents of fourteen- to sixteen-year-old girls complained that the girls often stayed out late at night and were difficult to discipline. The child welfare authorities attempted to solve these problems by putting children into the care of the state for a short period of time and offering them further education at the children's home.[87] The propagation of state supervision over child welfare became particularly important toward the end of the 1950s because the official organs of administration sought to demonstrate that they were taking the concerns of the citizenry seriously, in contrast to the regime of the early 1950s.

A child was placed in state care for "reasons of health" when one of the parents—usually the mother—suffered from a contagious disease requiring hospitalization and no one was left to look after her child. As late as 1960, cases of tuberculosis and hepatitis were found in virtually every district of Sztálinváros.[88] When state care was deemed necessary for health or moral reasons, the parent was compelled to pay a custody fee that was equal to the amount of child support settled by the court (20 percent of the person's average monthly income). When determining child support the family's social conditions and number of dependent family members were also taken into consideration. Mothers who paid the custodial fees all held jobs, generally blue-collar jobs, and many of them were employed in the catering trade and construction industries. Most of them resided in the Technikum District or the L-buildings.[89]

In rare cases the child welfare authorities returned a child to the parents' custody. In 1957 state care was suspended for the children of eight Sztálinváros individual parents. In the majority of the cases parents who were unemployed had found a job or a missing parent had been found. The same year twenty-five adoptions took legal effect, but only eight of these children had been in state care. Most adoptions of children who had not been in state institutions took place after a divorce when either the mother or the father had remarried. The process of adopting a child who was in state care generally began with placement of the child with the chosen parents immediately after he or she had been taken into state care. If the family became attached to the child and if the child adapted well to them, the adoption took place.[90] Nevertheless, the adoption process was highly complicated and entailed numerous impediments, as indicated by the fact that in the fall of 1959 only nine children who had been in state care were living with families in Sztálinváros.[91]

A 1957 presentence report on the placement of a child in state care describes the living conditions of Ilona K., who cohabited in the South Side barracks with György Á, whose name the child, Gábor (born in 1956), bore. The father worked for the Hungarian Railway as a yard master, where he earned 1,000–1,100 forints a month. The mother was an operator at the 26/1 Plant Construction National Enterprise. Her monthly income was 700–800 forints, roughly the national average, but slightly under the Sztálinváros average among women. They lived in a one-room family lodging equipped with company furniture and bedding. The mother believed "she would work three shifts, and thus could not take care of the child." At the age of eight months the baby was placed in the Rácalmás home and the parents had to pay a monthly custody fee of 200 forints, which was covered by the mother. According to the justification for the decision, "the mother was a single woman who was unable to offer proper care for the child due to her working conditions. The father is married and has one child."[92] The records indicate that the child remained in state care until he turned eighteen.

Figure 4.7. A Sztálinváros district nursery.

The majority of families first encountered the institutionalized system of family protection through district nurses. In 1954, four district nurses were working in Sztálinváros. They visited 738 families every month (484 of these visits involved families with a child younger than age one). In addition, nurses conducted an average of 45 counseling sessions for pregnant women every month.[93] This means that the district nurses met with virtually every family with infant children. Most Sztálinváros women attended counseling meetings at least three times during their pregnancies. On February 7, 1953, the Sztálinváros Center for the Protection of Pregnant Women was opened in the polyclinic.[94] A 1956 report states that future mothers attended counseling between three and seven times a week, and the relatively high infant mortality rate was allegedly not due to the lack of care but to the "inadequate social conditions" at some residences.[95]

According to the 1959 statistics of the City Council Health Department, high infant mortality rates were more common among families in which the mothers had physical blue-collar jobs (unskilled worker, cleaner) and the fathers were either unskilled workers (they constituted the majority) or skilled workers. In terms of residential areas, infant mortality was highest among commuters from nearby villages and families residing in the barracks in the South Side.[96]

The state punished alleged negligence of childrearing, supervision, and care by pursuing charges of crimes against youth. The primary aim of these proceedings was to set an example, since they were given relatively widespread publicity. "Childrearing" was seen as a chain of systematic influences based on exemplary behavior, "child care" as the assurance of the necessary conditions for normal physical development, and "supervision" as continuous, uninterrupted oversight.[97] The physical decline of a child for want of adequate nutrition was the most positive proof of this crime. In addition, the courts also blamed parents if the child spent entire days in the streets, although in the poorer districts of the city this was common.[98]

Conflicts between parents and state institutions responsible for child care most often arose with regard to opening hours of kindergartens and schools and allegations of child abuse. The first Sztálinváros nursery (which had thirty-five children) and the first kindergarten (which had eighty) were opened as early as the fall of 1951. These institutions provided care for the children of workers employed at the construction site. Parents dropped children off "at dawn, while it was still dark," and "took them home in the evening, when it was already dark."[99] The opening hours of kindergartens and schools were not adjusted to the working hours of the majority. Parents complained about this, but generally to no effect.[100]

As of 1953 and 1954, with the influx of families into the city, the number of children skyrocketed. This posed a seemingly insoluble problem for kindergartens and schools. Although by January 1954 Sztálinváros had four all-day kindergartens, they were all full, so newly arriving families had no place to send their children during working hours.[101] One solution was simply not to allow unemployed mothers to enroll their children, although there was demand. Many dependent mothers requested that their children be accepted in the kindergartens "for a few hours while we see to our daily tasks."[102] This indicates that, distrust for state institutions notwithstanding, day nurseries and kindergartens were relatively popular even among unemployed women. In December 1955, 1,500 children between ages three and six lived in Sztálinváros, but only 450 of them were able to attend one of the six kindergartens operating at the time.[103] In Sztálinváros schools the number of children grew more quickly than the number of classrooms.[104] In 1958 leaders of the City Council proposed the establishment of separate classes for boys and girls due to "moral considerations." This question was often raised, but no serious attempts were ever made to implement it as a policy.[105]

Parents rarely hesitated to enroll their children in school. In the 1955/56 academic year only 2.4 percent of school-age children were not enrolled. According to a council report, the majority of them lived in the South Side and Radar, where children often ran away from their families and their homes. Due to the highly fluctuating population of the city, the proportion of "student transfers" was also quite high in local schools. For example, in 1955, of the 1,120 students at the Pál Vasvári Elementary School (the largest elementary school in the city), 144 were new to the school and 184 left it. According to the City Council Cultural Department the majority of children leaving elementary schools could not pursue secondary education or find jobs, so many of them essentially became street urchins, mostly in the workers' districts.[106] The education available at the elementary level roughly met the needs of the population, but the capacities of the institutions at the secondary level were extremely limited.

In the records of the council meetings child abuse appears to have been a problem that varied from district to district. Downtown parents complained primarily about teachers who allegedly beat children, while according to the teachers in the barracks and old village schools the parents were abusing children. Naturally, the explanation for this lies not in any significant difference in the perceptions or training of teachers in different districts, but rather in the fact some social groups saw child abuse as "venial sin," while parents who led a more urban life (mainly in the downtown district) were described as considering child abuse a crime. Occasionally, if a child was given poor marks, parents would beat not the child but the teacher.[107]

The relationship between parents and teachers was good in the old village and strained in the new districts. According to council reports, the explanation for this was that the schools in the new districts were transitory, so there was no chance for stable relationships to develop between children and teachers. According to one report, "although the use of corporal punishment was by no means as widely practiced as the complaints (made primarily by parents living in the city) generally claim, our disciplinary methods must be perfected."[108] Some city leaders specifically blamed the loose morals of parents for the difficulties they faced with discipline (they claimed the children were "impossible to rear"). According to Jenő Tapolczai, parents were not strict enough with their children and this was why they got bad grades and took to stealing.[109]

In her memoirs, one teacher emphasized the differences between her approach to rearing children and the methods used by parents. She emphasized the "chaotic family relationships" she witnessed when visiting parents of children living in the Radar barracks:

> When I told the mother about my problems with the child, she reassured me that when Karcsi [the boy] was mischievous she would always give him a good beating! But to no avail. She cannot handle him, he is always running off. No wonder, the only thing you could do with a home like that would be to run off! . . . The J. family's apartment was tidy and neat, though they have six children. That's why the mother cannot find a job. One child is young, the other even younger. We discussed a lot of things, and I asked her what she gave all these children to eat. Her response shocked me. For lunch they had bread

with plum jam, but she had no idea what she would give them for dinner because they had run out of bread, she had no money, and her husband would only be paid a few days later.[110]

In the barracks several conflicts arose between parents and the school on the issue of child labor, usually because parents either failed to enroll their children or the children had unexplained absences. It was common practice for twelve- to fourteen-year-old children in the barracks to work as sharecroppers at harvest time, do laundry at various buildings, do housework, cook, or babysit their younger siblings, and, consequently, miss school.[111] No serious conflicts arose concerning this issue. Functionaries who worked in offices seem to have found it natural that children of poorer families worked and contributed to the family's income. After they left school and took jobs in industry, young adults did not immediately become self-supporting. Most of the time they continued to reside with their parents for years and spent part or all of their salaries on family expenses.

In Sztálinváros as in other communities, childhood seems to have been seen as coming to an end around the age of ten, followed by adolescence, which lasted until the age of fourteen. As an illustration of this, one could mention the view of someone who spoke up at a 1954 council meeting, insisting that given their "ill manners" and "insolence" boys between the ages of ten and fourteen should not be taught by young female instructors.[112] Similarly, many parents treated daughters between the ages of ten and fourteen as adults, assigning them essentially the same household duties and chores as their mothers.[113]

After the mid-1950s, a new concept of childhood was emerging, however, according to which children should spend their free time engaged in activities radically different from the pastimes of adults, but at the same time should be carefully preparing for adulthood and should not spend time in places of potentially ill repute. In the series of articles published in the local newspaper in 1957, titled "Children of the Night," two pedagogical principles clashed. According to one, to some extent children should be treated as adults, while according to the other they should be dealt with based on a distinctly different set of norms. In an article in which the first view prevailed the author mentioned, among other things, the regrettably "common sight of children romping about late at night or watching the swirling jazz music atmosphere in Sztálinváros restaurants and music bars."[114]

Despite the public warnings, Sztálinváros restaurants and clubs were full of "children of the night," although as the newspaper pointed out, "children should be in bed by 8:00 PM." Parents who took their children when they went out were considered immoral on other grounds as well. As an illustration of her alleged moral failings, The *Sztálinvárosi Hírlap* illustrated the alleged moral failings of one such mother, writing that since January 1957 she had not been employed, but her child had often been seen in the buffet of the Golden Star Hotel. In other cases the paper described how the "alcoholic Radar parents" would often take their children with them to the bars and taverns.[115]

Given the limited number of available places in kindergartens, primarily mothers of lower social standing were forced to come up with makeshift solutions. A 1954 council report states, "there is an increase in the number of occasions when a mother leaves her children at home and locks them in the room; consequently she is less able to perform at work because she worries about her children. Occasionally the mother may take the child with her to her workplace." Parents with a permanent job and residence had the best chance of successfully enrolling their children in one of the kindergartens. In 1954 one-third of the children attending kindergarten did not have a permanent place of residence and 40 percent of the parents of children on the waiting list had only a temporary address.[116] According to council reports, most of the children living in the working class districts were still "growing up in the streets."[117]

Despite the lack of available spots in kindergartens, the council wanted to demonstrate the efforts that had been made in regard to child care. To demonstrate this, in 1954, when several districts still lacked public roads and street lighting, the city already had two playgrounds. The fact that they went essentially unused did not discourage the aldermen, so in the spring of 1956, six new Sztálinváros playgrounds were opened. However, the situation did not improve, and in May 1957, Jenő Tapolczai sadly admitted that although several playgrounds had been made available, children preferred to go out into the streets to play. Children of L-building residents did not sit on swings, but instead played with building materials left behind at abandoned construction sites, smashed artificial stone slabs and cellar windows, smeared walls with filth, pulled up shrubs, broke electric bulbs with slingshots, or waged war on the young gangs living in the Technikum District. The Sztálinváros playgrounds, which remained unused for years, became urban architectural symbols of pedagogical ideals. In 1954 the council considered introducing more severe measures. Parents were to be instructed not to allow their children to leave the house after 7:00 PM and police officers were to escort children found in the streets home. But at 7:00 PM a parent working an afternoon or evening shift was not at home, but at the factory.[118]

Several aspects of children's everyday lives were to be strictly supervised. For example, hygiene (hand washing and disinfection) was inspected at schools, meals were centrally regulated, kindergarten and school dress codes were standardized, discipline and reward forms were hierarchically structured, and a strict daily schedule was adopted. Children's time, their appearance, and the spaces and objects they used were all under supervision. These regulations and controls affected the parent–child relationship as well. Parents embraced many of the pedagogical principles proclaimed at schools, which not only supported the strict measures but also shaped the policies regarding child care.

Conclusion

Marriage remained one of the principal institutions that helped to reproduce social hierarchies in Sztálinváros. Residents chose mates with whom they shared similar social backgrounds. The overlapping interests of the state and society determined the depictions of female workers and the ideal of childrearing. The ideal working woman, who was almost a new hero of the propaganda in the early 1950s, had become a fashionable housewife by the end of the decade. This transformed image better corresponded to the traditional expectations of the locals. In addition, the attempts made to create jobs for women in the city at the end of the 1950s indicate the municipal leaders' realization that they could not simply ignore the problem of unemployment among women. The two new factories created at the end of the decade specifically to provide jobs for women, and the clear emphasis placed on state supervision of the institutions of child welfare both functioned as expressive gestures with which the city administration demonstrated its break with the approaches that had characterized the regime in the early 1950s. This helped create stability in the everyday life of the city and made the system itself more durable. It was virtually impossible to obtain housing without a marriage certificate. Here cohabitation did not represent an alternative to marriage, but instead constituted a transitory and "unsettled" family model between two marriages. The primary function of the official stigmatization of single mothers and couples living together out of wedlock was to elevate the status of "respectable" citizens who lived in apartments they had been allocated through the centralized housing distribution system and in marriages, a relationship that was more easily overseen and regulated by the state. In other words, the state took deliberate measures to elevate the status of the "good" residents of the city, who became the basis of the new regime after 1956.

In Sztálinváros marriage was an essential prerequisite of social integration. Given the high level of female unemployment, if women sought to become "respectable members" of local society most of them had little choice but to marry. Because of industrialization, urbanization, large-scale migration, and high social mobility, the selection of a spouse was not arbitrary in Sztálinváros. On the contrary, social status was a good predictor of whom a female construction worker or a clerk would marry, or whom an engineer or bricklayer would choose for a wife. Indeed, it was also predictable what kind of housing they would be allocated and in which district, if they were given housing at all. The majority of people in Sztálinváros were married, but not necessarily or not only because the institution of marriage corresponded perfectly to their expectations and hopes. Couples also

Figure 4.8. Idealized image of a married couple in their home in Sztálinváros.

married because it was the only way of securing the acknowledgment of the larger community around them, which in turn furthered their social integration, not to mention the acknowledgment of the state, which discriminated in favor of married couples, particularly in the distribution of housing. Officially, almost everyone was married, but this did not necessarily mean that everyone lived together with his or her spouse, and Sztálinváros residents took advantage of this, finding back doors in the housing distribution system, though marriages in Sztálinváros remained more traditional than anywhere else in Hungary.

The relationships between families and social institutions were profoundly influenced by the fact that, in the decades following World War II, women's assumption of wage labor became an everyday phenomenon (though this varied from social class to social class). Once the first stages in the construction of the city had been completed and investment funds began to dwindle, the need for a large female workforce declined, and this led to high unemployment among women. In the wake of this shift, the separation in the discourse of wage labor and the tasks related to reproduction and childrearing served to deprive women of any chance of asserting their interests in conflicts between state enterprises and female members of the workforce. Business enterprises would justify the dismissal of women from their jobs by arguing that women played more important roles as mothers and caregivers.

The mystification of motherhood or, in contrast, the emancipation of women closely intertwined with the principles of childrearing expressed in the discourses of various state institutions (such as district nurses, nurseries, kindergartens, schools, parents' associations, and children's groups such as scouts). As in Budapest and other large industrial cities, in Sztálinváros the institutions designed to offer care for children were never able to meet the demand. It was more difficult for women to find work and send their children to kindergarten than it was to simply accept the traditional role of women, which the state began to propagate again in the mid-1950s.

Families had to be made supporting pillars of the system, not enemies. The measures taken by the state, however, created a foundation for a compromise between families and the state after the 1950s not only through state provision of child welfare or increased acknowledgment and respect for the roles of women in the home but also through two turns that could hardly be considered conservative. As of the mid-1950s, abortion performed by medical professionals in a hospital became widely available and the procedure for obtaining a divorce also became considerably simpler because of changes to practices in the courts. Paradoxically, these two changes in state policies were made to better respond to the demands of families on the one hand and to safeguard the transforming families according to Stalinist policies on the other.

Notes

Epigraph: FML, f. XXXI-18, b. 9.

1. Cf. Konopasek and Andrews, "A Cautious Ethnography of Socialism," 98; Betts, *Within Walls*, 7–8.

2. Keefe, "The Myth of the Declining Family."

3. *Sztálinvárosi Hírlap*, January 4, 1952, 3.

4. *Sztálinvárosi Hírlap*, August 28, 1953, 1.

5. In 1953, 732 babies were born in Sztálinváros and 186 weddings took place. In the last two months of 1952, there were only 67 newborns, in 1953 a monthly average of 60–70, while in the first half of 1954 there were more than 80. Nurseries and kindergartens designed to address the needs of permanent residents failed to meet the demand as the requests submitted to the local council demonstrate. FML, f. XXIII-502, b. 7, March 3, 1954, and June 9, 1954.

6. In 1960 among the male population above age fifteen the proportion of married men was 68 percent, while for women the figure was 75 percent. In 1960 the national average was 71.5 percent for men and 64.4 percent for women. Balázs, "A házasságkötések alakulása." Like other industrialized cities, Sztálinváros was among the youngest Hungarian cities from the perspective of the average age of its citizens. (Even as late as 1960, only 5 percent of the population was over age sixty.) *1960. évi népszámlálás. Fejér megye*, 47–49. In 1960, 89 percent of Sz-

tálinváros men between ages twenty-five and fifty were married, as were 88 percent of women between ages twenty and forty. Based on the figures in *Dunaújváros. 1950–1965*, 24.

7. *Sztálinvárosi Hírlap*, February 22, 1957, 2.

8. FML, f. XXIII-506, b. 24, 1958 housing requests.

9. Ibid.

10. For a more detailed analysis, see the section "Before the Registrar" in this chapter.

11. *1960. évi népszámlálás. Fejér megye*, 167.

12. FML, f. XXIII-505, b. 5, 1957.

13. In 1964, 1,525, and in 1967, 2,402 people. FML, f. XXIII-502, November 14, 1967.

14. Cf. Kotkin on the correlations between the Magnitogorsk housing system and family life. Kotkin, *Magnetic Mountain*, 194.

15. Samples were collected from FML, f. XXXIII-25, Dunaújváros (Sztálinváros) Birth and Marriage Record Duplicates, 1953, 1954, 1958, Sztálinváros registers of marriage. I analyzed data on 450 couples, 121 marriage certificates from 1953 and 105 from 1958, and 117 birth certificates from 1953 and 107 from 1958.

16. The national average that year was 28.6 and 24.7. Pallós and Vukovich, "A magyar házassági mozgalom."

17. Balázs, "A házasságkötések alakulása," 25.

18. Ibid.

19. In the group of intelligentsia, I included occupations that required greater than a high school education: teacher, engineer, physician, technician, and so on.

20. Skilled worker: 28.6%; office–administrative: 17.9%; unskilled worker: 17.9%; managerial: 14.3%; members of the intelligentsia: 7.1%.

21. Pápay, *Rang, párválasztás, közvélemény*, 117.

22. Sárkány, "A lakodalom funkciójának megváltozása falun."

23. There were sixty-one weddings in the winter, ninety-nine in the spring, sixty-two in the summer, and ninety-two in the fall.

24. *Sztálinvárosi Hírlap*, October 29, 1954, 3.

25. Ibid., November 16, 1954, 3.

26. On the wedding traditions of female workers who immigrated to Budapest, see Tóth, "Parasztlányokból munkásasszonyok." After Saturday was designated a weekend day, virtually every wedding was held on a Saturday (from 1968 to 1981, every other Saturday was a nonwork-day, and as of 1981 every Saturday became a weekend day).

27. Balázs, "A házasságkötések alakulása," 30.

28. Pallós and Vukovich, "A magyar házassági mozgalom," and "Munkaülés. A házasság és válás társadalmi-foglalkozási összefüggései," 368.

29. Bukodi summarizes possible interpretations of marriage homogamy and heterogamy. Bukodi, "Ki, mikor és kivel házasodik?" 56–58.

30. *Sztálinvárosi Hírlap*, September 12, 1958, 5.

31. Ibid.

32. Ibid., September 19, 1958, 5.

33. Ibid.

34. This was before the so-called kitchen debate, which changed the discourses on domestic life in state socialist countries. After that, the "mechanization of housework" meant much more—namely, everything from specific new appliances to the broader visions of a new way of life, de-Stalinization, and so on. See Susan Reid's work and books on these discourses in the Soviet context in particular. Reid, "Cold War in the Kitchen."

35. *Sztálinvárosi Hírlap*, March 15, 1957, 4.

36. Ina Merkel discerns a similar shift in the image of the ideal man. She analyzed the worldview and gender constructions of illustrated magazines published in the 1950s in the German Democratic Republic. The East German ideal man contributed more to tasks that involved childrearing, even if his primary identifying feature remained work. In addition, Merkel discovered two basic types of terminology: one was the "more productive," "heroic workman"; the other was "the educated man." Both are characterized by the fact that their social position is determined by their occupation, whereas their domestic position is defined by their willingness to help. Merkel, . . . *und Du, Frau an der Werkbank*, 109–15.

37. *Sztálinvárosi Hírlap*, March 15, 1957, 6; March 19, 1957, 4; March 22, 1957, 4.

38. See Fidelis, *Women, Communism, and Industrialization*, 3; Betts, *Within Walls*, 135; Lebow, *Unfinished Utopia*, 122–23.

39. *Nők Lapja*, May 19, 1960.

40. On the political representation of women and women's rights in Hungary, see Pető, *Women in Hungarian Politics*.

41. Valuch, *Magyarország társadalomtörténete*, 266.

42. *Sztálinvárosi Hírlap*, June 26, 1953, 2.

43. *Nők Lapja*, March 3, 1960.

44. FML, f. XXIII-502, b. 13, September 13, 1957.

45. Antal Apró (1913–94) was deputy chairman of the cabinet in 1957 and János Kádár's "right-hand man" responsible for industrial affairs. He actively participated in the post-1956 retaliations and personally oversaw the show trial of Imre Nagy.

46. FML, f. XXIII-502, b. 13, January 17, 1957; February 7, 1957; May 3, 1957.

47. FML, f. XXIII-505, b. 5.

48. FML, f. XXIII-502, b. 16, April 17, 1959. In 1960 Sztálinváros national enterprises kept records of only 5,669 economically active women, and many of them were not local residents but commuted to work from neighboring villages. In the same year, the number of Sztálinváros women between the ages of twenty and fifty-nine was 7,841, thus women employed in paid jobs constituted 72 percent of Sztálinváros female residents. The same proportion for men was 117 percent, which originated in the large number of commuters to Sztálinváros. *Dunaújváros. 1950–1965*, 24–26.

49. FML, f. XXIII-505, b. 5, April 13, 1958.

50. *Sztálinvárosi Hírlap*, July 30, 1954, 4; October 22, 1954, 3; February 19, 1957, 4; April 19, 1957, 6; May 10, 1957, 6; May 14, 1957, 4; June 11, 1957, 2.

51. FML, f. XXIII-502, b. 18, November 6, 1960.

52. On the cyclical nature of planned economic production, see Kornai, *A hiány*, specifically 224–29, and on the effect of cycles on the labor market, 251–79.

53. *Sztálinvárosi Hírlap*, June 17, 1958, 3.

54. Cf. Ferree, "Working Class Jobs"; Oakley, *The Sociology of Housework*.

55. Keresztesné Pataki, *A dolgozó nő háztartása*, 9–12.

56. Ibid., 65–66.

57. *Sztálinvárosi Hírlap*, March 1, 1957, 2.

58. Ibid., October 26, 1954, 4.

59. After introducing a hiring freeze at construction sites and prior to the establishment of light industry plants in Sztálinváros.

60. *Sztálinvárosi Hírlap*, March 1, 1957, 2.

61. FML, f. XXIII-502, b. 13, August 2, 1957.

62. FML, f. XXIII-502, b. 15, October 31, 1958.

63. *Sztálinvárosi Hírlap*, November 4, 1958, 2.

64. FML, f. XXIII-502, b. 16, November 9, 1959, Report on the condition of barracks, 3.
65. FML, f. XXIII-510, b. 3, September 5, 1957.
66. FML, f. XXXI-18, b. 6, unit 5/2, the case of István Sz.
67. FML, f. XXXI-18, b. 1, unit 1/13, The case of Mrs. Isván S.; and unit 1/17, Lajos T., both from 1957.
68. FML, f. XXVI-108, b. 2–3. In addition to council reports, the number of siblings indicated in school records also suggests a large number of children. Every year the proportion of dependent women in the school records exceeded 70 percent, but when one examines the lives of individuals, it was not rare for someone to be identified as "home-employed" one year and "unskilled worker" or "cleaner" the next. Naturally, a woman recorded as dependent was able to take temporary jobs, but this was not recorded in the statistics, not to speak of the more exhausting reproductive work of rearing children shouldered by women residing in the barracks.
69. FML, f. XXIII-502, b. 2, February 16, 1952.
70. FML, f. XXIII-502, b. 3, January 7, 1953.
71. FML, f. XXIII-502, b. 7, March 3, 1954.
72. FML, f. XXIII-502, b. 7, June 16, 1954.
73. FML, f. XXIII-502, b. 15, May 9, 1958.
74. FML, f. XXIII-502, b. 7, June 16, 1954; and b. 13, October 11, 1957.
75. Ibid.
76. FML, f. XXIII-502, b. 1, September 29, 1951.
77. FML, f. XXIII-502, b. 3, January 7, 1953.
78. Ibid.
79. FML, f. XXIII-502, b. 7, January 25, 1954.
80. FML, f. XXIII-502, b. 7, June 16, 1954.
81. FML, f. XXIII-502, b. 11, March 1, 1956.
82. *Sztálinvárosi Hírlap*, February 15, 1957.
83. FML, f. XXIII-502, b. 11, January 12, 1956.
84. FML, f. XXIII-502, b. 13, October 11, 1957.
85. *Sztálinvárosi Hírlap*, October 8, 1954, 3.
86. Ibid.
87. FML, f. XXIII-502, b. 13, October 11, 1957.
88. FML, f. XXIII-510, b. 4, 1959–60.
89. FML, f. XXIII-505, b. 4. Public records of people in state care.
90. FML, f. XXIII-502, b. 13, October 11, 1957.
91. FML, f. XXIII-510, b. 4, 1959–60.
92. FML, f. XXIII-510, b. 3, 1955–58.
93. FML, f. XXIII-502, b. 7, June 2, 1954.
94. *Sztálinvárosi Hírlap*, February 13, 1953, 2.
95. FML, f. XXIII-510, b. 3, 1955–58.
96. FML, f. XXIII-510, b. 4, 1959–60.
97. Egeli et al., *Büntetőjogi Döntvénytár*, 1324–30.
98. FML, f. XXV-24, Criminal proceedings, b. 4, 1958, B. 314 / 1958, Mrs. Géza P.
99. *Sztálinvárosi Hírlap*, November 1, 1952; June 19, 1953, 4.
100. Ibid., November 29, 1956, 3. Day nurseries and kindergartens opened at 6:30 AM, and closed at 5:00 PM. This mostly suited members of the intelligentsia and parents working in administrative positions at national enterprises, while it was by no means suitable for parents starting the morning shift at 6:00 AM.

101. FML, f. XXIII-502, b. 7, January 13, 1954.

102. FML, f. XXIII-502, b. 7, November 11, 1954.

103. FML, f. XXIII-502, b. 10, December 1, 1955.

104. In the academic year of 1954/55, 2,313 students attended Sztálinváros elementary schools, in 1955/56, 2,677, and in 1956/57, 3,200. In 1957/58, 243 students enrolled in the high school and 215 in the metallurgic secondary school of engineering. FML, Executive Committee, b. 10, May 12, 1955; FML, f. XXIII-502, b. 11, August 18, 1956.

105. FML, f. XXIII-502, b. 15, April 18, 1958.

106. FML, f. XXIII-502, b. 11, September 9, 1956.

107. FML, f. XXIII-502, b. 7, November 11, 1954; *Sztálinvárosi Hírlap*, December 18, 1953; March 4, 1958, 3.

108. FML, f. XXIII-502, b. 7, January 13, 1954.

109. FML, f. XXIII-502, b. 7, April 14, 1954.

110. FML, f. XXIII-508, b. 60. A work submitted under the category "Aster" at the contest titled "Living in a Young City" organized by the City Council, 1980.

111. FML, f. XXVI-108, b. 1. South Side elementary school. Justification of school absences. FML, f. XXV-24, Criminal proceedings, 1960, b. 6. Mrs. János B.'s negligence of duties in child-rearing; ibid., 1963, b. 11. József K. Crime against youth.

112. FML, f. XXIII-502, b. 7, January 13, 1954.

113. FML, f. XXV-24, 1963, b. 11, B III.130. Testimony of Etelka J.

114. *Sztálinvárosi Hírlap*, June 11, 1957, 2; June 14, 1957, 1; June 28, 1957, 5.

115. *Sztálinvárosi Hírlap*, April 15, 1958, 3; August 29, 1958, 3.

116. FML, f. XXIII-502, b. 7, June 9, 1954.

117. FML, f. XXIII-502, b. 11, March 1, 1956.

118. FML, f. XXIII-502, b. 7, April 21, 1954; May 26, 1954; b. 11, April 12, 1956; b. 13, May 3, 1957; *Sztálinvárosi Hírlap*, May 9, 1958, 4.

5   Abortion

I'm certainly scared of having a fourth one.

Excerpt from a mother's letter in *Sztálinvárosi Hírlap*, January 29, 1957, 2

While the baby was in the caul you could see it move. Then Mrs. P. cut it open, and I saw it was a boy. I could make out his fingers and toes, even the nails. When I saw the baby I said it must have been at least four months. Rózsi confessed that she was in her fourth month. I asked Rózsi how much she had paid for the abortion. She said she had paid Mrs. P. 400 forints to perform the abortion. After that, around the end of February, Rózsi and László Gy. moved out of our house. About six weeks later I met her and she complained that she was still bleeding. She went to see a doctor, but she did not tell him that she had had an abortion.[1]

Rózsi was eighteen years old at the time, and continued to live with László Gy. after the abortion. She claimed that she had not wanted the baby because it would have been the offspring of a previous relationship. Since childhood Rózsi had worked in the fields, and later as an unskilled worker at the construction site. Before 1945 her father was an agricultural laborer. Her father and youngest brother remained in their Fejér County village; Rózsi moved to Sztálinváros along with four of her siblings, and worked there beginning in the mid-1950s. László Gy. was not divorced from his wife when he and Rózsi moved in together, so they rented a room in the Technikum District. Rózsi had decided to terminate her pregnancy in the hope of safeguarding her newly entered cohabitation relationship. She knew abortions were only performed at the hospital and only for women who already had at least three children. Rózsi was afraid that László Gy. would leave her, as had the former lover who had impregnated her. She wanted to have children, but under different circumstances and by László Gy. Although at first sight it may seem paradoxical, she had an abortion specifically because she hoped to be able to start a "respectable" family acceptable to the outside world.[2]

Although abortion was legalized in the Soviet Union in 1955, and most of the Eastern bloc countries quickly followed suit, officials in these societies generally depicted abortion as a practice threatening to family life.[3] The primary reasons for this were pronatalist policies of these states and the mystification of motherhood. The role of the mother is mystified and romanticized through the perception of motherhood as a natural and fundamental part of a woman's everyday life that should be encouraged and supported.[4] In Sztálinváros the local administration judged women fundamentally on the basis of whether they were capable of performing this reproductive role. Those who did not wish to have children had to face many social sanctions. For Sztálinváros women becoming a mother was almost mandatory, both because of their socialization and because motherhood was still interpreted within a normative context, which demonstrates an overlap between state and society. However, as I will argue in this chapter, the state policy regarding abortion changed in the mid-1950s not only because the state administration realized that the restriction of abortion had no significant effect on the birthrate but also because in most cases people sought abortions to limit large family sizes, not to terminate a first pregnancy.[5]

However, according to the communist propaganda motherhood made a woman's life joyful, meaningful, and complete. This image represented a highly conservative aspect of Stalinist policies. The administration accepted abortion to reach an agreement with families who wanted to control family size. In regard to the pronatalist policies of the state, the aim of which was to increase the number of births, the most important task of the family and, of the woman within the family, was to give birth, so abortion, childlessness, and contraception considered harmful to families. In this interpretative context, from the moment of conception a woman does not have exclusive authority over her body because it is serving "higher" social goals, including familial unity, the population of the country, or the greatness of the nation.[6] Nevertheless, in the 1950s (and ever since) the manner in which the question of abortion was raised separated the control of sexuality from the control of reproduction. In this respect, the debates were not simply about control of the female body but also about power relations and the system of gender roles.[7]

Why did the pronatalist state allow abortions, and why were there so many abortions in the "model city" of Sztálinváros? How could these abortions contribute to the stability of the regime, and how could the Sztálinváros locals influence the work of the Abortion Committees? This chapter explores how in Sztálinváros abortion became almost the exclusive means of birth control, and why this was characterized in the official discourse as a symptom of the alleged collapse of family life, in spite of the fact that most of the women seeking abortions were married and already had children. I maintain that the high abortion rate in Sztálinváros was the product of an unofficial agreement between state policymakers and the local residents. With the liberalization of abortion the state sought to bring abortions that were being performed in secret under its oversight and thereby to bring birth control under its purview. This chapter demonstrates that the legalization of abortions in the mid-1950s was a tool with which the authorities sought to legitimize the modernist principles of Stalinist policies. Moreover, families with more than one child often felt the need for legalized abortion because they had no other effective means of contraception. This need, which was supported both by families and state policies, should have been respected when the regime endeavored to stabilize its rule and reload Stalinist policies.

The Ban on Abortion and the Myth of the Ratkó Children

State control of abortion was founded on a principle that deprived women of the right to decisions about their own bodies and at the same time determined their place in society. It is hardly a coincidence that abortion became a crucial issue of women's emancipation movements, since the limits that were and are placed on the practice of abortion are seen as limits on the rights of women to choose their own social roles (motherhood or life without children).[8] Even today the issue of abortion and the ways in which it was addressed in the 1950s still serve as reference points in Hungarian history.[9] Criminal cases involving abortion, the Ratkó law in February 1953 (which prohibited abortion and encouraged childbearing even outside of wedlock), and later the legalization of abortion in the second half of the 1950s (and the concomitant rise in the number of abortions, which came to exceed the number of births) all indicate the collision of opposing forces. The emphasis on the high number of abortions, which authorities tended to explain as a symptom of the "disintegration" of the family and the spread of "careless" relationships, played a crucial role in the myth of declining family life.

In Hungary the abortion provisions of the 1878 Csemegi code remained in effect until 1956. In other words, neither the drastic redrawing of the country's borders that took place after World War I nor the communist takeover of the country after World War II brought about changes in the provisions of the code regarding abortion, which therefore constitute some of the most enduring legal measures in the history of Hungarian law. A woman who deliberately had an abortion could be sentenced to two years in prison if she conceived out of wedlock and three years in prison if she was married (there were penalties for those who performed the abortion and the woman who had it). According to estimates by demographers, however, 100,000 illegal abortions were performed in the 1930s and 120,000–140,000 in the second half of the 1940s. At the beginning of the 1950s, an estimated 110,000–120,000 abortions were performed in Hungary (unofficially, of course).[10] Although it was implemented in the year of Stalin's death, the Ratkó law is referred to as a symbol of the Stalinist ban on abortion in Hungary, which came into effect on February 1, 1953, as a simple directive issued by the Ministry of Health.[11] Anna Ratkó, the first Hungarian woman minister and a reliable party worker of Rákosi's Stalinist regime, made only one substantial change to the provisions of the Csemegi code: the obligation to report an abortion was made stricter. The Ratkó ministerial directive thus merely strengthened the enforcement of a law that was almost eighty years old. This amendment gave the law a Stalinist spin by emphasizing mutual surveillance and widening the category of the guilty. In the meantime, the number of people convicted for obtaining illegal abortions increased, a tendency that clearly demonstrates the effects of the state ban on abortion. The essence of the prohibition was simply that abortion was permitted far more rarely than before, and in 1953 and 1954 almost never. However, the number of illegal abortions did not significantly decrease, so the austere directive was relaxed as early as 1954, and after June 1956 abortions performed in state institutions were allowed almost universally, partly because the termination of a pregnancy had been liberalized in the Soviet Union in 1955.[12] In addition, the ban on abortion had not brought about any significant growth in the number of births, such as the growth observed in the Soviet Union in 1936.[13]

Until abortion was legalized, however, the number of cases of illegal abortions and infanticides was high. Concealing a pregnancy was one of the ways for a pregnant woman to escape the social control of her body. In the majority of cases, women who committed infanticide had been abandoned by their partners. A 1955 infanticide case reveals that the accused, who had managed to conceal her pregnancy, committed infanticide for fear of contempt. According to one witness, the accused considered the burden of infanticide less difficult to bear than the stigma of being an "unmarried mother."[14]

> I was a few steps away when I heard the child cry and I saw a woman peering out from behind the door. I wanted to enter, but the outhouse doors on the opposite side were opened in such a manner that I could not go in. When I finally entered the woman was standing in the last stall. I yelled at her, asking what she had done, [and whether she] had she killed the baby. I called her "missus," but she said *she was not a missus, she was still unmarried*. I told her that she should feel ashamed for having killed her baby. She said it was none of my business and that her mother would definitely kill her if she found out about the child. I looked into the toilet and saw the baby crying in the pit. The woman did not even shed a tear. I told her I would go to the post office and use the phone there to call an ambulance to save the child. She clasped her hands together and begged me not to do this to her. But she had killed her child and I refused not to report her. I cried and fainted.[15]

The fire department arrived soon and extracted the child from the pit, but they were unable to save the infant, who had been born two months premature.

Initially the mother claimed not to have known that she was giving birth. She claimed simply to have gone to the outhouse when she had felt the pains of labor. For months she refused to reveal the name of the father, but she confessed that he was a married man. When the name of the father was eventually revealed the woman also said they had begun a sexual relationship within a month of having met each other and the man had promised to marry her. "When I discovered I was pregnant I also learned that the father was married, and although he had previously told me he was divorcing his wife I did not tell him or anyone else about the pregnancy."

As of June 1954 the twenty-year-old woman was working as a clerk at the Sztálinváros Radar post office. She resided in the L-buildings, where she met the man, who was one of her neighbors, in July. In September she discovered she was pregnant. She regularly visited her mother, who lived alone in their native village. On the morning of the delivery she had returned from the village to Sztálinváros. In the courtroom she contended that she had wanted to give birth in Budapest, but since she was only due in May she did not consider labor pains at the end of March anything particularly important. Of her acquaintances, her supervisor tried to dodge responsibility by recalling having seen that the woman was pregnant and having ordered her to see a doctor, which, however, she had not done.[16]

The liability of the father or the woman's immediate environment was not even brought up at court, but this was not the point of the trial. The point of the trial was to demonstrate that the mother had no right to decide whether to allow the baby to live or not. The severity of the measures taken against infanticide may have originated in part in the fact that even in the interwar period, the practice was still common as a means of birth control in some villages.[17]

After 1956 similarly liberal regulations were adopted in Eastern Europe, the Soviet Union, Bulgaria, and Hungary. In Poland and Czechoslovakia the termination of a pregnancy was allowed on "social grounds," broadly interpreted, in other words for those who claimed the birth of another child would confront them with financial difficulties. However, official data show considerable differences among countries. In 1959 in Poland there were ten times as many births as abortions, while in Bulgaria and Czechoslovakia there were only three times as many and in Hungary the number of abortions actually exceeded the number of births.[18]

Several demographic studies have shown that the "Ratkó law" barely affected the number of births. In 1953 the number of live births per thousand people in Hungary increased by 10 percent in 1953 and by 6 percent in 1954. Many attributed this tendency to the administrative measures adopted by the state. This increase in the birthrate was due in no small part to the rise in the number of marriages, in particular in the case of first children. In contrast to the majority of European countries, Hungary experienced no significant increase in births (no baby boom) right after World War II. The baby boom was belated, and this partly explains the increase in the number of births in 1953–54 in Hungary.[19]

The "Ratkó law" had a greater effect on births in urban communities than in villages. The birthrates in villages barely changed. This suggests that while the means of birth control (contraception or abortion) used in rural communities were not influenced or barely influenced by administrative measures, these same measures had a considerable, if temporary, effect on birthrates in urban areas. Naturally, a mother of several children responded differently to the strict ban on abortion than did a university student with no children, so the effects of the ban and the ways in which it was perceived differed among various social groups and generations. It was much easier for a mother living in a marriage with the father of her children to obtain permission to have an abortion than it was for an unmarried woman. Only 1,717 induced abortions were reported in 1952, but this number increased to 82,500 in 1956.

In the meantime, there was no significant change in the number of live births in 1952 and 1956 (186,000 and 193,000, respectively). Since no significant changes took place in the methods and incidence of contraception in the course of those four years (indeed presumably the use of contraception was less widespread in 1952), one can conclude that approximately 80,000 illegal abortions were performed in 1952, even if they do not show up in statistics. Otherwise it would be difficult to explain the insignificant difference between the numbers of births in 1952 and 1956. It is also highly likely that tens of thousands of abortions were performed illegally prior to World War II, the high birthrates notwithstanding (for instance, 182,000 births in 1938).[20]

In 1953, the state attempted to transform the system of birth control by completely prohibiting abortion, but this was an utter failure. Indeed, as of 1956 abortion performed in a hospital officially became the preferred method of birth control in Sztálinváros. Yet while officially abortion was accepted, it was nonetheless still condemned in the local press, which indicates that the state accommodated itself to the customs of the ordinary people of city society, and the ordinary people in turn were increasingly likely to choose hospitals and physicians when seeking an abortion instead of relying on the practices of midwives.

The Sztálinváros Abortion Committee

The measures adopted by the state regarding abortions did not significantly influence the number of abortions in Sztálinváros. The only major change was that after 1956 the abortions formerly performed in secret became more "visible." Prior to the liberalization of abortion in 1956, estimates indicated at least one abortion for every live birth in Sztálinváros, but this fact only appeared in statistics after 1956.

In the first half of 1954 the Fejér County Appeal Committee on Abortions received several requests, so on July 9, 1954, the Health Department of the Fejér County Executive Committee established the Sztálinváros Abortion Committee. Regrettably, the documents of the Sztálinváros Abortion Committee were not preserved and one must rely on other council documents when attempting to draw conclusions concerning its operations. The makeup of the committee was constantly changing, but for the most part so-called social organizations delegated the members (such as the Communist Youth Organization, the Women's Alliance, the trade union, and the local council of the Communist Party). Most of the work done by the committee, which met once a week, was a formality, since in 75 percent of cases it gave permission for an abortion on the basis of social circumstances (meaning financial difficulties).[21]

A directive issued by the Ministry of Health on June 24, 1956, made the high number of legal abortions possible. However, abortion had been widespread in Sztálinváros before liberalization. According to the report compiled by the Abortion Committee for the January 12, 1956, council meeting, the council met every Wednesday and on average thirty-eight to forty requests were reviewed at each meeting." If we assume that the meetings lasted eight hours with no breaks, the requests were discussed for an average twelve minutes. Based on the report, in 1955 the thirty requests that were accepted each week added up to 1,500 abortions. The same year 1,094 babies were born in the local hospital. This would suggest that the number of abortions almost equaled the number births. On the basis of the committee's next report, between January 1 and August 18, 1956, 531 pregnancies were terminated and 687 babies were born.[22] But even prior to the liberalization of the abortion policy on June 24, 1956, about one abortion was estimated for every birth.

In 1957 women almost besieged the Abortion Committee, which was not prepared for such a massive number of requests. Following the liberalization of abortion policy, within nine months the committee approved 1,571 requests for permission to have an abortion (we do not know how many were submitted), which was approximately a threefold increase compared to previous data. In January 1957 the Sztálinváros chief medical officer complained in a letter to his superior, the Fejér County Hospital Superintendent, about the "unbearable conditions" in regard to the Dunapentele Hospital Abortion Committee: "a large number of applicants are arriving, last Wednesday there were eighty-five of them in a day."[23] Requests were hastily reviewed, with roughly five minutes devoted to each case. However, the birthrate did not decrease. On the contrary it rose, which suggests that with the legalization of abortion earlier abortions (performed in secret) became visible to the authorities. In other words, women who earlier had an abortion performed in secret were now more likely to choose to have an abortion in a hospital, which offered a significantly greater degree of medical safety. In 1957 within the space of a single year one in seven women in the overall population of Sztálinváros was given permission to have an abortion (though again, we do now know how many requests were submitted).[24]

One especially grave problem for members of the Sztálinváros Abortion Committee was that fourteen- or fifteen-year-old girls would appear before them without being accompanied by their parents because "they did not want the parents to know [about the pregnancy]."[25] Based on a circular issued by the chief medical officer, in order to prevent this, as of 1960 the legal guardian (parent, adoptive parent, or guardian) had to provide written consent if a minor requested an abortion.[26] Thus the committee and parents or guardians shared the right of minors to control the practice of abortion. This is illustrated in the case of Mária S., a fourteen-year-old at the time who appeared before the Sztálinváros Abortion Committee accompanied by her mother on October 8, 1958, and requested an abortion. "The girl named above was born on October 4, 1944, and the physician examining her stated that she was already in the third month of her pregnancy. Thus at the time of copulation Mária S. was 13 years and 9 months old." On account of this fact the local chief medical officer requested that the police launch an investigation and charge the unknown father with a crime against youth. Within a rather brief period of time the police learned that Mária S.'s baby had been fathered by seventeen-year-old Sándor F. He could not be accused in a criminal procedure unless Mária S.'s legal guardians, in this case her parents, reported him to the police. However, the parents did not wish to press charges.[27] There are several possible explanations for their reluctance. They may have accepted the sexual relationship between their daughter and Sándor F. or they may have been afraid that a trial would be given considerable publicity and both they and their daughter would be condemned in the court of public opinion.

Younger women who did not yet have children and were requesting permission to have an abortion, however, were much rarer than women who already had three or more children. Almost half of the approximately two thousand women submitting requests already had at least three children.[28] In these cases, husbands could also play a significant role in the process. Husbands were entitled to request the termination of an unwanted pregnancy. A letter to the committee from a father with many children offers an illustration. The man blames his wife for her "careless" behavior:

> I am a father of six children, I am the only bread winner in the family, my monthly income is 1,600 forints plus child benefits.[29] My wife is about four or five months pregnant. Out of carelessness she has not come to the Abortion Committee. And I only learned this yesterday. She led me to believe that the pregnancy would be terminated by surgical intervention, and that the operation would prevent further pregnancies. I am now requesting your consent to terminate my wife's pregnancy. My request is based on the following facts: the 1,600 forints I earn is insufficient to provide for a family of nine, my children already live in a state of privation. It would be irresponsible to bring another child into this dire poverty.

At his request, the husband, who resided in the Technikum District, was called in by the committee for a hearing.[30] The available documents do not reveal whether the pregnancy was terminated or not, but they do indicate that the husband's actions in regard to his wife's pregnancy were considered legitimate. The husband contended that his wife had been careless and inconsiderate and that she was incapable of fulfilling her duties as a mother. For this very reason she had absolutely no right to decide between life and death. This argument may have met with approval among the members of the committee because the abortion committees themselves also referred to the alleged "carelessness" of women as justification for their prerogative to make the final decision regarding the termination of a pregnancy.

At the meeting of the City Council, Executive Committee members of the Abortion Committee remarked that most women sought to have an abortion because of their "carelessness."[31] According to this logic, women are incapable of reaching decisions on their own and the committee must act on their behalf. Some members wanted to include "education of pregnant women in the interests of prevention" among the tasks of the committee, though it is not immediately apparent what this "education" would have consisted of, since reliable contraceptive devices for women were not available (the only two available methods at the time were coitus interruptus or abortion). Rózsi and other mothers of three knew perfectly well how they had become pregnant, but apart from abstinence they had no means of preventing conception. As had been the case for their mothers, abortion was the only effective way to avoid having many children.

In 1960, by November 16, 1,731 abortion requests had been submitted, thus the annual average of 2,000 remained essentially unchanged. There were two abortions for every live birth in Sztálinváros at the time. The majority of women requesting abortions were still mothers of two or more children, with only 12 percent of the abortion requests filed by women who had no children already. The number of abortions rose in direct proportion to the number of children, and it reached its peak among mothers of three or four children, as was the case in other East European countries.[32] Thus the main functions of these abortions were to limit family size.

Determent and Contraception

Time and time again various offices raised the question: would the number of women requesting abortions decrease if women were informed of the dangers of the procedure?[33] On this topic the local newspaper, which was a mouthpiece of "socialist morals," merely reported that given the large number of surgical interventions, in the view of the chief medical officer: "Certain social and official measures are required. With regard to the high number of operations it was proposed that medical committees throughout the country not only decide on whether or not they should grant requests but also should undertake widespread efforts to educate the public. Women must be informed of the dangers of the procedure."[34]

"Education" did not imply spreading knowledge regarding the use of modern contraceptive devices, but rather informing women of the risks of abortion and deterring them from seeking abortions. Determent also included publicizing trials involving illegal abortions.

The widely publicized trial of Mrs. Albert B. and her alleged "accomplices" by the Sztálinváros Municipal Court on January 24, 1957, is an example of the "determent" discourse. At the time, abortion was accessible for most women at the Sztálinváros Hospital, so the article can be interpreted as an argument in support of the officially accepted way of obtaining an abortion and against unofficial (criminal) abortions. The subject of the case was an illegal operation that had ended in the death of the patient. Mrs. Albert B. performed abortions for many women at her apartment on May 1 Street. After one such operation on December 19, 1956, the patient, Mrs. János B., died. Five women were charged who, according to the police, were operating a "criminal gang" that performed illegal abortions. Women paid 250–500 forints for the procedure. Three of the five accused were tried as intermediaries and two as passive parties to the crimes (i.e., the women on whom the abortions had been performed). Mrs. P. was responsible for the "easier" cases, but if she proved unable to perform the task she would send her clients to her more "experienced" acquaintance, Mrs. B. Another of the accused, Mrs. János K., admitted to having performed twenty-four illegal abortions.[35]

She was sentenced to two years in prison, Mrs. Albert B. to twenty months, and Mrs. Gyula P. to eighteen months. The sentence for the intermediaries was between six months and eight months, but the sentences were suspended for three years.[36] The aim of the sentences was to reduce the number of "illegal" abortions, in other words abortions that were performed outside of institutional controls.

In the same issue of the newspaper containing extensive coverage of the trial an article by head physician Dr. Dezső Kiss on abortions was published. The primary aim of the article was to deter women by identifying the possible outcomes of an abortion, which included infection and infertility. Dr. Kiss described some of the "reprehensible examples." One woman had requested abortions on thirteen separate occasions. Another woman who had had three abortions explained simply that "we don't want children," in spite of the fact that she lived in a three-room apartment with her husband. Echoing the prevailing discourse of the time, Dr. Kiss explained the high number of abortions as a symptom of an "immoral lifestyle."

It is not immediately apparent what he meant by this, since he himself had acknowledged that most of the women requesting abortions were married. Taking into consideration the interests of the hospital, he further complained that the "abnormally high number" of women requesting abortions was a hindrance to the care of people who were "really" sick, since "women waiting for abortions take up the beds" and the surgical procedures consumed a great deal of the doctors' and gynecologists' time.[37] In spite of the fact that abortion was legalized (and thereby brought more under the supervision of the state), it was nonetheless seen as a "lesser" sin only if the woman in question had already fulfilled her reproductive role, that is, if she had given birth to at least two or three children.

Presumably also under external pressure, the editors of the *Sztálinvárosi Hírlap* initiated a debate on the abortion question, titled "Let's Talk about What We Don't Talk About." The first letter to the editor was written by a mother of three:

> So far I have never thought about abortion because my husband and I believed we could raise three children. But now I am afraid to have a fourth child. I am not scared of pregnancy or delivery, but I am truly worried about the financial challenges of bringing up a baby. I believe that terminating a pregnancy is a source of great anguish for every mother, but which course am I to choose— financial difficulties and even more work, or abortion? I would not choose either, but rather a third possibility: prevention. But how? Why are safe contraceptives not put on the market? . . . We will soon be able to travel to the moon, so in my humble opinion a problem of this significance could also be solved through relatively simple means. However, the cries of wives and women fall on deaf ears: help us, come up with something for prevention.[38]

Within a few days the newspaper carried a "letter" from a "father of four" who had arrived at the same conclusion.[39] Some people suspected that these "letters to the editor" were at times written by the editors of the paper themselves, though this would be hard to demonstrate persuasively.[40] It was characteristic of the double nature of public space that what could not be written down officially in the newspaper was written in the form of letters to the editor, and what was not written in letters to the editor was given voice in lectures presented to educate the general public, lectures on which the newspaper sometimes reported.

The "letters to the editor" cited above supported the argument that it was not terribly difficult for those who already had children to avoid having more. In regard to this group, abortion was cast primarily as a health hazard and not as a social problem. At the same time the tone of the letters to the editor was used to show changes in attitudes,[41] but the letters do not reveal any larger shift in people's opinions on abortion; rather, they indicate the change that took place in the official views of the state organs. As of 1957, the authorities considered abortion a forgivable sin.

In Dr. Dezső Kiss's view, the roots of the "problem" lay in the fact that, according to the regulations, abortion within the first trimester qualified as a private affair, and if a woman was older than forty or already had two children there was no reason to reject her request for the termination of a pregnancy. He never responded to the questions related to the issue of prevention.[42] Fundamentally, he saw abortion as a means of extending state control, and he urged that it be viewed as a "public affair." The state strove to exercise increased control over pregnancies, an effort that had origins in its pronatalist policies.

Sex education propaganda on contraception was launched in the summer of 1958. The Women's Council organized a presentation titled "Birth Control" in the house of culture of the Hungarian Young Communist League in the stigmatized South Side area of the city.[43] The lecture was held in the South Side because at the time 55 of the women in the 410 families in the district were pregnant, and the South Side was already known for the high birthrates among its residents.[44]

In his letter to the Health Department of the Executive Committee of the Sztálinváros City Council, the superintendent of the Fejér County Hospital ordered the purchase of "sample pessaries" to be distributed to gynecologists. According to the letter, "it is the duty of gynecologist offices to educate women on means of contraception and the possible dangers and risks of abortion. I am again attaching the necessary brochures for this, and I request that you forward them to the heads of all the specialist physicians' offices. It is also necessary, in order to popularize the 'pessaries' now available at every pharmacy, for the physicians to be able to show one to women in order to demonstrate their importance and use. Therefore, I order that a sample pessary be purchased and supplied to every gynecological specialist."[45]

In 1959 the Health Department of the Sztálinváros City Council "distributed sex education brochures to be given to women appearing before the abortion committee." In the same year at national enterprises employing a large number of female workers (such as the Undergarment Factory, today owned by Triumph and the Worsted Mill) ten-minute "antiabortion" films were shown.[46]

The limited effect of this "educational propaganda" clearly indicates the hasty and slapdash nature of the entire effort. In 1958 the Abortion Committee approved 2,271 requests for abortions, and in 1959 it received 828 requests within less than six months.[47] The use of contraceptive devices was propagated among rather narrow circles at public lectures, but the *Sztálinvárosi Hírlap* reported on the locations of lectures of "great public interest." In 1958, when the issue first began to be given official attention, the local newspaper mentioned not a single mode of contraception by name and gave no information regarding the incidence of use, even though precise data were available on the legal marketing of "condoms" or "pessaries" nationwide. The column "Let's Talk about What We Don't Talk About" was canceled. One cannot avoid the impression that the continuing use of hospital resources for women seeking abortions was more acceptable to the communist ethic than the sale of condoms. Although birth control pills caused a drop in the number of abortions, these pills were only brought onto the market in 1967 and then again in 1972. The propagation of birth control pills in Hungary began in 1972 in the wake of a decision of the Communist Party.[48]

Presumably, the most widespread form of birth control was also the oldest: coitus interruptus. According to a 1958 national survey, 56 percent of women used this method, and 19 percent (also a high proportion) used vaginal douches as a means of contraception. Most of these were workers, clerks, and members of the intelligentsia. Among "agricultural workers" these were the only significant means of contraception besides coitus interruptus. Only 5.6 percent of women used the pessary, the widely propagated birth control device of the time, and they were primarily people among the intelligentsia. The proportion of women using preventive contraception was especially low among blue-collar workers. The use of condoms was not uncommon among members of the urban population, but they were used by a significant proportion of the population only among the intelligentsia (42 percent) and office clerks (34 percent). In contrast, only 6 percent of "agricultural workers" and 15 percent of workers used them.[49] The extent to which condoms were purchased in various countries is one measure of the availability of effective birth control and the acceptance among men of some responsibility for contraception. Consumer data reveal that in 1960 in France and Hungary a man purchased hardly more than one condom per year, compared with eleven to thirteen condoms per year in the United States, ten in Sweden, eight in Japan, and five in England and West Germany.[50]

Women Who Had Abortions

The practice of performing criminal abortions at private residences continued even after abortion was liberalized.[51] In Sztálinváros most of the women who sought illegal abortions either had their requests rejected by the Abortion Committee due to the advanced nature of the pregnancy, heard rumors that "no anesthesia is used in the hospital and the surgical intervention is very painful," and thus decided not to go there, or they simply did not know about legal abortions performed at hospitals.[52] In 1957–58 women paid 300–400 forints to Mrs. P. in the Technikum District for an abortion, which was only a little more than 210–300 forints, the cost of an abortion at the hospital.[53] Indeed, the cost of the procedure in the hospital was the most burdensome for families whose primary motivation for deciding to seek an abortion involved social reasons. Since members of these groups were part of the least-educated stratum of the city, they virtually used only abortion as a means of birth control. A "surgical intervention" by Mrs. Mátyás N. was much less costly, even if all the more dangerous: the majority of those testifying in court paid her only 100–150 forints.

In general the police only found out about people who performed criminal abortions after a patient required hospitalization and care as a result of unprofessional treatment. In Sztálinváros in 1959 and 1962 women who had been performing illegal abortions for years were charged with "feticide."[54] During the trials several women were interrogated whose pregnancies had been terminated by the accused. For this reason, the records of the hearings of the trials contain more data on the women who performed the abortions than they do on the women who sought them, because the latter only appeared in the summary reports compiled by the Abortion Committee.

The women who sought abortions were between the ages of seventeen and thirty-five. The majority had several siblings (they came from families with four to six children, and in some cases as many as eleven, and most of them had either two children or none. Most identified the occupation of the father of the unborn child as "hired man" or "agricultural laborer." The majority of the partners and husbands were unskilled workers, but there were some skilled workers among them as well. Married or cohabiting women were dependent, while the group of single women included unskilled workers, kindergarten teachers, and clerks. Thus, with regard to occupation they formed a rather heterogeneous group. Of the characteristics listed above, occupation bore the least significant relationship with the decision to seek an abortion.

Alongside the factors of family size and profession, personal motivations for deciding to seek an abortion varied widely as represented during the trial.[55] As one young woman recalled: "In the morning when I was taking milk home from the store I met a woman named Mrs. B. in Gábor Áron Street. We stopped to chat. She inquired about my little boy, who was three months old at the time. I told her he was fine and I also complained that I was pregnant again. She responded that it was no reason to be sad because she knew a woman who could terminate pregnancy with some medication."[56]

The fact that the young mother did not want the second child was entirely understandable to Mrs. B. In fact, she offered the woman assistance in seeking an abortion. The reports on illegal abortions show a considerable degree of solidarity and discretion among women. They suggest, indeed, that women formed "secret alliances" in the neighborhood communities. Women of May 1 Street, the downtown area, the L-buildings, and the Technikum District turned to different women for help when seeking an illegal abortion.[57] The women who performed the abortions often came to the aid of the women seeking their help (who usually lived in the same building or a neighboring street) for free or for a reduced fee. They characterized the act as paid assistance: "I told Mrs. Zs. to go to the hospital for an abortion, but she said she was afraid because she had heard from others that no anesthesia or painkillers were used there, so the procedure was very painful. Pregnant women were begging me to terminate their pregnancies, so I did, because I wanted to help them. They said the price did not matter, whatever the cost, just bring the pregnancy to an end."[58]

Women were afraid to go to the hospital. One of the main reasons for this may have been that childbearing and abortion had only come under the supervision of physicians and hospitals comparatively recently. For centuries women had used various means to exercise some control over their bodies, reproduction, and childbirth. By establishing abortion committees and legalizing abortions performed by certified physicians, the state managed to institutionalize not only childbirth but also the practice of induced abortions, which previously were often performed by midwives. The control of a pregnant woman's body became a medical issue. Delivery and abortion were moved from the private sphere, where they were performed by women, into the semipublic space overseen primarily by male doctors. Thus the meanings of both were altered.

This may be one of the reasons that a mother of two who had already had several abortions at the hospital was nevertheless reluctant to go to the hospital again and instead sought the assistance of Mrs. P.

> In September 1958 I missed my period. I was scared that I was pregnant again so I went to the local gynecologist. After the examination the doctor said I was not pregnant but when I started menstruating I should see him again and I would receive some kind of radiation treatment since I had previously had four curettages.[59] Two weeks passed and my period still didn't come, I was afraid of the curettage, and since I had heard from women who were strangers to me that Mrs. P. performed abortions, and I vaguely knew her, I went to her home and asked her to help me terminate my pregnancy.[60]

As one consequence of the official condemnation of abortion, rumors circulated about the people who had been granted permission to have an abortion by decisions of the Abortion Committee. Rozália P. mentioned this: "Since I was not yet married to László Gy. and he did not father my baby, I was not going to give birth to the child. I intended to have my pregnancy terminated in the hospital, but I thought only women who already had three children were allowed to have an abortion."[61]

A year prior to this event, the wife of the abovementioned László Gy. had an abortion that she concealed from her husband. The young kindergarten teacher told Mrs. P. that she could not have her pregnancy officially terminated because her husband would learn about it.[62] The fear of a husband's response and the desire to keep an abortion secret is demonstrated in several reports of women who describe how they subjugated themselves to the expectations of their husbands, families, and those around them when they chose to have an abortion.

The personal motivations of women who sought abortions included fear of disgrace, fear of "becoming an unmarried mother,"[63] fear of "poverty,"[64] and in some cases simply the fact that the baby had not been fathered by the woman's husband or partner.

According to the woman who was performing the abortions, her husband was not aware of what she was doing; he only knew that she was making her own income. "My husband thought I had more money because I was doing needlework for others after I became unemployed." It is of course quite possible that she said this in order to save her husband from having to face criminal charges. She performed abortions in a rather primitive way: "At a course of instruction in Szeged I had heard from midwives that by injecting a diluted solution of soap and iodine pregnancy can be terminated. The gadget was a rubber pump with the appropriate glass tube usually found in every home."[65] The other accused used a different method: "Mrs. N. told me to lie on the bed, and then she took out the bound hollyhock root that she had placed underneath the pillow. She brought a wash bowl in which she prepared water with iodine, she washed the hollyhock in this solution and then inserted it into my womb. She told me not to remove the hollyhock until I started bleeding."[66]

These archaic methods of abortion continued to be used in several regions in Hungary for quite a long time.[67]

In comparison with practices at the time, the court gave the principal defendant a relatively light sentence of one year in prison and three years of probation. In the cases of the other defendants, the court brought the proceedings to an end without establishing guilt or issuing sentences. The court argued that Mrs. P. was facing financial difficulties (her husband earned only 1,200 forints a month) and that "she committed the offenses at the requests of women seeking her help, and not for business." The court did not enforce any penalties for the rest of the accused because "the Council of Ministers' directive states that from July 1, 1956, a pregnant woman is entitled to terminate a pregnancy, so in the view of the court the offense is of such minor significance that even the lightest sentence seems superfluous."[68] The same argument could have been used in the 1957 proceedings against Mrs. Albert B. and her alleged accomplices, but it was not. One reason for this may have been that by 1959 abortion was much more acceptable than it was two years earlier, when one of the defendants received a two-year jail sentence. The other explanation is much more down-to-earth: the defendant in the previous trial was held responsible for a woman's death.

The more severe sentence issued in the course of the proceedings in 1962 should not be interpreted as a sign that abortion had come to be seen as a more serious crime at the time. Rather, the state condemned Mrs. Mátyás N. for having performed abortions using "quacksalver methods and almost medieval tools" that were "dangerous for society" and that caused many women to be hospitalized. The court also considered the fact that Mrs. N. allegedly had an "appropriate income" and "performed some of the abortions out of greed" an exacerbating circumstance (which meant that she received payment for the perfomed abortions). Accordingly, Mrs. Mátyás N. was sentenced to eighteen months in prison.[69] Thus in this case the state sought not only to exercise control over the practice of abortion but also to oversee the health of women seeking abortions.

Conclusion

According to a 1960 survey of 26,000 women conducted with questionnaires in Hungary, economically active women generally wished to have smaller families. The income of the family did not affect the birth of the first child, but the decision to have a second child and income level were inversely related—that is, the lower a family's income the more likely they were to have a second child.[70] While income could have an important effect on the number of abortions sought in Sztálinváros, the overlapping interests of the local families and the administration were a more important factor in the high number of abortions.

In Sztálinváros for most families the family-based economy ended in the 1950s because most of the positions were given to husbands, and thus their wives, who usually could not get a job, became unemployed housewives. Children younger than fourteen were not permitted to work. Kin or nonkin strangers living with large, extended families was a very rare occurrence, even in the South Side. Most families in the cities lived in small family units. Only 11.2 percent of families shared their residences with relatives in Sztálinváros in 1960.[71]

After 1953 and especially after 1956, the wages of the husbands were increasing, and many cheaper consumer goods became available, mostly because of the legitimization campaigns of the new governments (Imre Nagy and, after 1956, the Kádár regime).[72] Within this "family consumer economy" as Louise Tilly and Joan Scott have argued, the family was centered on collecting and consuming the goods that had become available.[73] Consequently, after applying successfully to the City Council for an apartment (for which usually two or three children in one family were enough), there was no other reason to have more children. The family's consumption level could not rise because of more children, it could only fall. This family model based on consumption patterns seemed to be more reliable as a support for the regime than the other one based on economic production, and the state subsidized this family model with various forms of family allowances in the 1960s (in Hungarian, this is referred to as *családi pótlék*, meaning quite simply "family allowance").[74]

The families and the state had overlapping interests during the stabilization of the renewed regime. Accordingly, new factories for female workers were created in Sztálinváros, because the policymakers realized that women (and the family as the new consumer) needed more places to work and not more children. The "family consumer economy" had the support of the state, which allowed abortions in order to ensure that the family would not become so large as to be economically unviable. The portrayals of breadwinning husbands and fashionable housewives in the local newspaper after the mid-1950s not only exemplified the popularized constructions of the policymakers but also demonstrated the willingness of the Stalinists to compromise, as they sought now to build a more stable society than the one that had emerged in the tumultuous years of the early 1950s. The rise in the standard of living at the end of the 1950s did not encourage childbearing, but rather offered families opportunities to adapt more rapidly to the widely propagated consumer norms and habits associated with the new urban lifestyle.

Abortion was overseen by several parties: husbands and partners, the state, and physicians. A woman who sought to escape this oversight undertook the risk of serious legal consequences. Prior to the liberalization of abortion in 1956, at least 100,000 abortions were performed every year in Hungary. Demographers contend that according to official data one out of every two women in Hungary had an abortion in the second half of the twentieth century, and most of them did so before the pill became widely available in the 1970s. Legal abortion in the local hospital became an everyday practice among all social strata of the city. However, although abortion had been legalized, it did not become publicly acceptable. The legalization of abortion and the public treatment of the issue itself became important elements of a power hierarchy founded on gender roles in which motherhood remained a woman's primary social obligation.

Because of the transformation of the subjective image of female roles, the prevalence of birth control depended primarily on the number of children a mother already had. The growth in the use of birth control and the decline in interest in starting a family (both of which were due primarily to a sense of instability) stemmed essentially from the transformation of the frameworks of family life and changes that took place in the structure of families as they gradually adapted to the urban environment and lifestyle. The only relationship between family planning and standard of living was that as incomes rose the number of children declined. In terms of birth control, Sztálinváros was "rural," whereas with regard to childbirth it was an "urban" settlement,[75] where abortion was virtually the only means of birth control in widespread use.[76]

In addition to the high abortion rate, Sztálinváros was also seen as a city of divorcees.[77] The high number of divorces notwithstanding, a remarkably large proportion of the city's inhabitants were married, which was due in part to the system of housing distribution and in part to the rapid rate of remarriage.[78] In Sztálinváros society, which had undergone dramatic shifts tied to social and geographical mobility, the actual structures of families and the ever-shifting relationships of family members to one another corresponded less and less to the static image of marriage and the family fashioned by the state. The residents of the city, however, were able to shape this static image, especially the women, who had always been more likely to file for divorce than the men.[79] How can we understand the growing number of divorces in the context of the consuming families in "the most socialist city" in Hungary?

Notes

1. FML, f. XXV-24-a, Criminal proceedings, b. 5, unit III. 144/1959, Proceedings against Mrs. István P. and accomplices on the charge of feticide (hereinafter, Mrs. István P. and accomplices).

2. Ibid., Testimony of Rozália P.

3. Cf. Lapidus, *Women in Soviet Society*, 239; McLellan, *Love in the Time of Communism*, 58.

4. On the history of motherhood and the mystification of the mother–child relationship, see Badinter, *Mother Love*.

5. The prohibition of abortion did not stop falling birthrates in the Soviet Union either. See Goldman, *Women, the State and Revolution*, 291–93.

6. Cf. the representation of women in Nowa Huta, Lebow, *Unfinished Utopia*, 98–101.

7. Cf. Pető, "Women's Rights in Stalinist Hungary."

8. Beginning in the 1960s, the interrogation of the mystification of motherhood was a central element of the second wave of the women's movement, and this contributed to a shift in the polemics on abortion. Baber and Allen, *Women and Families*, 102–25, 145–46.

9. Even if data analyzed so far were almost exclusively of a demographic nature. See Pongrácz, "A Ratkó-korszak."

10. Kamarás, "Terhességmegszakítások Magyarországon." For one of the most comprehensive studies on the topic, see Kamarás, *Terhesség–megszakítások–tanulmányok*.

11. Ministry of Health Directive no. 8100-2/1953. For a detailed presentation of the 1952–53 population policy, see Moingl, *Az 1952–1953. évi népesedéspolitikai program*.

12. Ministerial Resolution no. 1047/1956, June 3, 1956, in Miltényi, "Népesedéspolitikánk néhány kérdése."

13. Lapidus, *Women in Soviet Society*, 114; Goldman, *Women, the State and Revolution*, 293.

14. A 1964 study shows that this was the primary incentive in two-thirds of infanticide cases. Raskó, *A női bűnözés*, 451.

15. FML, f. XXV-24-a, Criminal proceedings, b. 1, 1954–56, Éva M. infanticide, 453/1955, Testimony of Mrs. István H. (emphasis added).

16. Ibid., Record of evidence, June 22, 1955.

17. Tárkány Szücs, *Magyar jogi népszokások*, 116, 212. After the liberalization of abortion the number of court decisions in cases of infanticide and child abandonment significantly decreased: between 1922 and 1944 the annual average of guilty verdicts numbered fifty-four, between 1951 and 1955 it was fifty-eight, and in the period of 1958–62 it was "only" twenty-nine. A 1964 study shows that the majority of perpetrators (more than half) lived in villages or moved to urban areas from villages (80 percent of the perpetrators). The most common means (as the case above indicates) was drowning. More than half of the crimes involved drowning (and the most common method of drowning was simply delivery in the outhouse, toilet, or a bucket). Raskó, *A női bűnözés*, 441, 459–60.

18. Tietze and Lehfeldt, "Legal Abortion in Eastern Europe."

19. Klinger, "Magyarország népesedése."

20. Barsy and Miltényi, "A művi vetélések kérdése, " estimate the number of concealed abortions at an annual 100,000 between 1950 and 1952. Klinger, "Magyarország népesedése"; Miltényi, "Népesedéspolitikánk néhány kérdése," 17–21.

21. FML, f. XXIII-502, b. 11, January 12, 1956; August 18, 1956; b. 13., April 12, 1957.

22. Ibid.; FML, f. XXIII-510, b. 2, July 20, 1954.

23. FML, f. XXIII-510, b. 3, January 14, 1957.

24. FML, f. XXIII-502, b. 13, June 21, 1957. Report on social conditions in Sztálinváros.

25. FML, f. XXIII-502, b. 16, June 26, 1959.

26. FML, f. XXIII-510, b. 4, December 23, 1960.

27. FML, f. XXIII-510, b. 3. October 14, 1958; and October 20, 1958.

28. FML, f. XXIII-502, b. 13, June 21, 1957. Report on social conditions in Sztálinváros.

29. At the time this was a below average income.

30. FML, f. XXIII-510, b. 3, January 7, 1958; January 11, 1958.

31. FML, f. XXIII-502, b. 18, November 22, 1960.

32. Ibid. Cf. the data for Poland in Fidelis, *Women, Communism, and Industrialization*, 196; for the Soviet Union, in Goldman, *Women, the State and Revolution*, 279. The 1960 Sztálinváros statistics approximately match the 1957 national data. More than 40 percent of the abortions performed in the countryside involved mothers of three or more children. Barsy and Miltányi, "A művi vetélések kérdése." Hirschler, "Hozzászólás."

33. FML, f. XXIII-502, June 21, 1957.

34. *Sztálinvárosi Hírlap*, June 28, 1957, 4.

35. Ibid., January 25, 1957, 2.

36. Ibid., January 29, 1957, 3.

37. Ibid., January 25, 1957, 2.

38. Ibid., January 29, 1957, 2.

39. Ibid., February 8, 1957, 4.

40. József Karalyos, the photographer for *Ifjúsági Magazin* (Youth magazine, a socialist tabloid intended for youth), recalls the practice of the editorial staff writing the letters to the editor. Tóth and Murai, *Szex és szocializmus*, 63–64.

41. In the Soviet Union changes with regard to this subject were also indicated by the publication of letters to the editor that struck a new tone. Lapidus, *Women in Soviet Society*, 113.

42. *Sztálinvárosi Hírlap*, February 5, 1957, 2.

43. Ibid., June 13, 1958, 6.

44. Ibid., November 4, 1958, 2.

45. FML, f. XXIII-510, b. 4, September 20, 1958, Dr. Imre Péntek, Chief medical officer.

46. FML, f. XXIII-510, b. 4, May 22, 1959.

47. FML, f. XXIII-502, b. 16, June 26, 1959.

48. MNL OL. f. 288–41,unit 191, October 25, 1972. 5.

49. Acsády and Klinger, "A termékenység, a családtervezés."

50. K., M., Review of Tietze, Christopher, "The Condom as a Contraceptive," 395. Between 1957 and 1959 the sale or distribution of some contraceptive devices considered effective increased (for example, the number of condoms sold increased from 4,500,000 to 6,000,000), and the use of other birth control devices decreased. Miltényi, "Művi vetélések Magyarországon az 1957–1959";,Miltényi, "Népesedéspolitikánk néhány kérdése," 22.

51. Barsy and Miltényi, "A művi vetélések kérdése."

52. FML, f. XXV-24-a, Criminal proceedings, b. 5, 1959. III. 144, Mrs. István P. and accomplices, Testimony of Mrs. István P. and Rozália P.

53. Miltényi and Szabady, "Az abortuszhelyzet Magyarországon."

54. FML, f. XXV-24-a, Criminal proceedings, b. 10, Mrs. István P. and accomplices, 1962, III, 116; Proceedings against Mrs. Mátyás N. and accomplices on the charge of feticide.

55. According to the 1957–58 National Survey, the most common explanation women gave for using birth control was the desire to limit the number of children because of "financial difficulties" (38 percent) or "housing problems." Among the individual subjective motives, the proportion of women who stated that their husbands did not want children was remarkably high (10 percent). Raics and Árvay, "A terhesség művi megszakítása."

56. Mrs. István P. and accomplices, Testimony of Mrs. János H.

57. Clients of Mrs. István P. came from the Technikum District. Mrs. Mátyás N. "practiced" in the L-buildings and Mrs. Albert B. in May 1 Street. Mrs. Mátyás N. and accomplices. *Sztálinvárosi Hírlap*, January 25, 1957, 2; and January 29, 1957, 3.

58. Mrs. István P. and accomplices. Testimony of Mrs. P. at the hearing.

59. According to her testimony at the trial she had had five or six.

60. Mrs. István P. and accomplices. Testimony of Mrs. Béla H.

61. Mrs. István P. and accomplices. Testimony of Rozália P.

62. Mrs. István P. and accomplices. Testimony of Mrs. László Gy.

63. Mrs. Mátyás N. and accomplices. March 3, 1962.

64. Mrs. István P. and accomplices. Trial records. May 14, 1959. Testimony of Mrs. István P.

65. Mrs. István P. and accomplices. Trial records. May 14, 1959. Testimony of Mrs. István P.

66. Mrs. Mátyás N. and accomplices. Testimony of Aranka F. February 10, 1962.

67. Valuch, *Magyarország társadalomtörténete*, 35; Gémes, *A népi születésszabályozás*.

68. Mrs. István P. and accomplices. Decision no. III. 144 / 1959 / 5.

69. Mrs. Mátyás N. and accomplices. Decision no. III. 116 / 1962 / 3.

70. Miltényi, "A születéskorlátozás szociális és lélektani háttere."

71. *1960. évi népszámlálás*, 167.

72. For more on the rise in workers' incomes, on which the "consolidation" of the new regime was based, see Pittaway, *The Workers' State*, 233.

73. Tilly and Scott, *Women, Work and Family*, 176. For an assessment of this in Hungary, see Gyáni, "Patterns of Women's Work in Hungary"; and Nagy, "A nők keresőtevékenysége Budapesten."

74. Horváth, *Két emelet boldogság*, 169–84.

75. There were more pregnant women in provincial cities than in villages in 1960, and the lower birthrates in the cities were due only to the significantly higher proportion of induced abortions. Miltényi, "A születéskorlátozás szociális és lélektani háttere".

76. At the time, legal abortion (i.e., performed by physicians employed by the state) was also the most widely used means of birth control in other East European countries. Lapidus, *Women in Soviet Society*, 299.

77. Miskolczi, *Város lesz csakazértis*, 253.

78. High marriage and divorce rates were also seen in Poland during the period of rapid industrialization. Cf. Fidelis, *Women, Communism, and Industrialization*, 175.

79. This was the case in many countries, including the German Democratic Republic; see McLellan, *Love in the Time of Communism*, 77.

6   Divorce

> I will be sad, because I long for a neat, warm home, a pure life, love, and at such times, if I close my eyes, I see the gleam of your wedding ring. This gleam haunts me, and the fear of the future disturbs me. I want you to burn my letters. I'm afraid one day your wife will discover them, and I think that would create a big scandal.

THESE LINES WERE written by a married man's lover in 1954.[1] Naturally there was a scandal, but only years later, in 1957. Having discovered that her husband had had several lovers, the wife filed for divorce at a time when they still shared an apartment on paper but were living separately. (Many "separated couples" continued to share an apartment after a divorce because the state housing policies did not enable them to get two apartments instead of one.) In her petition she cited serious physical abuse she had suffered by her husband's hand, not his affairs. The story of divorce may seem ordinary, but there are innumerable variations. In the case of this particular story there were adequate grounds (lovers, physical abuse) for the courts and public opinion to consider it necessary to dissolve the marriage. However, several marriages were not dissolved in spite of such circumstances.

In Hungary in the decades following World War II the number of divorces rose significantly primarily in industrial cities, in particular in the new "socialist" cities. This chapter shows that the rise in divorce rates was caused not only by the increased acceptability of divorce in general among more layers of society but also by the changing expectations of state institutions concerning gender roles within the family. Divorce suits submitted by attorneys contain portrayals of women as relatively independent members of society, and of course the primary purpose of these suits was to persuade the courts to grant the divorce, so naturally they had to meet the expectations of the judges. The more the courts expected the women of the city to seem independent, the more independent they seemed in the courts.

Although the institution of divorce had seemingly been liberalized under socialism, it was nonetheless assessed negatively by the state, as indicated by judicial practices in divorce cases in the immediate aftermath of World War II. Divorce cases indirectly allow for a study of the conflicts considered worth presenting to the courts by spouses. Furthermore, they reveal how the state-propagated image of the "ideal family" influenced the arguments used by the parties to a divorce.

Couples who were seeking a divorce accommodated themselves to the changes in state expectations and the discourses used in the courts, which made divorce possible for far more people than it was earlier. Gail Savage argues that the legal system can itself facilitate the spread of divorce.[2] However, this was not the only factor that led to a rise in divorce rates. The language used by those seeking a divorce in Sztálinváros also shifted as it adapted to the change in the expectations of the state, and this too contributed to the increasing number of divorces. In the early 1950s, the state institutions regarded divorce as a grave sin, but by the end of the decade this was no longer the case, and thus the courts were not unduly hesitant to take the final step and bring a marriage to a legal end.

This chapter explores the changes in the narratives and language used by the courts and the wives in divorce files, as well as the ways in which the residents of the city were able to accommodate to a new language by repressing family relations. As I demonstrate, the courts expected descriptions of women in the files submitted in divorce cases as increasingly emancipated members of society who shared responsibilities as income earners and homemakers. The divorce courts were one of the most popular state institutions, alongside the registrar in Sztálinváros, and both were used by the residents to get help either in registering a marriage before applying for an apartment or in solving domestic conflicts. Paradoxically, however, the divorce courts intended to strengthen and stabilize the families in Sztálinváros by showing them the "proper" way of life, in which women have the right not only to care for the household and children but also to work. Thus, like many other state institutions, the divorce courts also had "didactic functions," and both the courts and the couples seeking a divorce were capable of learning each other's expectations. The reconstruction of the family and its new forms "as a key instance in the 'search for normality'" was a widespread phenomenon in postwar Europe.[3] The most striking feature, however, was the new language used by wives in the courts, which expected them to use this language of complaint about the patriarchal attitudes of husbands.

"Socialist Morals"

In 1894, the Hungarian state made divorce possible by accepting Act XXXI, which remained in effect until 1952 with only slight modifications.[4] The new law on families, which was shaped largely by the conservative Stalinist model, was adopted in 1952 (IV. Law), and it included provisions on divorce. According to this law, a court was only entitled to grant a divorce "in cases in which, because of the lasting and severe worsening of the marriage, there is no chance for the restoration of married life." This law compelled the courts to "discover" the "real" grounds for the collapse of a marriage, thereby making it the court's responsibility to intrude into the intimate lives of people seeking divorces in order to find necessary grounds for separation. In other words, the court had to find fault in the marriage before granting a divorce, and there was no such thing as no-fault divorce.

Consequently, the court records, which contained dutiful investigations of "deviant" behavior, led demographers to fascinating conclusions—for example, that the incidence of alcoholism among married couples grows with the number of children. In cases of couples with four or more children, one-third of the divorces were granted on grounds of "alcoholism," but alcoholism was the alleged cause of divorce in only 12 percent of the cases involving couples without children. Naturally, this did not mean that the more children a family raised, the more the parents drank. Rather, it was presumably related to the fact that among groups in which birthrates were higher (generally groups of lower social status), alcoholism was more frequently cited as grounds for divorce. The reason for this was that the parties would cite alcoholism, even if it was not an issue, in order to find a fault and satisfy the rules of the court so that they would be granted a divorce. This also suggests that the growth in the number of people who were characterized as "deviant" in the demographic data was merely a product of the use by people seeking a divorce of terms that would meet the expectations of the courts.

Often the courts sought forms of "deviant" behavior behind the reasons given for dissolving a marriage. Since the attorneys were seeking to persuade the state to grant a divorce, they had to conform to the expectations of the court, so they adapted their arguments to these expectations. It is therefore not surprising that studies of the causes of divorce often concluded, on the basis of the decision of the court, that the divorces had been caused by the "deviant" behavior of at least one of the two parties.[5] In his 1965 study András Klinger identified marriages contracted "at an early age without due consideration" as the primary explanation for the high proportion of divorces in Hungary, and he also added "excessive alcoholism" and "abuse" that was frequently due to alcohol consumption as causes.[6]

By establishing exemplary norms concerning the ideal family life, the state intervened in the practices of divorce through the courts. This is illustrated by the fact that in several cases divorce was not granted on account of the person's social status. In one of its rulings rejecting a university professor's petition for divorce, the Supreme Court offered the following reasoning:

> As a highly cultured individual, the petitioner is rightfully expected by society to conform to state and social discipline and fulfill his moral duties. On account of his profession, the petitioner is to set an example of the rise of moral standards in society. It is possible that the love he now feels for a woman twenty years his junior has emotionally estranged him from the respondent and he therefore finds cohabitation with her difficult. But precisely because of his

erudition, he should know that marriage not only secures rights but also entails obligations, and in order to fulfill these obligations he must make the sacrifice of holding on to his family, even if he is emotionally attached to another woman.[7]

While the occasionally sarcastic phrasing of the above citation captures the clerk of court's flair for style, the ruling was, quite simply, a rejection. According to "socialist norms," an extramarital relationship was "irresponsible," and in particular people of higher social status (especially those belonging to the "intelligentsia") should remain aware that they cannot violate this rule, for their marriages were supposed to be exemplary.

The term *socialist norm* refers essentially to all the concepts and ideals by which the authorities attempted to "civilize" the "lower classes." While this was by no means an exceptional practice on the part of an authoritarian or even democratic government (one could cite numerous analogous endeavors in Western Europe before 1945), in the case of socialist Hungary the effort to civilize the population, which was centered on *kul'turnost'*, was based on a Soviet model.[8] As I have demonstrated in the previous chapters of this book, there was a distinctive conservative turn in Hungary, which, together with the de-Stalinization campaign, propagated essentially traditional values after 1953 and 1956, such as traditional gender roles for women, which included cooking, raising children, and dressing fashionably. Thus the meaning of the term *socialist norm* continuously shifted. By the end of the 1950s, it was far more traditional from the perspective of gender roles and family life than it was at the beginning of the decade.

This is clearly demonstrated in a petition for divorce submitted by a Stakhanovite man who contended that the disorderly state of his family life was an impediment to his performance at work. The Supreme Court rejected his request with the following explanation: "As a valuable workman educated by the People's Republic the petitioner is bound not only to build socialism on the production front, but also to assert the norms of socialist morals in his domestic life. This means carefully protecting the purity of family life and remaining devoted to the family. And if these emotions rise to the surface in the petitioner and he ceases his impermissible relationship, the restoration of domestic harmony will not be hopeless. Indeed, this is the primary obligation of the petitioner toward his family and our society."[9]

Thus holding a family together and preventing divorce appear as "social obligations" in the court discourse. In the 1950s, the persecution of churches by the state made it almost impossible for churches to give an opinion concerning, for instance, the question of divorce. As a partial consequence of this, sometimes the court acted as the patron saint of families and refused to grant divorce for "demographic" reasons: "Today the husband may believe that he is unable to break up with his new partner and return to his family. However, the court does not dissolve the marriage, for it knows by experience that marriages of such great disparity in age as the one the husband is planning with his partner are very rarely successful." The same court decision indirectly declared the system of child support insufficient, and also used this as a reason for not granting divorce: "Children born to married couples require paternal guidance. How does the husband, who claims to love his children, wish to provide this guidance? Does he believe that child support is sufficient? These questions automatically lead to the conclusion that the husband did not thoroughly consider his intention of dissolving the marriage." In its pronouncement, the court also condemned the husband's new partner: "the court also wishes to provide the husband's partner with an opportunity to consider what she has done to the life of a family with four children."[10]

In most cases one finds, behind the "most common grounds for divorce," the basic schema expected by the court in order for it to dissolve a marriage. Erika Rév, who relies in her book on her own experience as a judge, believes that in the 1950s and 1960s the courts treated some complaints as virtual guarantees of a grant of divorce. These included alcoholism, permanent separation, lasting extramarital relationships, and abusive treatment.[11] Roughly half of the reasons given for requesting a divorce in 1957 conformed to the expectations of the court. One explanation for this was that the attorneys often deliberately exaggerated these reasons so that the court would dissolve the marriage. On the other hand, these "causes" were the ones considered the least forgivable according to official "Socialist" morals, because they were problems that would disappear with the coming of communism, or at least so the officials contended, and possibly even believed.

Divorce at the City Council

As a follow-up to its attempts to present the regime as sensitive to social issues and tensions, the Sztálinváros City Council started to deal with divorces in the city as of 1956, and every year the local court submitted a report to the council on the city's divorce cases. These reports demonstrate how the renewed state policies concerning families adopted a new interpretation of divorce and how socialist forms of divorce were accepted as social practice. In its 1956 report to the City Council the Sztálinváros City Court, acting in defense of the family, arrived at the conclusion that the underlying cause of the majority of divorces was "irresponsible" behavior:

> Unfortunately there are many people who, often after long years of married life, destroy domestic peace and abandon their families without any real reason, in most cases for some passing sensual craving. Such cases, we can affirm, are almost everyday affairs at the court. In such instances the court attempts to reconcile the spouses and make them aware of the responsibilities they have to their children and each other. Unfortunately, these efforts rarely yield positive results. Nevertheless, the attention of the party and social organizations must

Figure 6.1. A Sztálinváros couple portrayed in the movie *Kiskrajcár* (Little Denier, 1953, directed by Márton Keleti).

be called to this unwholesome and common phenomenon so that we can fight it through education and other means.[12]

The court itself realized that the function of a substantial proportion of divorces was to bring an end to legally recognized relationships (i.e., marriages) that were no longer part of actual everyday life and no longer corresponded to the ways in which families lived, but nonetheless constituted a hindrance to everyday affairs, for instance, preventing people from obtaining permanent residences. Consequently, these cases were treated differently from those in which one of the parties objected to the dissolution of the marriage.[13]

As was the case in other industrialized cities, in Sztálinváros the divorce rates were rather high. According to the 1956 judicial report, the court dissolved 35 marriages a month on average, which means an annual average of 420 divorces per year (over the course of the following year 105 couples married in the city, but most of the families came to the city as married couples).[14] In 1957, petitions were filed for the dissolution of 200 marriages that had been concluded in Sztálinváros (this number does not include the significant number of petitions for divorce filed in Sztálinváros involving marriages that had been concluded elsewhere).[15]

Naturally, the high divorce rate in Sztálinváros may partially be due to the quite high proportion of married adults in the city's population, which is higher than the national average (three out of four people were married).[16] At the time, divorce rates were highest in Budapest and in cities inhabited primarily by miners, while with a few exceptions they were low in cities categorized as provincial.[17] The especially high divorce rate in Sztálinváros may also have been because divorce was always more common among younger couples. In the 1950s this tendency became more pronounced, as did the drop in average ages at the time of marriage, presumably not coincidentally.[18]

Two out of three causes of divorce can be traced back to the transformation of families into consumer units, and this figure differed strikingly from the "national average." The Sztálinváros court attributed divorces to three major reasons: "financial difficulties," housing problems, and "irresponsibility."[19] This is in contrast to the conclusion of former judge Erika Rév concerning the national average. According to Rév, alcoholism, extramarital relationships, and abusive treatment were the three most important causes of divorce.

The increase in the number of divorces granted on grounds of "extramarital relationships" and "alcoholism" was in all likelihood not due solely to the decisions of the attorneys to craft petitions that conformed to the expectations of the courts. For example, in cases involving property rights the question of who was "at fault" in a divorce was of major significance. A husband considered an "alcoholic" had very little chance of keeping his position as the primary leaseholder in an apartment. Consequently, the petitions submitted by divorce seekers contained numerous signs of exaggeration. Attorneys' documents reveal that the story told by the petitioner was modified by the attorney to highlight factors that would be considered "well-founded causes" by the courts.[20] As close study of the divorce files reveals, however, whereas in the course of the proceedings the husbands would often blame their wives for having neglected their "traditional" duties, wives blamed their husbands for failing to help with precisely these same tasks. They frequently contended that their husbands "refused to help with household chores and did not participate in childrearing."

The Complaints of Wives and Husbands

The complaints made by husbands regarding their wives' failure to see to their domestic tasks seem to have been accepted by the court, since petitions drafted by attorneys are full of references to "negligence of the duties of a housewife." One infuriated foundry man stated that his wife "left a note saying that she had arranged food for me, which was a big bowl of cumin soup," and he added, "While we were living together my wife turned out to be untidy and indolent, she did not perform her duties, did not prepare proper food, and was always out."[21] The following complaint embodies what a presumably average Sztálinváros husband would have expected of his wife in regard to traditional domestic duties:

> My wife neglected household chores. She never packed an afternoon snack for me. . . . She shuddered at the thought of doing household tasks, never performed them, and I was the servant at home. I did the shopping, did the dishes, cleaned the house, and cooked, just to spare her. She went to the hairdresser, the beautician, and recently she pushed the task of doing the laundry on me as well. . . . She lived an unbelievably extravagant life; from stockings to pants all her clothes were made of nylon. . . . She did not care for the children at all.[22]

The attorney made these complaints the focus of the husband's petition, which implies that such pleas sometimes influenced the court's decision.

Although rarely, on some occasions wives would reprove their husbands' "callousness" toward the children. The attorney for one wife in a divorce case included the following detail from her account in the petition: "Shortly after I left the hospital my husband started complaining that the baby's crying annoyed him, and he did not like my physically weak condition either. So on May 31 he sent me packing, back to my mother." However, even this petition emphasizes first and foremost "abuse" and only then "callousness" as grounds for divorce. This indicates that courts did not consider a husband's failure to adapt to family life and participate in managing the household and rearing the children "absolute grounds" for divorce.[23]

In the statistics the amount of time that passed between the wedding and the divorce determined whether a case was categorized as "divorce as a consequence of impetuous marriage." However, if one examines the actual primary sources pertaining to the cases, a far more complex image emerges. Cohabitation prior to marriage was by no means uncommon in Sztálinváros. In addition, in several cases the marriage of a husband and wife who had lived together for just a short period of time was only dissolved years after separation because the parties did not feel that divorce was necessary. Thus the actual divorce proceedings did not significantly delay the dissolution of a marriage, since according to court records in 1956 and the preceding years 90 percent of divorce cases were closed within six months of submission of a petition (three-fourths of the cases were closed within less than three months). Only 1.5 percent of the cases took more than a year to close.[24]

In October 1952 Mrs. István S. married an unskilled worker two years younger than she. They lived together until October 1954 and then separated. They did not have children and the husband did not contribute to household expenses, but she only filed for divorce in February 1957 because by then she was living with a man she intended to marry. (Her husband had also been living with another woman since 1955.) Thus the marriage seems to have been quite short. The period of time in which the couple lived under the same roof as husband and wife was shorter than the period of time between their separation and the filing for divorce. According to the wife's account, the husband's transfer to a job in another town also contributed to their separation. However, this marriage cannot be considered "impetuous" because the spouses had lived together for three years before getting married. This demonstrates that in certain walks of life cohabitation may have played a more crucial role in starting a family than marriage. For example, at age twenty-five Mrs. István S. moved in with her future husband and lived together with him for three years before they actually married. They separated after only two years of marriage. Then she lived—as a "married woman"—with another man for three more years until her divorce was granted, and she presumably filed for divorce only because she intended to marry her partner.[25] Although divorce is generally seen as a termination of family life, several separations were not "ends" but "beginnings" for those who fled from the pressures of institutionalized family life.

Childless couples often cited the "failure to produce offspring" in court. This suggests that reasoning based on the notion of the reproductive role of the family conformed to the strict conditions set by the court. Preparation for "mandatory motherhood,"[26] that is, that a woman or rather a wife must bear children, has always been and continues to be part of the socializing process for women. A marriage that failed to produce offspring was considered dysfunctional by the husband, the wife, the people in their surroundings, and even the court. In one petition for divorce a woman wrote of the difficulties she faced because of her husband's infertility:

> From the moment I learned about his illness my husband changed. He continuously humiliated me, and kept repeating that this marriage was not worth anything, because sooner or later I would cheat on him. He reproached me for wanting children more than he did, even though I never brought up his infertility against him. My sense of myself as a woman was hurt by the idea that we were not blessed with children because of my infertility, and from the moment I became aware of my husband's illness I instinctively sensed that our life together was unable to fulfill the real duty of the institution of marriage.[27]

Thus childlessness could be presented as "an absolute grounds for divorce," because in this case the woman founded her argument on a child-centered concept of marriage. This cause of divorce, which was traditionally accepted socially and legally, was also part of the pronatalist state policies. Thus the expectations of the court and the complaints filed by people seeking a divorce in this case overlapped. The state institutions insisted that the country needed more children and the wives echoed this view by complaining about their husbands' infertility.

A childless woman was also less dependent on her husband because her own income was generally sufficient. As a matter of fact, descriptions of marriages in divorce petitions often presented husbands as more of a burden than a help in caring for children. This was the case for Mrs. László T.:

> In . . . April 1954 my son was born. From that moment on I saw my husband as useless. I spent every moment with my son. His birth entailed additional expenses, so I told my husband that I could not afford to make more money available to him. When he was in the army barracks my husband started gambling,[28] which required a lot of money. Since I could not support him financially, he started borrowing sums of 50 and 100 forints from our neighbors, which eventually I had to repay. On such occasions we always had ugly fights. In the end he reproached me for caring more for my child than I did for him. . . . On one Sunday evening, November 14, he took my last penny, so the next day I could not even buy milk for my son.[29]

Extramarital relationships were presented as "absolute grounds for divorce," as the Stalinist divorce courts had resolved to make putting an end to male promiscuity one of their responsibilities.[30] However, some case reports suggest that it was not uncommon for spouses, including husbands, to forgive infidelity, even in the courts. Indeed, one husband was willing to allow his wife to have a lover simply to save the marriage. Before Gábor Sz. finally filed for divorce, his wife had been living with her lover for months. According to him, "My wife was struggling with herself that is clear, because she was unable to decide between her impetuous love and her children and their father. She got to the point that on May 23 she ingested poison to kill herself, and on our way home from Budapest to Sztálinváros she told me that I would not find much joy in her return, since she had poisoned herself.

Nevertheless, the two of them continued to live together for months, even though he was aware of her extramarital relationship.[31]

Extramarital relationships were the most common cause of divorce in Sztálinváros. Most of these relationships were not simply "impetuous affairs" or conflicts that arose because of a sudden passion or indulgence. Generally they were relationships (some of which involved cohabitation) that lasted for years, sometimes with the full awareness of the spouse. The petition for divorce was not always filed by the partners who had been "cheated on," but if they did request a divorce it was usually only when the unfaithful spouse had already moved out or they wanted to end the marriage anyway. Frequently marriages were only dissolved when one of the spouses cohabiting with someone in a separate household decided to remarry. At the time, this occasionally led to a kind of "bigamy" because people who had married in other parts of the country thought that these marriages would not be discovered when they remarried in Sztálinváros without having divorced their spouses.

"Occasional adultery" seems to have been viewed as a "forgivable sin" by the court, because no available divorce records indicate that divorce was sought on these grounds. In many cases the reason for this was that although many mothers had jobs they were still financially dependent on their husbands. "For the time being my client condones and forgives her husband's affairs—though not happily—and is waiting for him to realize that his place is by the side of his three children."[32] In other cases the husband held the title to the apartment, so the wife had to choose between becoming homeless with children or tolerating her husband's behavior. (If a wife did not have a workplace, she was unable to request an apartment through her employer. She had to turn to the council for assistance, but given the huge number of requests for apartments, she had little chance of success.) This was especially true of working men in Sztálinváros who entered into a marriage primarily to obtain an apartment. In her petition one wife who had been lured to Sztálinváros to help a man obtain an apartment offered the following account: "The few months that we spent living in harmony were merely due to his fascination with a young woman. When the attraction of a new lover was gone, my love virtually became merely a burden instead of part of the intimacy of married life. He already had an apartment, so the next question was how to get rid of me. The methods did not matter as long as they did not create a scandal. There was no scandal, but spiritually I was crushed, humiliated, elegantly dismissed, never to be taken back."[33]

The references to "harmony" and "intimacy" indicate that for the Sztálinváros courts these represented important elements of a marriage. In their petitions for divorce, wives often expressed their wish to find husbands who, breaking with traditional models, offered more help with household chores and child care. In contrast, in their petitions the husbands seemed to hope to find wives who tended to the housework, reared the children, and anticipated their husband's every need. The petitions submitted by husbands and wives were crafted to meet the expectations of the courts, even if they sometimes seemed to contradict each other. As far as the courts were concerned, they could justify their decisions with references both to overly flagrant transgression of traditional norms and exaggerated adherence to inherited models. In other words, a man could find himself faulted for having adopted an overly traditional approach to married life, while at the same time a woman might be criticized for having strayed too far from the traditional models.

Thus the Sztálinváros courts expressed their support both for women who were fighting for equal rights and for men who sought to preserve traditional gender roles. This represented a contradiction, although perhaps not as contradictory as it may seem at first glance. The court was simply more likely to grant a divorce if the two parties to the case cited problems allegedly brought about by the changing place of women in society. Problems that arose because of changes in gender roles could be presented to the courts as grounds for divorce. The courts thus contributed, at least for a time, to the preservation of traditional expectations concerning a woman's place, since a mere reference to the *absence* of change in gender roles—such as a woman's complaint regarding her husband's failure to do housework—was not sufficient to persuade the courts to grant a divorce. How did this influence the narratives and discursive modes used by people seeking a divorce, and how did it affect the portrayals they provided of their marriages in their submissions to the courts, whether the woman was presented as a victim or an independent actor? In what follows, I seek answers to these questions.

The Private Sphere before the Public Gaze

In some cases wives were almost completely dependent on their husbands, whether they had jobs or not. This does not mean that conflicts never arose regarding this question, but in most cases conflicts were "resolved" when the wife acquiesced, so they were rarely mentioned before the courts. Mrs. Elemér Zs. was a working wife, but the loss of her job following downsizing was one source of conflict in her marriage. However, she presented the problems so as to emphasize differences in worldview:

> In January 1957 I was dismissed as part of downsizing at the Engineering Head-quarters of the Stalin Ironworks and I became home-employed. My husband held it against me that I did not contribute to the family expenses and he had to support both me and my mother financially, and so he demanded complete obedience from us. Even when I did have a job he believed that since he was making more money he was entitled to order me around. On April 25, 1957, he caught his son praying with his grandmother. He threw a terrible tantrum and declared that he would not have his son learning prayers and my mother had better not go to church or pray. . . . Since then we have lived separately and have not reestablished our lives together as husband and wife.

Two weeks after her attorney had recorded the "state of affairs" the woman withdrew her petition for divorce, a decision that in all likelihood was prompted in part by her husband's intervention.[34] According to the wife, she had turned to the court as a last resort, and this had influenced her husband's conduct. The tolerance of religiousness as an acceptable explanation was a post-1956 development. Before 1956, one would not have been able to use religious belief as the foundation of an argument presented to the courts. Thus the expectations of the court helped families maintain a family life in which both of the spouses were working.

Consequently, one also comes across what might be characterized as "emancipated" attitudes in some representations of marriages. The Sztálinváros Court encouraged the attorneys for women to represent the wives not only as housewives who tended to housework, but also as independent, working women. Mrs. György

O. describes herself as someone who broke away from the traditions of her parents and, after she had divorced her first husband, she entered a new marriage based on love, equality, and mutual respect. She may have been more easily able to do this than Mrs. Elemér Zs. because she was better educated. She also had a relatively secure position at her workplace and at the time of her divorce she was already in a relationship with her future second husband. According to the account she gave at the attorney's office, she had found the traditional role of the wife unbearable.

> We were constantly fighting, our children did not hear anything but quarreling. Generally the main reason involved financial issues. My husband handled our family budget and he only gave me money for food, but never enough. My husband was a radio amateur and he devoted every moment of his life to this hobby. As soon as he came home he immediately began working on the radio. He never played with the children, and he never went anywhere with me. If I wanted to go out, he told me to feel free to go but he never joined me. Slowly this fully estranged me from him.[35]

Whereas in the first case the wife is presented as a victim, in the second she is portrayed as someone who acted independently and of her own will. Divergences in the narratives crafted by the lawyers of women seeking divorces were based first and foremost on references to family background, education, and the positions of wives in the workplace. A wife who had some education was able to present herself to the courts as someone who acted with a significant degree of independence far more persuasively than a woman with little or no education. She did not have to portray herself as a victim to convince the court to grant her a divorce. In contrast, a woman who had lost her job and was religious, or in other words was more attached to traditional values and lifestyles, almost had to characterize herself as a victim in the petition in order to achieve her goal, even if she quickly withdrew the petition. This also meant that the court expected women who had jobs and some education to depict themselves as better educated than uneducated women who were seeking a divorce. Furthermore, the courts sought so strengthen the double role of wives as workers who also tended to household duties.

Very few sources include information on the private sphere of married life. At divorce hearings parties reveal "secrets" to the court that one would otherwise find only in diaries and private letters. If perhaps indirectly and somewhat resembling a mosaic, divorce records and their narrative style offer an image of what spouses regarded as "normal" or "abnormal" in sexual relationships. Wives complained of "hot-blooded" husbands, much as husbands were tormented by "licentious" wives. At the same time, property rights issues were often causes for divorce allegedly grounded in problems with a couple's sexual life. Problems in sexual life could be represented also as grounds for divorce at the court. Mrs. Sándor Sz.

excused her own adultery by referring to her husband's attitude toward sex, and she represented their sexual life as a primary ground for divorce:

> I was twenty years old at the time [of our marriage] and my husband was twenty-eight. My husband was rather hot-blooded; he constantly desired sex, a desire I found difficult to satisfy. He often demanded that we have sex when I was menstruating, and he was very rude to me when I refused. . . . Because of my husband's forceful behavior I became pregnant on two other occasions, but I requested an abortion in both cases. . . . In the summer I had a crush on a man younger than me whom I believed I could love because his tenderness felt good. I spoke about him to my husband and added that although I would never even think of abandoning my two children, I did like this man. My husband attacked me, beating me so brutally that bruises were visible for days.[36]

According to the husband, who in his petition emphasized property rights, "Although the question is not closely tied to the problem, I wish to note that our sex life meant that I sought sexual satisfaction from her twice a week and this was absolutely sufficient for me. . . . the rest is all lies." Of course petitions for divorce do not offer an objective account of a couple's sex life, but they do shed some light on what was deemed "immoral" by the courts and in the public eye, and what could therefore be cited as possible grounds for divorce. After 1956, domestic violence was mentioned more often during divorce proceedings, and the failure of husbands to do work around the house was a common motif in the narratives of wives. This shows that although the traditional roles for women continued to be propagated after the mid-1950s, the courts intended to help women put an end to domestic abuse and mitigate the burdens they faced because of being expected to simultaneously hold jobs and maintain a household.[37]

In many cases various charges were alleged by the parties to a divorce only to ensure that following the dissolution of a marriage the other spouse would not be designated the proprietor of the apartment. Attorneys who represented wives seem to have preferred to emphasize sexual exploitation, which indicates that the court was likely to decide in favor of the wife on these grounds. Although the parties to a divorce probably had not heard of the legal concept of "domestic violence," it was one of the causes cited most frequently by their legal representatives in petitions submitted to the courts.

In her petition one wife provided a detailed description of the rough treatment she suffered at her husband's hand, and only then did it come to light that she was not merely filing for divorce but also wanted to take out a restraining order to prevent him from entering the apartment. Like the petition cited above, her account makes clear that wives and their attorneys considered it a woman's natural right to have a balanced sex life in her marriage. The absence of a "normal" sex life was presented as dysfunctional even if in the majority of existing marriages the conduct of a wife in intimate matters was subordinated to the will of her husband, so it could hardly have been considered "balanced." The prudishness of the times notwithstanding, in many of the petitions submitted to the court a satisfying sex life was seen as the cornerstone of a happy marriage.[38] In this case, the courts met the expectations of the couples for more open talk about a husband's and wife's sex life, and the courts also seemed to be more "enlightened" warriors in the cause of sexual equality.

In their petitions husbands only rarely stated that they found their sex lives unsatisfying. Husbands more often cited their wives' "licentiousness" or "domestic negligence" as a primary cause for divorce. For instance, in his petition Vince Cs. offered the following account:

> When I got married I had not known a woman before, and I had moral principles with regard to marriage. On the basis of these principles I found it offensive and insulting that my wife dared to lean out of the window wearing only a full slip and at her workplace dared to work in nothing more than a swimsuit in the presence of male coworkers. . . . I left my wife, and I had other sound reasons to do so, in addition to these. For example, she was untidy, neglected household duties, and she regularly failed to prepare a hot meal for me.[39]

The petition implies that in the eyes of the court a woman's "failure" to cook for a husband was a more definite sign of the disintegration of a marriage and more serious grounds for divorce than her refusal to sleep with him.

Differences in lifestyle also seem to have been considered acceptable grounds for divorce in the eyes of the court. This arose in a conflict (the crafting of which was partly the work of the attorney) between an urban man and a village-born woman for whom "family solidarity" was an important ideal. Two weeks after the wedding, the wife brought her brother and his wife into the apartment, followed later by her sister and the sister's two-year-old son.[40] Allegedly the apartment soon began to look like a flophouse and the husband's "anxiety" became so acute that he soon divorced his wife. Differences in occupational status were rarely cited in petitions for divorce, but references to practices deemed "rural" or "backward" increased, in contrast to the "urban" lifestyle. This does not necessarily mean that different backgrounds or different lifestyles necessarily caused genuine problems between spouses. It might simply indicate that these differences harmonized with the official discourse regarding the tensions between "rural" and "urban" life.

Conclusion

The difference between the legal and spontaneous process of separation and the tendency to solve marital and cohabitation problems without pursuing legal measures grew stronger as women began to earn their own incomes and a more urban lifestyle began to prevail. According to the 1960 census, despite the high number of divorces, the proportion of divorces was 1.2 percent among men and

2.3 percent among women.[41] This indicates that second marriages often began relatively soon after a divorce, which can only have been the case if legally married individuals had already begun cohabiting with someone else prior to divorce. The majority of divorces were followed by a new marriage, and divorced men were more likely to enter second marriages than divorced women.

The 1955 marriage statistics indicate that, in comparison with thirteen other European countries, Hungary had the highest proportion of second marriages in the total number of marriages.[42] In Hungary and in particular in Budapest and the industrial cities (i.e., Sztálinváros among others), divorce became a factor that deeply affected the forms of family life much earlier than it did in several other European countries. One fundamental reason for this was presumably that traditional roles (primarily those of husbands and wives) could not be adapted rapidly enough to keep pace with the ever-changing environment, which was being transformed by the effects of accelerated urbanization and industrialization. The frequency and gradual acceptance of divorce contributed to a profound shift in the image of the family. At the same time, an essentially negative view of divorce in general (a view that influenced judicial practices) continued to constitute an obstacle to couples seeking to bring their legal status (married or single) in line with their actual day-to-day family lives.

In everyday life the relationship between the "patriarchal" husband and the "overly emancipated" wife was by no means as rife with conflict as the documents submitted to the courts and shaped to meet their expectations might suggest. At the same time, the underlying problem in marriages that were founded on a notion of male "supremacy" or, in contrast, equal partnership may simply have been that husbands and wives who were increasingly earning their incomes independently of each other had divergent priorities when it came to family life and consumer habits.

However, due to contemporary notions of the functions of the family, judicial divorce practices did not afford parties much opportunity to describe their separation as a natural outcome of a marriage or a legal process that simply marked a new phase in their lives. Thus in the official discourse the increase in the number of divorces was cast as a symptom of the disintegration of family life allegedly caused by urbanization, industrialization, or "modernization." Anthropologist Nigel Rapport touches on this when he states that in an era of mass social mobility and migration the home and the family are easier to define in the context of continuous movement and transformation than as static notions.[43]

The diversity and transformation of the families that migrated to Sztálinváros in the 1950s and underwent unprecedented social change were characterized by dynamic interpersonal relations (cohabiting partners, divorcing couples) that contrasted starkly with the expectations and images of officially supported legal institutions at the beginning of the 1950s. Yet the system of state redistribution of housing encouraged residents of the "city of divorced couples," when at their places of work or submitting requests for housing, to describe their shifting relationships as static. In court cases the parties to a divorce were pressured to describe their marriages as an idyllic and stable state of affairs that had been upset by some unexpected "deviant" act, such as an affair, alcoholism, domestic abuse, or the scandalous behavior of a licentious wife. After the middle of the 1950s, the discourse on the institution of the family changed, and women searching for jobs or a better life without domestic violence found a forum in which they could express their needs: the divorce attorney and the divorce court. Because divorce became available to members of all social groups in Sztálinváros, women got an institution where they had the right to complain about the problems in their personal lives and the expectations that were placed on them. They also got a virtual shelter for their family life, namely, the possibility to file for divorce.

The language used in the petitions for divorce was crafted to meet the expectations of the courts. By accepting new grievances such as domestic violence as grounds for divorce, the court also provided spouses with new tools to protect the family. After the mid-1950s, the state adopted policies intended to nurture intimacy and harmony in family life. Accordingly, in the petitions for divorces in Sztálinváros family happiness and harmony became two of the most important things to be safeguarded. Thus, divorce became a tool to prevent the disintegration of family life by encouraging the "modernization" of family life. This meant putting an end to promiscuity, domestic violence, and alcoholism, giving wives a chance to have a workplace, encouraging husbands to take part in household chores, and providing a tool with which to get rid of the "most notorious" patriarchy. The didactic functions of the court could also be understood as a tool of kul'turnost', that is, a quest to educate and uplift families so that they might lead a proper life according to the "socialist norms." The courts appear to have been flexible enough in divorce cases to come to the aid of women, whether they were seeking more support for housework or help with the burdens they faced as members of the workforce, whichever happened to be necessary in the given case. The language of divorce in Sztálinváros was shaped both by the reloaded Stalinist policies regarding family life and by couples in court, which made it highly flexible and capable of safeguarding the family as a consumer unit.

Notes

1. FML, f. XXXI-18, b. 7, 8/13.
2. Savage, "Divorce and the Law," 500.
3. Cf. Betts, *Within Walls*, 89, 101.
4. Law of domestic relations. Nagy, "One Empire, Two States."

5. Department for Population Statistics and the Demographic Research Institute of the Hungarian Central Statistical Office representative data from 1957 and 1962 regarding grounds for divorce. The findings were published under the title *A válások okai*.

6. Klinger, "A válások okaira vonatkozó vizsgálat."

7. Klinger, *A válás*, 165–66.

8. For more on the origin of the "socialist norm" regarding marriage at this period, see Carlbäck, "Lone Mothers and Fatherless Children," 86–88.

9. Klinger, *A válás*, 165.

10. Ibid., 164.

11. Rév, *Válóperek krónikája*, 112.

12. FML, f. XXIII-502, b. 11, July 26, 1956. Report on the operation of the court.

13. Ibid.

14. FML, f. XXXIII-25, 1958.

15. FML, f. XXIII-502, b. 15, May 9, 1958. Report on the 1957 operation of the court.

16. Balázs, "A házasságkötések alakulása."

17. Klinger, *A válás*, 36–37.

18. Ibid., 40.

19. FML, f. XXIII-502, b. 11, July 26, 1956, Report on the operation of the court; b. 15, May 9, 1958. Report on the 1957 operation of the court.

20. FML, f. XXXI-18, Documents of Attorney Dr. Endre Tirpák.

21. FML, f. XXXI-18, b. 6, 5/2.

22. FML. f. XXXI-18. b. 9, Mrs. Mihály V.

23. FML, f. XXXI-18, b. 6, 5/13.

24. Klinger, *A válás*, 81. More than half of the divorced couples had not lived together as husband and wife for more than five years at the time of the divorce. *A válások okai*, 1965.

25. FML, f. XXXI-18, b. 1, 1/13.

26. See Gordon, *Women's Body, Women's Right* on this concept.

27. FML, f. XXXI-18, b. 1, 2/3.

28. He was doing his compulsory military service.

29. FML, f. XXXI-18, b. 5.

30. Cf. Goldman, *Women, the State and Revolution*, 341.

31. FML, f. XXXI-18, b. 6, 5/9.

32. FML, f. XXXI-18, b. 8.

33. FML, f. XXXI-18, b. 8. Mrs. Ádám Sz.

34. FML, f. XXXI-18, b. 6, 5/11.

35. FML, f. XXXI-18, b. 6, 5/16.

36. FML, f. XXXI-18, b. 7, 8/1.

37. The same was true in Poland and the German Democratic Republic in the 1950s and 1960s; see Betts, *Within Walls*, 110–11; Fidelis, *Women, Communism, and Industrialization*, 178.

38. E.g., FML, f. XXXI-18, b. 9, Mrs. Mihály V.

39. FML, f. XXXI-18, b. 10, Vince Cs.

40. FML, f. XXXI-18, b. 6, 5/2.

41. *1960. évi népszámlálás* , 62–63.

42. Pallós and Vukovich, "A magyar házassági mozgalom"; cf. Chester, *Divorce in Europe*.

43. Rapport, *Transcendent Individual*, 64–79.

PART III

HIERARCHY

This is the buffet, waiters running to and fro,
Grinding, steaming coffee, rushing as they go,
One measures rum, one wipes blood up with a curtain,
One makes a hole in a spoon just to be certain.
The others are customers. One munches on some bread,
One steals a glass; one hits another on the head,
One kicks one of the waiters in the face.
One runs for the doctor. The square is named Peace Place.

Excerpt from an "anti-skit" on Sztálinváros, 1954
(FML, f. XXIII-508, b. 60)

7 Bars

The usual weekend bustle on Béke [Peace] Place. People were climbing up onto trucks that had been covered with tarpaulins or boarded over to make little huts. Everyone was gray and green in their Soviet quilted jackets, their rubber boots all muddy and dusty. The girl was reluctant. She did not want to go with me into Késdobáló [the Knife Thrower], which stretched long on the opposite side. It was cowering under a red, dust-covered roof, with its tattered entrance and barred windows facing the street. Some people were lingering under the young leafless poplars in front of it. A small stocky unshaven man was howling, "My room is full of tears." Though he didn't have a room. He lived in Radar in a room stuffed with bunk beds.

THE EXCERPT IS part of a "recollection" novella submitted for a 1980 literary contest organized by the City Council.[1] The author, conforming to official expectations, attempts to reconstruct the atmosphere of the most infamous Sztálinváros bar, the so-called Késdobáló, which means "knife thrower." The first-person narrator begins his description of the city with the chaos on Béke Place, followed immediately by a description of the bar, which is crowded with "deviants." He later mentions May 1 Street, which was considered to have been the first fully completed street of the city, with its journalist residents, who were regarded as illustrious. The author also describes the crowded workwomen's hostel, contrasting it with the peaceful and "intimate" atmosphere of the village, the Old Town. Later the protagonist also enters the entirely different world of the managers' canteen, where, in his narrative, the local "elite" are making merry.[2] The bar counter, engineers, the waltz, and the twist make clear to those who enter that the norms here differ entirely from those in Késdobáló with its zither band. On Béke Place people are "gray and green in their Soviet quilted jackets," while Mara, the protagonist's beloved, is trying on a two-piece suit and evening gown in the managers' canteen.

The narrator knows the regulars in Késdobáló well, but he "refuses to recognize them" when he is with Mara, as she is hesitant to enter the place with him. In contrast, he boasts about his metallurgical engineer pal and his circle of friends, and she gladly goes with him to spend time with them and, indeed, mixes and mingles with them: "she visibly felt at ease among people not garbed in Soviet quilted jackets." By contrasting the two settings, the author depicts the differences, according to public opinion, between the groups of people who frequented them. In the managers' canteen gentlemen are discussing weighty topics, while in Késdobáló drunken barrack residents are singing popular songs. However, although he pretends to be a stranger to the two places, the narrator himself is trapped in both worlds. As spirits rise, the protagonist and some members of the "elite" group, which is composed mainly of technical specialists, break into drunken song, just as the "tippler" does in front of Késdobáló.

There are innumerable works of historical and urban anthropological secondary literature on the power of bars, taverns, and the leisure-time activities of workers as forces of integration in the life of a city, as well as on the ways in which these institutions are depicted in various discourses.[3] As "masculine" institutions, bars posed a significant challenge for the local administration, both because of the changes that took place in the mid-1950s, when family life in Sztálinváros became officially supported, and because bars represented an opposition to a prevalent value system that had the support of the authorities. This provides a provocative perspective from which to consider the ways in which, for new arrivals in industrial cities, the bar symbolized the transformation and sustenance of the values of the village community. In this chapter I argue that the conflicts between members of the local administration and patrons of the bars represent the changing social environments of the socialist city and a struggle between the "old" and "new" management of the city, which changed in 1953/54, when officials in the local council obtained more power than they had had previously. The symbolic war between the officials and the bars in Sztálinváros represented the struggle between the "old" citizens (the builders) and the newcomers (the skilled workers employed at the factory) and the change in the official municipal policy. This story also exemplifies change in the representation of the "urban" and "villager" lifestyles in Sztálinváros.

By the end of the 1950s, the city was no longer the "leavening" or the "melting pot" of a homogeneous urban society, but rather the dwelling place of strikingly different social groups. The sharp social divides were manifested in shifts that took place in the circles of people who frequented the various restaurants and bars. The dividing lines that were blurred at the beginning of the decade were relatively rigid by its end. This made the city sustainable and functional in the eyes of the officials and the residents, and it also made the social hierarchy itself enduring. The story of the growth and demolition of the old bar Késdobáló and the construction of the new Hotel Golden Star (which was intended to function in part as a representation of the status of the city) demonstrates not only how the local policies regarding leisure were shaped both by the inhabitants of the city and the original Stalinist plans, but also how conflicts arose between various members of the administrations. This chapter explores how the former social hierarchies were reproduced in the leisure culture of bars and how the Stalinist

Figure 7.1. Outdoor bar by the new buildings in Sztálinváros.

policies regarding leisure were shaped by the new consumer lifestyle at the end of the 1950s. It also examines how all this made the practices of socialism more sustainable.

Késdobáló Bar and Béke Place

In the symbolic struggle between the planned and (to borrow the terminology of Tibor Weiner, the chief architect) the "growing" elements of the city of Sztálinváros,[4] the infamous Késdobáló played a significant, distinctive role. Opened in one of the first barracks, the bar, which also functioned as an eatery, was run by the state-owned building enterprise responsible for the construction of the residential buildings in Sztálinváros. When most of the buildings were ready in 1953, the Mine Works Supply of the Ministry of Domestic Trade, which was responsible for public catering in Sztálinváros, was tasked with running the bar in order to mitigate the problems that had arisen around it. The members of the Sztálinváros City Council, who for the most part began their work in 1954, had always seen the bar as an enemy of civilized urban life; in contrast, the managers of the national enterprises saw it as an important institution with which to address some needs of the workforce. In spite of the intentions of the council officials, Késdobáló became one of the informal centers not simply because workers arriving in the city alone or in gangs frequented it to drink, but also because many of them did their shopping and boarded there. Many workers made friends and met with them in Késdobáló, and it was often here that people learned of better employment opportunities. In other words for many workers of Sztálin-város, Késdobáló was a "gateway."

The history of Késdobáló goes back to the "heroic" age of the founding of the city of Sztálinváros. In 1950 the site that was to become Béke Place was little more than cornfields. The first construction workers arrived here and constructed the first barracks, including the barrack of the Késdobáló next to Lajos-kő, or Lajos Stone. Lajos-kő is a monument marking the spot where Hungarian king Lajos rested with his army before the Battle of Mohács (1526), in which the Hungarian armies were defeated by the Ottomans, bringing about the fall of the Medieval Hungarian Kingdom and ushering in a century and a half of Ottoman rule. The first barrack beside the Lajos Stone also provided space for offices and lodgings. In 1950, Késdobáló was opened in one of the first barracks to have been completed. Toward the end of 1953, the local newspaper printed the following description of the bar: "The passing of time left the buildings a bit worn, so it is hardly surprising that workmen enter the rooms, which are always sooty and filled with smoke, with some trepidation, even when simply coming to have a drink."[5]

The construction work at what was to be Béke Place gave the impression that the site was going to be the center of the city. Many believed that the "heart of the construction was throbbing" here. The first grocery store was also opened at the site.[6] The first canteen, which provided meals for the workers, was located nearby.[7] So new arrivals in Sztálinváros had good reason to think that Béke Place was the center of the new city, although according to the final plans it was located outside the future downtown area.

The first residential quarters "sprang up" west of Béke Place: barracks, the József Attila House of Culture (located in the barracks at that time), the grocery store, and the Medical Examination Center were all nearby. The construction area—the buildings of the future city were being built first—was east of Béke Place, so the first residents employed at the construction site crossed Béke Place on their way to work. The buses used by workers who had been given accommodations in nearby villages also departed from here. Thus Béke Place became one of the first symbols of Sztálinváros, with Késdobáló at its "heart."

For people arriving in or departing from Sztálinváros, the first and last impression of the city was the crowd milling about the bar on Béke Place. The recollections of one worker offer a vivid example: "At about 5:00 in the afternoon vehicles were waiting at Béke Place. People coming from the construction site were congregating here. Good Lord, what a hullabaloo it was! In front of the door of the barrack operating as a grocery store people were standing in long queues."[8]

Késdobáló, the bar in the barracks, first attracted the attention of the local newspaper in 1953, which indicated that tensions had already arisen between the regular customers of the bar and the officials. According to the newspaper account, the bar was packed with drunks whose howling and singing disturbed the peace of the neighborhood. Those who happened to be in the vicinity were in danger of being beaten or even stabbed by drunken men who had lost all sense of self-control. The risks and hazards of loitering in the area were aggravated by the fact that the bus station was nearby. According to the paper, Késdobáló had become a place for vagrants, drunks, and thugs.[9] The author of the article was particularly outraged by the fact that patrons harassed passersby, and in doing so ruined the atmosphere of the entire neighborhood.

Anyone who spent time in Sztálinváros soon learned of Késdobáló, and many thought that those living in Sztálinváros must have resembled the people frequenting the notorious bar, "people with criminal records." In addition, Béke Place was a popular site for beggars, especially on busy market days.[10] Although people tended to believe that workers were arriving in the city from every corner of Hungary, this image begs some clarification. For the first phase of the construction work, bricklayers had indeed arrived with village brigades of construction workers, but when the first factory was built in 1952–53 a large number of workers arrived from provincial cities (primarily from the Rimamurány region, an industrialized area in northeastern Hungary) and from Budapest.

According to a sample of 448 employees of the Engineering Works of the Stalin Foundry, in 1952–53 only 43 percent of the skilled and unskilled factory workers who eventually settled in Sztálinváros (construction workers were only rarely given accommodations in the buildings designated as permanent) came from villages; 29 percent had been born in Budapest (the remaining 28 percent came from provincial cities); and 58 percent of the skilled workers were from Budapest (the remaining 42 percent came from villages and provincial cities). Only 8 percent of unskilled workers were from Budapest, but unskilled workers were far less likely to be given housing.[11] The majority of the better-educated workers coming to the factory were from Budapest and provincial cities, so in terms of behavior they were urban. In contrast, the majority of earlier immigrants to Sztálinváros were construction workers with rural backgrounds.

Due to the investment freeze in 1953 construction work in Sztálinváros came to a standstill, so a significant proportion of the construction workers, who were seen as geographically mobile, left the city. In addition, in 1953 members of the educated working class who had urban origins started to gain prominence, so it became increasingly necessary for the local officials who were also living downtown to "cleanse" the city, especially the downtown area.

In 1953 the city of Sztálinváros must have resembled something of a "surreal dream." The writer Bulcsú Bertha (1935–97) came to Sztálinváros in 1953, immediately after graduating from high school in a traditional provincial town, Keszthely, and he had clear recollections of Béke Place and Késdobáló thirty years later. Indeed, he seemed to identify the city with the bar, which was quite typical of the post-1956 recollections on the early years of the city: "Right behind Béke Place bar there was a forest of saplings with recently planted 3–4 meter trees. The back windows of the bar faced this forest. When big fights broke out in the bar the windows were opened and the winners of the brawl or the waiters threw the defeated into the forest. By the time the police arrived everyone was quietly sipping their wine, or, to be more precise, their beer with rum, because that was the fashion at the time."[12]

At the time, the bar was one of the larger places of its kind in the city. Though it could hardly have held more than fifty or a hundred people, even if the tables and chairs that were still in working order were taken outside, there were nonetheless few places in the city where so many people would have found room to gather at one time, whether sitting or standing. By 1953 regular police inspections were conducted at Késdobáló. This is hardly surprising, since in August 1953 the new local council head, Jenő Tapolczai, had arrived in the city. His first measure, as a "novice" in comparison with the old leaders (e.g., Ambrus Borovszky [1912–95], head of the Foundry, who had not considered Késdobáló a cause for any great outrage and himself had frequented it[13]), was to address the issue of bars.

> For years, police reports . . . described our city as one of the most tainted in the county. . . . Struggles to close all the bars and restaurants that are dominated by suspicious people were continuous. . . . In fact, rumor had it that before you entered "Lepra" [the Bum, another nickname of Késdobáló] you had to fire a bullet into the place, and if no shots were fired back, you could enter. The closing of "Lepra," the den of the Sztálinváros underworld and a place that required constant readiness on the part of the police, posed a serious challenge for the local council. As our first measure we closed down the temporary bus station located in some of the barrack buildings near Lepra, and then we took steps to have the diner closed, which was far from easy.[14]

In his recollections Tapolczai depicts himself as the most ardent opponent of the bar, to which he and council meeting records refer as "Lepra,"[15] but which in other sources is more frequently called Késdobáló. He did this in part to present himself as a representative of the fight carried out by the local council against alcoholism.

The Fight against Bars

By 1953 the downtown residential district had been completed, and the old image of Béke Place, which was at one of the corners of the district, failed to meet the expectations of the council, which was attempting to propagate an "urban" lifestyle. According to articles in the local newspaper and recollections of the local elite, the bar on Béke Place was frequented by residents of the neighboring "bar-

Figure 7.2. Jenő Tapolczai, the local council head, welcomes Nikita Sergeyevich Khrushchev, First Secretary of the Communist Party of the Soviet Union, in Sztálinváros in April 1958. In the 1950s country leaders coming to Hungary regularly visited the country's first socialist city during their official program.

rack settlement" and "villagers" commuting from nearby villages. Thus the struggle against Késdobáló turned into a symbolic battle between the "urban" and the "rural" in the eyes of the local administration, which drew a sharp distinction between these two lifestyles.

In the winter of 1953 the building that housed Késdobáló was remodeled and its windows were made larger in the hope that the renovation of the building would drive away "undesirables."[16] But the attempt failed (even if it was a bit easier to throw drunks out of the windows). The police saw one indication of this failure in a huge brawl in February 1954 during which one of the accused made political statements considered criminal. Several witnesses testified that police intervention itself was behind the outbreak of the brawl and that police officers had "deliberately" provoked the "breach of peace" in the vicinity of the bar. As one witness described it:

> I noticed that two men were holding each other up. That is, one of the men, the one with curly hair, was drunk as a skunk and the other, his foreman, was trying to take him home. But the drunken man did not want to go, and he cursed

at the man [his foreman] who was trying to help him. Soon the police officer comrade arrived and asked about the people who had been fighting. We showed him where the two people were standing and the officer comrade and my friend and I also went there. The officer comrade told the two people to stop fighting, and in response the drunken man hit the foreman and the officer comrade too.[17]

The accused man was taken to the police station, and for obvious reasons, he was protesting and cursing at the police officers. When he was sentenced to ten months in jail, the political statements he made in the course of all this (for example, "they have handcuffed a workman") were quoted by the court as evidence of his most serious transgression. All the witnesses were residents of barracks and the surrounding villages, and they were all unskilled workers, which indirectly gives an impression of the bar's clientele.[18]

On March 2, 1954, while the hearings were under way, the local newspaper published an article titled "Order Must Be Restored in the Béke Place Buffet." The article reveals that the "buffet" was the most popular of the public catering businesses in Sztálinváros, but its "reputation is not worthy" of the city because it was a scene of continuous uproar and brawls. Even during the day it was packed with rowdy drunkards, and clothes, shoes, and stolen goods were available for purchase within its walls. "At dinner time business begins in a relatively friendly and orderly manner, but every thirty minutes the place begins to seethe as scandals erupt. After the guests have consumed enough alcohol, at approximately 10:00 PM, the various songs are mixed with yelling and squabbling. 'Prowess' is stronger than common sense and fights break out all of a sudden. . . . Gypsy music plays continuously,[19] the staff watches helplessly, and on several occasions a bleeding head, knocked out teeth, and torn clothes indicate that harmless entertainment has escalated into a fight in the crowd."[20]

Since the Public Catering Enterprise (under the supervision of the Ministry of Domestic Trade) was compelled to increase business, several staff members were on friendly terms with regulars, and various credit systems were used. The newspaper, under the supervision of the local council, noted that as a kind of final epilogue, drunkards who had been driven out into the street from the semilit restaurant would hold farewell brawls in front of the entrance.[21] Until 1954, the Public Catering Enterprise's interests enjoyed more importance.

Codes of behavior and a "cleansing" process were introduced in other downtown restaurants as well. In 1954 the management of Béke Restaurant decided to prohibit the intoxicated, people wearing untidy clothes, and "those wearing caps" from entering. "We hope Béke Restaurant will become a popular place for workers who wish to enjoy decent amusement," the manager of the restaurant stated.[22]

Neither the remodeling nor the police raids yielded any result in Késdobáló, and in June 1954 a fatal brawl took place in front of the bar.[23] Meanwhile Sztálin-

Figure 7.3. The Béke (Peace) Restaurant.

város aldermen were in a dispute with the Management of the Mine Works Supply of the Ministry of Domestic Trade, which had overseen Késdobáló since 1953. The management had filed several appeals protesting the closing of Késdobáló, arguing that the measure would seriously hinder the completion of revenue plans.[24] Nonetheless, the new leaders of the council won, and national enterprise was given compensation at a new site for a restaurant not far from the home of the council itself. Eventually the council, which referred to the increase in alcoholism, prevailed, and on October 8, 1954, the *Sztálinvárosi Hírlap* reported that Késdobáló—also known by the nicknames "bum," "howling," "spitting," and "little tango"—was closed down.[25]

The Golden Star Hotel and Restaurant

Six weeks after Késdobáló had been closed down, the Golden Star Hotel and Restaurant was opened in the "most impressive building" in the city at the other end of the downtown area.[26] The restaurant, which was designed to seat two hundred people, was intended to meet the high standards of the local elite. At the opening the managing director barred people wearing "Soviet quilted jackets" and "overalls" from entering on account of their attire. Even the *Sztálinvárosi Hírlap* noted that customers were expected to behave modestly and decently: it was "no place for drunkards." The newspaper described the Golden Star Hotel as the most impressive gathering place for Sztálinváros society.[27]

Within a week of opening, managers of the restaurant were inviting customers for a Sunday afternoon "five o'clock tea" (the fee to be paid for the compulsory cloakroom was 5 forints).[28] The downtown area seemed to have been "cleansed" of undesirables. However, this idyllic state lasted only until the Arany Csillag Népbüfé, or Golden Star People's Snack Bar, was opened behind the Golden Star Hotel. The People's Snack Bar was established in part to replace Késdobáló by the same state-owned enterprise (the Mine Works Supply of the Ministry of Domestic Trade) that operated Késdobáló on the other side of the downtown area.

For the grand opening of the Golden Star Hotel a small reception was meticulously organized by Sztálinváros aldermen. Officials of the Domestic Trade Ministry suggested that waiters should be brought from Budapest if the goal was to create a refined catering trade. And indeed waiters were transferred from the Gundel Restaurant, which to this day remains one of the most prestigious restaurants in Budapest. Jenő Tapolczai, the local council head made a deal with Ferenc Lombos, the secretary of the Sztálinváros party commission, that customers would be served before party officials. Waiters were also present at this negotiation. One of them, a man named Sanyi (the short version of the name Alexander in Hungarian), asked for permission to speak and stated that in the old days, during the precommunist era in the 1930s, when he had worked at prestigious banquets, whatever high-ranking guest happened to be visiting the capital, he had always served the mayor first and only then waited on others. Tapolczai seemed to convince Sanyi that things were to be done differently in Sztálinváros, but Sanyi proved more stubborn than the council head realized. A few days later, when a high-ranking delegation was received at the new hotel, the staff began waiting on them according to the old routine. Local leaders were served food and drinks first. Tapolczai summoned Sanyi and asked if he had forgotten their talk. Sanyi replied that he most certainly had not, but then whispered in the Tapolczai's ear, "these gentlemen are leaving within an hour, but we will remain here." Tapolczai replied to the obstinate waiter's remark with a short curse.[29]

Of course this is Tapolczai's version of the story, and I have not found any other account. However, as his retelling makes clear, Jenő Tapolczai (1911–76) belonged to the group of leaders in Sztálinváros who were proud of the fact that they were able to keep their positions in part because of the social acceptance they had won among the people of the city. In other words, they had not simply been given their positions by people at the top of the party leadership. And while he was removed from his position as head of the Sztálinváros City Council in 1956, Tapolczai was given back his place in 1957 as a reformer in the newly forming Kádár regime—that is. as someone who both maintained order and listened to the voice

Figure 7.4. The waiters of Béke Restaurant.

of the people. He held this position until 1967, when he became president of the county council.[30]

In his 1959 "summary," which met the expectations of the Ministry of Interior, András Sándor also described the Golden Star Hotel as a place where the "local elite" entertained themselves:

> People who were like-minded and close in age, who knew and trusted one another, either met at one another's places of residence or passed their time in the Golden Star Hotel. . . . (Typically workmen were looked down on by the Golden Star, and the manager of the restaurant deliberately aimed to keep the working class out, running a standing-only bar for workers in the back, in the backstreet. On another occasion, when an engineers' ball was organized in the first-floor reception rooms of the Golden Star Hotel, a big fight broke out, and although no invitation was required to enter, they did not allow workers appearing at the entrance to come in and tried to drive them out by force.) Generally, huge sums were written on the headwaiter's bills in the Golden Star, and one could clearly sense in the atmosphere of the place the stuffiness of the awakening bourgeois world.[31]

The practice of creating what essentially amounted to separate classes of leisure-time places (not to mention separate classes of residential districts) was adopted in other socialist cities as well. At the beginning of construction in Magnitogorsk in the Soviet Union a separate district was created for American engineers and experts working in the city (Amerikanka, or American city), who, as one functionary recalled, had no particular aversion to vodka and who "danced the foxtrot to balalaika music." In 1932 the American professionals left the city, and high-ranking party officials, administrative and industrial managers moved into their apartments (at this point the name of the district was changed from Amerikanka to Berezka, or "Little Birch," owing to the its oasis-like character within the industrial city). The local elite enjoyed a relatively luxurious life, residing in detached houses, doing their shopping in special stores, and often riding in Fords driven by a driver. Essentially they lived much the way that the former American residents had lived. In 1936 the local newspaper reported that engineers' wives were organizing a fancy-dress ball for the local elite. However, as happened later on several occasions in Sztálinváros, the organizers had to cope with the problem that "undesirable persons" (even—horror of horrors— workmen), who had been deceived by the propaganda message of social equality, wished to join the party. The authorities prevented this by reprinting the tickets and soliciting the assistance of the police, but the ball was still something of a disappointment in part because the guests "wore very few creative costumes," according to the local newspaper, the *Magnitogorsk Worker.*[32]

Regarding local privileges, Stephen Kotkin argues that "privilege had from the beginning been an integral part of life in Magnitogorsk," but the local elite "aspired to an upper-class lifestyle in what was supposed to be a proletarian town."[33] In comparison with Sztálinváros, the former hierarchies of industrial workers and technical professionals (such as engineers) were transformed by the demolition of Késdobáló and the construction of the Golden Star Hotel. Both places represented different privileges and lifestyles, and both served the goals of the local council because they created a physical context for and manifestation of the sharp divide between residents of the city with urban backgrounds, on the one hand, and rural backgrounds, on the other. The discourses in the local press and the steps taken by the authorities regarding Késdobáló and the Golden Star Hotel helped the townspeople carve virtual lines in the society of a highly chaotic construction site.

In the fourth quarter of 1955 more than half (52 percent) of total sales of alcohol at the People's Snack Bar located at the back of the illustrious Golden Star Hotel came from sales of hard liquor (mainly rum and the hardest and cheapest sweet liquor, *kevert*), which indicates that consumers of strong drinks in the downtown area came to this bar. In contrast, in the restaurant on the other side of the building the consumption of hard liquor was only 11 percent of total alcohol sales. Here bottled wine, which was rather expensive, was first on the list.[34] The prestigious restaurant and the People's Snack Bar, which replaced Késdobáló and was kept under stricter control, worked well together, in close proximity, even if the two places were frequented by people belonging to entirely different social groups. As in the case of Késdobáló, on several occasions steps were taken because

Figure 7.5. Ball in the Golden Star Hotel.

of events that transpired in the People's Snack Bar, as the following citation illustrates: "intoxicated people behaved boorishly and a fight broke out in the crowd between the staff and the drivers. People threw buckets, plates, and other objects at one another, and this caused injuries to the drivers, in particular Gábor Sz., whose nose was cut off, and a plate was thrown at Gyula Cs.'s forehead, causing him injury."[35]

In this case it was noted that a bar ruffian already known from Késdobáló (where he had attempted to make his point with a winch) had come to the People's Snack Bar, and that cooks and waiters also joined in the fight. One can conclude that some of the old Késdobáló customers had begun frequenting the People's Snack Bar in the back of the Golden Star Hotel, but the Snack Bar never had the same image as Késdobáló.

The closing down of Késdobáló and the opening of Golden Star Hotel in 1954 (and the opening of the People's Snack Bar) were symbolic gestures of the ways in which the two establishments, each of which had acquired symbolic value for the denizens of the city, themselves changed as part of a general shift in the perception of city spaces. In the course of this process, the assertion of norms began with the closing of the "village-like" Késdobáló and the opening of the Golden Star

Hotel, which represented the "bourgeois idyll," and the People's Snack Bar as a place that had the potential to "civilize" its visitors. These were not the first institutions in Sztálinváros with didactic functions, but they were among the first to spread a "civilized manner" of consumption. Although the "cleansing" of the downtown area was not achieved in its entirety, Késdobáló, which for a time was a metonym for Sztálinváros, was replaced by the snack bar behind the Golden Star Hotel in the public mind. The social hierarchies at places of leisure reproduced themselves not in a planned way, but according to the expectations of the city's inhabitants, including the downtown residents and officials on the local council, who were themselves also "ordinary people."

"Downtown" Bars and Bars on the "Outskirts"

The closing of Késdobáló contributed to social segregation, which was becoming increasingly visible in Sztálinváros in the mid-1950s. Beyond the "boulevard" that encircled the downtown area (Szórád Márton Street–Építők [Builders'] Street–Stalin Avenue–Kossuth Lajos Street), the semirural and rural bars still thrived. They included the 103 Liquor Store—which had been opened by the same state-owned enterprise under the supervision of the Ministry of Domestic Trade as had the other bars in the city—in a first-floor corner apartment in Gorky Square, the old town Dúlás (Plunder), or by its official name Felszabadulás (Liberation) Diner and the Kék egér (Blue Mouse), the Radar Lepra (Bum) snack bar, the Technikum Aranykapca (Gold Foot Rag), and the South Side bar.[36] In 1955 the Management of the Mine Works Supply of the Ministry of Domestic Trade (Belkereskedelmi Minisztérium), which ran the Sztálinváros bars and restaurants, had also given up hope that bars on the "outskirts" would function as "refined restaurants." On account of this, Felszabadulás and Vasmű restaurants stopped serving cooked meals.[37]

> A Wild West atmosphere was typical in these bars. . . . On entering the place one could easily be served a slap or two with the goulash offered on the menu from morning till night. Gorilla, Wooden Leg, Jocó, Horse head, Big Checkered, and other wild characters all knew the police well. At the time the great attraction of these bars was Csöpi, the tallest man in Hungary, and Jancsi, who had beaten the midget in the traveling circus by two centimeters. . . . Cékla [Beet root] also lived around the snack bars, and since he was a kid who had run away from the orphanage, he was loved, coddled, and fed by everyone.[38]

In earlier times people had a very different image of the old town establishment, Felszabadulás, characterizing it as an old-style restaurant: "It was a very good place for the young stomach and mouth, because it was inexpensive and tasty. One had to take the stairs up; there was a door and a cloakroom, and no bouncers. The restaurant operated as an enterprise. Even by my high standards it was very good. My mother was a very good cook, but we still often went there. There were Swabian musicians, because the Swabians were related to the old town. And those Swabians could play. One could tell that we came from the city. And they were just villagers."[39]

Driving out bars regarded as village-like from the downtown area contributed to the formation of distinctive local cultures. At the end of December 1956, two months after the revolution in Hungary, two downtown customers were beaten in the South Side catering establishment because they were singing communist propaganda songs. The two men, who had been sipping wine, attempted to call the police, but the manager of place told them that he would not let them do this because the people who had started the fight were his best customers. At this point the two men who were beaten still had enough strength to go to the neighboring "people's store," but the manager there gave them a similar response.[40]

For the local council, closing down Késdobáló did not mean that the rural lifestyle was replaced by an urban one, but indicated rather that this symbol and crucible of the rural lifestyle had been driven out of a particular district. At first a factory culture club and later a workshop canteen were opened where Késdobáló had been. The bustle of the square still attracted beggars, and some of the former patrons of Késdobáló became regulars at the snack bar located at the bus terminal.[41] Another group started frequenting the 103 Liquor Store in Gorky Square, which within a short period of time became a target for council members and people who lived "decent" lives. The 103 was closed down at the end of 1956, when Kohász Restaurant opened in the Technikum District (the "prole" district).[42] Regulars of the bar very soon began frequenting the Kohász Liquor Store, located right next to the Kohász Restaurant, that is, outside the downtown limits. When at the end of 1959 the Kohász Liquor Store was also closed down there was nowhere else to go, so its patrons (who presumably had earlier been regulars at Késdobáló, the People's Snack Bar, and 103) started going to the neighboring confectionery not with the intention of eating cake, but because confectioneries became the "black markets" of liqueur.[43] The bars that had the worst reputations were gradually driven out of the downtown area. The old town Felszabadulás Diner and bars located in the South Side and Radar barracks were also considered disreputable places, but they were tolerated because they were located outside the limits of the planned socialist city.

Patrons of the downtown Béke Restaurant also came from increasingly "prestigious" circles, as indicated by the residential and occupational data of witnesses in a 1958 court case. The case involved a man who had suffered grievous injury after having been kicked out of the restaurant for drunkenness by the waiters, who had thrown him down the stairs, and he later died in the hospital. The witnesses included several downtown residents, members of the intelligentsia, and skilled workmen. The intoxicated man was thrown out of the restaurant because he had "disturbed" the other patrons, who were enjoying an evening of various performances, with his interruptions. The doctor on duty irrigated the man's stomach, but he had also suffered fractures to his cranium and ribs, and these injuries, which led to his death, were only noticed the next morning. One of the waiters who now stood accused of lethal assault was Sanyi, who prior to and after World War II had worked in places such as the Margitszigeti Nagyszálló (the Grand Hotel on Margaret Island in Budapest), the prestigious Hungária (Hungary) and Gundel restaurants in Budapest, and in fact had run his own restaurant in Újpest. Another waiter employed at Béke Restaurant had earlier worked in the Budapest Karaván (Caravan) and Anna Coffee Shop, which were among the most prestigious coffee shops and restaurants in Budapest.[44]

Since they were located far from the downtown area, which was designed to be impressive and respectable, the restaurants and bars on the outskirts of the city were categorized as "tolerated" (later there were three such categories in the cultural policies of the Kádár regime: forbidden, tolerated, and encouraged[45]). Consequently, scandals at the Felszabadulás Diner were still on the agenda of council meetings as late as 1961.[46] In one of his remarks István Takács, a member of the Sztálinváros City Council, complained that although the Executive Committee of the Sztálinváros City Council had passed a resolution to close down Felszabadulás Restaurant and to fight against alcoholism, no measures were actually taken.[47]

István Sófalvi agreed with Takács that the Sztálinváros catering trade was "oversized," but "until we are able to sway people, we need liquor stores, with which we achieve the aim that in other catering establishments there is no indecent behavior and the number of drunks is insignificant.... Indeed, the Executive Committee passed a resolution to convert Felszabadulás Restaurant into a house of culture, but experts found that the material with which the building was built made it impossible to remodel, since it has walls that would not bear any alteration."[48]

At the end of the official debates about alcohol, it was decided to ban its consumption. One finds a similarly ambiguous situation in the Soviet socialist city of Magnitogorsk, where during the first years of construction alcohol consumption was officially forbidden. Vodka was nonetheless easy to purchase, in spite of the ban, so as was later done in Sztálinváros, the authorities attempted to raise the standards (where *kul'turnost'* came into play) in the bars and taverns that officially functioned as liquor stores and thereby to exert some influence on the alcohol consumption of the city's denizens. The beer house Amerikanka, which opened its doors in April 1936, was one such bar, a site where new habits of alcohol consumption were to be promulgated among local residents. Naturally, of the coffeehouses that were opened in order to raise the "cultural standards of

Figure 7.6. Paying in a liquor store (*italbolt*) in Sztálinváros.

the city," those where beer, wine, and vodka were served with appetizers continued to be more popular than those where coffee, tea, and alcohol-free beverages were served.[49] In both cases the idea of raising the level of *kul'turnost'* was a decisive factor in the steps taken by the local administration regarding the regulation of bars. In Sztálinváros, however, alcohol consumption was limited and restricted, but never banned.

Actions taken by the Sztálinváros City Council to fight alcoholism and the pressure placed on the Catering Trade Enterprise to meet the economic plan had contradictory effects. The conflict notwithstanding, alcohol was served in all Sztálinváros restaurants, and this was only raised as a problem in May 1957 during a session of the council.[50] The police took harsh measures against "intoxicated persons," the council often initiated misdemeanor proceedings, and the *Sztálin-városi Hírlap* published their names. These measures further stigmatized regular patrons of bars.[51]

Owing to the processes of social mobility that had taken place in Sztálin-város, liquor stores, snack bars, and coffee shops attracted different customers, so residents of the city had different views of the establishments. The snack bar of the Golden Star Hotel was frequented by members of virtually every social stratum, as was Béke Restaurant. A person who was a regular at the Kohász may well have gone to a "more elegant" place for a special occasion. Nonetheless, Késdobáló and the restaurant in the Golden Star Hotel represented two entirely different lifestyles, and this view was shared by officials on the local council, the national building enterprise, and the guests of these institutions.

Conclusion

The struggle to "cleanse" bars further strengthened the distinction between the downtown area and the outskirts. According to the policy of the local council, in Sztálinváros certain bars and bar pastimes had special meanings. Bars and their patrons were branded unworthy of Sztálinváros and socialism itself, since according to official perceptions bar life was fundamentally opposed to "socialist morality" and a "decent" lifestyle. Furthermore, bars were depicted in the local press as if they were destroying proper family life, which became a cornerstone of the new policies after the mid-1950s. Thus the fight against the bars was also supported by the families living in the downtown apartments.

In spite of all this, many local leaders (especially the older ones, such as Borovszky) did not want to take up arms against the bars. The changes implemented after 1953/54 and the relegation of old leaders to the background after 1956 were both palpable in the fight against the bars. New leaders alluded to the importance of maintaining order, while the old leaders dwelled on lost revenues and lost productivity. By the end of the 1950s, the municipal leadership had become more independent of the factory. The city was no longer merely an accoutrement of the factory, and city leaders sought to pass regulations independently of the interests of industry.

Accordingly, several campaigns were launched to subdue social life in bars. Debates were launched by the local newspaper, the names of people who had been caught drunk were made public, and police and court proceedings were initiated. The bureaucracy of the local council—and not the national enterprise—started to regulate public life in the city after the mid-1950s. This maintained the local social hierarchy in a renewed form and helped raise a more stable system of identifying sites affiliated not with places of leisure, such as bars, but places of consumption, such as the cinema, shops, and restaurants.

Figure 7.7. Furniture store in Sztálinváros in 1960.

Beginning in 1954, when the social structure of the population of Sztálinváros began its transformation (a consequence of the high demand for skilled
labor), a peculiar informal classification system emerged in the measures taken
by the Sztálinváros police against bars. Based on this, the police considered some
bars acceptable and some unacceptable. Because their customers came from
higher social strata, catering establishments in the downtown area were treated
with more forbearance, whereas bars frequented by unskilled workers (who from
the perspective of the authorities were superfluous after the new constructions
were finished) were subject to frequent police raids. Council and police measures
were fundamentally shaped by the belief that the downtown area was the most
significant district of Sztálinváros, and accordingly it was crucial to ensure that
the institutions located there were cleansed of "undesirables." The police and the
City Council hoped to realize the vision of the planners of the socialist city, according to which the everyday activities of local residents should be subject to oversight and control, in part through the fight against bars in the downtown area and
attempts to "cleanse" them. At the same time, by stigmatizing bars and their customers, the state policies did exert an influence on members of younger generations, for whom more modern forms of recreation, such as movie theaters and
dance halls (the latter were usually in one of the houses of culture in Sztálinváros),

came to function as the center of social life. On the other hand, younger and better-paid skilled workers were more likely to frequent establishments that were transformed from bars into places that offered "music and dancing" (e.g., Béke Restaurant). When young skilled workers went out, they did not necessarily insist on going anywhere in particular (a bar), but rather were drawn to a given place by the music or the outfits that were considered fashionable (e.g., the garb of the teddy boy). One can also discern the effects of this process in the fact that the more modern consumer culture exerted a considerably more palpable influence on the habits and identities of members of the younger generation than it did on the habits of the first arrivals in the city, including, for instance, the patrons of Késdobáló. The main unit of consumption became the family, not the head of the family. Accordingly, places where people spent their free time (such as bars) had to be transformed as well. This was a challenge for the younger generations, whose members had been born before the war but socialized during the establishment of the communist regime. They were the most important group of consumers in Sztálinváros.

Eventually the building in which Késdobáló had been located was demolished, along with the barracks of Béke Place. On the site of the first barrack a public pool was built, a typical symbol of the "urban, modern" lifestyle. The site where the foundations of the barrack called Késdobáló were found was preserved by the City Council during the construction of the public pool.

Notes

1. FML, f. XXIII-508, b. 60. A 1980 short story submitted under the category "Solus eris" for a literary contest titled "Life in a Young City."

2. One frequently finds descriptions of the setting, which included bars and restaurants, in other recollections as well. For example: "At the time Erkel Place was located near Liszt Ferenc Place, May 1 Street and its vicinities, Golden Star Hotel and its surroundings, and Béke Restaurant and its vicinity were all considered illustrous. The downtown area, with its 3–4 story buildings, of a provincial city. And later the construction of the Technikum District began." Interview with János B., March 26, 2001.

3. Examples include: Hutt, *The Death of the English Pub* discusses competition among bars and the decline of bar culture; Burke, *The English Inn* regards bars as a cultural historical phenomenon and not as social phenomenon; the changing roles of nineteenth- and early twentieth-century workers' bars in a midsize industrial town (Worcester); Rosenzweig, *Eight Hours for What We Will*, esp. 35–64, 93–126, 183–90. In Hungary primarily sociographers have addressed the topic of the leisure-time activities of workmen, for example, Litván, *Magyar munkásszociográfiák*; Tomasz, "A pesti kocsmák világa."

4. Weiner, "Sztálinváros," 38.

5. *Sztálinvárosi Hírlap*, December 31, 1953, 5.

6. Miskolczi, *Az első évtized*, 37.

7. Ibid., 39.

8. Quoted in Miskolczi, *Város lesz csakazértis*, 20.

9. *Sztálinvárosi Hírlap*, October 20, 1953, 2.

10. FML, f. XXIII-509, b. 1, Taken from the minutes of minor meetings on council resolutions, September 18, 1954.

11. At the time the number of employees at the first plant was between 1,200 and 1,500 people, so the samples include more than 30% of them. In the sample that was examined, unskilled workers made up 36%, employees in administrative positions 21%, skilled workers 22%, and technical specialists and other managers 21%, which approximately reflects contemporary employment conditions. Source of samples: MNL OL, Duna (Stalin) Foundry, f. XXIX-F-2-a., b. 10, 20, 73, 74, 76, 84.

12. Bertha, "A legendás város."

13. Ibid., 15.

14. Tapolczai, *Egy elnök naplója*, 43.

15. The infamous bar located in the Radar barracks was also referred to by the derogatory nickname "Lepra" (Bum). Miskolczi, *Az első évtized*, 72.

16. *Sztálinvárosi Hírlap*, December 31, 1953, 5.

17. FML, f. XXV-24, Criminal proceedings, 1954–56. Emánuel L. provocation and violence against authorities, 146/1954.

18. Ibid.

19. During the daytime the gypsy band also played to accompany production competitions.

20. *Sztálinvárosi Hírlap*, March 2, 1954, 4.

21. Ibid.

22. Ibid., February 23, 1954, 2.

23. Ibid., June 25, 1954, 4.

24. Tapolczai, *Egy elnök naplója*, 44.

25. *Sztálinvárosi Hírlap*, October 8, 1954, 3.

26. Ibid., November 26, 1954, 2.

27. Ibid., November 30, 1954, 3.

28. Ibid., December 12, 1954, 4.

29. Tapolczai, *Egy elnök naplója*, 44–45.

30. Tapolczai, *Egy elnök naplója*.

31. ÁSZTL, file O–13582, 5.

32. Kotkin, *Magnetic Mountain*, 125–28.

33. Ibid., 128.

34. MNL OL, f. XIX-G-4-rr, b. 14, Domestic Trade.

35. FML, f. XXV-24, Criminal proceedings, 1954–56, László G., László V. and Gyula Cs. criminal damage, unit 137/1955.

36. Tapolczai, *Egy elnök naplója*, 44; Miskolczi, *Az első évtized*, 72.

37. MNL OL, f. XIX-G-4-rr, b. 8, Domestic Trade.

38. Miskolczi, *Az első évtized*, 72.

39. Interview with János B., March 26, 2001.

40. *Sztálinvárosi Hírlap*, January 12, 1957, 3.

41. FML, f. XXIII-502, b. 8. Meeting on September 30, 1954, no. 225/1954. Executive Committee resolution; FML, f. XXIII-502, b. 11, Meeting on February 9, 1956. Executive Committee meeting; b. 16, April 24, 1959, Executive Committee meeting.

42. FML, f. XXIII-502, b. 11.

43. FML, f. XXIII-502, b. 18.

44. FML, f. XXV-24, Criminal proceedings, Gyula Sz. and accomplices, fatal assault and battery, b. 48/1958.

216 of Stalinism Reloaded

45. This cultural policy was known as the "Three T's," "tiltott" (forbidden), "tűrt" (tolerated), and "támogatott" (encouraged). It was formulated in the summer of 1957 as part of a plan for reform and it is usually associated with György Aczél, who later served as minister of culture. Eörsi, "Ideológiai pragmatizmus és (Ön)cenzúra."

46. Felszabadulás Diner was nicknamed "Plunder," a pun based on the last two syllables of the world, *dulás,* which when written with a long "ú" means plunder. The slang term for the restaurant transforms the name, a reference to the alleged liberation of the country by Soviet troops, into a reference to the plunder of the country by the Russian army.

47. Manager of a smaller store or catering establishment that operated on free accounting (*szabadkasszás*) or leased on this term.

48. FML, f. XXIII-502, b. 21. December 5, 1961.

49. Kotkin, *Magnetic Mountain,* 189–90.

50. FML, f. XXIII-502, b. 13, May 31, 1957.

51. FML, f. XXIII-502, b. 11, July 26, 1956. Examining the status of public security; b. 16, August 14, 1959.

8 Hooligans

In 1954, AFTER having fled across the border into Austria, four youngsters offered the following account of life in Hungary:

> We grew up together on the lot [square], went to the same school, and spent all our free time together. Despite our humble origins and the fact that we came from the working class, we did not like the paradise [people's democracy]. We did not want to become party toads or cogs [Stakhanovites], so we had no future ahead of us. We were bored with the heap of talk [propaganda], working the dead grind [workers competitions], and the whole of Hungarian life, it sucked. We short-waved [listened to the radio secretly] enough, and a relative also kept scribbling letters to us from B. so we would know how much cooler work life was in the West. We decided that as soon as we could we would make tracks and slip across the border. We were just waiting for the right opportunity. And the trick worked.[1]

Choice of style and vocabulary obviously in themselves constitute an expressive speech act. The use of language is an element of identity. Youngsters define their identities and their social orientations through their use of language and, of course, slang.[2] In the propaganda of the 1950s youth were portrayed as the most important audience and eventually crucible of the value system of the "socialist man." However, in Sztálinváros, in principle the most socialist of all Hungarian cities, it was the young who were generally "up to no good" and whose value system was a part of an alternative lifestyle that hardly corresponded to official expectations.

According to the propaganda, in Hungary the teddy boy was the epitome of the social clique of youth who constituted a negative example for their peers because they were adherents of the "capitalist" value system. The figure of the *jampec* (teddy boy) in common parlance meant a worldly, independent, extravagant lifestyle, and centered mainly on the flamboyant look of the mostly working-class boys, which were similar to the teddy boys in England. The teddy boy was a recurring character in socialist-realist films, the young embodiment of the image of the enemy, and until 1956 the fight against teddy boys overlapped with the fight against hooligans, which at the time meant youth who did not want to adhere to the socialist norms. According to the movie clichés, impressionable young people who had been misled and severed from their roots aspired to be a part of the world of the teddy boy.[3] But who were these young people who, according to the accounts in the *Sztálinvárosi Hírlap*, from time to time would besiege the house of culture, much to the astonishment of the people who lived by good, socialist values?

The image of the jampec in the 1950s originates in depictions of Western popular culture, centered around the importation of newspaper articles from the Western press, which were the products of Western moral panic as depicted in Westerns, gangster films, dime novels, and comic books.[4] The construction of the jampec in Hungarian films and newspapers was a product of the mixture and adaptation of instances of Western moral panic. According to Uta G. Poiger, who compared the influence of American culture in East and West Germany, contemporary West German experts and East German functionaries claimed that "after consuming westerns and gangster films, young male workers tried to relive 'Wild West', 'gangster' and 'desperado' feelings for such an extended time and so intensely that they became their 'basic outlook on life'."[5] The Hungarian functionaries and journalists, following this logic, created an anthropomorphic figure, the jampec, in order to explain the dangers of films, comics, and Western popular culture in general.

Katherine Lebow argues that the Polish counterpart of the Hungarian jampec, the *bikiniarze*, as a subculture was also linked to outlook and fashion.[6] In my interpretation, the teddy boys did not represent a subculture. Rather, they were a caricature of Western consumption created by communist propaganda. The use of the term *jampec* overlapped with the fight against hooliganism until the mid-1950s (a term taken from state discourses in the Soviet Union), but after 1956 these terms had two different meanings. The fashionable youth became more tolerated by the authorities. This, of course, did not mean that no people characterized themselves or the people around them as teddy boys. Accordingly, the term was shaped during the 1950s not only by the state propaganda and policies regarding youth but also by a new generation, socialized mostly after the communist takeover, which wanted to imitate something that seemed Western.

This chapter demonstrates that the shift in the portrayals of the city's young people and of a distinctive self-image were closely intertwined with the image of the youth depicted in in the *Sztálinváros Hírlap*. The teddy boys, who were a part of everyday life in the city, were key figures in the shift that took place in daily life because their customs and fashions represented not only the condemnation by the regime of Western consumption but also, after 1957, the gradual official acceptance of Western consumption. By the end of the 1950s, the Stakhanovite worker was no longer the role model for the youth, but rather the teddy boy, an archetype that was also created by the socialist propaganda, a figure who aped Western values and became a symbol of the culture of urban consumption. I will explore how this negatively depicted figure became a positive one in Sztálinváros at the end of the decade and how this was related to the changing roles of families.

A teddy boy followed not Western trends so much as the images presented in the communist propaganda of Western trends. In addition, the slang idealized by youngsters as a Western sociolect was cast as a form of resistance or opposition by the officials, although they had contributed to the creation of this slang with propaganda that represented the "bad habits of the youth." The teddy boy culture replaced the leisure-time culture centered around bars that had brought it into being and that had characterized the working class. The symbolic struggle against teddy boys can be interpreted as an extension of the fight against bars. By the time dangerous Sztálinváros bars were believed to have been done away with, new enemies had to be found in public spaces, and the teddy boys suited this purpose. At the end of the 1950s, the teddy boys disappeared from the newspapers, replaced by reports on the fight against youth violence and hooliganism (galeri). This shows how the regime reflected on and renewed Stalinist policies regarding generational problems, which also made the regime more sustainable than it had been before and reloaded Stalinism with new power.

The Invention of the Teddy Boy

In the creation of the hooligan in Hungary the notions of the teddy boy and the hoodlum were used, terms that before 1956 had been the most derogatory designations for the young.[7] The image of the teddy boy was made widely known in the first half of the 1950s in Hungarian movies, which were used as a means of spreading socialist propaganda. The most well-known teddy boy character was Swing Tóni (Imre Pongrácz), one of the most memorable characters of the 1950 movie Dalolva szép az élet (Life Is Lovely in Song). The main characteristic of the tongue-in-cheek Swing Tóni is his aping of Western fashion, founded primarily on American comic strip culture, language use, and dance.[8] The party newspaper Szabad Nép (Free People) also noted that in the movie "the reactionary music teacher and the teddy boy who imitates foreign cultures meet."[9] "Foreign" in this context refers to the West, or the image of the West as presented by the communist authorities. The depiction of the Western fashions aped by the teddy boy was a consequence of the sense of moral panic that emerged primarily because of comic strips, westerns, and gangster movies, a panic that won the attention of the Hungarian press as well. Of course, the teddy boy did not follow Western trends, but rather the image of Western trends as presented in the socialist media. This representation of the teddy boy in films had some unintended consequences for the regime. He represented a caricature of the protagonists of Western comic strips, westerns, and gangster movies; and because of this, he became a champion of "Western ideas" for the youth.

In the first half of the 1950s Szabad Ifjúság (Free Youth) and Budapest Est (Budapest Evening, the forerunner of Esti Hírlap [Evening News]) carried numerous articles and cartoons describing the allegedly detrimental effects of American pulp fiction, comics, and movies. In general, they adopted an argument that was used in media campaigns in the 1930s in Great Britain and the United States to justify the censoring of gangster movies. Behind the sense of moral outrage over the depictions of violence in movies and comic strips (a response still prevalent today), however, lay the business interests of competing representatives of the film industry, who used churches and politicians as mouthpieces to exert an influence on the market.[10] According to one of the main arguments used in the United States in the campaign against comics in the late 1940s and early 1950s, the genre contributes to violence among youths. The circulation of comics in the United States reached its climax in 1953–54, when seventy-five million comic books were sold each month. More and more articles were printed attacking them, and these articles drew sustenance in part from the paranoia of the McCarthy era.[11]

In March 1950 *Szabad Ifjúság* carried an article stating that "one of the main reasons for the moral depravity of Western European youth is the American 'cinematic arts,' radio, and pulp fiction."[12] The paper published other articles that month noting that in Budapest in front of Emke (a prestigious hotel in the Hungarian capital and a legendary meeting place for youth in Budapest) and at the "booth" of Mrs. Kardos on Blaha Lujza Square one could purchase this kind of pulp fiction for a pittance and choose from "the adventures of Buffalo Bill, Checkered Pierre, and other revolver-toting heroes."[13]

Szabad Ifjúság and *Budapesti Est* (the daily that most closely resembled the tabloid press in the 1950s) regularly covered moral campaigns in the West as well. For example, they reported on how in Canada parents protested against the violent books of "Winnipeg publishers." According to the parents, "having read such books, sooner or later our children themselves will become criminals."[14] Nonetheless, the moral outrage concerning violence among the youth in the early 1950s was given so much attention in the media that in 1955 even the United Nations placed "prevention of juvenile delinquency" on its agenda.[15] The subject of this campaign was used by the Hungarian socialist press to craft images of Western youth and the enemy among the youth in Hungary. This was often done by citing voices of moral outrage in the West.

The figure of the teddy boy was based on fictional characters. Swing Tóni embodied the clichés used to describe mainstream American heroes. The Hungarian word *jampec* is a compound of Yiddish origin. Its original meaning is "big dick" (one could compare it with the Hungarian word *balfasz*, or "left dick," which means "jerk"). Its first known use dates from 1928, but presumably the word existed before this. The semantic shift from "very dumb" to "dandy and fashion victim" also took place in Hungarian. According to the Hungarian historical-etymological dictionary, *jampec* means a frivolous, good-for-nothing young man who wears ostentatious attire and behaves oddly.[16] The character of the teddy boy is primarily associated with fashion. Prior to World War II, the term was used to refer to people who came from rich families and who distinguished themselves from their surroundings with their extravagant habits, their admiration of all things "modern" (such as "dance," crime stories, motorcycles, and Kodak), their unusual dance style, and their many lovers.

Comic Book Characters as Real Characters

The teddy boy was something of a comic book character, so he was distinguished primarily by his attire. Rather than garbing him in clothes that fit Western fashion trends, his creators dressed him based on what they saw in Western comic strips, westerns, and gangster movies. In their portrayals, the teddy boy wore black or colorful shirts, patterned neckties or red-dotted scarves, loose and sloping-shouldered jackets, slim-fit trousers, striped socks, colorful rubber-soled shoes, and cowboy hats. Teddy girls wore tight skirts and loose jackets, and generally wore their hair in a ponytail or permed. In the 1955 film *Egy pikoló világos* (A Small Glass of Beer) Julika Cséri (played by Éva Ruttkai) represents a caricature of the teddy girl who is saved from the lifestyle of "Beelzebub's daughters" by Marci Kincse, a young man with innocent eyes who is given permission to leave army headquarters temporarily.[17] In a review printed in *Béke és Szabadság* (Peace and Liberty) a film critic went so far as to note the disparity between the portrayal and reality: "Teddy boys slavishly copied from life come off as caricatures in the movie."[18]

"Wild dancing" became an attribute of Swing Tóni and other teddy boys because in movies and comic books gangsters listened to jazz music and danced to it wildly. Alongside his distinctive garb, the teddy boy was also characterized by his arrogant storytelling, in part due to the influence of the stories of Dick Tracy, one of the most well-known American comic-strip heroes. Noting this phenomenon, the officials constantly rebuked the slang used by the younger generation.[19] In 1954 *Szabad Ifjúság* launched a series of articles titled "Speak Hungarian!"[20] Some young people may have found the fictional character of the teddy boys as portrayed in socialist movies and journalistic feuilletons, which were rich with images of street life, quite appealing. In certain cases this may have influenced their choice of social identity, which was manifested first in the use of slang by the youth and later in clothing fashions.

The socialist regime attributed new meanings to words that officially were used by opponents of the regime. The language of the socialist regime became as much a factor in identity formation as the language of the Third Reich had been.[21] In this respect, one of the major functions of the slang attributed to young people was to represent, at least in the official discourse, the threat posed to the regime

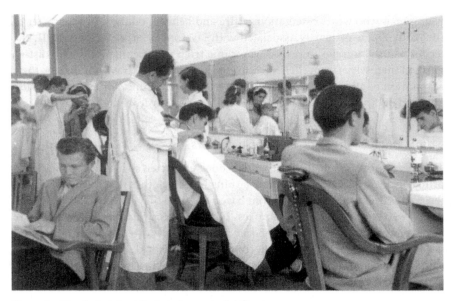

Figure 8.1. New hairstyle at the hairdresser in Sztálinváros.

by admiration of the West among the youth. The youth liked this language more than it liked socialist culture, although it was also a product of socialist propaganda.

Reports of the deeds and exploits of teddy boys also drew on stereotypes that contrasted the lifestyles of people who lived in working-class districts and residents of the downtown area. For this reason, the accounts usually described teddy boys who made appearances in the houses of culture of working-class districts.[22] The young Stakhanovite workman was a similar fictional character, the archetype of the socialist individual who fought the teddy boy spirit both in the factory and in the streets and the houses of culture.[23] In the contemporary propaganda the teddy boy represented the embodiment of all negative attributes, while the stalwart Stakhanovite was the embodiment of all things good.

For the young workmen who purchased their clothing on the black market, the garb of the teddy boy functioned as a symbol of status and urban culture, the feeling of belonging to a community, and adherence to Western trends. For instance, in the 1950s a man who at the time was a skilled worker in Sztálinváros and living in the L-buildings offered the following account:

> We were eyed suspiciously when we entered a place, although we were not showing off. But we were wearing teddy boy shoes with thick soles and a rubber welt. And they were not. . . . I never wore them to work, I saved them for

the weekend. We went out to have fun wearing our teddy boy shoes, loose leather jackets and everything. . . . There were three junk dealers in the South Side. I don't know their names, one of them was called something like Frici, and I think they had brought the stuff from Yugoslavia. . . . They must have been envious of others, wanting to know where they had bought the outfits. They were staring at the cool, slim-fit trousers.[24]

Individualistic attire and hairstyle, dance styles, and distinctive use of language all served as means of expressing social identities in the city of Sztálinváros. People who moved to Sztálinváros from Budapest also used these strategies to distinguish themselves from those around them, and they set examples for the youth immigrating to Sztálinváros from villages. In the public space the means adopted by youngsters to express themselves also served to define their identities. With a change of hairstyle or clothing, a group of young people indicated to other passersby that they were off to revel and indulge, thereby withdrawing themselves for a time from the supervision they endured in the workplace and the oversight of the state and party.

Sztálinváros Teddy Boys in the House of Culture

Owing to the large number of young Sztálinváros immigrants and the state control of public spaces, articles on the "teddy boy spirit" appeared relatively early in the Sztálinváros press. In May 1951, when the town's first street was completed, one reporter from the local newspaper described how "teddy boys invaded the beer garden of the house of culture. One Sunday evening young workers warned one of the teddy boys not to jump about as he danced. 'I can't dance slower,' replied the man, who was wearing slim-fit trousers, 'see, brother no matter how I twist my feet I can't slow down,' and he started singing in a slurred voice."

The newspaper depicted teddy boys as people who needed guidance. Some of these poor young people had simply been misled, or so the argument went, and they might yet become useful members of society. However, even the journalist gave up on some of them, since in his view they had deliberately chosen to be "Chicago gangsters."[25]

According to the local newspaper, the "teddy boy spirit" was also spreading among women, and this was cited as an explicitly moral question in disciplinary proceedings. A female worker whose performance in the workplace was "negligent" was laid off because she "obstructed the decent entertainment" of youth as a regular customer of the canteen with her conspicuous behavior and "teddy boy" dancing.[26] Another youngster accused of being a teddy boy was particularly harshly criticized by the newspaper because in spite of the fact that he was a good Stakhanovite, he performed extravagant routines on the dance floor of the house of culture instead of setting a good example.[27] In addition to being a symbol of

Figure 8.2. Béla Bartók House of Culture in Sztálinváros.

moral depravity, the teddy boy was also branded by the newspaper as a representative of "antifashion." Furthermore, for most members of the local society the teddy boy symbolized the norms established by young gangs. If someone was derogatorily referred to as a teddy boy, he symbolically may have been considered a member of a gang that rejected the norms of the dominant culture and created its own codes instead.

For young workmen, the dance hall (in the house of culture) and the movie theater replaced the bar as the main venue for making new acquaintances, cultivating friendships, and securing a sense of intimacy. The emergence of the teddy boy image in public discourse was also prompted by the fact that for the young it represented an alternative lifestyle, in opposition to official expectations. For instance, the depiction of the teddy boy styles of dancing in the local press went hand in hand with renewed support for dance schools in which traditional "middle-class dances" were taught. Critics of teddy boy dances unanimously regarded folk dance, the waltz, tango, and slowfox as acceptable dances, and after some hesitation even the fox-trot, although a couple of decades earlier these dances were also objects of reprehension. According to an article written at the time, the "boogie-woogie" and "hand jiving" were "filthy and unimaginative" dance routines. Furthermore, "the only thing these young people know about love is what they have learned from dirty jokes." According to the article, the teddy boy spirit primarily corrupts young workmen and women, who usually spend their new incomes on themselves, donning slim-fit trousers, sloping-shouldered jackets, in other words the standard teddy boy outfit.[28]

In depictions of hooligans and teddy boys youth violence was not a real issue in Sztálinváros until 1956. It found its place, rather, in the discourse on state child care. At a 1955 Sztálinváros council meeting the formation of a South Side gang was attributed to a boy in the care of the state. Members of the gang, described as "truants," were often alleged to run away from the family home and not return for two or three days.[29] Nobody called these boys hooligans or teddy boys at the council meeting. Council meetings primarily addressed the question of street gangs as an issue of "gangs of teenagers."[30]

According to the *Sztálinvárosi Hírlap*, the Béla Bartók House of Culture was one of the major meeting places for teddy boys in the city. When the ballet school and folkdance groups performed, boisterous youngsters generally dressed in the latest teddy boy fashion and dancing in the teddy boy style would occupy the houses of culture on weekends.[31] Similarly, owing to the dance events on Saturdays and Sunday, houses of culture in the South Side and the Radar barracks also became a favorite place for teddy boy youngsters. Since the South Side house of culture had not been renovated, it collapsed, and young people in the district were left with nowhere to dance. At the end of 1959 the council official in charge of social affairs suggested that one or two entertainment places in the barracks should also be allocated for the youth loitering in the streets. However, no new house of culture was built because according to the long-term plans the barracks were to be abolished.[32]

Teddy boys were associated with the distinctive language described in part at the beginning of this chapter, and several articles were published in the local newspaper rebuking this slang, including expressions like *csoda jó csaj* (wondrous hot chick), *himbál a flamó* (I am dizzy with hunger), *lóvé* (dough, cash), *salni* (shoe), *bré* (beret), and many other examples. The word *duma* was used to mean talk or chatter, *piás* to mean drunk, and *pipás* to mean angry.[33] The squares, dance halls, and bars, as the sites where young people socialized, recurred with particular frequency and sometimes with particularly imaginative designations. In order to make the fairly simple statement, "even in December there are many workers vacationing in Siófok, so there are lots of guys hanging out in the bars at night," the youths cited at the beginning of this chapter said the following: "Siófokon decemberben is sok melós nyaral, így a csehókban éjjel is sok ürge tanyázik." Words like *melós* (worker), *csehó* (dive, joint, bar), and *ürge* (gopher, but here meaning guy or dude) are examples of the slang used by the youth and frowned on by the regime.

One group of youths in Sztálinváros was able to portray themselves as urban by borrowing words and phrases from Yiddish and Budapest slang. This enabled

Figure 8.3. The House of Culture in the "Old Town" of Sztálinváros.

young people of peasant descent arriving from the Hungarian Plains and nearby villages to feel more welcome in the city. One can also discern in the use of language a rejection of the language and worldview of the propaganda. A radio, for instance, was called a "blabber box" (*hadova láda*), the workers competitions were referred to as the "dead grind," the minister of the interior was given the name of a figure from folk tales, the "stone-hearted man," and members of the secret police were called "mochas," a reference to their brown shoes. The meals served in the plants were referred to as "swill," a party functionary as a "party mickey," the peasant as a "clodhopper," and the Communist processions as "poorhouse parades." Mátyás Rákosi was called "the bald coconut" (a reference to his baldness) and the free food served on May 1 was "Turkish food," a reference to the occupation of the country by the Ottoman Turks in the fifteenth and sixteenth centuries (implicitly equating the occupation of Hungary by the Soviet army with the occupation of the country by the Ottomans).[34]

The use of slang, adherence to a dress code created by the movies and caricatures, and the purchase of clothes on the black market represented an alternative lifestyle for the youth of Sztálinváros. With the exception of having articles published in the local press on this youth culture phenomenon, the Sztálinváros authorities never took any official steps against the new style or the teddy boys. After the mid-1950s, not only did the authorities become increasingly tolerant of the consumption of "extravagant" clothes, but gradually the articles concerning teddy boys disappeared from the local newspaper. The image of the "city of families," which was based on the family as the unit of consumption, could also include the teenage consumers who came from families with more and more income.

Tolerating Consumption

By 1957 the rock and roll craze had reached Sztálinváros. The *Sztálinvárosi Hírlap* carried a report on the dangers of this new fashion:

> Distorted faces, disheveled hair, twisted limbs, and wild moves. . . . These are the characteristics of rock and roll, the latest dance of the season. Rock and roll makes youth crazy. In Western Europe films about rock and roll are generally accompanied by the unruly mischief of teddy boys. Fights are everyday events in dance halls, and often the police have to intervene. What are the reasons for the detrimental effects of rock and roll? The music is a kind of "stimulant," a musical narcotic. Its rhythms resemble the ever louder rattle of a feverish engine, it practically shackles the mind and brings savage instincts to the surface.[35]

This officially negative image of rock and roll and its fans, however, changed very quickly. Although on January 10, 1958, the *Sztálinvárosi Hírlap* reported with a slightly negative tone that teddy boys had learned the latest dance routines from the newsreels in which rock and roll was stridently condemned, and they had perfected them on the dance floor, this article really only demonstrated that a rock and roll concert had been allowed in Sztálinváros.[36] Rock and roll had won acceptance as part of the popular culture that enjoyed the support or at least tolerance of the state, and the Hungarian Young Communist League was even allowed to organize rock concerts. One of the first contemporary Hungarian rock bands, Metro, held one of its first concerts outside of Budapest in Sztálinváros. The rock band played a gig in the house of culture of the Stalin Foundry at the invitation of the local Hungarian Young Communist League (KISZ).[37] The KISZ organized the show in part to popularize itself, which was an attempt by the regime to co-opt youth culture. This can be seen as part of a larger process whereby the public discourse became gradually more open to consumer goods coming from the West. By the end of the 1950s, the consumption of Western-style music was tolerated, and the garb worn by the teddy boys was regarded as increasingly common.

The teddy boys of Sztálinváros were less and less an unusual site. It was perfectly acceptable for a young girl or boy to wear clothes depicted by the press as part of "Western fashion" or to listen to the music broadcast from the West. The representations of the generational gap were appropriated by the regime, and by the end of the decade many consumer habits that would never have been tolerated ten years before were now acceptable. In 1958 the *Sztálinvárosi Hírlap* carried a general description of the teddy boy:

> He differs from ordinary men in every possible respect. His appearance, language, and manners are refined. His attire also implies sweeping eccentricity. Green shoes, plum-colored trousers, a yellow tie, and perhaps a brown coat, or as he calls it, a "jakó" [a conspicuous loan word in Hungarian implying by its mere use the aping of Western fashions]. He is very scrupulous about this. He even pronounces the word like this (with a "j" as in jacket instead of an "y" sound, which is the usual pronunciation of the letter "j" in Hungarian). When he was a child, his parents chased him around the piano for not smoking Caro and Mistral, naturally not inhaling deeply, just a little. He is very familiar with English traditions, but he pronounces the word lady "laudy" and with the heavy accent of the Hungarian Plains. As long as other men have wives, he will not marry, but if he does "lose his mind," he will only marry a true lady who is, first and foremost, a gifted piano player, understands abstract art, and is a damn good dancer.... He admires the composer of the masterpiece Jim Single-Eye, the Baghdad carrot thief.[38]

The teddy boy became a snob in this new depiction, and it was his snobbery and "dandyism" that made him distinctive, not his consumption of Western goods. Consumerism was no longer such an important problem. A few weeks later the journalist reported something scandalous, namely, that he had been threatened for having written the article: "they threatened to fix me," that is, to beat him brutally.[39] According to the article, teddy boys sought to distinguish themselves from Sztálinváros society through their "otherness," and their eccentricity no longer meant listening to Western music or wearing Western-style clothes, but rather indicated their views of themselves as part of an imagined elite.

In the same year that the *Sztálinvárosi Hírlap* published the article on this new type of teddy boy, the paper also covered the local show of "official" fashion that took place in the building of the Sztálinváros elite, the Golden Star Hotel. Every single article of clothing represented the standard of classic stylishness. Models walked out onto the catwalk to the sweet, smooth melodies played by the band of the Golden Star Hotel and stepped onto the stage under the captivated gaze of the audience. The latest dinner dresses and high-heel fancy sandals were on display, as the newspaper reported. The audience had a chance to see elegant tweed suits and a suit of export quality in a double-breasted cut from a fine fabric also used for the dress uniform of Hungarian Army officers. The dinner jacket, which again had come into fashion and is elegant attire for a ball, theater performance, and wedding party, was met with rhythmic applause.[40]

This fashion embodied the "decent urban lifestyle," which made the slim-fit trousers and sloping-shouldered jackets of the teddy boy even more exclusive (in both the fashion sense and the political-social sense). However, slim-fit trousers were replaced by jeans in the dreams of teenagers as a symbol of the West, and this time the symbol was coming not from depictions of the teddy boys crafted by the communist propagandists, but from items purchased on the black market.[41]

Conclusion

By 1958, the consumer habits of the teddy boys and the families of Sztálinváros had essentially won the acceptance of the regime. To view the teddy boy fashion as a mere imitation of Western trends would disregard several other important aspects of the phenomenon. For new arrivals in Sztálinváros, the teddy boy culture constituted an opportunity to craft an image and reading of urban life that differed from the official expectations. The teddy boy character was a means of manifesting otherness, and it enabled youth to distinguish themselves from the mass of urban residents, on the one hand, while at the same time they were able to be a part of the eddies and flows of urban culture without losing their distinctive identities, on the other.

The teddy boy (jampec) phenomenon was more complex than this might suggest, however. The teddy boy was also present in villages in Jászság, a rural region in the Hungarian Plains. Slim-fit trousers, plum-colored shoes, sloping-shouldered jackets, and teddy boy "behavior" were brought to the settlements of the Jászapáti district by young men and women who worked in the cities, in industrial plants, and often in Sztálinváros, according to *Népszabadság*, the daily of the party central committee. The newspaper article stated that rural parents generally disapproved of teddy boys. One father in Jázsdózsa expressed his distaste for the fashion by tearing up a pair of slim-fit trousers. Several parents in the village, however, were proud of their children's teddy boy attire, the journalist reported.[42]

One of the major functions of the official image of the teddy boy was to personify unacceptable norms and express the official expectations placed on the youth. Naturally, this does not mean that there were no young people who, in their choice of dress or lifestyle, did not conform to the features described by the contemporary press as characteristic of the teddy boy. In the propaganda, the alleged strength of Sztálinváros was embodied in the characterization of the new urban community as the city of the young. Descriptions of the "heroic construction men" and "classless society" were also recurrent images in the propaganda. In contrast, the image of the teddy boy became part of the propaganda and articles in the press because by crafting this portrayal the regime was able to draw a sharp distinction between the forms of conduct that were to be followed and those to be rejected. The teddy boy lifestyle was presented as a foil to official norms because this enabled the propaganda machine to stigmatize any distinctive feature of contemporary cultural and social life that had not emerged as part of the planned economy but rather as a manifestation of Western influence. The fight against the teddy boy was also a war on individualism. This was one means of justifying both collectivism and the alleged equity of socialist society, in contrast to the "capitalist" social order. The teddy boy was important as a notion in the first years of the 1950s because Sztálinváros was to become a model socialist city in which Western tendencies and lifestyles simply were not tolerated.

At the end of the 1950s, the teddy boys disappeared from the news. They were replaced by other groups, in Hungary mainly by juvenile gangs (*galeri*), which were accused of committing criminal acts as descendants of the armed groups of the 1956 revolt. These discussions served a similar function, except that some aspects of the consumer habits of the teddy boy gradually became more acceptable.[43] Rock and roll and brushed-back hair were less and less regarded as sins, even if in official places (at the workplace or at school) long-haired youth garbed in inappropriate attire were still reprimanded. Young people who had earlier listened to Western radio stations to hear rock and roll music were now able to attend "youth clubs" run by the KISZ instead of hanging out on the street corner or going to the house of culture.[44] And with the propagation of consumer socialism, colorful clothing was no longer so striking. With the gradual spread of Western consumer habits onetime teddy boys found themselves purchasing refrigerators and watching pop music on television. They were able to listen to the newer (though still censored) versions of the songs that in the 1950s had won them the reproaches of officials. As it was to some extent in the West,[45] the teddy boy image gradually lost its connotation as an expression of protest, and slowly the people who had fed the fashion adapted to the value system of emerging "refrigerator socialism." The epithet refers to the large number of refrigerators sold in the 1960s and 1970s. Although the refrigerator was not a product intended specifically for young people, it came to be understood as a symbol of the new consumer culture. These politics of consumption depended significantly on the construction of the teenager as a principal target group, a process visible in all postwar societies, whether in the Eastern bloc or in the West. Social hierarchies among families and members of different generations were reproduced via this new cultivation of consumerism, but also by the changing functions of poverty, which was an effect of the controversial and unequal welfare policies of the authorities.

Notes

1. The source is available in Katona, "Krina, franko, mikulás." The text is available at Open Society Archives, f. 300-40, b. 4/7. The meaning of slang words is explained in the "slang dictionary" attached as an appendix to the source: *klatyó*—square; *paradicsom* (paradise)—people's democracy; *miki, mikulás* (Santa, Santa Claus)—man, dude; *élskerás*—Stakhanovite, champion

worker; *albérleti duma*—Communist propaganda; *hullameló* (dead grind)—workers' competition; *tré* (shit)—bad; *kacsázni*—listen to Western radio channels; *skribolni*—write; *frankó* (cool)— good, appropriate; *meghúzni a zamzigot*—escape; *átgémblézni*—cross; *taccs*—border, iron curtain; *kocogni* (trot)—come, go, progress.

2. Widdicombe and Wooffitt, *The Language of Youth Subcultures*, 55–75.

3. Teddy boys are portrayed in the following movies: *Dalolva szép az élet* (Life Is Lovely in Song, 1950), *Kiskrajcár* (Little Denier, 1953), *Ifjú szívvel* (With a Youthful Heart, 1953); see Szilágyi, *Életjel*, 275.

4. About these moral panics, see Springhall, *Youth, Popular Culture and Moral Panics*, 121–46. On the term *moral panics*, see Cohen, *Folk Devils and Moral Panics*, 9.

5. Poiger, *Jazz, Rock, and Rebels*, 67.

6. Lebow, *Unfinished Utopia*, 142–45.

7. On the origins of the term and its Russian adaptation, see Pearson, *Hooligan*, 74–86; Neuberger, *Hooliganism*.

8. *Dalolva szép az élet*, directed by Márton Keleti. Magyar Filmgyártó Nemzeti Vállalat (Hungarian National Film Production Enterprise / Hunnia Filmstúdió [Hunnia Studio]. Magyar Nemzeti Filmarchívum [National Hungarian Film Archives], record no. HF 763.

9. László Kürti, "Dalolva szép az élet," release of the latest Hungarian movie, *Szabad Nép*, September 17, 1950, 10.

10. Springhall, *Youth, Popular Culture and Moral Panics*, 98–120.

11. Ibid., 121–46.

12. "A bűn forrásai" [The Roots of Crime], *Szabad Ifjúság*, March 17, 1950, 16.

13. "Made in USA," *Szabad Ifjúság*, March 3, 1950, 13.

14. "Kanadai 'Gyermekmulattató'" [Canadian "Children's Entertainment"], *Szabad Ifjúság*, November 24, 1950, 9.

15. United Nations, *Prevention of Juvenile Delinquency*.

16. Benkő, *A magyar nyelv történeti-etimológiai szótára*, 258–59.

17. *Egy pikoló világos*, directed by Félix Máriássy, 1955.

18. *Béke és Szabadság*, December 28, 1955. Hungarian National Film Archives, record no. HF 668.

19. See, for example, Lajos Sirokmány, "Budapesti jegyzetek: A nyelvrontókról" [Budapest notes: On language corruptors]. *Budapesti Est*, June 28, 1955, 2.

20. Words like *dumcsizni* (chat), *frankó* (cool, awesome), *bikás* (hard-hitting), *kajolni* (to love), *kóser* (kosher, in this context meaning okay or acceptable), *csörögni* (dance), *pipec* (fizzy), *csaj* (chick, girl), *hadova* (bullshit), *krapek* (dude), and *rendicsek* (okeydoke) were considered unacceptable slang. *Szabad Ifjúság*, February 21, 1954, 8.

21. Klemperer, *The Language of the Third Reich*.

22. See, for example, M. L., "Egy kultúrház és amiért nem látogatják" [A house of culture and the reasons for its abandonment], *Budapesti Est*, July 31, 1952, 4. József Horváth, "Budapesti jegyzetek: 'Szvingtónik' a Kultúrotthonban" [Budapest notes: "Swing Tónis" in the house of culture], *Budapesti Est*, May 6, 1953, 2. Mrs. Lukács Vince, "Budapesti jegyzetek. Jó lesz jelmeznek" [Budapest notes: It will make a good costume], *Budapesti Est*, May 15, 1953, 2.

23. A. B., "'Gépészmérnök akarok lenni': Egy ifjúmunkás-sztahanovista kultúrélete" ["I want to become a mechanical engineer": The cultural life of a young Stakhanovite], *Budapesti Est*, September 10, 1952, 4.

24. Interview with János B., March 26, 2001.

25. *Dunai Vasmű Építője* [Builder of the Duna Iron Mill], May 22, 1951, 4.

26. Ibid., June 5, 1951, 4.

27. *Sztálinvárosi Hírlap*, September 11, 1953, 2.

28. Ibid., March, 26, 1954, 4.

29. FML, f. XXIII-502, b. 10, May 12, 1955.

30. FML, f. XXIII-502, b. 11, September 6, 1956.

31. *Sztálinvárosi Hírlap*, February 9, 1954, 1; September 7, 1954, 4; September 28, 1954, 4; December 17, 1954, 3.

32. FML, f. XXIII-502, b. 16, November 9, 1959.

33. *Sztálinvárosi Hírlap*, September 28, 1954, 4.

34. For more examples, see Csaba Katona's contemporary dictionary of slang terms. See also Katona, "Krina, franko, mikulás."

35. *Sztálinvárosi Hírlap*, February 22, 1957, 3.

36. Ibid., January 10, 1958, 3.

37. Ibid., January 31, 1958, 2.

38. Ibid., January 31, 1958, 5.

39. Ibid., February 28, 1958, 3.

40. Ibid., March 4, 1958, 3.

41. Interview with János B. (March 26, 2001), who regarded himself as a teddy boy in Sztálinváros in the 1950s and purchased his first pair of jeans, which had been smuggled in from Yugoslavia, on the black market.

42. *Népszabadság*, April 16, 1958, 2.

43. Disputes generated by the regime about "gangs" led to the publication of books such as Huszár, *Fiatalkorú bűnözők*, and Molnár, *Galeribűnözés*.

44. Gradually "Halbstarke" culture also moved into accepted dance halls. Adam, "Rocker in einer Großstadt des Ruhrgebiets."

45. Cremer, *Die Subkultur der Rocker*, 58.

9 Slums

In 1962 Etelka J., a fourteen-year-old girl living in Sztálinváros [at the time already Dunaújváros], gave the following account at the police station:

> My mother and my foster father changed residences several times in the South Side. . . . Usually we lived at the same place for six months or a year. . . . My winter clothes were the same clothes that I was wearing in the summer, a sleeveless dress. I did not have a winter coat or shoes. I wore slippers to school, and sometimes I had stockings, but sometimes I only wore socks. Although I was enrolled, I only rarely attended school because I had to stay at home to cook, clean the house, babysit children, and occasionally I had to gather firewood. This year my mother sent me out twice to steal, once to steal baby corn and the second time to steal wood from the construction site of a straw pulp plant. . . . Mihály C. [district commissioner] saw me coming home carrying wood. He asked me who had told me to go and steal fuel. We replied that it was my mother. Mihály C. told my mother not to send us out to steal because there would be trouble to pay. My mother told Mihály C. that she wouldn't take orders from anyone, and it was none of his business where she sent us.[1]

Officially there was no poverty under the socialist regime. However, in Sztálinváros, the city designed to be the model socialist urban community, members of some social groups frequently found themselves compelled to rely on the charity of the family, the neighborhood, the community, the city, or the state. Officially Etelka was entitled to social care for several reasons. She lived in a state of permanent privation, she had been abandoned by her parents, and her opportunities to earn an income were limited. Occasionally she received assistance from distant relatives or neighbors, and for a while she was placed in the care of the state. However, state institutions took action to improve Etelka's situation only after the girl brought charges of rape against her foster father. At the appeal hearings, Etelka's reliability was questioned, presumably because several neighbors had spread the rumor that she had visited the unmarried workmen's quarters to offer sex for money.[2] Her foster father admitted that he had regularly beaten the girl with a rubber hose when she was disobedient. The neighbors testified that this meant Etelka had refused to satisfy his physical desires. However, because she was suspected of having engaged in prostitution, Etelka lost the right to make a claim for mercy from the community. Her foster father was released and Etelka was left to return to the "family nest."

The narrowest definitions of poverty focus on the income or property of individuals or families and are generally confined to determinations of the level of bare necessity and "standard of living." They often attempt to identify "what percentage of the population was poor at a given time." In addition to income, a more complex version of the same definition also considers "consumption" when defining the "poverty threshold."[3] A broader definition considers the poor to be those who are deprived of opportunities and social, economic, or cultural capital. Research based on a definition of poverty as deprivation also focuses on the absence (and dispossession) of physical amenities, health, security, and the sense of security, "welfare goods," and "status goods."[4] Hungarian research on poverty moved roughly within these ranges, reforming the above definitions during the socialist and postsocialist regimes: Zsuzsa Ferge's studies in the field concentrate on occupational status, Iván Szelényi's on the effects of redistribution on the growth of social inequalities, and István Kemény's on way of life.[5]

In Sztálinváros the barracks, as part of the "grown" city, were viewed by the local authorities as hotbeds of poverty and "deviance" because the local administration had to deal with the everyday problems faced by residents of Radar and South Side. The council, police, and court proceedings against barrack residents determined who was eligible to claim social welfare and who was not.[6] From time to time, the norms that served to distinguish between "honest" and "disreputable" poverty were regulated.

This chapter examines the relationships between state welfare policy and poverty in Sztálinváros through the story of a woman living in the barracks, who had legal action taken against her. My intention is not to present a "typical case" of destitution in Sztálinváros, since the existence of any such "typical" cases is doubtful. Rather this chapter describes the process by which a person lost the opportunity to make a claim for assistance from the state or the community. Furthermore, I offer a description of the methods used by the state to draw a distinction between "honest" poverty and "disreputable" poverty, a practice with roots that stretched back to the precommunist era. I will argue that because state institutions dealt primarily with cases of "disreputable" poverty, most local administrative sources contain information on this phenomenon and its characteristics. The tens of thousands of residents who were believed to live an "honest" life appear only occasionally in these sources. Thus the story of Mrs. P. is an "illustration" not of poverty, but of the process by which "poverty" was assessed and categorized.

The chapter also demonstrates that this practice became part of everyday life in Sztálinváros at the end of the 1950s, when the municipal bureaucracy resolved to "cleanse" the city of "unhygienic" social groups.[7] The "public welfare politics" that came in the wake of 1956 made the poor a target and scorecard for the bureaucrats who sought to implement social reforms. Poverty in the city was treated

Figure 9.1. Police photo of an apartment in the South Side.

as a security and health issue, an approach with traditions in precommunist times. State institutions sought, on the one hand, to create a welfare state, and on the other, they adopted aggressive measures when dealing with the destitute, and the state saw these steps as part of the maintenance of one and the same utopia.[8] The measures that were taken in the fight against poverty were acceptable to the inhabitants of the downtown area, the residents of the city who led "proper" lives, and they found support among the general populace. In this case, social solidarity proved weaker than the forceful acts of the state institutions.

The substance of the terms *poverty* and *social policy* changed. The pursuit of one's interests in the face of the paternalist state became almost the only mode of achieving one's aims. Thus in this context, any reference to social policy is little more than a euphemistic allusion to a state of affairs in which the regime both giveth and taketh away. Because of this, the people who lived in the slums of Sztálinváros and who had the least means of asserting their own interests were obvious targets of the "cleansing" campaigns of the municipal administration. The protagonist of this chapter, a woman who was raising her children entirely on her own, was one of these people. The interests of the local administrative bodies that treated poverty as a security issue again overlapped with the interests of those living in the downtown area who led a "proper" life. Thus the state's efforts to deal with poverty contributed to the reproduction of social hierarchies and the implementation of measures that would meet with the approval of the downtown residents. The Stalinist policies, which until 1956 denied the very existence of poverty, were shaped in part by local residents who had been able to obtain an apartment from the City Council in the downtown area. The people living on the periphery of the city became "useful" victims in the process of establishing the downtown norms and the "proper way of life" in a socialist city.

The Sztálinváros Slum

The shared lavatories, paper-thin walls, and windows that looked directly out on one another brought many families and single people into close and almost continuous contact in the South Side and in Radar, the slums of Sztálinváros. Events that would have belonged to a family's private sphere often took place on a kind of shared stage. This led to numerous conflicts, the prevalence of which did not signify the disunity of the community but, on the contrary, its interdependence. These conflicts often culminated in legal proceedings that expressed the expectations neighbors placed on one another, along with the expectations the state placed on the residents of the barracks. An analysis of these court cases offers a more nuanced understanding of the state's expectations and the interrelationships of poverty and state intervention, which are discernible beneath the thin veil of welfare policies.

The main character in the story is a young woman, Mrs. P., who during the legal proceeding against her was labeled by the authorities and neighbors "an alcoholic," "a prostitute," "a negligent mother," and "a bad wife," among other things. Of these accusations, the court could only prove the charge of "negligent mother," so Mrs. P. was charged with having committed a "crime against youth."[9] Her life story up to the criminal proceedings included the landmarks (loss of parents, village poverty, migration to the city, and marriage at a young age) common to the lives of most of the people who moved to Sztálinváros and were considered poor by the other residents of the city.

Mrs. P. was born in 1934 in a village in Szabolcs County in northeast Hungary, one of the country's poorest regions. She lived there until 1954. Her father worked as a farmhand on an estate for the "squires." He did not own land either before or after 1945. Until the age of twenty Mrs. P. worked at home. Then her father died. The same year she married, and in the fifth month of a pregnancy she had a miscarriage. In the spring of 1955 she became pregnant again, and that summer she moved to Sztálinváros with her husband. Her husband worked as a driver and she was employed in a canteen. In late November 1955 her first daughter was born, and she claimed that after she gave birth she discovered that her husband was having an affair.

After this, she quarreled regularly with her husband, who had several extra-marital relationships. Mrs. P. began to go out on her own, without her husband. In early October 1956, her husband was transferred to Budapest, and although he returned home only once a week, he regularly sent her all his earnings. Rows and fights continued between them. Mrs. P. became pregnant again in the fall of 1956. In the summer of 1957 she gave birth to her second daughter. Before her baby was born Mrs. P. had already been a regular at Sztálinváros restaurants and bars. That summer she gave up her job because her workplace was moved to Pécs, a city 130 kilometers from Sztálinváros, which by that time was no longer the focus of investment. Employees of the national building enterprise had to choose: either they followed the enterprise to Pécs (or other regions in Hungary for other construction projects) or they would be laid off. The majority of the 1957 downsizings were not politically motivated, but rather were a consequence of economic considerations, and they mainly affected the less skilled members of the workforce.[10] Since they were bound to the town by their temporary yet sole residences, most of the residents of the Sztálinváros barracks had to search for new jobs.

After losing her job and giving birth to her second child Mrs. P. began to lead a life of indulgence. She consumed more and more alcohol and witness reports suggest that she had several sexual partners. In the winter of 1957 this began to arouse the suspicions of neighbors, with whom she had regular altercations. The first source available on Mrs. P. was written shortly after these events. Her life story was documented precisely because of the legal action taken against her. Mrs. P. resided in the Sztálinváros Radar barracks, approximately two kilometers from the center of town, next to the ironworks. (Today the only thing left of the barracks is the Radar Bar at the head of the subsidiary road that once led to the barracks.)

Brick barracks stood ten meters apart from one another along an inner macadam road. Initially the buildings had been designed to provide accommodation for eighty to one hundred residents. In 1953 some of the houses were rebuilt by the Stalin Ironworks Trust. A single-wing plan was developed, and by building a longitudinal partition wall a hallway was constructed off of which the rooms opened. One barrack building contained five 7×7 meter rooms, which opened directly onto the outside yard.[11]

Several reports suggest that in general residents of the barracks occupied their "apartments" without actually having obtained an official allocation certificate, so if someone caused "trouble" he or she could easily be evicted. The authors of these reports also stated that "families living in the barracks generally do not have a residence permit, and their permanent residences registered on their identity cards are located in different districts of the city and have long been occupied by others." In their view, "workers living in the barracks have rather limited needs. They are content to have a roof over their heads and they themselves do not bother to improve their situations. People who do not have jobs also take refuge here. They cover their minimum needs by taking occasional jobs or stealing shared property (such as the theft of firewood from the areas around the barracks).[12] Naturally, there are also residents in the barracks who, considering the circumstances, keep their apartments tidy and neat and live an honest life."[13]

The contention that "there are honest poor people too" has been part of the discriminative discourse on poverty since the nineteenth century, and was as typical of the writings of Sztálinváros journalists and employees of social welfare institutions as it had been of factory inspector reports in the nineteenth century, the authors of which drew a distinction between "honest" and "disreputable" workers. The basis of distinctions drawn between the workers was first and foremost normative and moralistic. Education and training counted less.[14]

A 1956 proposition by the Social Policy Department at the Health Department of the Sztálinváros City Council attempted to solve the problems faced by families by investing enterprises with the right to "reassess" employees with families on the basis of their work performance. The council suggested that those whose performance was deemed unsatisfactory be sent back with their families to their original homes after having been laid off. This bundle of measures included a proposition that national enterprises would not allocate residences in the barracks to workers with families. The only exception was for workers who had been evicted from an apartment in the city with their families due to layoffs.[15] As often happened, this idea was never implemented (except for the evictions). Not a single council or national enterprise official dared take responsibility for displacing thousands of families that had been designated as poor.

Mrs. P. and the Authorities

The council and the court took action against residents of the barracks not out of goodwill, but because of the requests made by neighbors. State welfare agents intervened in the private lives of residents of the barracks only in extreme cases. This is what happened to Mrs. P. Action was taken against her at the initiative of neighbors, not the authorities. Neighbors ostracized her, considering her a negligent mother, an alcoholic, and a woman of loose morals. As far as the authorities were concerned, the residents of the barracks were all similarly penurious.

The report on the barracks claims that "children grow up in the streets." In Mrs. P.'s case, the same claim became an accusation. The report said that families and single-parent families made a living by doing odd jobs, which was deemed a criminal act in Mrs. P.'s case, since for more than a year she had not held a permanent job. Contradictory rumors spread by neighbors, the questions posed by the police (which were based on stereotypes and formulated as accusations), and sensational descriptions by journalists left the accused, who was already ostracized, utterly defenseless.[16] This was exacerbated by the inconsistencies of the authorities (police records reveal that the investigation took only a few days, the appointed attorney failed to appear at the hearings and sent his clerk to substitute for him, and the hearing lasted hardly longer than three hours, including the rendering of judgment). Thus the trial drew a symbolic dividing line between "honest" poverty and the "disreputable" lifestyle. In the eyes of the court, the behavior of the accused, though it stemmed in part from the poverty in which she lived, constituted a criminal act.

One of the neighbors who pursued criminal proceedings against Mrs. P. was Mrs. József B. This neighbor was originally from Kisbajom, a village in South Hungary, where women still remembered the story of Lidi Zsobrák, who had allegedly been taken in a hansom cab to see her lover in Pécs, the largest city in that region. Even fifty years after the affair, Kisbajom women still told of a famous beautiful woman: "Lidi Zsobrák's lover was an officer. She was driven in a curtained cab to see him in Pécs." According to the account, "Immoral young women were made to sit on the bench of shame. Zsobrák's mother, Lidi Zsobrák also had to sit there. There were some who didn't, who killed themselves. Jumped into the well. Good looking young women, immoral ones had a separate bench. It was located underneath the organ loft. Lidi Zsobrák, and I don't remember the names of the others, but they were standing there. Womenfolk, the harlots had to sit there. Church elders made them do so."[17]

The story was recorded by Ilona Dobos, a folklorist. It was told by Mrs. József Tót Szőke, whom she had met in the fall of 1953 in Sztálinváros. Mrs. Tót had followed her son to Sztálinváros. They were allocated a small kitchen in one of the quarters where they lived together.

One finds the same motif in the story of Mrs. P., a modernized version of the tale of Lidi Zsobrák. Neighbors claimed that Mrs. P. was taken in a cab, and the journalist writing an article about the case of Mrs. P. said she was taken in a car, to Budapest, in all likelihood to see her lover. For many people in the 1950s, a car was like a hansom cab, a sign of wealth (and party leadership status). It was viewed as a status symbol.[18] However, the sources neglect to note that at the time, Mrs. P.'s husband was working as a driver in Budapest, and he may well have simply taken his wife for a drive.

In the eyes of the neighbors, Mrs. P.'s most heinous transgression was that she received male visitors at her apartment. In other words, like Lidi Zsobrák, she behaved like a "whore." The neglect of the children was presented as a major crime in the records after the child welfare authorities and the police had "taken measures." In contrast, the police officer who originally brought action against her had not even mentioned the care she gave the children. Like the neighbors, the police also considered "fornication" with "various men" her most serious crime. To prove this, the authorities conducted a supplemental investigation in the course of which it became apparent to the officers taking the testimony of witnesses that Mrs. P. did not engage in "furtive sexual acts" for money. She seems rather to have acted on her own free will, having extramarital relationships much as her husband had done during her first pregnancy. It might be too simple an explanation, but in her testimony Mrs. P. claimed to have done what she did in order to take revenge on her husband. This part of the testimony demonstrates how Mrs. P. interpreted her own acts as "rebellion," whereas her neighbors considered them a crime. Mrs. P. rebelled against her husband and patriarchal norms, while her neighbors were able to exclude her from their community by calling on the organs of the state bureaucracy that dealt with poverty for help, and in doing so ensuring that she would be forever branded as poor. The norms of the neighbors overlapped with the norms of the government bodies. They were able to choose from among the various principles suggested by the bureaucracy when condemning the woman.

In other words, the norms offered by the state made it possible for the community to legally drive a woman raising her children on her own from her home. In this interpretative framework, Mrs. P. began frequenting bars, spending time away from home, failing to prepare hot meals, having love affairs, getting intoxicated, and getting involved in fights, just as men did. But these acts were not regarded as grave "crimes" (and possibly not as crimes at all) when performed by a husband, provided he contributed his income to the family budget.[19] Despite his extramarital affairs, drinking habits, and fights, because Géza P. sent his earnings home, neither his neighbors nor the authorities labeled him a criminal. The fact that he regularly abused his wife further verified for the court and neighbors that Mrs. P. was the sole "culprit."

The husband's responsibility was further extenuated in his assessment (and the assessments of the neighbors and the court) by the fact that from time to time he went home and ordered his wife to "do the laundry," and, furthermore, he forbade his wife to see her best friend, Mrs. Á., who according to the reports was Mrs. P.'s drinking buddy and was believed to have tempted Mrs. P. to indulge in wanton and criminal acts. So in the eyes of the court Mrs. P. was at remiss in her duties, and the husband had the right to reprimand her. Mrs. P. adopted "masculine" habits that were seen as unworthy of a "respectable" mother. Texts written during the proceedings suggest that it was the sole responsibility of the mother to care for children. By punishing her, the authorities defined what a "respectable" mother was allowed to do and what she was compelled to do. The charges shed light on the expectations placed on Mrs. P. by both the state and the community around her. Thus the community was able to condemn her by referring to communal norms, which themselves were all the while being adapted to official expectations.

The court stated that Mrs. P. had virtually admitted to committing a crime against youth. This was, of course, far from reality from Mrs. P.'s perspective. She pleaded guilty to having neglected her children, but she denied charges of having had sexual relationships with various men. According to the court, however, her denial was undermined by the facts that the police patrol had warned her to change her lifestyle and that "neighbors had seen strange men visiting her at her home—clearly, not because they had nothing to do with the accused." Mrs. P. also denied that there had been worms in her child's bed, but Mrs. B. claimed that it was so (and the court believed her). Initially, the accused also denied that her children had gone hungry. She claimed that this accusation was fabricated by hostile witnesses. The court claimed that the medical evidence gathered when the children were placed in the care of the state proved that they were malnourished. The underlying reasons for all this (malnourishment, the unhealthy conditions in the apartment, and the motivations of the families that had moved in), however, were not investigated by the court. The court also did not consider why Mrs. P. had remained in Sztálinváros. Together with many other barrack residents she hoped to be allocated an apartment with central heating and a bathroom in one of the modern buildings she herself had helped to build.

Mrs. P.'s story can also be interpreted as an attempt by residents of a slum to establish norms. In this regard, the neighbors who pursued action against Mrs. P. ostracized her in part to contrast their images of themselves with an image of the "deviant" poor. The more one's own lifestyle resembled the lifestyle of the poor, the more important it was to insist on a distinction between the "honest" and the "disreputable" poor.

The Uses of Poverty

Poverty existed in Sztálinváros because it was "useful," that is, it had numerous beneficial functions for several social groups. What does "useful" mean in this context? The "radical functionalist" approach to poverty and the ways in which poverty can be "useful" was first explained in a 1972 article by Herbert Gans, and this model offers insights into the Sztálinváros policies regarding poverty.[20]

The poor perform the physically demanding, dangerous, seasonal, underpaid, and undervalued "dirty jobs." Consequently, economic undertakings that are based in part on "dirty jobs" depend on the poor and poverty. In Sztálinváros, construction work was one such "dirty job." Generally, construction offered employment opportunities for social groups that were considered poor. Without the barracks, which provided housing for the people who did "dirty jobs," there would have been no easily available workforce willing to do these tasks, and without this workforce, plans for investment in construction would have been more difficult to realize. Although officially and publicly both the City Council and officials at the ironworks wanted to close the barracks, they were nonetheless bound to some extent by their direct interests to keep the barracks open and

Figure 9.2. House of Culture in the South Side.

functioning, as indeed is clear from the fact that the barracks remained in use until the 1970s.

Thus poverty secured a cheap labor force for projects, thereby indirectly supporting investments that generated benefits for people who were not poor. Such projects include the construction of apartment houses and apartments equipped with modern conveniences in Sztálinváros, which were generally built by barrack residents and occupied by technical specialists or skilled workers of higher social status.

The existence of poverty leads to the creation of welfare institutions and thereby the creation of jobs for those whose task it is to deal with the poor. Had there been no poverty in Sztálinváros, many jobs would not have come into being—for example, positions in the social and health departments of the council or national enterprises. In addition, poverty also creates jobs for people who are responsible for "cleansing" the slums—for example, police or those working in the Management Department (Igazgatási Osztály) of the council. The proceedings against Mrs. P. secured incomes for many officials, including the functionary in charge of child welfare, the district nurse, several police officers, journalists who wrote about "social issues," and the presiding judge. They were all paid for a few days of work to address her case.

The poor also consume products that the well-to-do refuse to purchase (for example secondhand clothing). At Sztálinváros fairs many substandard and secondhand items were exchanged, and this created a market for goods that would otherwise have been difficult or impossible to sell.[21]

In addition to playing these economic roles, poverty serves many other social-cultural functions. Among these, perhaps the most important is the part it plays in legitimizing norms by creating the norms of the poor, who can be identified and, if necessary, stigmatized as deviants. Similarly, the existence of "slums," with their "deviant" residents, legitimized the code systems of the "elite" parts of the city. In this manner the Sztálinváros barracks and the (mis)conduct of their occupants helped stabilize the "respectable" norms of the downtown area. Poverty strengthened the sense of spatial divisions in Sztálinváros and the conceptual segregation of the downtown area and the outskirts.

The existence of poverty also creates opportunities for social groups to do "charity" work. In addition, members of groups willing to offer "charity" may feel themselves fortunate not to be poor, which strengthens their perceptions of their own status (an interplay that is quite palpable in the relationship between the residents of the downtown area in Sztálinváros and the residents of the barracks). Most of the people who moved to the city came from villages or workers' colonies, and if they were given their own apartments and well-paying jobs, as far as they were concerned the move to the city represented a step up in the social hierarchy. This perception was strengthened by the fact that some people were given housing in the barracks. People who were allocated "urban" housing in one of the better neighborhoods of the city may have considered themselves particularly fortunate.

People who live comfortable lives can observe from a distance the actions and events that are so often attributed, at least in part on the basis of stereotypes, to the poor. For instance, according to a prevalent stereotype, alcoholism is more common among the poor and the poor are, in general, more licentious. For this reason, articles reporting on the proceedings against Mrs. P. tended to highlight these motifs, and presumably contemporary "downtown" readers also "reveled" in these details. Whether the poor actually consume more alcohol or are more licentious is neither here nor there. For several social groups, stereotypes serve to prove the existence of norms about which they only fantasize. Sensationalist journalism about slums was related to the contemporary discourse that propagated the welfare policies of the Kádár government, thereby clearly distinguishing the pre-1956 and post-1956 eras. The sensationalist articles written about the case of Mrs. P. used a language in which poverty is sensational and the only person bearing any responsibility is the accused.[22]

In a society in which social mobility is a significant goal and people consider it important to make their rise in the social hierarchy visible to others, poverty also enables those who do not consider themselves poor to differentiate them-selves from the impoverished, and thereby affirm their social status. This is particularly significant for members of groups that are considered poor by the majority but who do not view themselves as such. In Mrs. P.'s story this distinction is palpable in the manner in which neighbors distinguish their "respectable" life-style from her "deviant" lifestyle, and they create a norm via, for example, legal proceedings shaped by them and the local authorities.

Conclusion

Under the socialist regime the centralized treatment of poverty could not be made public because officially poverty did not exist. In a similar fashion, the labeling of Sztálinváros barracks as slums was possible only if this designation attracted little publicity. This essentially determined the discourse on poverty and slums, as well as the institutional welfare network. The issue was such a taboo that even the City Council was officially not allowed to include it on its agenda. Characteristically, in Sztálinváros for a long time the Social Policy Department functioned (as if under cover) within the administrative framework of the Health Department, which of course did not mean that it did not have numerous problems to solve or a wide range of responsibilities. The Social Policy Department played a primary role in child welfare proceedings. Yet in the administrative discourse Mrs. P.'s case was treated as a problem of "administration," "child welfare," "health," "po-lice supervision" (and within this, police who dealt with prostitution), and "crim-inal law," and not as a welfare issue, even though the majority of people involved in the prosecution designated Mrs. P.'s case as an example of the effects of "poverty."

When declaring the verdict and sentence in Mrs. P.'s case, the court primar-ily relied on the officially accepted stereotype that many parents in Sztálinváros, and especially in the barracks, failed to provide and care for their children, and so these children became criminals. In cases of juvenile delinquency in Sztálin-város, the court claimed to have ascertained that if a minor committed a crime, this was first and foremost due to the failings of his or her parents. However, in the case of Mrs. P., the fact that she had no previous convictions and was a mother were both regarded by the court as mitigating circumstances.

Mrs. P. was given a one-year jail sentence, and she was forbidden to exercise her rights as a parent for two years. A long article on the trial in the *Sztálinvárosi Hírlap* stated: "The law on which the proceedings against Mrs. P. were based is an old one. The previous society disregarded the directives included in it. But social-ist society and socialist jurisdiction must enforce this law to its fullest."[23] The ar-ticle held Mrs. P. solely responsible for the malnourishment of her children, the condition of the apartment, and her alcoholism. The proceedings against Mrs. P.

conformed to Stalinist policies that blamed the poor for their poverty, insofar as the socialist state offered them every opportunity to escape penury. However, the ostracism and punishment of Mrs. P. specifically and the Sztálinváros poor in general served as examples and also had fundamental economic and social-cultural functions, which were part of the foundation of the state welfare system. The state disguised its control of welfare as housing policy, health care, child welfare, and the practice of criminal law, thereby defining poverty as an issue of housing policy, child welfare, and criminal justice, and circumscribing the group of people who were eligible for welfare. Welfare policy not only exerted a form of social control over the most defenseless social groups (the homeless, abandoned children, and the elderly), it also constantly redefined itself, enabling employees in the field to emphasize the relevance of their responsibilities. Poverty was primarily a police issue, as in the case of Mrs. P. She was abandoned not only by the state but also by the community, her social environment, her family, and her neighbors, as was her mother, who was left without care after her daughter began her prison sentence.

Notes

1. FML, f. XXV-24-a, 1963, b. 11, B III.130.
2. Many of the people who gave testimony vouched for the truth of these claims. However, it cannot be determined with any certainty whether Etelka had sexual intercourse with residents of the workmen's hostel for money or, as she contended, simply went there to collect the men's clothes to wash them for money. The gynecologist's report reveals that Etelka was not a virgin when the proceedings began.
3. For a summary of the history of this definition, see Fields, *Poverty, Inequality, and Development*.
4. Anthony Forder and Robert Holman each offer a more detailed summary and essential bibliography of the above definitions, see Forder, "Explanations of Poverty," and Holman, *Poverty*. On the Hungarian uses of the definition of poverty based on deprivation see Bokor, *Depriváció és szegénység*, and Bokor, *Szegénység a mai Magyarországon*.
5. Ferge, *Fejezetek a magyar szegénypolitika történetéből*; Szelényi, *Új osztály, állam, politika*; Kemény, *Szociológiai írások*.
6. On the interrelationships between social welfare, poverty, and notions of deviancy prior to World War II in Hungary, see Gyáni, "Könyörületesség, fegyelmezés."
7. On the use of "cleansing" and "hygiene" as pretexts for state violence in the early Soviet period, see Holquist, "State Violence as Technique."
8. On the goals of the communist "welfare" programs, see Hoffmann: *Cultivating the Masses*, 306–8.
9. FML, f. XXV-24-a, Criminal proceedings, b. 4, 1958. B. 314 / 1958, the Case of Mrs. Géza P., Crime against youth.
10. Layoffs for political motivations attracted more attention—both at the time and in historical sources—than the "downsizing" of the unskilled labor force, whose members obtained jobs due to the 1950s industrial expansion. Zsuzsanna Kőrösi and Adrienne Molnár analyze

the experiences of layoffs as a consequence of involvement in the events of 1956, in *Carrying a Secret in My Heart.*

11. FML, f. XXIII-502, b. 11, Report on the Radar barracks compiled by the Social Department for the May 17, 1956, Executive Committee meeting.

12. The writer of the report uses "communal property" to refer to stolen objects and utensils that were communally used by barrack residents.

13. FML, f. XXIII-502, b. 11, Report on the Radar barracks.

14. Litván, *Magyar munkásszociográfiák*, 34–70.

15. FML, f. XXIII-502, b. 11, .

16. *Sztálinvárosi Hírlap*, July 18, 1958, 2; September 12, 1958, 5.

17. Dobos, *Egy folklórgyűjtő feljegyzései*, 81.

18. On the shifting meaning of the car and driving and their roles as status symbols after World War II, see Majtényi, "Életstílus és szubkultúra."

19. "Folk disciplinary traditions" also regarded frequenting bars and having extramarital relationships as far more serious sins if committed by a wife rather than a husband. Tárkány Szücs, *Magyar jogi népszokások*, 783–84.

20. Gans, "The Positive Functions of Poverty."

21. FML, f. XXIII-502, b. 7, May 5, 1954.

22. *Sztálinvárosi Hírlap*, July 2, 1957, 2–3; July 18, 1958, 2.

23. Ibid., September 12, 1958, 5.

10 Prostitution

> By the standards at the time, she was a relatively well-educated woman. She was single, in her thirties. That is, she was older than I was. And she was awfully held back. There were these moral preachings as well. Then she met a German mechanic, she was initiated into the world of sex, and after that she had a sex life that was so active that it showed that people found a strange and peculiar freedom in this world. This strange freedom does not mean liberty in the political sense. But it refers to how people would break away from the general sociological environment and get a taste of independence, independently reached decisions, and opportunities in every field of life, from progress at the workplace to the variety of jobs to sexuality.

Sztálinváros was widely seen as the embodiment of "sin city," a characterization that was supported in part by the perception that the people of the city had libertine sex lives. How can the official image of the relationships of the people of the city be reconciled with the images people had of the intimate relationships of the men and women in Sztálinváros? In this chapter I address this question primarily in regard to the attitudes of the official organs in Sztálinváros toward prostitution, which was seen as the greatest threat to family life, and how prostitution and these attitudes influenced the definitions of acceptable and unacceptable forms of sexuality.

Sexuality is the most important factor in power relations between the sexes. Public discourse on sexuality plays a crucial role in gender constructions. In the public discourse in Sztálinváros sexuality figured primarily in connection with criminal acts and moral questions, which was not uncommon in other places either.[1] The threat of women driven by the Stalinist labor policy taking jobs traditionally performed by men, however, had an important influence on the discourse of sexuality in Sztálinváros. Official discourse distinguished between legitimate and illegitimate sexuality, including prostitution, which was seen officially in every socialist country as a symptom of capitalist society that had no place in the East.[2] The construction of legitimate sexuality, however, was determined by what was labeled deviant and reprehensible. Socialist morality tied legitimate sexuality to the institution of marriage, and often illegitimate forms of sexuality were also defined in relation to marriage (one thinks of the terms "premarital" and "extramarital" sex).

This chapter will explore how the local authorities (especially the vice squad) saw prostitution as the most menacing threat to family life, and thus prostitution became the central theme of official and unofficial discourses on sexuality after family life became the cornerstone of local policies in the mid-1950s (see chapter 4). The main reason for this was that images of prostitution conformed perfectly to the discourse in which sexuality virtually only emerged as a theme when it was considered deviant, reprehensible, violent, and immoral. Another reason was that the officials in Sztálinváros, and in particular the people working in the security organs of government, liked to deal with the anomalies in city life. Thus issues related to sexuality appear in the documents because of the questions at hand, which were often hardly ordinary. Furthermore, prostitution was closely tied to unemployment among women.[3]

Nonetheless, the stereotype of sexuality as representing a free space for contemporaries in an unfree society under the socialist regimes is pervasive.[4] This stereotype, I argue, is misleading at best. The image of sexual freedom actually facilitated the condemnation of women as lascivious because, after the conservative turn, it functioned as a counterpoint to the revival of traditional and enduring gender roles. The labeling of women as inappropriately immodest or licentious was a product of a traditional gender hierarchy that stretched back to well before the communist era. This hierarchy was challenged in early Stalinist labor policies and in particular in campaigns to create new occupations for women, but during the process of de-Stalinization, protests were made against the image of the woman who sought work in positions traditionally occupied by men. Indeed women who worked ran the risk of being labeled prostitutes, and not only by male managers but even by journalists.[5]

The image of female workers as half-prostitutes was also shaped by the official campaign to safeguard family life and the fight against promiscuity after the mid-1950s. One of the symbols of promiscuity was prostitution, which was officially under constant attack. However, it became apparent by the end of the decade that it was accepted, even in the workplace, where women had only a limited space to achieve their goals. Furthermore, the authorities (mostly the police dealt with this issue) characterized prostitution as the product of "deviant" female conduct observed primarily among working-class women.[6] Because prostitution was depicted as a type of female hooliganism, control over prostitution and promiscuity was mostly a didactic task for the police. Thus the police were given didactic functions via the vice squad and the constant struggle against prostitution, as if the prostitutes were selling their bodies because they had failed to obtain a proper education. In the early stages of construction of the city, the rights of female workers were much more important to the authorities, as the disciplinary proceedings at one workplace show. After the mid-1950s, however, characterizing female workers as lascivious, and blurring the distinction between prostitution and the sexuality of working women helped revive and reinforce the traditional gender hierarchy in the workplace.

Female Workers and Prostitution

The police, all too willing to accept prevalent stereotypes, regarded women in blue-collar jobs as likely future prostitutes. According to one report, 85 percent of the cases of prostitution occurred in Sztálinváros because "the job opportunities attract women who arrive here from villages and other settlements in the hope of finding a job. Sooner or later some of them get into the company of prostitutes and because of their ignorance or the easy income they themselves become prostitutes."[7]

As noted above, in the early 1950s the rights of female workers in the workplace were an issue of importance, as evidenced by disciplinary proceedings in workplaces. In the case in question, chief foreman László H. was determined to behave "arrogantly with unskilled female workers, using the rudest words and expressions, and when they failed to make him tea or prepare scrambled eggs and bacon for him on time during working hours he spoke of them as prostitutes." One witness stated that László H. had expressed his wish to bring his wife to the city, but she had not liked the idea.[8]

Another case offers a clear example of an explicit promise of promotion in exchange for sex and the official condemnation of this transgression. Chief foreman technician Elek G. "made unethical offers to retrainee lathe operator women at his post, inviting them to his apartment, and during working hours he conducted himself in an unacceptable manner with them." Margit Sz., a thirty-year-old witness, offered the following account: "Elek G. was my foreman. . . . He asked why my sister was so silly to go hungry instead of visiting his apartment, where they would have a great time. . . . On one occasion I heard him remind my sister that they were meeting at 8:30. But my sister did not show up. Ever since he has been ridiculing my sister by calling her 'little eight-thirty.'"

A twenty-five-year-old lathe operator retrainee was also summoned as a witness. He made the following claim, quite possibly out of jealousy: "My wife told me that Comrade G. would promote her to the position of operator if she went to see him in his apartment one night." Elek G. was dismissed on the grounds that "[although] our constitution secures a woman's equality and right to work, Elek G. belittles the female workforce."[9] Elek G. was dismissed in 1952, when the propagation of the image of female workers performing tasks in industry was still often on the agenda. The language used during the proceedings suggests that something else must have been going on in the background, and the disciplinary procedure was only a pretext for his dismissal. However, the pretext itself proved so effective that feminist principles were presented as part of the socialist ethic.

Prostitutes and female workers who did heavy physical labor both earned their incomes with their bodies, so according to stereotypes at the time women who worked as unskilled laborers had a great deal in common with prostitutes. Police reports reveal that for many women prostitution was only a temporary phase until they found a job, and some women workers used prostitution to supplement their wages.[10] Mass unemployment among women in Sztálinváros made it more difficult for women who occasionally earned money as prostitutes to become workers again. In Sztálinváros the transformation of the attitude toward prostitution involved the assertion of a clear distinction between prostitution and the sexuality of working women, a distinction that was necessary if the socialist state was going to either glorify or stigmatize the working woman.

There were many myths of legendary Sztálinváros prostitutes, and these myths influenced the identity of Sztálinváros residents. A person who left town recalled that "according to public belief at the time it was impossible and indeed improper to return unspoiled from Sztálinváros. A man who left the city without taking with him a memorable experience was an idiot. Those who were less fortunate left with other stuff as well."[11]

Since the nineteenth century, public discourse has presented prostitution as a police and health issue. Accordingly, the major responsibility of the state is to protect its citizens' health (mainly from venereal diseases, stereotypically spread by prostitutes) and, in addition, to protect families and marriages from the moral morass of an unrestrained sex life. The tasks assigned to the vice squad, which was instituted purportedly to protect families, included the following: maintaining vice squad records (who posed a threat to families and how?); arresting people who had contracted venereal diseases (especially syphilis); tracking down homosexuals; pursuing charges of prostitution; tracking down brothels and keeping them on record.[12]

In Sztálinváros the number of prostitutes on record and the extent to which the police regarded the city as "infected" was determined largely by the number and intensity of police raids. Officers themselves admitted that the number of women listed in vice squad records within a given area did not necessarily rise or fall because the number of prostitutes grew or shrank, but because police officers were inexperienced, conducted fewer raids, or were asked to submit fewer reports at a given moment.[13]

Tracking down prostitutes and penalizing them were listed as important tasks quite early. The existence of prostitution was interpreted in several ways by members of the vice squad, the most common of which was to explain the number of prostitutes by the weather or changes in job opportunities. In the winter of 1952 police accounted for the increase in the number of prostitution cases with the contention that women and their customers "sought mutual satisfaction in their living quarters because of the cold weather, so oversight and arrests were much more efficient." On another occasion warmer weather was cited as the reason for the increase in the number of prostitutes because, according to the police, in good weather the number of single construction workmen grows, so demand grows too.[14] The police found brothels in half-completed Sztálinváros buildings, accommodations located on neighboring farms, mass housing projects, near to bars and "watering holes," and in the private hostels on the outskirts of the city. The majority of prostitutes placed on record in January 1952 were underage, the explanation for which was intriguing: "cold weather had set in, and since they have a bad attitude toward work, they start to live an immoral life, which briefly improves their financial situation." The police regarded public humiliation and assistance with finding employment as the most effective deterrents against prostitution. They achieved this by giving more attention in the press to the cases tried in court.[15]

In Fejér County in the spring of 1952, within a month the number of women arrested for prostitution decreased by twenty. The police explained that a new officer had taken charge of the vice squad: "He has recently been transferred here, and therefore he is not yet adequately familiar with the people and places."[16] The person who was previously in charge of the vice squad had for a long time released prostitutes without launching any kind of proceedings. He explained this by saying he would "soon leave to attend the Communist Party school anyway."[17] Furthermore, according to the police one of the obstacles they faced in the entire county was that although relations with the Hungarian Army had improved, "often comrades, especially officers, are reluctant to turn prostitutes on record over to the prosecuting police officer."[18] Army officers were regular customers of other prostitutes as well, which made the work of the police more difficult, since the army officers did not want their favorite prostitutes to fall into police hands. This happened with the H. girls, who, despite the protests of neighbors, regularly hosted in their apartment Soviet soldiers, who brought food and drinks: "Their sexual relationships with men are arranged by their mother, Mrs. Miklós H., who on one occasion also participated in an orgy with the Soviet soldiers. As compensation for sex, the girls were given watches, see-through stockings, and chocolate. The H. girls sold these items to neighbors."[19]

In the spring of 1952 a new vice squad officer was appointed to address the problems, but he also failed to meet his superiors' expectations, because he did not penalize recidivist prostitutes strictly enough, that is, he did not have them imprisoned.[20] An indication of the transformation in the Sztálinváros vice squad's work is that in the spring of 1952 only one-third of the women arrested were underage, and minor offense proceedings were launched against 60 percent of those arrested, who were charged with vagrancy and public menace, "as it was impossible to convict them of prostitution, since they all demonstrate a bad attitude toward work, they feign illness and on this pretext stay at home. While their coworkers were at the workplace, these women used their lodgings to host men with whom they had sex, but they were not placed under the surveillance of the public health authorities."

No one was placed under police supervision either, nor was anyone banished from the city, and none of the accused was interned. One-fifth of them were given jobs and had to start working. Those who were charged with minor offenses were given jail sentences of five to twenty months per verdict. There was no record of any man "who lived off the earnings of a woman paid for prostitution."[21]

After the Fejér County Central Police were condemned for inefficiency, raids were initiated targeting primarily the "hiding places of prostitutes." The Sztálinváros police department followed the supervisors' instructions on prostitution control and managed to produce appropriate reports. "Efficiency" was demonstrated by the increase in the number of women arrested. In addition, proceedings were launched against a greater number of them.[22] In the second half of 1952 more and more prostitutes were imprisoned, and the following year the police report on the work of its vice squad in 1952 contained the following remark: "last year work performance at the department on prostitution control showed a rise in figures, both in the number of women on record and in the number of legal proceedings." According to police reports, in the second half of 1952, "the solution to the social problems, job placement, and housing of people against whom action has been taken has also improved. However, one deficiency in the vice squad's work is that it only deals with people who are destitute or who are already known to the police, but has not yet tracked down the circle of upper-class whores."[23]

The police observed a close connection between the number of prostitutes and the layoffs from factories in which a large female workforce was employed.[24] Accordingly, women in blue-collar jobs were treated as potential prostitutes. This also surfaced in systematic raids at some of the female workers' hostels and the arrest of women for having "received male visitors late at night at the hostel that had been allocated as accommodation."[25]

The county summary report was content to affirm that "there are no police stations in the county anymore that would not initiate proceedings against prostitutes."[26] Officers of the vice squad regularly checked the people on record and compiled reports on how they performed at their workplaces.[27] Yet oversight and the systematic maintenance of records were made difficult because of the fact that many prostitutes often changed their places of residence.[28]

The Vice Squad and "Cleansing"

A police officer's work performance was regarded as efficient if he wrote several reports, placed as many women as possible on record for prostitution, and attempted to initiate proceedings against them. So the primary interest of Sztálinváros vice squad officers was to show an upward trend in the number of prostitutes on record, because they were rewarded for this. One reason for this was that in an ideal socialist city sexual norms were supposed to be under stricter control. Furthermore, the police ascribed to the stereotype according to which the city attracted prostitutes. The police effort to arrest as many prostitutes as possible was in part a response to the expectations placed on the ideal socialist town. Thus, paradoxically, in Sztálinváros the number of women on record showed an increase because, according to official expectations, under socialism, and consequently in a socialist town, prostitution did not exist.

Due to the increase in unemployment among women, as of 1954 fewer reports were published on how women placed on record as prostitutes were "assigned a job." Police sanctions were rather varied. The most lenient punishment was to require a woman to submit to an examination for sexually transmitted diseases. This could be followed by the assignment of a workplace, banishment from the city, legal proceedings on grounds of vagrancy and public menace (which usually entailed several months of imprisonment), and, finally, internment. However, occasionally (and naturally in secret) the arrest of a prostitute generated conflicts between the police and some powerful local potentate, so as of the mid-1950s prostitutes were given lighter punishments.[29] Operative reports in 1956 state that in the majority of cases, prostitutes were still warned or compelled to find a job by an assigned date.[30] In 1958 the bulk of the proceedings were limited to placing prostitutes under the supervision of the health authorities.[31] In contrast, the most serious punishment for people who paid for sex was to have their personal data recorded or, very rarely, to be subpoenaed as witnesses in some other criminal case. Only the prostitute was to be penalized for prostitution, not customers, which implies that the elimination of prostitution was not really a serious goal of the local police.

The vice squad was also responsible for tracking down homosexuals, but as they stated in 1953: "In Sztálinváros one such person was sentenced to ten months in jail, and the verdict was public knowledge. Ever since, we have not encountered such crimes. In the course of our investigations, we have not obtained information implying the commission of other criminal acts by homosexual individuals."[32] In January 1952 the police tracked down three homosexuals,[33] but they were unable to find one in 1953. Presumably, the number of homosexuals in Sztálinváros had not decreased, rather in all likelihood, owing to public deterrence, they were keeping a low profile. On the other hand, vice squad officers were unlikely to regard finding homosexuals as the most significant part of their jobs. The police attempted to bring homosexual acts to light by investigating other charges among people suspected of homosexuality. In other words, they ascribed to the stereotype that homosexuals were prone to commit other crimes as well. However, as they were unable to prove the commission of other criminal acts, the police were unable to launch proceedings against alleged homosexuals. Nevertheless, occasionally the police took the opportunity to banish people considered homosexual from the city.[34]

As of 1954, Sztálinváros was to become the city of families, so the vice squad and centers for the control of sexually transmitted diseases were given further assistance in the fight against prostitution. In June 1954, at the meeting of the Executive Committee of the City Council, the following contention was made: "The social factors (unemployment) that in a capitalist society are sources of the spread of venereal disease have partly been eliminated."[35] The association of venereal diseases with unemployment also served as grounds to stigmatize patients affected with such diseases. The argument was that one could only contract a sexually transmitted disease if one led an immoral life. This was part of the official ideology that made marriage the exclusive sphere of sexual life.

The "cleansing" of bars and taverns was also launched in 1954, and this effort was closely related to measures taken against prostitution, since according to council officials, "there are many suspicious women in bars and restaurants."[36] In the first half of 1955 the measures targeted hostels, where twenty-eight of the seventy-eight women on vice squad records resided. The report on this emphasizes that these women were easier to "handle" because they were employed, although very often they "lived a life of sloth and licentiousness."[37]

By 1959 authorities had managed to make the outskirts the most tainted districts "with regard to vice squad issues," meaning the old town, the barracks, and Szalki Island.[38] The police seem to have tolerated prostitution in these districts. While they were aware of the brothels operating there, they did little to eliminate them.[39] Voluntary patrolmen in the barracks regarded it as one of their main responsibilities to arrest prostitutes and people visiting the women's lodgings. Patrolman K. captured and arrested a person who "was intoxicated and made improper advances to women." He also captured Klára M., "the infamous whore in the district, and together with the evidence he took her to the criminal subdivision. For his unhesitant and courageous act Patrolman K. was disparaged by a South Side council member named Németh."[40] "Voluntary patrolmen Mihály Sz. and E. arrested a harlot who for a long time had been working in the Radar district. In addition, they also arrested a man who in an intoxicated state entered a women's lodgings and lay down in a bed. The patrolmen were only able to remove and take him to the police station by force." Voluntary patrolmen received money in recognition of their work. Some other patrolmen were to be rewarded at their workplace, but this did not always go as planned because at the workplace "people were thrust into the background and despised for being voluntary patrolmen."[41]

By the end of the 1950s the problem of prostitution for the most part was believed to have been solved, as demonstrated by the increasing occupation of vice squad officers with the sex lives of young girls. For example, they attributed the fact that "recently in several cases young girls contracted venereal deceases" to the disintegration of family life. With the astuteness characteristic of the police, they contended that this was because "it is mainly older men who wish to have sex with young women."[42]

Sztálinváros police had a considerable amount of information on the exact locations where people engaged in prostitution, women who worked as prostitutes, and the social backgrounds of the customers. The punishment a prostitute was given depended in part on this information. Street prostitution did not exist in Sztálinváros because it was prohibited. Prostitutes appearing in public places were quickly and severely punished, primarily to preserve the image of the socialist city. In this informal classification system, the second most persecuted districts were those frequented by people of lower social status. Prostitutes in the old town and barracks were the most systematically subjected to police oversight, yet they were also the most tolerated. The most common form of prostitution involved bars and restaurants, but it was the reputation of the given place that determined the extent to which the police kept it under surveillance. Inspections were systematic in bars frequented by people of lower social status, and prostitutes doing business there were arrested the most often. Thus they were stigmatized very early. In contrast, in the Golden Star Hotel no raids were conducted to eliminate prostitution. In all likelihood, this was why the importance of intensifying the "struggle against upper-class whores" (*úri frankák*) continuously remained on the agenda. Naturally, no measure was ever actually taken in this direction.

Prostitution was generally tolerated in semipublic places (such as bars and workers' lodgings), and little attention was given to prostitution that took place in private homes and buildings, far from the public eye, even if the police knew the addresses of the "secret" brothels. For example, in 1956 in Székesfehérvár, which in comparison with Sztálinváros was known as a conservative city, dozens of prostitutes and brothels were on record, all tolerated by the police.[43] It may well have been in the interests of the police that prostitutes met their customers in the places that were kept on record, because in that way they could regularly target the same places when organizing raids. This may also have enabled them to maintain oversight over places where, at least in their perception, sexually transmitted diseases were being spread by prostitutes.

Women who went to bars, restaurants, dance halls, and the like by themselves also risked being labeled prostitutes. A police report dated October 8, 1956, offers an illustration of the criteria on the basis of which the police would have presumed someone to be a prostitute: "I carefully examined the woman sitting alone. She was dressed rather flashily, but her hands, shoes, and handbag were not tidy. Her behavior and gestures resembled the deportment of women who pick up men in these kinds of bars and coffee shops and practice their 'profession' with them. . . . I took [her] to the police station, where she told me that she was an orphan, no one had taken care of her, and often she had resigned herself to downfall and degradation, and she had even wanted to commit suicide because life had defeated her."

The police officer seems to have been more preoccupied with the Budapest address and the other various details noted above than he was with the fact that the woman—who was taken to the station and later released—was a shorthand typist on commission in Sztálinváros. She filed a complaint in which she claimed to have been writing in her pocketbook to avoid the "watchful gaze of the men."[44] Although in principle socialism sought to ensure women equal rights, including the right to work, most women did not even have the right to go to a restaurant without a male companion unless they were willing to tolerate the suspicion that they were prostitutes. Accordingly, measures taken by the state to control and punish prostitution, and rumors that were spread about the sex lives of women with jobs served as safeguards with which to bolster gender hierarchies.

Conclusion

In Sztálinváros in the 1950s the temporary industrial workforce had become a permanent industrial labor force, and due to new immigrants arriving in the city the proportion of people doing odd jobs showed a downward trend. Owing to this process and the transformation in state regulations, the gap dividing prostitutes and working women also widened in Sztálinváros. Instead of frequenting labor hostels and downtown bars and restaurants, women who earned a living by prostituting themselves moved to the outskirts to continue their work. By the end of the 1950s the number of prostitutes who were being arrested had declined and the sanctions against them had relaxed. However, by this time the police did not consider it their responsibility to provide job placement for women convicted of prostitution, and thus they passed this task on to the women themselves. In view of their stigmatization and the high rates of unemployment among women, it was virtually impossible for these women to find jobs (at the most, they may have "found" fictitious jobs).

As of 1954, with growth in the number of families in Sztálinváros, the temporary population of unmarried men decreased, which also reduced the demand for prostitution (even if the majority of customers had not been unmarried men). Because it became increasingly difficult for a woman to move between the two spheres (legal employment and work as a prostitute), numbers dwindled on the "supply side" too. By the end of the 1950s the police had most of the remaining prostitutes under control, and prostitution was tolerated and sanctioned less severely.

Measures targeting prostitution served in part to make people regard extramarital sex as something extraordinary and even a form of deviance. However, it was not in the interests of the state to eliminate prostitution entirely. By subjecting prostitutes to aggressive legal proceedings, intense police surveillance, and stigmatization in the public discourse, and also by failing to prosecute people who paid for sexual gratification, the state ensured that prostitutes would be almost inescapably on the margins of society, and in doing so actually ensured that there would always be a kind of stable reserve of prostitutes.[45]

The contemporary descriptions presented the sex lives of Sztálinváros women as unusually licentious because in the "model city" the state intended to exercise stricter control over people's sexual activity, especially given the intention of the authorities to create a "city of families." Moreover, the primary goal of measures allegedly taken to control prostitution was actually to fortify representations of working women in Sztálinváros as lascivious tramps and to safeguard the positions of male workers at workplaces, which had been threatened by the early Stalinist labor policies. The reproduction of the gender hierarchies at the shopfloor level after the mid-1950s and the segregation of female workers in factories in light industry helped reload Stalinism with policies that were more acceptable to the male workers and thus to establish a more sustainable regime.

Notes

Epigraph: Interview with Tibor V., March 28, 2001.
1. Baber and Allen, *Women and Families*, 61.
2. McLellan, *Love in the Time of Communism*, 174.
3. Similarly, the connection between prostitution and unemployment during the New Economic Policy in the Soviet Union has been highlighted in numerous studies. Goldman, *Women, the State and Revolution*, 119.
4. Cf. Betts, *Within Walls*, 115; Miskolczy, *Város lesz csakazértis*, 33.
5. A similar tendency was observed in Poland in the 1950s, see Fidelis, *Women, Communism, and Industrialization*, 127, 241.
6. Cf. Fenemore, *Sex, Thugs and Rock 'n' Roll*, 23.
7. FML, XXIV-11, b. 9, 1957–58. Report on the second half of 1958.
8. MNL OL, f. XIX-F-2, b. 73, 1952.
9. MNL OL, f. XIX-F-2, b. 68. b. A case from 1952 without date.
10. As was found to have been the case in the Soviet Union in a study from 1923. Goldman, *Women, the State and Revolution*, 120.
11. Miskolczi, *Város lesz csakazértis*, 33.
12. FML, f. XXIV-11, b. 2, 1952.
13. The same is true of other crime and police statistics. For example, the growth in the number of minor offenses was attributed to the fact that "compared to the past three months during this quarter-year, liquor stores, bars, and restaurants where minor offenses were found to have been committed were more frequently inspected." FML, XXIV-11, b. 17, 1962.
14. FML, XXIV-11, b. 2, 1952. Report on April 30, 1952.
15. Ibid., b. 3, 1952. Report on January 30, 1952.
16. Ibid., b. 2, 1952. Report on May 3, 1952.

17. Ibid., b. 2, 1952, Report on April 1, 1952.

18. Ibid., b. 3, 1952, Report on February 5, 1952.

19. Ibid., b. 12, 1959, Report on June 23, 1959. Their file was opened on November 18, 1958.

20. Ibid., b. 2, 1952, Report on May 2, 1952.

21. Ibid., b. 2, 1952, Report on April 30, 1952.

22. Ibid., 3. b. 1952: "The quality of vice squad proceedings has improved substantially and significantly. Prosecution was efficient against approximately 90 percent of the women arrested. This work must be improved similarly by increasing the number of women arrested with at least the same percentage of proceedings. Furthermore, the initiation of administrative procedures must also be increased." Cf. in Nowa Huta 10 percent of female hostel dwellers were labeled "prostitutes or half-prostitutes" in 1955. Lebow, *Unfinished Utopia*, 120.

23. FML, XXIV-11, b. 4, 1953.

24. Ibid., b. 3, February 1, 1952.

25. Ibid., b. 3, January 30, 1952.

26. Ibid., b. 4, 1953, Report on January 12, 1953.

27. Ibid., b. 3.

28. Ibid., b. 3, 1952, Report on the January 1952 work of the Adony District Police. Among the women arrested there was one who arrived in Adony from Sztálinváros.

29. Ibid., b. 8, 1956. In 1952 action was taken against 45 percent to 62 percent of the women arrested (the proportion varied monthly). Ibid., b. 2, 1952.

30. Ibid., b. 8, 1956.

31. Ibid., b. 9, 1957–58, 1958 report on the second half of the year.

32. Ibid., b. 2, 1952.

33. Ibid., b. 3, 1952, Report on January 30, 1952.

34. Ibid., b. 3, 1953.

35. FML, f. XXIII-510, 1954, b. 2.

36. FML, f. XXIII-502, b. 7, November 11, 1954. Ibid.: Forty-eight women are listed in the vice squad records.

37. FML, f. XXIII-502, b. 10, August 18, 1955.

38. FML, f. XXIII-502, b. 16, August 14, 1959.

39. Ibid. Speech by György Csavajda. "Secret brothels" in the old town were found in many other cases, but police rarely initiated any proceedings. FML, XXIV-11, b. 8, 1956.

40. Presumably there was some kind of clash of interests.

41. FML, f. XXIII-502, b. 21, September 12, 1961.

42. FML, f. XXIII-502, b. 18, October 11, 1960.

43. FML, XXIV-11, b. 7, 1956.

44. FML, XXIV-11, b. 7, 1956.

45. Uta Falck arrives at similar conclusions in her analysis of state measures targeting prostitution and the role played by the state in sustaining prostitution in the German Democratic Republic. Falck, *VEB Bordell*, 37–72.

Conclusion

Dᴜʀɪɴɢ ᴛʜᴇ ᴛᴇɴᴛʜ anniversary celebrations of the founding of the city of Sztálinváros on July 17, 1960, thousands of workers gathered by the gigantic gate of
the ironworks to listen to the speech of János Kádár, the first secretary of the Hungarian Socialist Workers' Party. After the passing of a decade that had left hardly
any residents of the city certain about its future, the anniversary celebrations
broadcast by the newsreel demonstrated that the first socialist city in Hungary
was and would remain one of the most important investments of socialist Hungary. The ironworks would work and the city would flourish in the new era, an
embodiment of the triumph of the new order. The people living and working in
the city again would feel the importance of their efforts, although the city represented a Stalinist past that was hardly a distant memory, and after 1956 the Kádár
administration always strove to draw a clear distinction between the "Stalinist
years" and the new "human face" of socialism. The Kádár era and de-Stalinization,
however, ushered in an era of relative security and even prosperity compared to
the years before 1957.

The picture sequences of the newsreel created to capture the story of the anniversary presented a city that exemplified the aspirations of the socialist modernization campaign, including land surveyors, smoking factory chimneys, and
steel rolling machines. Kádár and other prominent members of the government
are depicted watching the machines with looks of gratified satisfaction on their
faces. One sees a diesel locomotive and shots of the local Pioneer Railway. Kádár
travels alongside children in a city that is home to happy, optimistic families.
Kádár inspects an open-air stage and an anniversary competition at the public
pool, which is a site of both learning and leisure, since sports are useful, hygienic,
modern pastimes that represent healthy alternatives to taverns and bars. Kádár
visits the housing estate, and his visit illustrates that everyone in the city has a
workplace and housing. Socialism guarantees every citizen a job and an apartment. A pillar bearing advertisements, street lights, and images of the city bathed
in the glow of lamps at night are tokens of modernity, stability and consumption,
and also motifs of an inspiring vision of postwar society.[1]

In 1960 not only the city of Sztálinváros seemed more stable but also the socialist regime itself, and not only in Hungary, but in all the countries of Eastern
Europe. According to Mark Pittaway, the political crisis of the mid-1950s "stabi-
lized the regimes by encouraging a climate in which populations learned to

Figure 11.1. János Kádár, First Secretary of the Hungarian Socialist Workers' Party, at the tenth anniversary of Sztálinváros.

accept the permanency of their socialist political orders."[2] Furthermore, in Hungary after the "instability of the thirteen years since 1945, the regime remained stable . . . for the following three decades."[3] At the end of the 1950s, according to Czesław Miłosz it became axiomatic for the people of the "East" that "the basic means of production should belong to the State, that they should be regulated according to a planned economy, and that their proceeds should be used for hygienic, cultural, scientific, and artistic ends."[4] The legitimacy of the regime, however, rested not only on the ways in which people accommodated to the new circumstances but also on the integration of traditional practices into the Stalinist policies. As Miłosz poetically describes it, "they have set out to carve a new man much as a sculptor carves his statue out of a block of stone, by chipping away what is unwanted."[5] This book, however, has looked at how the unwanted parts of the stone were integrated into the "new man" and how the state tolerated and, indeed, in some ways accommodated these formerly unwanted parts. In other words, it examined how the statue began to breathe and act as a historical agent, carving out spaces that also served as stones in the foundations of a long-lasting regime.[6] This Eastern European Pygmalion effect on the men of marbles,[7] who were building the new regime, played a significant part in making the regime stable and sustainable.

In this book I have explored the processes that helped the new regime stabilize itself on the everyday level. Specifically, I examined how the policies of the state and the habits and practices of ordinary citizens exerted mutual influences on each other, leading to the creation of a tacit social order in an artificially created community, which in the end actually became a real city. An understanding of this process helps us better account for why the regime lasted as long as it did, and it is also offers insights into why it was eventually abandoned in 1989/90.

As historian László Borhi has persuasively argued, the key factors in the maintenance of Soviet rule in Hungary were "military occupation coupled with the ideologically motivated loyalty and voluntary obedience of the Hungarian leadership."[8] These factors were palpable in other East European countries under Soviet rule. However, endogenous factors also played an important role in enabling the regime to survive for so long and in the construction of cities like Sztálinváros. In Stalinist policies regarding both social hierarchies and family life, significant shifts that were implemented by the authorities in the mid-1950s in part in response to the needs of ordinary people, also played a crucial role in this process. Because it examines the ways in which important segments of Hungarian society were complicit in the maintenance of the regime in Hungary, this book is part of the larger trend that began to emerge in the historical scholarship on Central Europe specifically and the study of autocracies in general in the 1990s. This trend rejects the totalitarian paradigm, which rests on a simplistic opposition between powerful perpetrator and powerless victim, and examines instead the limits of state control. By shedding light on the ways in which locals acted as historical agents and the extent to which they were able to influence and even reshape state policies, this book offers a nuanced understanding of how Sztálinváros became a real, functioning city.

Sztálinváros was considered a city not only by the authorities, including polemical institutions, but also by the inhabitants of the city. When asked whether or not he regarded Sztálinváros as a city, Tibor Vámos, an engineer who had worked there, offered the following reply in 2001:

> The city is a place where people can choose between numerous theaters or concert halls. There are entire institutions. It took a long time before these began to take shape, before the city had a museum, and a lot of other things. I was born in Budapest, and I always lived in Budapest, I was raised in Budapest. If I call Budapest a city, or even Pécs, then I cannot consider [Sztálinváros] a city. If I compare it with the old Pentele or any other city that I knew at the time, then I consider it a city. It depends on one's perspective. . . . The whole thing took shape as the situation consolidated. A construction site was turned into a well-organized large-scale industrial works, with a consolidated labor force

Figure 11.2. Stalin Avenue in 1958.

and local members of the intelligentsia. It was an enormous transformation, and it was constantly under way.[9]

People's views of the city were fundamentally determined by their assessments of the regime, since the city was seen as one of the creations of the regime. This was true even though the city was not built entirely in accordance with the original plans, with the exception of some of the plans for the buildings and roads. The "growing" city eventually swallowed the "planned" city (to borrow the terms used by Tibor Weiner, the chief architect of the city), and the original Stalinist policies were transformed by the residents and the ever-changing conditions. The state authorities were nowhere near as able to control the social processes that were taking place in the city as they had assumed they would be, and the limits of the dictatorship were shaped not only by ordinary people but also by members of the state administration and intelligentsia who were locked in seemingly endless debate with one another. As I have shown, these debates played a seminal role by creating divergent images of the city.

The contradictory images of the city strongly influenced the identities of the residents of Sztálinváros and the depictions of the urban spaces. The city, which in principle was intended to be homogeneous, was broken into different sections that symbolized divergent values. According to the conservative turn in officially supported values and beliefs in the mid-1950s, these diversifications helped reproduce the social hierarchies that were based on the renewal of family-based policies. This contributed to the emergence of social distinctions, a process that took place in socialist cities no less than in cities in the West, but at the same time, somewhat paradoxically, it also furthered the development of a sense of home within the different districts. However, the official distinction between urban and rural, which was much blurred at the everyday level, also played a role in the stabilization of city life by shaping the language used by the inhabitants in their official claims.

In the official rhetoric the urban lifestyle was contrasted with the rural lifestyle in much the same way that, when industrial cities emerged, a distinction was drawn between the people living in the city, who represented a kind of cultivation, on the one hand, and the "uncivilized" immigrants flocking to the city, on the other. The discourse of the socialist state transformed this worn opposition, which had been created to protect "urban values," to "civilize" the immigrants by adopting the Soviet model of *kul'turnost'*, and to educate the city's inhabitants. References to "proper" family life also played an important role in this didactic function of the city. Family bonds and traditional hierarchies within families were not weakened by the regime, especially after the mid-1950s. Furthermore, the high rate of abortions and divorce did not weaken family life, and not only because of "the importance of mutual support in difficult conditions."[10] The Stalinist policies were reshaped by the residents and by the authorities so that the family, as a unit of consumption, was safeguarded by the official propaganda as well as by the measures taken by local authorities. The renewed Stalinist policies regarding the family were intended to serve as a basis for legitimizing and sustaining the socialist regime.

The filmstrip that was published for the city's tenth anniversary was intended to demonstrate that socialist Hungary had caught up with industrialized countries in the West (e.g., "the high-speed train shortens the time need to travel to 70 minutes between Sztálinváros and Budapest") and also to show symbols of modernity and family life. The filmstrip also focused on the urban spaces of consumption and state welfare institutions.[11] Urbanity was represented by the number of residents of the city ("almost forty thousand people living there"), the main road (Stalin Avenue), public statues, the decade-old May 1 Street, and the public parks. The state welfare institutions included kindergartens, a new hospital, a doctor's consulting room, and different types of public schools, which produced the new intelligentsia. The spaces of consumption in the filmstrip included supermarkets and furniture and clothing stores for housewives (the term *housewives* was used again at the end of the 1950s), who while shopping also "visited the confectioner's shop" as well as the toy shop, the amusement park for families, restaurants, and

Figure 11.3. Flag on the water tower of Sztálinváros (view over May 1 Street).

fancy bars for couples. And last but not least, the film also presented the light industry factories, which provided jobs for unemployed women. Whereas in a 1952 newsreel the new women managers (Johanna Wolf, Zsófia Tevan)[12] at the Sztálinváros construction site represented the new class of female workers as the members of the new technical elite,[13] in a 1958 newsreel the recently built light industry factories of the city represented the exemplary sites of labor for females, factories in which women worked primarily as unskilled laborers who were separated from male coworkers.[14]

The "widespread popular support for Stalinism's promised social revolution" identified by Katherine Lebow in her examination of this history of Nowa Huta in Poland was also palpable in Hungary,[15] especially among members of the new intelligentsia and bureaucrats who cherished visions of a new age of "cultural enlightenment." This support, however, did not last long, and indeed it may well never have existed among the bricklayers and industrial workers living in the barracks in Sztálinváros. These social groups came to the city under construction to escape the postwar economic crisis, unemployment, and a shortage of housing that prevailed both in old industrial cities and in rural areas in Hungary.

For the young generation arriving in Sztálinváros the economic crisis and chronic unemployment of the 1930s were still vividly remembered childhood experiences, as were the suffering and extreme privations endured during the war. Consequently, the communist regime could seek legitimacy by providing work and housing in Sztálinváros, much as mobilization on the production front provided legitimacy for the communist takeover and the ensuing campaigns of rapid industrialization.[16] However, as I have endeavored to demonstrate, ultimately the creation of new workplaces and new apartments did not constitute a stable foundation for the legitimacy of the regime and the new social order, not only because of the flaws in the system of centralized housing distribution but also because of the inequalities in this system and the decline in investments at the construction site between 1954 and 1958.

Old habits that die hard created more problems for the new technical elite tasked with building a city from scratch than the thick mud that covered everything at the construction site. Accordingly, not only did the local authorities have to find new ways to appease the demands of the residents and to achieve their goals, the residents of the city had to accommodate to the new circumstances in order to obtain a position in the factory or a new apartment. Both the authorities and the locals (some of whom worked for the authorities) were reshaping each other during the process of construction of the city. After the mid-1950s, the fragile legitimacy of the regime rested on the reshaped Stalinist policies, which included more and more issues relating to the private sphere, including family-based rhetoric and initiatives.[17] As a consequence of the conservative turn that took place over the course of the 1950s, by the end of the decade the socialist regime propagated not industrial production, but rather growth in patterns of consumption among families and stable family life, and this was true even in the case of Sztálinváros, a city that originated in early visions of an urban center based on heavy industry. This is one of the reasons that, ultimately, nostalgic memories of communism in Hungary and other countries of Central Europe "tended to focus on domestic life."[18]

The city came into being as an embodiment of the communist utopian ideal, and its decline was also a consequence of this ideal. The origins of the violent rise of the state bureaucracy, which had the realization of a communist society as its goal, and the creation of a paternalistic "welfare state" (a term used with some irony in this context), which sought to reshape society using didactic tools, lay in the utopian aspirations of the communist vision. All this harks back to a notion that emerged during the Enlightenment, according to which society is not given, but can be shaped and transformed to embody our ideas and our ideals. According to David L. Hoffmann, "communist officials and non-Party specialists shared a belief in the rational management of the population, a reliance on statistics to represent society, and a highly medicalized language to depict social problems and interventionist solutions."[19] The creation of Sztálinváros was indeed a stage (possibly even a late stage) in this process of social engineering that was rooted in the Enlightenment.

Since the rise of the revisionist school of historians, dominant trends in historical scholarship on postwar Europe have not only replaced the totalitarian paradigm, which emerged in the Cold War era, but have also rejected the model of a "dictatorship based on consensus," which depicts the communist regimes as systems of social consensus and compromises. The inadequacies of both the totalitarian paradigm and the notion of dictatorship based on consensus become apparent when one ceases to examine the system in Hungary on the normative level and instead attempts to understand the ways in which the system functioned by examining social practices at the micro level.[20] This is because the state itself frequently changed its stance on the question of how it related to the fundamental principles necessary for the realization of a communist utopia, as did the "ordinary people" who were compelled to adapt to the dictatorship.

From the perspective of the Communist Party, the goal of the paternalistic alms or the construction of Sztálinváros was not to legitimize the use of violence by the state or violent nationalization, but to create the communist utopia. Following Stalin's death, leaders old and new, including Imre Nagy and János Kádár, did not "loosen" the dictatorship's grasp on the people, even if this may have seemed to be the case at the time.[21] Rather, they simply adopted new methods in the creation of the envisioned utopia. Both state violence and state paternalism were methods intended to lead toward the same goal, the creation of a communist utopia. Both were regarded as legitimate tools from the perspective of the party, and both were used at various times, depending on what seemed the most expedient means for the authorities to achieve their goals.[22] Thus the methods that were adopted were used not simply because "depraved villains" were running the country, as institutions that have catalogued the sins of communism have tended to claim.[23] Nor for that matter were they used because the regime that sought to create a communist utopia classified the inhabitants of the country in a manner that differed strikingly from the classifications used in modern welfare states.[24]

Beginning with the establishment of the socialist regimes, members of the party bureaucracy characterized violence as a tool used by the (Stalinist) state to create a better society and also to "educate" this society.[25] And while authoritarian systems of rule were hardly new to the region, the rise to power of the communist regimes, their increasingly well-organized bureaucracies, and the ability to keep society under complete and continuous observation and supervision had been more an aspiration than part of everyday practice. Until the end of World War II, the threat of upheaval and disarray was always far more imminent than the threat of omnipresent state oversight.[26] After 1945, however, in Hungary and the other countries of East Central Europe the best organized state bureaucracies the region had ever known were established in the interests of furthering the creation of a communist utopia. However, as I have attempted to demonstrate, at least in Hungary, it was able to shape the society's perception of itself through social accommodation.

As historian János M. Rainer has observed, Kádárism itself and the Kádár era represented a break with classical Stalinism in its presentation of the world and its discourses on social experiences: "Kádárism—to the extent that this is a scientifically precise term—is also a kind of perception of the world that gave rise to a general social condition. It is a system of continuous parallels and comparisons, which create an interpretive domain that is broad in space, time, and terminology."[27] This break, however, was slow and painful, lasting many long years. First, the language with which experiences could be expressed (and thereby created) had to be changed. Thus "Soviet collectivization" became "the formation of a cooperative," the peasant became "the working peasantry," a violent measure became an "administrative initiative" or simply "organized agitation," the overzealous implementation of which could threaten the "faith" of the "workers" in the party. The creation of a communist utopia began with the transformation of language, long before the first brick of Sztálinváros had been laid. One clear sign of the retransformation of this language came in 1989, when Imre Pozsgay, "state minister" at the time, suddenly announced on the radio that 1956 had been an uprising, not a counterrevolution. This was a clear sign that even party leaders had ceased to believe in the attainment of a communist utopia.

The changes made to the language affected the name of the city as well, When the city was named after Stalin in 1951, on the anniversary of the Great October Socialist Revolution, a celebration was held in Dunaújváros that was attended by thousands and featured several national party leaders.[28] Ten years later, *Magyar Közlöny*, an organ of the media that published government decrees, informed its readership that in accordance with the decision of the Presidential Council held on November 25, 1961, the name of the city had been changed to Dunaújváros, a name that was suggested by the Sztálinváros City Council. The city was quietly given a new, neutral name, just as the Stalinist policies were also quietly reshaped and new policies were presented. Other names were suggested that emphasized the production of steel, such as Steel City (Acélváros), Danube Iron

City (Dunavasvár), Foundry City (Kohászváros), and even Steel Fortress (Vasvárad), but the City Council rejected these names and chose the politically neutral Dunaújváros.

After November 25, 1961, the next issue of the *Sztálinvárosi Hírlap* was published under the new title *Dunaújvárosi Hírlap*. It contained an explanation for the change of name, which was characterized as a symbolic break with the past: "The old name was formally an expression of an era in which the foundation stone of the city was laid and the work of millions and millions was stamped with the name of a single man. The labor movement has since broken fundamentally with the cult of personality and has successfully eliminated its remains, and it now fights to erect insurmountable obstacles to the return of this cult. This is why the name of the city was changed."[29]

The prosperous period of the city's history is intricately intertwined with the socialist system. By 1986, its population had swollen to sixty-two thousand. In 2013, however, this number had dropped to forty-five thousand, in part because people had left the city for the surrounding villages and in part because given the high rates of unemployment people had left to find work elsewhere. Compared to national averages, the population of the city is old. It has the lowest birthrate for a community of its size and the highest number of per capita deaths. Of the cities with county rights, Dunaújváros has the highest rate of unemployment among the youth and, over the past decade, the lowest number of newly constructed apartments. It also has the greatest number of pensioners and the fewest functioning economic enterprises. The city of youth in the 1950s has become a city of the elderly, and birthrates have continued to drop. In recent years, it had one of the highest emigration rates of all the cities in Hungary. The population of the city is one of the oldest in Hungary, with some fifteen people older than age sixty-five for every child.[30]

In the end, the successor company to the Stalin Ironworks, which was built according to Soviet plans, ended up in Russian hands. Following a crisis in the steel industry, the ironworks, which kept the city alive, was given the politically neutral name "Dunaferr," and in 2004 it was privatized and became a member of the Industrial Union of Donbas. Since 2008, the company has lost money every year and the number of workers has been cut. Vnesheconombank, which owns the company and is headed by the Russian government, nonetheless does not wish to sell it to the Hungarian government, which in 2013 announced its intention to purchase the ironworks "in the interests of saving workplaces." At the time, the ironworks employed less than seven thousand people, just over half of the thirteen thousand who were employed there in the 1980s.[31] In 2001, Triumph, which is known for its lingerie and linens, built a new factory in the city. For years it thrived, but in 2015 the Hungarian branch was closed because of the high costs of production in Europe.[32]

Figure 11.4. Flying Lenin. (After demolishing the sculpture of Lenin according to the decree of the City Council in 1990, it was placed in Intercisa Museum, which was planned in 1950 as the headquarters of the Hungarian Communist Party.)

The Sztálinváros Sanitary Station, where new arrivals were checked for infectious diseases at the beginning of the 1950s, became a symbol of the city. In its place, a Heating Center was later built to provide residents of the city with central heating. In 1983, a Skála shopping center was opened on the site, a three-story department store that was a mecca of consumerism in the socialist era, where loudspeakers were used to announce the newest sales. In 2002, it was bought by a Chinese husband and wife, who renamed it Hong Kong Shopping Center.[33] The utopia of the first Hungarian socialist city seems to have ended not with a bang but with a whimper.

The story of Sztálinváros also symbolized the transition from Stalinist "chaos" to a de-Stalinized, sustainable "normality," from traditional to modern, from the nonsocialist to the socialist world. Sztálinváros became a symbol of the

1950s, however, in part because the history of the city was a pithy portrayal of both the strivings of the party-state and the limits of its power. Nevertheless, Stalinization in Hungary changed the methods of "human gardening," including the creation of a new microcosmos of socialism like Sztálinváros, and the de-Stalinization campaign transformed the ways that ordinary people perceived their place in society and how they reflected on state policies. These limits notwithstanding, the Stalinization that took place in Hungary was a drastic experiment in social engineering that left permanent marks on its physical and cultural landscape. The history of Sztálinváros, which was an embodiment of both the visions and the failures of socialism, provides a case study of the interplay between government power and social power, and their mutual accommodation. By exploring this interplay in the case of what was to have been an exemplary model of the power of the state to shape society, I hope to have furthered an understanding of ways in which ordinary people perceive, negotiate, and renegotiate their places in society, both adapting to and transforming the policies of the state.

Notes

1. Magyar Filmhíradó [Hungarian Film Newsreel] 1960/30. July 21, 1960.
2. Pittaway, *Eastern Europe 1939–2000*, 143.
3. Pittaway, *The Workers' State*, 257.
4. Miłosz, *The Captive Mind*, 38.
5. Ibid., 238.
6. For the term "carve out space," see, Lebow, *Unfinished Utopia*, 182.
7. *Man of Marble* (in Polish *Człowiek z marmuru*) is a 1976 Polish film directed by Andrzej Wajda about a Polish bricklayer working at the construction site of Nowa Huta.
8. Borhi, "Hungary's Role in the Soviet Bloc," 94.
9. Interview with Tibor Vámos on March 28, 2001, by the author.
10. Cf. Fitzpatrick and Lüdtke, "Energizing the Everyday," 284.
11. *Sztálinváros 10 éves* [Sztálinváros 10 years old] (Text: Irén Mérei, edited by Sándor Ják) (Budapest: Magyar Diafilmgyártó Vállalat [Hungarian Slide Factory], 1960).
12. Vámos, "Wolf Johanna."
13. Fitzpatrick, *The Cultural Front*, 177.
14. Magyar Filmhíradó, 1958/39. September 1958.
15. Lebow, *Unfinished Utopia*, 182.
16. Cf. Pittaway, *The Workers' State*, 265.
17. Cf. Valuch, *Magyar hétköznapok*, 325.
18. Betts, *Within Walls*, 229.
19. Hoffmann, *Cultivating the Masses*, 12.
20. Sabrow, "Der Konkurs der Konsensdiktatur"; Pollack, "Die offene Gesellschaft und ihre Freunde," 195; Bauerkämper, *Ländliche Gesellschaft in der kommunistischen Diktatur*, 499.
21. Cf. Ormos, "A szuverenitásról."
22. On the tools used in the creation of a communist Utopia, see Bauman, *Socialism, the Active Utopia*.

23. Of course, the processes of lustration vary from country to country. For a comparison, see Stan, "Explaining Country Differences."

24. On the debate concerning this, see Hoffmann, "European Modernity and Soviet Socialism."

25. Holquist, "State Violence as Technique."

26. Deák, "How to Construct a Productive, Disciplined, Monoethnic Society," 206.

27. Rainer, *Bevezetés a kádárizmusba*, 144.

28. Magyar Filmhíradó 1951/46. November 1951.

29. *Dunaújvárosi Hírlap*, November 28, 1961, 1.

30. Pekarek, "Szomorú adatok Dunaújváros népességéről"; *Megyei jogú városok*, 6–10.

31. *Heti Világ Gazdaság*, July 9, 2014, 52–53.

32. *Dunaújváros*, March 25, 2015. http://dunaujvaros.com/hirek/201503/mellbevago_a _Triumph_170_embert_kuld_el_a_varosi_gyarbol, accessed April 18, 2016.

33. *Dunaújvárosi Hírlap*, February 16, 2002, 1.

Bibliography

Archives

Állambiztonsági Szolgálatok Történeti Levéltára (ÁSZTL)
[Historical Archives of the Hungarian State Security]

3.1 O (Objektum [Target]) and M (Munka [Work]) files

Budapest Főváros Levéltára (BFL) [Budapest City Archives],
Fővárosi Tanács [City Council]

fond (f.) XXIII-101-a. Budapest Főváros Tanácsa tanácsülési jegyzőkönyvei [Minutes of
the Meetings of the Budapest City Council]

Magyar Országos Levéltár Fejér Megyei Levéltára (FML)
[Fejér County Archives]

f. XVII-904. Dunaújvárosi Népi Ellenőrzési Bizottság, 1958–60 [People's Oversight
Committee of Dunaújváros]
f. XXII-117. Dunapentele nagyközség iratai, 1946–50 [Documents of the Dunapentele
Township, 1946–50]
f.XXIII-230. Dunaújvárosi Járási Tanács Végrehajtó Bizottsága, Igazgatási Osztály,
1952–66 [Executive Committee of the Dunaújváros District Council, Management
Department]
f. XXIII-501. Dunaújváros (Sztálinváros) Városi Tanács üléseinek jegyzőkönyvei, 1951–62
[Minutes of the Meetings of the Dunaújváros (Sztálinváros) City Council]
f. XXIII-502. Dunaújváros (Sztálinváros) Városi Tanács Végrehajtó Bizottsága (VB),
ülések jegyzőkönyvei, 1951–62 [Minutes of the Meetings of the Executive Committee of the Dunaújváros (Sztálinváros) City Council]
f. XXIII-504. VB. Titkárság, 1951–62 [Secretariat]
f. XXIII-505. VB. Pénzügyi Osztály, 1951–62 [Treasury Department]
f. XXIII-506. VB. Igazgatási Osztály, 1951–62 [Management Department]
f. XXIII-507. VB. Műszaki Osztály, 1951–62 [Technical Department]
f. XXIII-508. VB. Művelődési Osztály, 1951–80 [Educational Department]
f. XXIII-509. VB. Termelés–Ellátás felügyelő (Kereskedelmi- és Begyűjtési) Osztály,
1951–62 [Production–Department of Supervision of Supplies (Trade and
Acquisition)]
f. XXIII-510. VB. Egészségügyi Osztály, 1951–62 [Health Department]
f. XXIII-511. VB. Terv és Beruházási Osztály, 1951–66 [Planning and Investment
Department]
f. XXIII-512. VB. Óvárosi kirendeltség, 1951–62 [Old Town Office]
f. XXIII-724. Dunapentelei Községi Tanács, 1950–51 [Dunapentele Municipal Council]

f. XXIV-11. Fejér Megyei Rendőr-főkapitányság (=Rendőrség) [Fejér County Police Headquarters (=Police)]

f. XXV-24. Dunaújvárosi (Sztálinvárosi) Városi Bíróság(=Bíróság), 1954–72 [Dunaújvárosi (Sztálinváros) City Court (=Court)]

f. XXV-151. Dunaújvárosi (Sztálinvárosi) Állami Közjegyző (=Közjegyző) 1954–70 [Dunaújváros (Sztálinváros) Notary (=Notary)]

f. XXVI-61. Dunaújvárosi Münnich Ferenc Gimnázium, 1959–68 [Ferenc Münnich High School]

f. XXVI-108. "Délivárosi" Általános Iskola, 1954–65 ["South Side" Elementary School]

f. XXVI-110. Dunaújvárosi "kisegítő" Általános Iskola, 1961–68 ["Ancillary" Elementary School in Dunaújváros]

f. XXVI-112. Ságvári Általános Iskola, 1959 [Ságvári Elementary School]

f. XXVI-113. Szórád Márton Általános Iskola, 1949–58 [Szórád Márton Elementary School]

f. XXVI-114. Vasvári Általános Iskola, 1952–66 [Vasvári Elementary School]

f. XXVI-702. "Bartók Béla" Művelődési Központ, 1954–60 [Documents of the Bartók Béla Cultural Center, 1954–1960]

f. XXIX-104. Dunaújvárosi Kereskedelmi Vállalat, áruforgalom, májusi vásár, 1955 [Dunaújváros Trade Enterprise, Circulation of Commodities, May Market, 1955]

f. XXXI-18. Dr. Tirpák Endre ügyvéd iratai, 1957–59 [Documents of Attorney Dr. Endre Tirpák, 1957–59]

f. XXXIII-25. Dunaújvárosi (Sztálinvárosi) születési és házassági anyakönyvek másodpéldányai, 1953, 1954, 1958 [Dunaújváros (Sztálinvárosi) Birth and Marriage Record Duplicates, 1953, 1954, 1958]

Magyar Nemzeti Levéltár Országos Levéltára (MNL OL)
[Hungarian National Archives]

f. XIX-G-4-rr. Belkereskedelmi Bányaellátó Igazgatóság [Management of Domestic Trade Mine Supplies], 1954–55

f. XXVI-D-8-f. VÁTI [Institute for Urban Planning]. Tervtár [Plans]

f. XXIX-F-2 Dunai (Sztálin) Vasmű központi iratai, 1948–70 [Central Documents of the Danube (Stalin) Ironworks]

Management Documents; Production affairs; IX. Administrative affairs; Security affairs; Education and social affairs; Affairs related to movements; Documents of the engineering department; Documents pertaining to personnel and labor affairs

f. 288–41. MSZMP Agitációs és Propaganda Osztály. [Documents of the Agitation and Propaganda Department of the Hungarian Socialist Workers' Party]

Politikatörténeti és Szakszervezeti Levéltár (PSzTL) [Political History
and Trade Union Archives]

f. I-658. Pártok, Szociáldemokrata Párt [Parties. Social Democratic Party]

f. XII-16. Fejér SZMT, Szakszervezetek Fejér Megyei Tanácsa, 1952–60 [County Council of the Fejér County Trade Union, 1952–60]

f. XII-33. Építők, Építőipari Dolgozók Szakszervezete, 1950–58 [Trade Union of Builders and Construction Industry Workers, 1950–58]

Oral History Archives in the Institute of 1956

Interview 57 with Zsófia Tevan
Interview 99 with Ambrus Borovszky
Interview 237 with András Sándor
Interview 316 with Tibor Vámos

Organs of the Print Media

Budapesti Est [Budapest Evening], 1952–55
Építés–Építészet [Construction–Architecture], 1950–51
Esti Hírlap [Evening Post], 1957–58
Nők Lapja [Women's Magazine], 1951–62
Szabad Nép [Free People], as of 1956, *Népszabadság* [People's Liberty], 1951–62
Sztálinvárosi Hírlap [Sztálinváros Herald], 1950–60 (previously 1950–51: *Dunai Vasmű építője* [Builder of the Danube Ironworks]; 1952–53: *Sztálin Vasmű Építője* [Builder of the Stalin Ironworks]; 1954–56: *Sztálinváros*; November 1956–March 1957: *Dunapentelei Hírlap* [Dunapentele Herald]

Print Sources

1960. évi népszámlálás: Fejér megye [1960 census: Fejér County]. Budapest: Központi Statisztikai Hivatal, 1961.
A válások okai [Causes of divorce] (without author). Budapest: Központi Statisztikai Hivatal, 1965.
Acsády, György, and András Klinger. "A termékenység, a családtervezés és a születésszabályozás néhány kérdése" [Some questions of fertility, family planning, and birth control]. *Demográfia* 2, nos. 2–3 (1959): 176–216.
Adam, Clemens. "Rocker in einer Großstadt des Ruhrgebiets" [Rocker in a city of the Ruhr area]. PhD diss., University of Bochum, 1972.
Alexander, Anthony. *Britain's New Towns: Garden Cities to Sustainable Communities.* London: Routledge, 2009.
Anderson, Jessica. "Columbia Association to Drop 'People Tree' from Logo." *Baltimore Sun*, January 31, 2012. Accessed April 24, 2016. http://articles.baltimoresun.com /2012-01-31/news/bs-md-ho-columbia-logo-change-20120130_1_columbia -association-the-people-tree-new-logo.
Assmann, Jan. *Das kulturelle Gedächtnis: Schrift, Erinnerung und politische Identität in frühen Hochkulturen* [Cultural memory: Writing, memory, and political identity in early high cultures]. Munich: C. H. Beck, 1992.
Az 1956-os Forradalom Adattára [Documents of the 1956 Revolution]. Budapest: Országos Széchenyi Könyvtár Történeti Interjúk Tára, 2006. CD-ROM.
Baber, Kristine M., and Katherine R. Allen. *Women and Families: Feminist Reconstructions.* New York: Guilford Press, 1992.
Badinter, Elisabeth. *Mother Love: Myth and Reality: Motherhood in Modern History.* New York: Macmillan, 1981.

Bailey, James, ed. *New Towns in America: The Design and Development Process*. New York: Wiley, 1973.

Baksay, Zoltán. *A munkaerőhelyzet alakulása és a munkanélküliség felszámolása Magyarországon 1945–1949* [Transformation of the labor force and the elimination of unemployment in Hungary 1945–1949]. Budapest: Akadémiai, 1983.

Balázs, József. "A házasságkötések alakulása Magyarországon a II. világháború után." [Weddings in Hungary after World War II]. In *Emlékkönyv Dr. Kemenes Béla egyetemi tanár 65. születésnapjára* [Book for the sixty-fifth birthday of Professor Béla Kemenes]. Edited by Károly Tóth, 19–37. Szeged: József Attila Tudományegyetem, 1993.

Barsy, Gyula, and Károly Miltényi. "A művi vetélések kérdése az 1957: évi adatok tükrében" [The question of abortion based on data from 1957]. *Demográfia* 1 (1958): 226–48.

Bauerkämper, Arnd. *Ländliche Gesellschaft in der kommunistischen Diktatur: Zwangsmodernisierung und Tradition in Brandenburg 1945–1963* [Country society in the communist dictatorship: Forced modernization and tradition in Brandenburg, 1945–1963]. Cologne: Böhlau, 2002,

Bauman, Zygmunt. *Socialism, the Active Utopia*. New York: Holmes and Meier, 1976.

Békés, Csaba, Malcolm Byrne, and János M. Rainer, eds. *The 1956 Hungarian Revolution: A History in Documents*. Budapest: CEU Press, 2002.

Belényi, Gyula. *Az alföldi városok és a településpolitika (1945–1963)* [The cities of the Hungarian lowlands and settlement policy (1945–1963)]. Szeged: Csongrád Megyei Levéltár, 1996.

———, ed. *Munkások Magyarországon 1948–1956: Dokumentumok* [Workers in Hungary 1948–1956: Documents]. Budapest: Napvilág, 2000.

Benda, Gyula. "Budapest társadalma: 1945–1970" [The society of Budapest: 1945–1970]. In *Magyarország társadalomtörténete. III: válogatott tanulmányok.* [The social history of Hungary. III: Selected essays]. Vol. 2, edited by Nikosz Fokasz and Antal Örkény, 8–31. Budapest: Új Mandátum, 1999.

Bender, Thomas. *The Unfinished City: New York and the Metropolitan Idea*. New York: New Press, 2002.

Benkő, Lóránd, ed. *A magyar nyelv történeti-etimológiai szótára* [A historical and etymological dictionary of the Hungarian language]. Budapest: Akadémiai, 1970.

Béres, Csaba. *A városfejlődés fordulópontján* [At the turning point of urban development]. Debrecen: Kossuth Lajos University, 1983.

Bernáth, Péter, and Laura Polyák. "Kényszermosdatások Magyarországon" [Forced bathing in Hungary]. In *Kényszermosdatások a cigánytelepeken, 1945–1985* [Forced bathing in the Roma settlements, 1945–1985], edited by Gábor Bernáth, 7–25. Budapest: Roma Sajtóközpont, 2002.

Bertha, Bulcsú. "A legendás város" [The legendary city]. In *Ipari közelképek* [Industrial close-ups], edited by István Matkó, 7–23. Budapest: Ipari Minisztérium, 1986.

Bessel, Richard, and Ralph Jessen, eds. *Die Grenzen der Diktatur: Staat und Gesellschaft in der DDR* [The limits of dictatorship: State and society in the GDR]. Göttingen: Vandenhoeck und Ruprecht, 1996.

Betts, Paul. *Within Walls: Private Life in the German Democratic Republic*. Oxford: Oxford University Press, 2012.

Bloom, Nicholas Dagen. *Suburban Alchemy: 1960s New Towns and the Transformation of the American Dream.* Columbus: Ohio State University Press, 2001.

Bodnár, Judit. *Fin de Millénaire Budapest: Metamorphoses of Urban Life.* Minneapolis: University of Minnesota Press, 2001.

Bokor, Ágnes. *Depriváció és szegénység* [Deprivation and poverty]. Budapest: Kossuth, 1985.

———. *Szegénység a mai Magyarországon* [Poverty in Hungary today]. Budapest: Magvető, 1987.

Borhi, László. *Hungary in the Cold War, 1945–1956: Between the United States and the Soviet Union.* Budapest: Central European University Press, 2004.

———. "Hungary's Role in the Soviet Bloc, 1945–1956." In *Imposing, Maintaining, and Tearing Open the Iron Curtain: The Cold War and East-Central Europe, 1945–1989,* edited by Mark Kramer and Vít Smetana, 87–97. Lanham, MD: Lexington Books, 2014.

Browning, Christopher R. *Ordinary Men: Reserve Police Battalion 101 and the Final Solution in Poland.* New York: HarperCollins, 1992.

Brunnbauer, Ulf. *"Die sozialistische Lebensweise": Ideologie, Gesellschaft, Familie und Politik in Bulgarien (1944–1989)* ["The socialist lifestyle": Ideology, society, family and politics in Bulgaria]. Vienna: Böhlau, 2007.

———. "'The Town of the Youth': Dimitrovgrad and Bulgarian Socialism." *Ethnologia Balkanica* 9 (2005): 91–114.

Buckley, Cynthia. "The Myth of Managed Migration: Migration Control and Market in the Soviet Period." *Slavic Review* 54, no. 4 (1995): 896–916.

Bukodi, Erzsébet. "Ki, mikor és kivel házasodik? A házasság helye az egyéni életútban és a történeti időben" [Who marries, when, and whom? The place of marriage in the individual's life and in history]. *Szociológiai Szemle* 10, no. 2 (2000): 28–58.

Burke, John Frederick. *The English Inn.* New York: Holmes and Meier, 1981.

Cabrera, Miguel A. *Postsocial History: An Introduction.* Lanham, MD: Lexington Books, 2004.

Carlbäck, Helene. "Lone Mothers and Fatherless Children: Public Discourse on Marriage and Family Law." In *Soviet State and Society under Nikita Khrushchev,* edited by Melanie Ilic and Jeremy Smith, 86–103. New York: Routledge, 2009.

Certeau, Michel de. *The Practice of Everyday Life.* Berkeley: University of California Press, 1984.

Chandler, Alfred Dupont. *Scale and Scope: The Dynamics of Industrial Capitalism.* Cambridge, MA: Harvard University Press, 1994.

Chester, Robert, ed. *Divorce in Europe.* Leiden: Martinus Nijhoff Social Sciences Division, 1977.

Clout, Hugh. "Rural–Urban Migration in Western Europe." In Salt and Clout, *Migration in Post-War Europe,* 30–51.

Cohen, Phil. *Subcultural Conflict and Working Class Community.* Birmingham: University of Birmingham—Centre for Contemporary Cultural Studies, 1972.

Cohen, Stanley. *Folk Devils and Moral Panics: The Creation of the Mods and Rockers.* London: MacGibbon and Kee, 1972.

Compton, Paul. "Migration in Eastern Europe." In Salt and Clout, *Migration in Post-War Europe,* 168–215.

Cremer, Günter. *Die Subkultur der Rocker: Erscheinungsform und Selbstdarstellung* [The subculture of the rocker: Forms of manifestation and self-expression]. Pfaffenweiler: Centaurus-Verlag, 1992.

Crouch, Christopher. *Design Culture in Liverpool, 1880–1914: The Origins of the Liverpool School of Architecture.* Liverpool: Liverpool University Press, 2002.

Csanádi, Gábor, and János Ladányi. *Budapest térbeni-társadalmi erezetének változásai* [Changes in the spatial and social networks of Budapest]. Budapest: Akadémiai, 1992.

Dallos, Ferenc, and Egon Szabady, eds. *Magyar városok* [Hungarian cities]. Budapest: Közgazdasági és Jogi Könyvkiadó, 1966.

Dániel, Zsuzsa. "Lakáspolitika, lakbér, lakáshiány" [Housing policy, rent, apartment shortage]. *Valóság* 20, no. 12 (1977): 93–100.

Davis, Belinda, Thomas Lindenberger, and Michael Wildt, eds. *Alltag, Erfahrung, Eigensinn: historisch-anthropologische Erkundungen* [Everyday, experience, "Eigensinn": Historical-anthropological explorations]. Frankfurt/Main: Campus, 2008.

Deák, István. "How to Construct a Productive, Disciplined, Monoethnic Society: The Dilemma of East Central European Governments, 1914–1956." In Weiner, *Landscaping the Human Garden,* 205–17.

Dobos, Ilona. *Áldozatok* [Victims]. Budapest: Kozmosz Könyvek, 1981.

———. *Egy folklórgyűjtő feljegyzései* [Notes of an ethnographic collector]. Budapest: Kozmosz, 1984.

Dowling, Timothy. "Building Socialism: Stalinstadt/Eisenhüttenstadt as a Model for (Socialist) Life in the GDR." PhD diss., Tulane University, 1999.

Downs, Roger M., and David Stea. *Maps in Mind: Reflections on Cognitive Mapping.* New York: Harper and Row, 1977.

Dunaújváros: 1950–1965. Székesfehérvár: KSH Fejér Megyei Igazgatóság, 1966.

Egeli, László, Sándor Halász, György Rácz, and György Sömjén, compilers. *Büntetőjogi Döntvénytár: Bírósági Határozatok, 1953. október–1963. október* [Criminal legal records: Judicial rulings, October 1953–October 1963]. Budapest: Közgazdasági és Jogi Kiadó, 1964.

Ember, György. *Sztálinvárosiak* [People of Sztálinváros]. Budapest: Művelt Nép, 1953.

Engel, Helmut, and Ribbe, Wolfgang, eds. *Karl-Marx-Allee–Magistrale in Berlin: Die Wandlung der sozialistischen zur Hauptstrasse des Berliner Ostens* [Karl-Marx-Allee–Magistrale in Berlin: The transformation of the socialist avenue into the main street of East Berlin]. Berlin: Akad. Verl., 1996.

Engelhard, Jutta-Beate. *Nachbarschaft in der Großstadt: Neuere Initiativen, dargestellt am Beispiel der Stadt Münster* [Neighborhood in the big city: New initiatives, as embodied by the city of Münster]. Münster: F. Coppenrath Verlag, 1986.

Eörsi, László. "Ideológiai pragmatizmus és (Ön)cenzúra: A három 'T' kultúrpolitikája" [Pragmatic ideology and (self-)censorship: The three-T cultural policy]. *Világosság* 49, nos. 11–12 (2008): 73–96.

Erdős, Ferenc. "Dunapentelétől Sztálinvárosig" [From Dunapentele to Sztálinváros]. In Erdős and Pongrácz, *Dunaújváros története,* 243–80.

Erdős, Ferenc, and Zsuzsanna Pongrácz, eds. *Dunaújváros története* [The history of Dunaújváros]. Dunaújváros: Dunaújváros Megyei Jogú Város Önkormányzata, 2000.

Falck, Uta. *VEB Bordell: Geschichte der Prostitution in der DDR* [VEB bordello: The history of prostitution in the German Democratic Republic]. Berlin: Links, 1998.

Fenemore, Mark. *Sex, Thugs and Rock 'n' Roll: Teenage Rebels in Cold-War East Germany.* New York: Berghahn, 2007.

Ferge, Zsuzsa. *Fejezetek a magyar szegénypolitika történetéből* [Chapters from the history of the politics of poverty in Hungary]. Budapest: Magvető, 1986.

Ferree, Myra Marx. "Working Class Jobs: Paid Work and Housework as Sources of Satisfaction." *Social Problems* 23, no. 4 (1976): 431–41.

Fidelis, Małgorzata. *Women, Communism, and Industrialization in Postwar Poland.* Cambridge: Cambridge University Press, 2010.

Fields, Gary S. *Poverty, Inequality, and Development.* Cambridge: Cambridge University Press, 1980.

Figes, Orlando. *The Whisperers: Private Life in Stalin's Russia.* New York: Metropolitan Books, 2007.

Fitzpatrick, Sheila. *The Cultural Front: Power and Culture in Revolutionary Russia.* Ithaca, NY: Cornell University Press, 1992.

———, ed. *Stalinism. New Directions.* London: Routledge, 2000.

Fitzpatrick, Sheila, and Alf Lüdtke. "Energizing the Everyday: On the Breaking and Making of Social Bonds in Nazism and Stalinism." In *Beyond Totalitarianism: Stalinism and Nazism Compared,* edited by Michael Geyer and Sheila Fitzpatrick, 167–301. New York: Cambridge University Press, 2009.

Földes, László. *A második vonalban* [In the second line]. Budapest: Kossuth, 1984.

Forder, Anthony. "Explanations of Poverty." In Anthony Forder, Terry Caslin, Geoffrey Ponton, and Sandra Walklate, *Theories of Welfare,* 203–26. London: Routledge and Kegan Paul, 1984.

French, Richard Antony, and Ian F. E. Hamilton. "Is There a Socialist City?" In French and Hamilton, *The Socialist City,* 1–21.

———, eds., *The Socialist City: Spatial Structure and Urban Policy.* Chichester: John Wiley, 1979.

Gábor, Eszter. *A CIAM magyar csoportja* [The Hungarian Group of the CIAM]. Budapest: Akadémiai, 1972.

Gaborit, Pascaline. *European New Towns: Image, Identities, Future Perspectives.* Brussels: Peter Lang, 2010.

Gádoros, Lajos. *A korszerű lakás térszükséglete és berendezése* [Furnishings and the lack of space in the modern apartment]. Budapest: Országos Építésügyi Kormánybiztosság, 1946.

———. "Lakásépítkezésünk eredményei és tanulságai" [The results and lessons of apartment construction]. *Építészet-építés* 1, nos. 1–2 (1949): 11–18.

Gádoros, Lajos, Jenő Kismarty-Lechner Jr., and Imre Perényi, eds. *Családi lakóház* [The family dwelling]. Budapest: Építéstudományi Központ, 1948.

Galantay, Ervin Y. *New Towns: Antiquity to the Present.* New York: G. Braziller, 1975.

Gans, Herbert J. "The Positive Functions of Poverty." *American Journal of Sociology* 78, no. 2 (1972): 275–89.

———. *The Urban Villagers: Group and Life of Italian-Americans.* New York: Free Press, 1962.

Gémes, Balázs. *A népi születésszabályozás (magzatelhajtás) Magyarországon a XIX–XX. században* [Birth control (abortion) in Hungary in the nineteenth and twentieth centuries]. Budapest: MTA Néprajzi Kutatócsoport, 1985.

Gerasimova, Katerina. "Public Privacy in the Soviet Communal Apartment." In *Socialist Spaces: Sites of Everyday Life in the Eastern Bloc*, edited by Susan E. Reid and David Crowley, 207–30. Oxford: Berg, 2002.

Germuska, Pál. "A szocialista városok helye a magyar urbanizáció történetében: A magyarországi szocialista városok kialakulása" [The place of socialist cities in the history of urbanization in Hungary: The evolution of Hungarian Socialist Cities]. PhD diss., Eötvös Loránd University, Faculty of the Humanities, Budapest, 2001.

Glenn, Justin. *The Washingtons: A Family History*. Vol. 5. El Dorado Hills: Savas, 2014.

Gmelch, George. "Migration and the Adaptation of Migrants to City Life: Introduction." In Gmelch and Zenner, *Urban Life*, 188–95.

Gmelch, George, and Walter P. Zenner, eds. *Urban Life. Readings in Urban Anthropology*. Prospect Heights, IL: Waveland Press, 1996.

Goldman, Wendy Z. *Women, the State and Revolution: Soviet Family Policy and Social Life, 1917–1936*. Cambridge: Cambridge University Press, 1993.

Gordon, Laura. *Women's Body, Women's Right*. New York: Viking, 1976.

Gregory, Paul R., and Irwin L. Collier. "Unemployment in the Soviet Union: Evidence from the Soviet Interview Project." *American Economic Review* 78, no. 4 (September 1988): 613–32.

Gyáni, Gábor. *Az utca és a szalon: A társadalmi térhasználat Budapesten (1870–1940)* [The street and the bar: The social use of space in Budapest (1870–1940)]. Budapest: Új Mandátum, 1998.

———. *Bérkaszárnya és nyomortelep* [Tenement building and slums]. Budapest: Magvető, 1992.

———. "Könyörületesség, fegyelmezés, avagy a szociális gondoskodás genealógiája" [Mercy, discipline, or the genealogy of social welfare]. *Történelmi Szemle* 41, nos. 1–2 (1999): 57–84.

———. "Patterns of Women's Work in Hungary, 1900–1930." *European Review of History*. 5, no. 1 (1998): 25–36.

———. "Sorskérdések és az önmegértés nemzeti diskurzusa a globalizáció korában" [The national discourse on vital questions and self-understanding in the age of globalization]. In *Mi a magyar most?* [What does Hungarian mean now?], edited by Sándor Iván, 21–46. Bratislava: Kalligram, 2011.

Gyáni, Gábor, György Kövér, and Tibor Valuch. *Social History of Hungary from the Reform Era to the End of the Twentieth Century*. Boulder, CO: Social Science Monographs, 2004.

Gyarmati, György, and Tibor Valuch. *Hungary under Soviet Domination, 1944–1989*. Boulder, CO: East European Monographs, 2008.

Haeder, Sonja. *Schülerkindheit in Ost-Berlin: Sozialisation unter den Bedingungen der Diktatur (1945–1958)* [School-age childhood in East Berlin: Socialization under the conditions of the dictatorship]. Cologne: Böhlau, 1998.

Hamilton, Ian F. E., and Alan D. Burnett. "Social Processes and Residential Structure." In French and Hamilton, *The Socialist City*, 263–304.

Hannerz, Ulf. *Exploring the City: Inquiries Toward an Urban Anthropology.* New York: Columbia University Press, 1980.

Harris, Steven. *Communism on Tomorrow Street: Mass Housing and Everyday Life after Stalin.* Washington, DC: Woodrow Wilson Center Press, 2013.

Harrison, Martin. *Young Meteors: British Photojournalism: 1957–1965.* London: Jonathan Cape, 1998.

Heineberg, Heinz. "Service Centres in East and West Berlin." In French and Hamilton, *The Socialist City*, 305–34.

Hellbeck, Jochen. *Revolution on My Mind: Writing a Diary under Stalin.* Cambridge, MA: Harvard University Press, 2006.

Hirschler, Imre. "Hozzászólás 'A művi vetélések kérdése az 1957. évi adatok tükrében' című cikkhez'" [A remark on the article "Abortions in the mirror of statistics in 1957"]. *Demográfia* 2, nos. 2–3 (1959): 375–78.

Hoffmann, David L. *Cultivating the Masses: Modern State Practices and Soviet Socialism, 1914–1939.* Ithaca, NY: Cornell University Press, 2011.

———. "European Modernity and Soviet Socialism." In *Russian Modernity: Politics, Knowledge, Practices*, edited by David L. Hoffmann and Yanni Kotsonis, 245–60. New York: Palgrave Macmillan, 2000.

———. "Moving to Moscow: Patterns of Peasant In-Migration during the First Five-Year Plan." *Slavic Review* 50, no. 4 (1991): 847–57.

———, ed. *Stalinism: The Essential Readings.* Malden, MA: Blackwell, 2003.

Holman, Robert. *Poverty: Explanations of Social Deprivation.* Oxford: Martin Robertson, 1978.

Holquist, Peter. "State Violence as Technique: The Logic of Violence in Soviet Totalitarianism." In Weiner, *Landscaping the Human Garden*, 19–45.

Horváth, Sándor. *Kádár gyermekei: Ifjúsági lázadás a hatvanas években* [Children of Kádár: youth revolt in the 1960s]. Budapest: Nyitott Könyvműhely, 2009.

———. *Két emelet boldogság: Mindennapi szociálpolitika Budapesten a Kádár-korban* [Two-story happiness: Everyday social policy in Budapest in the Kádár era]. Budapest: Napvilág, 2012.

Huszár, Tibor. *Fiatalkorú bűnözők* [Juvenile offenders]. Budapest: Tankönyvkiadó, 1964.

Hutt, Christopher. *The Death of the English Pub.* London: Hutchinson, 1973.

Jajeśniak-Quast, Dagmara. *Stahlgiganten in der sozialistischen Transformation. Nowa Huta in Krakau, EKO in Eisenhüttenstadt und Kunčice in Ostrava* [Steel giants in the socialist transformation Nowa Huta in Kraków, EKO in Eisenhüttenstadt and Kunčice in Ostrava]. Wiesbaden: Harrassowitz, 2010.

Jarausch, Konrad H., ed. *Dictatorship as Experience: Towards a Socio-Cultural History of the GDR.* New York: Berghahn Books, 1999.

Jones, Polly. *Myth, Memory, Trauma: Rethinking the Stalinist Past in the Soviet Union, 1953–70.* New Haven, CT: Yale University Press, 2013.

K., M. "Review of Tietze, Christopher, *The Condom as a Contraceptive* (New York: National Committee on Maternal Health, Inc., 1960)." *Demográfia* 4, no. 3 (1961): 395.

Kamarás, Ferenc. ed., *Terhesség–megszakítások–tanulmányok, adatok, jogszabályok, hazai és nemzetközi trendek* [Abortions–studies–statistics, law, domestic, and international trends]. Budapest: KSH, 2000.

———. "Terhességmegszakítások Magyarországon" [Abortions in Hungary]. In *Szerepváltozások: Jelentés a nők és férfiak helyzetéről* [Changing roles: Report on the situation of women and men], edited by Tiborné Pongrácz, and István György Tóth, 190–216. Budapest: TÁRKI&Szociális és Családügyi Minisztérium, 1999.

Kántor, Balázs. *Így épült a vas és acél országa* [Building the country of iron and steel]. Accessed April 25, 2016. http://mult-kor.hu/20130313_igy_epult_a_vas_es_acel _orszaga?pIdx=2/.

Kato, Yuki. "Planning and Social Diversity: Residential Segregation in American New Towns." *Urban Studies* 43 (November 2006): 2285–99.

Katona, Csaba. "Krina, franko, mikulás–Egy határátlépés története budapesti szlengben" [Story of a border crossing in Budapest slang]. *Archivnet* 2, no. 6 (2002). Accessed May 2, 2011. www.natarch.hu/archivnet/. Also published as Csaba Katona, *Egy illegális határátlépés története–budapesti szlengben, 1954* [Story of a border crossing in Budapest slang, 1954]. In *Tanulmányok az 50 éves Bana Jocó tiszteletére* [Collection of essays for the fiftieth birthday of Jocó Bana], edited by Csaba Katona, 63–80. Győr: Palatia, 2006.

Keating, Peter John. *The Working Classes in Victorian Fiction*. London: Routledge, 1971.

Keefe, Susan Emley. "The Myth of the Declining Family: Extended Family Ties among Urban Mexican-Americans and Anglo-Americans." In Gmelch and Zenner, *Urban Life*, 308–22.

Kemény, István. *Szociológiai írások* [Sociological writings]. Szeged: Replika Kör, 1992.

Kenney, Padraic. *Rebuilding Poland: Workers and Communists, 1945–1950*. Ithaca, NY: Cornell University Press, 1997.

Keresztesné Pataki, Mária. *A dolgozó nő háztartása* [The household of the working woman]. Budapest: Közgazdasági és Jogi Könyvkiadó, 1950.

Kharkhordin, Oleg. *The Collective and the Individual in Russia: A Study of Practices*. Berkeley: University of California Press, 1999.

Kismarty-Lechner, Jenő Jr. *Városi lakástípusok* [Urban types of apartment]. Budapest: Országos Építésügyi Kormánybiztosság, 1947.

Klemperer, Victor. *The Language of the Third Reich. LTI, Lingua Tertii Imperii: A Philologist's Notebook*. London: Athlone Press, 2000.

Klinger, András. *A válás* [Divorce]. Budapest: Közgazdasági és Jogi Könyvkiadó, 1957.

———. "A válások okaira vonatkozó vizsgálat főbb eredménye" [The principal findings of the study of the reasons for divorce]. *Demográfia* 8, no. 1 (1965): 71–81.

———. "Magyarország népesedése az elmúlt negyven évben" [Growth of the population of Hungary over the course of the past forty years]. *Statisztikai Szemle* 63, nos. 4–5 (1985): 370–88.

Konopasek, Zdenek, and Molly Andrews. "A Cautious Ethnography of Socialism: Autobiographical Narrative in the Czech Republic." In *The Uses of Narrative. Explorations in Sociology, Psychology, and Cultural Studies*, edited by Molly Andrews, Shelley Day Sclater, Corinne Squire, and Amal Treacher, 92–103. London: Routledge, 2009.

Konrád, György, and Iván Szelényi. *Az új lakótelepek szociológiai problémái* [The sociological problems of the new housing projects]. Budapest: Akadémiai, 1969.

Kornai, János. *A hiány* [Economics of shortage]. Budapest: Közgazdasági és Jogi Könyvkiadó, 1982.

————. *The Socialist System: The Political Economy of Communism*. Princeton, NJ: Princeton University Press, 1992.

Korompay, János, ed. *40 éves a Dunai Vasmű* [The Danube Ironworks is 40 years old]. Budapest: Mercurius, 2000.

Kőrösi, Zsuzsanna, and Adrienne Molnár. *Carrying a Secret in my Heart . . . Children of the Victims of the Reprisal after the Hungarian Revolution in 1956: An Oral History*. Budapest: CEU Press, 2003.

Kotkin, Stephen. *Magnetic Mountain. Stalinism as a Civilization*. Berkeley: University of California Press, 1995.

Kotsonis, Yanni. "Ordinary People in Russian and Soviet History." *Kritika: Explorations in Russian and Eurasian History* 12, no. 3 (Summer 2011): 739–54.

Kott, Sandrine. "Everyday Communism: New Social History of the German Democratic Republic." *Contemporary European History* 13 (2004): 233–47.

Központi Statisztikai Hivatal [Central Statistical Office]. *Népszámlálás* [Census]. 1949.

————. *Népszámlálás* [Census]. 1960: Fejér County. Budapest: 1961.

Kramer, Mark. "New Evidence on Soviet Decision-Making and the 1956 Polish and Hungarian Crises." *Cold War International History Project Bulletin* 8, no. 9 (Winter 1996–97): 358–84.

Krylova, Anna. "Soviet Modernity: Stephen Kotkin and the Bolshevik Predicament." *Contemporary European History* 23, no. 2 (2014): 167–92.

Kuipers, Benjamin. "The 'Map in the Head' Metaphor." *Environment and Behaviour* 14, no. 2 (1982): 202–20.

Ladányi, János. *Lakóhelyi szegregáció Budapesten* [Residential segregation in Budapest]. Budapest: Új Mandátum, 2009.

Lane, Christel. *The Rites of Rulers: Ritual on Industrial Society—The Soviet Case*. Cambridge: Cambridge University Press, 1981.

Lapidus, Gail Warshofsky. *Women in Soviet Society: Equality, Development, and Social Change*. Berkeley: University of California Press, 1978.

László-Bencsik, Sándor. *Történelem alulnézetben* [History from below]. Budapest: Szépirodalmi, 1973.

Lázár, István. *Örkény István alkotásai és vallomásai tükrében* [István Örkény seen through his compositions and confessions]. Budapest: Szépirodalmi, 1979.

Lebow, Katherine. "*Kontra Kultura*: Leisure and Youthful Rebellion in Stalinist Poland." In *Pleasures in Socialism: Leisure and Luxury in the Eastern* Bloc, edited by David Crowley and Susan E. Reid, 71–92. Evanston, IL: Northwestern University Press, 2010.

————. *Unfinished Utopia: Nowa Huta, Stalinism, and Polish Society, 1949–56*. Ithaca, NY: Cornell University Press, 2013.

Lewin, Moshe. *The Making of the Soviet System: Essays in the Social History of Interwar Russia*. New York: Pantheon Books, 1985.

Lindenberger, Thomas. "Alltagsgeschichte und ihr Beitrag zur Erforschung der Sozialgeschichte der DDR" [History of everyday life and its contribution to research on the social history of the GDR]. In *Die Grenzen der Diktatur. Staat und Gesellschaft in der DDR* [Borders of dictatorship: State and society in the GDR], edited by Richard Bessel and Ralph Jessen, 298–325. Göttingen: Vandenhoeck und Ruprecht, 1996.

Lindner, Christoph. "The Death and Return of the New York Skyscraper." In *Urban Space and Cityscapes: Perspectives from Modern and Contemporary Culture*, edited by Christoph Lindner, 122–33. London: Routledge, 2006.

Litván, György, ed. *Magyar munkásszociográfiák* [Hungarian workers' sociographies]. Budapest: Kossuth Könykiadó, 1974.

Lozac'h, Valérie, ed. *Eisenhüttenstadt*. Leipzig: Leipziger Universität, 1999.

Lüdtke, Alf. *Eigen-Sinn: Fabrikalltag, Arbeitserfahrungen und Politik vom Kaiserreich bis in den Faschismus* ["Eigen-Sinn": Factory everyday, experiences of work, and politics from the empire to fascism]. Hamburg: Ergebnisse-Verlag, 1993.

———, ed. *The History of Everyday Life: Reconstructing Historical Experiences and Ways of Life*. Princeton, NJ: Princeton University Press, 1995.

Ludwig, Andreas, ed. *Fortschritt, Norm und Eigensinn: Erkundungen im Alltag der DDR* [Progress, Norm, and "Eigensinn": Investigation into the everyday in the German Democratic Republic]. Berlin: Links, 1999.

———. "'Traum der Zukunft—Wirklichkeit': Stadtgeschichte, Selbstbild, Fremdbild in Eisenhüttenstadt" ["Dream of the future—reality": Urban history, self-image, image of the other in Eisenhüttenstadt]. In Lozac'h, *Eisenhüttenstadt*, 9–20.

Lukácsy, András. *Felismerem-e Angyal Istvánt?* [Do I recognize István Angyal?] Budapest: Magvető, 1990.

Lynch, Kevin. *The Image of the City*. Cambridge, MA: MIT Press, 1960.

Major, Máté. "Előszó" [Preface]. In Kismarty-Lechner, *Városi lakástípusok*, 5–7.

Majtényi, Balázs, and György Majtényi. *A Contemporary History of Exclusion: The Roma Issue in Hungary from 1945 to 2015*. Budapest: CEU Press, 2016.

Majtényi, György. *A tudomány lajtorjája: "Társadalmi mobilitás" és "új értelmiség" Magyarországon a II. világháború után* [Ladder of science: "Social mobility" and the "New Intelligentsia" in post-1945 Hungary]. Budapest: Gondolat Kiadó–Magyar Országos Levéltár, 2005.

———. "Életstílus és szubkultúra: Az autózás története (1920–1960)" [Lifestyle and subculture: The history of motoring (1920–1960)]. *Korall* 1, no. 1 (Summer 2000): 101–18.

Massey, Douglas S., and Nancy A. Denton. "The Dimensions of Residential Segregation." *Social Forces* 67, no. 2 (1988): 281–315.

Matthews, Mervyn. "Social Dimensions in Soviet Urban Housing." In French and Hamilton, *The Socialist City*, 105–18.

Matussné, Márta Lendvai, and Zsuzsánna Pongrácz, *Dunaújváros története képeslapokon* [The history of Dunaújváros on postcards]. Dunaújváros: TSO Alapítvány, 2000.

May, Ruth. *Planstadt Stalinstadt: Ein Grundriss der frühen DDR–aufgesucht in Eisenhüttenstadt* [The planned city of Stalinstadt: The ground plan of the early German Democratic Republic]. Dortmund: IRPUD—University Dortmund, 1999.

Mayne, Alan. *The Imagined Slum: Newspaper Representation in Three Cities, 1870–1914*. Leicester: Leicester University Press, 1993.

McLellan, Josie. *Love in the Time of Communism: Intimacy and Sexuality in the GDR*. Cambridge: Cambridge University Press, 2011.

Megyei jogú városok [Towns of county rank]. Budapest: Központi Statisztikai Hivatal, 2012. Accessed April 18, 2016. http://www.ksh.hu/docs/hun/xftp/idoszaki/regiok /veszpremmjv10.pdf.

Megyei jogú városok a Közép-Dunántúlon, 2009 [Towns of county rank in Middle-Transdanubia, 2009]. Budapest: KSH, 2011.

Merkel, Ina. . . . *und Du, Frau an der Werkbank: [die DDR in den 50er Jahren]* [. . . and you, woman at the workers' bench: (The GDR in the 1950s)]. Berlin: Elefanten Press, 1990.

Mevius, Martin. *Agents of Moscow: The Hungarian Communist Party and the Origins of Socialist Patriotism, 1941–1953*. Oxford: Oxford University Press, 2005.

Mihályi, Péter. "Történeti szempontok a magyarországi lakáshiány értékeléséhez" [Historical perspectives in the assessment of dearth of housing in Hungary]. *Valóság* 20, no. 5 (1977): 48–59.

Miliutin, Nikolai. *Sotsgorod: The Problem of Building Socialist Cities.* Cambridge, MA: MIT Press, 1974. [Originally published as Sotsgorod: Problemy stroitel'stva sotsialisticheskikh gorodov (Moscow-Leningrad: Gosudarstvennoe izdatel'stvo, 1930).]

Miłosz, Czesław. *The Captive Mind.* New York: Vintage Books, 1955.

Miltényi, Károly. "A születéskorlátozás szociális és lélektani háttere. 26 000 nő kikérdezése alapján" [The social and psychological background of birth control based on the responses of 26,000 women]. *Demográfia* 5, no. 1 (1962): 33–72.

———. "Művi vetélések Magyarországon az 1957–1959. években" [Abortions in Hungary in 1957–1959]. *Demográfia* 3, nos. 3–4 (1960): 424–36.

———. "Népesedéspolitikánk néhány kérdése" [Some issues of population policy]. *Demográfia* 1, no. 1 (1958): 7–26.

Miltényi, Károly, and Egon Szabady. "Az abortuszhelyzet Magyarországon; demográfiai és egészségügyi összefüggések" [Abortion in Hungary: Demographic and health-related interconnections]. *Demográfia* 7, no. 2 (1964): 303–9.

Miskolczi, Miklós. *Az első évtized: Dunapentelétől–Dunaújvárosig* [The first decade: From Dunapentele to Dunaújváros]. Dunaújváros: Dunaújvárosi Tanács, 1975.

———, ed. *Új tavasz '80* [New spring '80]. Dunaújváros: KISZ Dunaújvárosi Bizottsága, 1980.

———. *Város lesz csakazértis . . .* [It'll be a city just to show 'em]. Budapest: Szépirodalmi, 1980.

Mlinár, Zdravko. "A bevándorlók baráti kapcsolatai Velenjében" [The friendships of immigrants in Velenje]. In Szelényi, *A szocialista városok és a szociológia*, 220–45.

Moingl, István, ed., *Az 1952–1953. évi népesedéspolitikai program Magyarországon. Dokumentumgyűjtemény* [National population policy in Hungary in 1952–1953]. Budapest: KSH Népességtudományi Kutató Intézete, 1992.

Molnár, József. *Galeribűnözés: Antiszociális fiatalkori csoportok, a fiatalkori csoportos bűnözés* [Gang crime: Antisocial youth groups, crime among young groups]. Budapest: Közgazdasági és Jogi Könyvkiadó, 1971.

"Munkaülés. A házasság és válás társadalmi-foglalkozási összefüggései: A termékenység és a társadalmi átrétegződés" [Social and professional aspects of marriage and divorce: Fertility and social realignment] (without author). *Demográfia* 6, no. 3 (1963): 366–80.

Nagy, Beáta. "A nők keresőtevékenysége Budapesten a 20. század első felében" [Income of women in Budapest in the first half of the twentieth century]. In *Férfiuralom: Írások nőkről, férfiakról, feminizmusról* [Male dominance: Writings about women, men, feminism]. Edited by Hadas Miklós, 155–75. Budapest: Replika Kör, 1994.

Nagy, Sándor. "One Empire, Two States, Many Laws Matrimonial Law and Divorce in the Austro-Hungarian Monarchy." *Hungarian Historical Review* 3 (2014): 230–61.

Nelson, Nici. "Surviving in the City." In Gmelch and Zenner, *Urban Life*, 259–77.

Neuberger, Joan. *Hooliganism: Crime, Culture, and Power in St. Petersburg, 1900–1914.* Berkeley: University of California Press, 1993.

Niethammer, Lutz, Alexander von Plato, and Dorothee Wierling. *Die volkseigene Erfahrung: Eine Archäologie des Lebens in der Industrieprovinz der DDR* [The experience of the people's enterprise: An archaeology of life in the industrial province of the German Democratic Republic]. Berlin: Rowohlt, 1991.

Oakley, Ann. *The Sociology of Housework.* New York: Random House, 1974.

Ogrezeanu, Andrea. "Mahala: The Slums of Bucharest. A Space of Urban Change." *Romanian Journal of Society and Politics* 2, no. 1 (2004): 62–81.

O'Hara, S. Paul. *Gary: The Most American of All American Cities.* Bloomington: Indiana University Press, 2011.

Örkény, István. *Babik.* [Babik] Budapest: Szépirodalmi, 1982.

———. "Sztálinvárosi képeskönyv, 1951–1953" [Sztálinváros picture book, 1951–1953]. In Örkény, *Visszanézve*, 346–81.

———. *Visszanézve: Arcképek, korképek* [Looking back: Portraits, depictions of an age]. Budapest: Szépirodalmi, 1985.

Ormos, Mária. "A szuverenitásról, különös tekintettel a 16-21. század magyar történelmére" [On sovereignty, in particular sixteenth–twenty-first-century Hungarian history]. *Magyar Tudomány* 174, no. 4 (2013): 422–31.

Pallós, Emil, and György Vukovich. "A magyar házassági mozgalom néhány jellegzetessége: házassági táblák" [Some distinctive features of the Hungarian marriage movement: Marriage tables]. *Demográfia* 3, no. 2 (1960): 159–91.

Palotai, Boris. "Egy nap Dunapentelén" [A day in Dunapentele]. In n. a., *Dunapentelén épül a békemű* [In Dunapentele the work of peace is being built], 8–17. Budapest: MNDSZ, 1951.

Pápay, Zsuzsa. *Rang, párválasztás, közvélemény* [Rank, selecting a mate, public opinion]. Budapest: Gondolat, 1989.

Papp, István. "Békés város tagozódása és a népesség szegregálódása" [The division of a peaceful city and the segregation of the population]. *Békési Élet*, no. 2 (1987): 191–206.

Pearson, Geoffrey. *Hooligan: A History of Respectable Fears.* New York: Schocken Books, 1983.

Pekarek, János. "Szomorú adatok Dunaújváros népességéről" [Sad statistics on the population of Dunaújváros]. *Dunaújvárosi Hírlap*, July 23, 2012. Accessed April 18, 2016. http://duol.hu/dunaujvaros/szomoru-adatok-dunaujvaros-nepessegerol-1049122.

Peltonen, Matti. "Clues, Margins, and Monads: The Micro-Macro Link in Historical Research." *History and Theory* 40 (2001): 347–59.

Perry, Clarence. *The Rebuilding of Blighted Areas: A Study of the Neighborhood Unit in Replanning and Plot Assemblage.* New York: Regional Plan Association, 1933.

———. *The School as a Factor in Neighborhood Development.* New York: New York City, Department of Recreation, Russell Sage Foundation, 1914.

Pertti, Ahonen et al., eds. *People on the Move: Forced Population Movements in Europe in the Second World War and Its Aftermath.* Oxford: Berg, 2008.

Pető, Andrea. *Nőhistóriák: A politizáló magyar nők történetéből (1945–1951)* [Women's histories: From the history of Hungarian women in politics]. Budapest: Seneca, 1998.

———. *Women in Hungarian politics, 1945–1951.* Boulder, CO: East European Monographs, 2003.

———. "Women's Rights in Stalinist Hungary: The Abortion Trials of 1952–53." *Hungarian Studies Review* 29 (2002): 49–76.

Pető, Iván, and Sándor Szakács. *A hazai gazdaság négy évtizedének története. 1945–1985. I. Az újjáépítés és a tervutasításos irányítás időszaka* [A four-decade history of the Hungarian economy, 1945–1985: The period of reconstruction and the command economy]. Budapest: Közgazdasági és Jogi Könyvkiadó, 1985.

Pike, Burton. *The Image of the City in Modern Literature.* Princeton, NJ: Princeton University Press, 1981.

Pittaway, Mark. "Control and Consent in East Europe's Workers' States." In *Social Control in Europe, 1800–2000,* vol. 2, edited by Clive Emsley, Eric Johnson, and Pieter Spierenburg, 343–67. Columbus: Ohio State University Press, 2004.

———. *Eastern Europe 1939–2000.* London: Arnold, 2004.

———. *The Workers' State: Industrial Labor and the Making of Socialist Hungary, 1944–1958.* Pittsburgh: University of Pittsburgh Press, 2012.

Poiger, Uta G. *Jazz, Rock, and Rebels: Cold War Politics and American Culture in a Divided Germany.* Berkeley: University of California Press, 2000.

Pollack, Detlef. "Die offene Gesellschaft und ihre Freunde" [The open society and its enemies]. *Geschichte und Gesellschaft* 26 (2000): 184–96.

Pongrácz, Tiborné. "A Ratkó-korszak" [The Ratkó era]. *Korfa. Népesedési Hírlevél* 13, no. 1 (2013): 1–4. Accessed April 26, 2016. http://demografia.hu/kiadvanyokonline /index.php/korfa/article/view/727/191/.

Power, Anne. *Estates on the Edge: The Social Consequences of Mass Housing in Northern Europe.* London: Macmillan, 1999.

Prakfalvi, Endre, and Virág Hajdú, eds. *Építészet és tervezés Magyarországon 1945–1959* [Architecture and planning in Hungary, 1945–1959]. Budapest: Országos Műemlékvédelmi Hivatal—Magyar Építészeti Múzeum, 1996.

Raics, Jenő, and Sándor Árvay. "A terhesség művi megszakítása kapcsán szerzett tapasztalataink" [Experience with the artificial termination of pregnancy]. *Magyar Nőorvosok Lapja,* no. 5 (October 1958): 249–60.

Rainer, János M. *Bevezetés a kádárizmusba* [Introduction to Kádárism]. Budapest: 1956-os Intézet- L'Harmattan Kiadó, 2011.

———. "The Hungarian Revolution of 1956: Causes, Aims, and Course of Events." In *The Hungarian Revolution. Hungarian and Canadian Perspectives,* edited by Christopher Adam et al., 12–31. Ottawa: University of Ottawa Press, 2010.

———. "Revisiting Hungarian Stalinism." In *Stalinism Revisited: The Establishment of Communist Regimes in East-Central Europe,* edited by Vladimir Tismaneanu, 231–54. Budapest: Central European University Press, 2009.

Rapport, Nigel. *Transcendent Individual: Towards a Literary and Liberal Anthropology.* London: Routledge, 1997.

Raskó, Gabriella. *A női bűnözés* [Crime among women]. Budapest: Közgazdasági és Jogi Könyvkiadó, 1978.

Reid, Susan E. "Cold War in the kitchen: Gender and the de-Stalinization of consumer taste in the Soviet Union under Khrushchev." *Slavic Review* 61, no. 2. (2002): 211–52.

Relph, Edward. *The Modern Urban Landscape*. Baltimore: Johns Hopkins University Press, 1987.

Rév, Erika. *Válóperek krónikája* [Divorce chronicle]. Budapest: Kossuth Könyvkiadó, 1986.

Romsics, Ignác. *Magyarország története a XX. században* [The history of Hungary in the twentieth century]. Budapest: Osiris, 1999.

Rosenzweig, Roy. *Eight Hours for What We Will: Workers and Leisure in an Industrial City, 1870–1920*. Cambridge: Cambridge University Press, 1983.

Rottenberg, Simon. "Unemployment in Socialist Countries." *Industrial and Labor Relations Review* 15 (1962): 536–38.

Saád, József. "A lakosság területi szegregálódása a városnövekedés folyamatában" [The segregation of the population by district in the processes of urban growth]. *Valóság* 20, no. 3 (1977): 78–87.

Sabrow, Martin. "Der Konkurs der Konsensdiktatur. Überlegungen zum inneren Verfall der DDR aus kulturgeschichtlicher Perspektive" [The bankruptcy of the consensus dictatorship: Reflections on the inner decline of the GDR from a cultural-historical perspective]. In *Weg in den Untergang: Der innere Zerfall der DDR* [Way into the downfall: The inner disintegration of the GDR], edited by Konrad H. Jarausch and Martin Sabrow, 83–116. Göttingen: Vandenhoeck und Ruprecht, 1999.

Salt, John, and Hugh Clout, eds. *Migration in Post-War Europe: Geographical Essays*. Oxford: Oxford University Press, 1976.

Sándor, András. *Sztálinváros*. Budapest: Népszava, 1951.

Sárkány, Mihály. "A lakodalom funkciójának megváltozása falun" [The change in function of the countryside wedding]. *Ethnographia* 94, no. 2 (1983): 279–84.

Savage, Gail. "Divorce and the Law in England and France prior to the First World War." *Journal of Social History* 21 (Spring 1988): 499–513.

Schildt, Axel, and Detlef Siegfried, eds. *European Cities, Youth and the Public Sphere in the Twentieth Century*. Aldershot: Ashgate, 2005.

Schneider, Peter. "Straßenfluchten und Fluchtstraßen: 'Boulevard' und 'Dorfstraße' in modernen Gesellschaften." [Roadblocks and escape routes: "Boulevard" and "village street" in modern societies]. In *Straße und Straßenkultur* [Street and street culture], edited by Hans-Jürgen Hohm, 217–31. Konstanz: Universität-Verlag Konstanz, 1997.

Scott, James C. *Seeing Like a State: How Certain Schemes to Improve the Human Condition Have Failed*. London: Yale University Press, 1998.

———. *Weapons of the Weak: Everyday Forms of Peasant Resistance*. New Haven, CT: Yale University Press, 1985.

Siegel, Achim, ed. *The Totalitarian Paradigm after the End of Communism: Towards a Theoretical Reassessment*. Amsterdam: Rodopi, 1998.

Simić, Andrej. "Bogdan's Story: The Adaptation of a Rural Family to Yugoslavian Urban Life." In Gmelch and Zenner, *Urban Life*, 210–27.

Simon, Zoltán. *A groteszktől a groteszkig: Örkény István pályaképe* [From the grotesque to the grotesque: The career of István Örkény]. Debrecen: Csokonai Kiadó, 1996.

Springhall, John. *Youth, Popular Culture and Moral Panics: Penny Gaffs to Gangsta-Rap, 1830–1996.* New York: St. Martin's Press, 1998.

Stan, Lavinia. "Explaining Country Differences." In *Transitional Justice in Eastern Europe and the Former Soviet Union Reckoning with the Communist Past,* edited by Lavinia Stan, 247–70. London: Routledge, 2009.

Standeisky, Éva. "Egy literátus ügynökről" [On a literate secret agent]. In *Az ügynök arcai. Mindennapi kollaboráció és ügynökkérdés* [The faces of the agent: Everyday collaboration and the agents], edited by Sándor Horváth, 319–54. Budapest: Libri, 2014.

Statisztikai évkönyv 1985 [Statistical yearbook 1985]. Budapest: KSH, 1986.

Strauss, Anselm L. *Images of the American City.* New York: Free Press, 1961.

Sudár, István. "Két nyár és az első tavasz" [Two summers and the first spring]. In *Tavasz '75: Találkozás a várossal* [Spring 1975: Becoming acquainted with the city], edited by Miklós Miskolczi, 37–41. Dunaújváros: KISZ Dunaújvárosi Bizottsága, 1975.

Suny, Ronald Grigor. "Stalin and His Stalinism: Power and Authority in the Soviet Union, 1930–53." In *Stalinism and Nazism: Dictatorships in Comparison,* edited by Ian Kershaw and Moshe Lewin, 26–52. Cambridge: Cambridge University Press, 1997.

Suttles, Gerald D. *The Social Order of the Slum. Ethnicity and Territory in the Inner City.* Chicago: University of Chicago Press, 1968.

Szabó, Zoltán. *Cifra nyomorúság* [Thinly veiled destitution]. Budapest: Akadémiai, 1986. [A reprint of works published in 1937 and 1938 by Cserépfalvi.]

Szelényi, Iván, ed. *A szocialista városok és a szociológia* [The socialist cities and sociology]. Budapest: Kossuth, 1971.

———. *Új osztály, állam, politika* [A new class, state, politics]. Budapest: Európa, 1990.

———. *Urban Inequalities under State Socialism.* Oxford: Oxford University Press, 1983.

———. *Városi társadalmi egyenlőtlenségek* [Urban social inequalities]. Budapest: Akadémiai Kiadó, 1990.

Szilágyi, Gábor. *Életjel: A magyar filmművészet megszületése. 1954–1956* [Sign of life: The birth of Hungarian film 1954–1956]. Budapest: Magyar Filmintézet, 1994.

Szirák, Péter. "A Grotesque Allegory of Human Dignity. István Örkény: Welcoming the Major." In *Visegrad Drama 3. The Sixties,* edited by Kamila Cerná, Zbynek Cernik, Anna Lakos, Kasia Ogidel, and Natália Mazanová, 183–212. Prague: Arts and Theatre Institute, 2009.

Szirmai, Viktória. *"Csinált városok"* ["Ready-made cities"]. Budapest: Magvető, 1988.

Sztálinváros: Első szocialista városépítkezésünk Sztálinváros [Sztálinváros: Our first socialist city construction] (no author). Budapest: Népszava, 1952.

Sztálinvárosi helytörténeti kiállítás [Sztálinváros local historical exhibition]. Budapest: Művelődési Minisztérium Múzeumi Főosztálya, 1954.

Tapolczai, Jenő. *Egy elnök naplója* [The diary of a president]. Budapest: Kossuth, 1977.

Tar, Sándor. "6714-es személy" [Train no. 6714]. In *Folyamatos jelen: Fiatal szociográfusok antológiája* [Continuous present: Anthology of young sociographers], edited by György Berkovits and István Lázár, 95–103. Budapest: Szépirodalmi, 1981.

Tárkány Szücs, Ernő. *Magyar jogi népszokások* [Hungarian legal folk traditions]. Budapest: Gondolat, 1981.

Tietze, Christopher, and Hans Lehfeldt. "Legal Abortion in Eastern Europe." *Journal of the American Medical Association* 175, no. 13 (April 1961): 1149–54.

Tilly, Charles. "Trust Networks in Transnational Migration." *Sociological Forum* 22, no. 1 (March 2007): 3–24.

Tilly, Louise A., and Joan W. Scott. *Women, Work and Family*. New York: Rinehart and Winston, 1978.

Tomasz, Gábor. "A pesti kocsmák világa" [The world of bars in Pest]. *Új Holnap* 46 (Autumn 2001): 64–95.

Tóth, Eszter Zsófia. "Parasztlányokból munkásasszonyok" [From peasant girls to working wives]. In *Paraszti múlt és jelen az ezredfordulón* [Peasant past and present at the turn of the millennium], edited by Miklós Cseri, László Kósa, and Ibolya T. Bereczki, 405–22. Szentendre: Magyar Néprajzi Társaság, 2000.

Tóth, Eszter Zsófia, and András Murai. *Szex és szocializmus* [Sex and socialism]. Budapest: Libri Könyvkiadó, 2014.

Tóth, Heléna. "Névadó, KISZ-esküvő, temetés: A társadalmi ünnepek kialakítása és a kollektivizálás, 1958–1962" [Name-Giving, KISZ Wedding, Funeral: The Transformation of Social Ceremonies and Collectivization, 1958–1962]. In *Állami erőszak és kollektivizálás a kommunista diktatúrában* [State violence and collectivization in the communist regime], edited by Sándor Horváth and József Ö. Kovács, 257–80. Budapest: MTA BTK Történettudományi Intézet, 2015.

Tóth, Pál. *Társadalmi kapcsolatok szerveződése és típusai a lakótelepeken* [The structures and types of social relationships in housing projects]. Miskolc: Nehézipari Műszaki Egyetem, 1978.

United Nations. Prevention of Juvenile Delinquency. First United Nations Congress on the Prevention of Crime and the Treatment of Offenders. Geneva, August 22–September 3, 1955. Accessed April 18, 2016. https://www.unodc.org/documents/congress//Previous_Congresses/1st_Congress_1955/018_ACONF.6.L.11_Prevention_of_Juvenile_Delinquency.pdf.

Valuch, Tibor. *Magyar hétköznapok: Fejezetek a mindennapi élet történetéből a második világháborútól az ezredfordulóig* [Hungarian everyday life: Chapters of everyday life from World War II until the turn of the century]. Budapest: Napvilág, 2013.

———. *Magyarország társadalomtörténete a XX. század második felében* [The social history of Hungary in the second half of the twentieth century]. Budapest: Osiris, 2001.

Vámos, Éva. "Wolf Johanna, az első sikeres magyar kivitelező építészmérnöknő" [Johanna Wolf, the first successful Hungarian woman architect]. In *Asszonysorsok a 20. században* [The fate of women in the twentieth century], edited by Margit Balogh and Katalin S. Nagy, 85–91. Budapest: BME Szociológia és Kommunikáció Tanszék, and Szociális- és Családvédelmi Minisztérium Nőképviseleti Titkársága, 2000.

Varga, Zsuzsanna. "The Appropriation and Modification of the 'Soviet Model' of Collectivization: The Case of Hungary." In *The Collectivization of Agriculture in Communist Eastern Europe*, edited by Constantin Iordachi and Arnd Bauerkämper, 497–534. Budapest: CEU Press, 2014.

Vogel, Brigitte. "Kulturelles Leben in Stalinstadt zwischen Politisierung und "Eigen-Sinn": Ansätze zu einem deutsch-deutschen Vergleich städtischer Kulturpolitik in den fünfziger Jahren." In Lozac'h, *Eisenhüttenstadt*, 21–32.

von Plato, Alice. "(K)ein Platz für Karl Marx: Die Geschichte eines Denkmals in Karl-Marx-Stadt" [A small place for Karl Marx: The history of a monument in Karl-Marx-Stadt]. In *Inszenierte Einigkeit: Herrschaftsrepräsentationen in DDR-Städten* [Staged unity: Representations of the regime in GDR towns], edited by Adelheid von Saldern, 147–82. Stuttgart: Franz Steiner Verlag, 2003.

Weclawowitz, Grzegorz. "A városok térbeni-társadalmi erezete Kelet-Közép Európában" [Spatial and social networks of Budapest]. *Tér és Társadalom* 6, nos. 3–4 (1992): 215–25.

Weiner, Amir, ed. *Landscaping the Human Garden: Twentieth-Century Population Management in a Comparative Framework.* Stanford, CA: Stanford University Press, 2003.

Weiner, Tibor. "Sztálinváros" [Sztálinváros]. In *Sztálinváros, Miskolc, Tatabánya: Városépítésünk fejlődése* [Sztálinváros, Miskolc, Tatabánya: The development of urban planning], edited by Aladár Sós, Kálmán Faragó, Géza Hermány, and György Korompay, 17–88. Budapest: Műszaki, 1959.

———. "Új forma új tartalom" [New form new content]. In n. a., *Üzenet* [Message], 83–91. Dunaújváros: Dunaújvárosi Tanács, 1963.

Welz, Gisela. *Street Life: Alltag in einem New Yorker Slum* [Street life: Day in a New York slum]. Frankfurt am Main: Institut für Kulturanthropologie und Europäische Ethnologie, 1991.

Widdicombe, Sue, and Robin Wooffitt. *The Language of Youth Subcultures: Social Identity in Action.* New York: Harvester Wheatsheaf, 1995.

Young, Michael, and Peter Willmott. *Family and Kinship in East London.* London: Penguin Books, 1986.

Zaborowska, Magdalena J. *How We Found America: Reading Gender through East-European Immigrant Narratives.* Chapel Hill: University of North Carolina Press, 1995.

Zibell, Barbara. *Frauen in Wohnumfeld und Nachbarschaft* [Women in the domestic world and the neighborhood]. Berlin: Institut für Stadt- und Regionalplanung, 1983.

Index

SÁNDOR HORVÁTH (PhD 2003), is Senior Research Fellow and Head of the Department for Contemporary History at the Institute of History, Research Centre for the Humanities at the Hungarian Academy of Sciences. He also serves as the founding editor of the *Hungarian Historical Review*, a peer-reviewed international quarterly of the Hungarian Academy of Sciences. He is the author of *Two Floors of Happiness: Everyday Practice of Social Policy in Budapest during the Kádár Era* (in Hungarian, 2012), *Children of Kádár: Youth Revolt in the 1960s* (in Hungarian, 2009), and a number of articles on social history and everyday life in the twentieth century in peer-reviewed international journals.

Lightning Source UK Ltd.
Milton Keynes UK
UKOW05f0918230317
297321UK00017B/77/P